CLASSIC 1-2-3 MACROS

Third Edition

E. MICHAEL LUNSFORD

John Wiley & Sons, Inc.

New York • Chichester
Brisbane • Toronto • Singapore

Publisher: Katherine Schowalter
Editor: Paul Farrell
Managing Editor: Micheline Frederick
Production & Design: North Market Street Graphics

Designations used by companies to distinguish their products are often claimed as trademarks. In all instances where John Wiley & Sons, Inc. is aware of a claim, the product names appear in Initial Capital or all CAPITAL letters. Readers, however, should contact the appropriate companies for more complete information regarding trademarks and registration.

This text is printed on acid-free paper.

This publication is designed to provide accurate and authoritative information in regard to the subject matter covered. It is sold with the understanding that the publisher is not engaged in rendering legal, accounting, or other professional service. If legal advice or other expert assistance is required, the services of a competent professional person should be sought.

Library of Congress Cataloging-in-Publication Data:

Lunsford, E. Michael.
    Classic 1-2-3 macros. Third Edition / E. Michael Lunsford.
       p.   cm.
    Includes index.
    ISBN 0-471-06398-3 (pbk. : alk. paper)
    1. Lotus 1-2-3 (Computer file) 2. Macro instructions (Electronic computers) 3. Business—Computer programs. 4. Electronic spreadsheets. I. Title. II. Title: Classic one-two-three macros.
HF5548.4.L67L853 1995
650'.0285'5369—dc20   94-30064
                                    CIP

Printed in the United States of America
10 9 8 7 6 5 4 3 2

To Merlyn, the love of my life.

C O N T E N T S

v

ABOUT THE AUTHOR

E. Michael Lunsford is an acknowledged expert on Lotus 1-2-3 and author of numerous articles as well as twelve books on spreadsheets and macros, including *Macros, Menus, and Miracles for Lotus 1-2-3*. He is also creator of several software programs, including *101 Macros for Lotus 1-2-3*. A software developer, teacher, consultant, and CD-ROM producer, Lunsford has been a featured speaker at user and developer conferences around the country.

Purchasing Software from the Author

Instead of keying each macro in this book into 1-2-3 for use with your own spreadsheets, you may be interested in obtaining the entire collection of macros, already pretyped and debugged, directly from the author, E. Michael Lunsford. For only $54.95 (includes shipping and sales tax), you can purchase discount copies of *101 Macros Plus for 1-2-3* at a **full 20 per cent off the usual retail price.** Simply fill out the coupon at the end of this book and send it with your check or money order to:

E. Michael Lunsford
656 Alameda
San Carlos, CA 94070

I N T R O D U C T I O N

Why Use Macros?

Like so many Lotus users, I worked with 1-2-3 for over a year before discovering macros. It wasn't that I hadn't heard of macros. From time to time my co-workers would wonder at my not using this powerful feature of 1-2-3. However, in spite of comments like, "Macros are real timesavers, why aren't you using them?", I always contended that I was already a fast typist and couldn't imagine that macros would really save enough time to make them worth the trouble.

I had no idea what macros were all about, of course, or how they could benefit me in my work with 1-2-3. The only macros I had seen were either extremely complex programs created by someone else for a specific spreadsheet or very simple macros that saved only five or six keystrokes. The first type seemed inapplicable to my work and the second type seemed only marginally faster than accomplishing the same tasks manually.

Then one day, as I was typing the @sum formula for the fortieth time on a single spreadsheet, it struck me that the 13 to 17 keystrokes it normally takes to type that formula should be automated. All I had to do was create a macro that would type the letters **@sum(** and paint in the range of the numbers to sum, then close the parenthesis, and press Enter. In no time I had

written my first macro that did exactly that—it summed any vertical range of numbers automatically and all I had to do was press a couple of keys.

Since that day, of course, Lotus has added an automatic Sum Smart-Icon that accomplishes the same task; but at the time, this first step into the world of macros represented an important turnaround in my use of 1-2-3. Before long, I had a collection of everyday macros that would help me in my work with all types of 1-2-3 worksheets, from balance sheets to financial analysis, from database worksheets to marketing forecasts. I realized that macros need not be complicated to save dozens of keystrokes. In fact, it seems the simplest kinds of macros get the most use.

In a short time, writing and using macros pushed me ahead in my overall knowledge of 1-2-3 and provided me with the means to do things in 1-2-3 that were not possible without macros. For example, I could create a macro to copy column widths from one range to another, as you normally copy data. Or I could develop a macro to subtotal all the like items of a database, automatically inserting rows where required. I could use macros to prompt for particular information, or present a custom menu of spreadsheet-specific commands, or even change the Ready indicator to display any type of message.

I wondered, though, why there was no resource for a set of prewritten macros that I could use with any spreadsheet. I imagined a collection of useful macro shortcuts that I could combine, modify, customize, and—most importantly—learn from. Finally, I published my own software package, *101 Macros for Lotus 1-2-3*. The success of the package was instantaneous, resulting in the development of similar macro collections for Excel, Quattro Pro, WordPerfect, and Microsoft Word. Also from that base was born the idea for a strong tutorial book titled *Macros, Menus, and Miracles for Lotus 1-2-3*, published by John Wiley & Sons.

Now, after years of improvements on the original collection, hundreds of requests and suggestions from macro users, and growth in Lotus' own macro capabilities, it has become apparent that spreadsheet users could benefit from a fresh approach to a long-standing problem: how to gain access to a collection of standard, generic, and proven *classic* macros that are presented in a clear, direct, simple-to-difficult sequence that anyone can understand. *Classic 1-2-3 Macros* was written to offer that double benefit—over 150 practical macros that you can use right away while gaining a thorough understanding of exactly how macros work.

Who Should Read This Book?

Whether you been exposed to macros before or have only heard about them, this book is for you. The macros presented in this book cover all releases of 1-2-3, for both DOS and Windows.

Spreadsheet users do not typically explore the world of macros until working with the spreadsheet for at least three months. This is primarily due to the perception that one must master the fundamentals of the program before launching into the more advanced subject of macros. This learning period is not necessary before exposure to macros, however. As you will see in the first few chapters, there are simple one-liners that can help the novice users eliminate unnecessary typing and menu steps from their first days with 1-2-3.

Intermediate users who have used macros written by others or created a few of their own will find a wealth of information in this book about the syntax of macro keywords, the combined use of menu steps and macro commands, and special tips and techniques for writing custom macros.

Advanced macro writers will be especially interested in the many uses of string formulas, self-modifying macro lines, and the use of advanced functions like @cell and @cellpointer in custom macros. The macros presented here are laid out and explained with a detail that makes them extremely easy to understand and modify. Working examples showing macro keywords in action provide a level of learning not found in simple descriptions in the Lotus 1-2-3 manual, and the advanced macros in the last few chapters teach a level of macro writing that can turn any average macro writer into an exceptional macro "guru."

What This Book Can Teach You

This book is divided into seventeen chapters, beginning with a chapter called "What Is a Macro?". In this first chapter, macros are defined in terms of their use in saving keystrokes and frustration, storing commands, adding new features not normally considered a part of 1-2-3, automating the spreadsheet, and adding custom menus to the spreadsheet. We point out that macros are also an excellent learning tool, since a healthy by-product of writing macros is a dramatic increase in your working knowledge of 1-2-3.

Chapter Two, "Writing Your First Simple Macro," covers the basics of how to create a simple macro and offers a few conventions for range-naming, what to do if nothing happens when you try to invoke a macro, how to stop and pause a macro, where to locate your macros, when to use lowercase and uppercase in macros, and different ways to invoke a macro.

Chapter Three, "A Few Short Macros," offers a few short one-liners, including a macro to insert a label prefix, macros to move your cursor to the left or right a designated number of cells, a macro to jump from your current cell to the top of the page, a macro to move to the lower left corner of your spreadsheet, a macro to widen the column by one space, format macros, an @sum macro, a macro to verify that the vertical sum of a column matches the horizontal sum, an @date macro, a macro to copy the data from the cell above, and automatic execution macros.

Chapter Four, "Using Step, Record, and Learn Keys," presents techniques for debugging your macros using the Step key, and methods for recording your keystrokes. In Release 2.x this is done by establishing a /Worksheet Learn Range and activating the Alt+F5 Learn Feature. The Record Buffer of Release 3 and higher, on the other hand, is a 512-byte area of computer memory in which 1-2-3 records all your keystrokes in the background as you type them.

Chapter Five, "The Macro Programming Commands," describes in detail the seven categories of advanced macro programming commands, including commands to control the screen, allow user input, control program flow, interrupt program flow, manipulate data, manipulate files, and access add-ins. The macros in this chapter include a Data Entry macro, a Save and Print macro with a simple subroutine, a File Combine macro, an Automatic Graph macro, a macro to jump to the leftmost column or topmost row, a menu macro to delete a row or column during Global Protection, a looping macro to prune files, and a File Extract macro.

Chapter Six, "The Art of Range-Naming," describes macros to jump around the spreadsheet, a self-modifying file retrieve macro, macro commands to turn off the screen refresh, instructions for using the @cellpointer command and {let} command, macros using subroutines with place-markers, macros to view or recalculate ranges of the spreadsheet, a macro to transpose a matrix of columns to rows, and copy command macros, including a macro to copy to alternate cells, macros to copy relative formulas as absolute, and Copy & Stay and Move & Stay macros that leave your cell pointer at the destination cell.

Chapter Seven, "Creating a Background Macro Library," explores the use of macro libraries in Release 2.2 and higher. And although Release 2 does not provide a way to operate your macros from outside the current worksheet, you can simplify the transfer of macros from worksheet files on disk to the current worksheet. In Release 2.x, you can use the MACROMGR. ADN application to hold macros in a type of hyperspace outside the current worksheet. Although Release 3 and higher do not have a Macro Library Manager add-in as found in Release 2.x, you can have background macros in two ways: either in an extra background worksheet in the same file, or in a separate active file.

Chapter Eight, "Toggles and the Macro Run Key," introduces the use of toggles in your macros, including a toggle to jump to often visited areas of your spreadsheet. Also covered are use of the Alt+F3 Macro Run key in Release 2.2 and higher, a Macro Launcher for Release 2 to simulate the Alt+F3 Macro Run key in Release 2.2 and higher, and ways to jump your cell pointer to special areas such as a notepad area, appointment calendar area, pop-up calculator window, and a custom help screen.

Chapter Nine, "Data Entry and Modification," explores use of the {if} command with the @cellpointer function to facilitate data entry and modification of data in your worksheet. We will also look at two prompt commands, {getlabel} and {getnumber}. The macros covered in this chapter include a label format macro, a number format macro, a macro to indent a column, a macro to add leading zeros, a rounding macro, a macro to eliminate the ERR messages in a spreadsheet, a data entry macro, a macro to modify cell data by a constant, a borders macro, and a financial functions macro.

Chapter Ten, "String Formulas and String @Functions," reviews the science of string formulas and the use of the special string manipulation features of 1-2-3 to combine two or more elements into a single word or phrase. It defines the string formula concept and the individual string @functions, and explores their purpose and application in spreadsheet cells to create variable entries and in macros that require variable or self-modifying lines. String @ functions used in combination with other @ functions of 1-2-3 in this chapter include @upper, @lower, @proper, @length, @find, @left, @right, @mid, @trim, @clean, @repeat, @code, @char, @exact, @replace, @value, @n, and @s.

Chapter Eleven, "Counters and the {for} Loop," shows ways to make your macro loop a designated number of times in one of two ways: by using {if} with the {let} command, or by using the more advanced {for} command. The macros covered in this chapter include macros to change the width of any number of columns; allow a type of slide show of your graphs; squeeze the filled cells in a column together into one contiguous range of viable data; change zeros in your worksheet to blank spaces; test a matrix of numbers for a particular value, and insert another value in its place; enhance the existing /Range Search capability by adding a new feature called Previous; change number-labels to values; vertically display a series of dates exactly one month apart; and add or delete a prefix in each entry in a column.

Chapter Twelve, "Using the {get} Command," defines and explores uses of the {get} command in combination with macro techniques and commands of previous chapters. You will see how {get} can be used to create a Yes/No prompt, quit a macro upon your press of the Escape key, create a special "action key," differentiate between a press of letter/number keys and directional or function keys, and evaluate and act on your response to special {indicate} prompts.

Chapter Thirteen, "Manipulating Strings in your Macros," explores the use of string technology to display a variable message in the upper panel, display changing choice explanations in custom menus, change case of a single-cell entry, change values to label-numbers, create a custom help screen, create a sum-and-stay macro, sum a series of ranges, display an absolute cell address as a relative address, create range names that change based on the counter in a {for} loop, and calculate and display a relative cell location based on your current cell address.

Chapter Fourteen, "Wysiwyg Macros," explores ways to speed up your spreadsheet publishing tasks using macros that access 1-2-3's Wysiwyg commands. Among these macros you'll find shortcuts for toggling between Wysiwyg attributes, frame types, display sizes, and printer orientations; automating the loading of Wysiwyg add-ins; changing Wysiwyg attributes the instant you retrieve a file; automating standard 1-2-3 /Copy and Wysiwyg :Copy commands; increasing the size of an outline box created with single, double, or wide lines; and instantly deleting a line that exists in both of two adjacent cells.

Chapter Fifteen, "Macros to Manipulate a Database," covers macros that use variable strings and the combination of several features including operators such as #not# and @functions such as @exact, @iserr, @value, and @choose to facilitate the use and manipulation of databases in 1-2-3. The examples we will look at include macros to create date headings or an entire worksheet matrix, automate data query setup, view duplicate entries, find a string within a string, delete blank or zero-value rows, and subtotal like items in a database.

Chapter Sixteen, "Using File Control Macros," takes a look at macros designed to switch your file directory instantly, automatically save a file, save a backup and beep when finished; present a message in your upper screen indicating the size of a file in bytes, list a file name table in your worksheet; create a table of active files in Release 3, and save a Macro Library .MLB file in Release 2.2.

Chapter Seventeen, "Creating Macro Applications," is the final chapter and covers the creation of special applications including a program to automate and maintain an address database, print form letters and address labels from that database, create a checkbook ledger, and automatically type out your checkbook amounts in words as they might be written on a check.

Acknowledgments

This book would not have been possible without the love and support of my wife, Merlyn, and my son, Hassin.

I would also like to acknowledge the following people at John Wiley & Sons for their help and support: Allison Roarty (Assistant Editor), Paul Farrell (Editor), and Micheline Frederick (Managing Editor).

1

What Is a Macro?

In the most basic terms, a macro can be described as a collection of saved keystrokes and commands that can be played back by pressing a simple, two-keystroke combination. In 1-2-3 for DOS, this means simultaneously pressing the Alt key and a single-letter key (Alt+A, Alt+B, and so on). In 1-2-3 for Windows, you press the Ctrl key and a single-letter key (Ctrl+A, Ctrl+B, and so on).

By *Classic 1-2-3 Macros* we mean the most commonly accessed macros that have been proven useful to all types of 1-2-3 users over the years, both as standalone utilities and as subroutines that can form a part of larger macro programs.

For example, it's invaluable to have a macro that can move the cell pointer down a column of numbers, making changes as required, and automatically quitting when it reaches the last number. It's a real timesaver to have access to a macro that can format a range, make certain cells bold, add lines and italics, and change column widths, all automatically. Imagine a macro that prompts you to enter values, text, or dates, checks their validity, modifies them in various ways, and places them in designated cells in a spreadsheet. Or consider a macro that can work in the background to retrieve a file, manipulate its data, and print the results; retrieve a second file, manipulate its data, print those results, and so on, until it processes an entire series of worksheets while you work on something else.

Even a simple playback macro can save hundreds of keystrokes over time. Suppose, for example, that you work for a company named MAR-VELOUS BOSS AND ASSOCIATES, INC. That's quite a few characters to type over and over; but you can enter it automatically if you store those keystrokes in a macro that you invoke by simply pressing Alt+M (or Ctrl+M in 1-2-3 for Windows). With such a macro, 1-2-3 will type your company name for you—and so fast, it doesn't look like typing at all. The company name just appears in the current cell, instantly.

Saved Keystrokes—and Saved Frustration

As you can imagine, saving yourself all those keystrokes also has the effect of saving much of the frustration that goes along with dull, repetitive work. Consider, for example, having a range of values that you want to convert to number-labels, and think of the frustration of having to type a label prefix (an apostrophe, for example) in front of every entry in that range. With a macro, you can automate the process so that 1-2-3 instantly converts the values to number-labels. Or you might want to do the opposite, changing a range of number-labels to their equivalent values. Since 1-2-3 has no range feature for accomplishing that task, it's ideal to have a macro that can handle the job for you.

What if you have an inventory database of part numbers and quantities, but you want to shorten the list by deleting all records that show a zero quantity? Moving down a database with your cell pointer and making those changes manually can be a tedious and time-consuming exercise; but a macro can take care of the task for you automatically and much quicker than the fastest typist.

Storing Commands

By storing keystrokes and commands, you can actually modify the way 1-2-3 works. For example, those of you who have used Microsoft Excel's F5 Goto key may appreciate the way Excel presents a history of the last cells you visited using F5. With the macro language, you can create a similar functionality in 1-2-3.

Imagine that your cell pointer is on cell R223 and you want to visit an area that's four screens down, three screens to the right, two columns to the left, and one row up. You press PgDn four times, Ctrl+Right Arrow three times, Left Arrow twice, and Up Arrow once (or, in 1-2-3 for Windows, you make the appropriate mouse clicks in the vertical and horizontal scroll bars) until you're finally there. You change a cell or just check its value, and now you want to return to your original location. What do you do?

Well, if you've forgotten the cell row and column location where you started (cell R223, remember), you'll probably press PgUp four times, Ctrl+Left Arrow three times, Right Arrow twice, and Down Arrow once.

Instead, you can use the Goto with History macro—it "remembers" where you were and presents you with a menu of up to seven of the last cells you visited using this macro, as well as the option to go to a new cell location. What's more, once you return to your original cell, you can always use the Goto with History macro to jump back and forth between the two locations with just a couple of keystrokes.

Adding Other New Features

In addition to storing keystrokes and commands, the 1-2-3 macro structure can actually be considered a programming language. In fact, some studies have shown that more people are programming with macros than with any other language.

As often short but powerful programs, macros can be used to provide a host of new features or to improve features already provided. For example, you might like to have a macro that automatically transfers your data from 1-2-3 to a word processor. Or perhaps you'd like a macro that prints alternate columns of a spreadsheet. You might appreciate a macro that automatically fills a range with certain data sequences specific to your company. And you'll probably get a great deal of use from a macro that accomplishes both a copy command and a special copy (complete with any top, bottom, left, and right lines) all at once.

Automating Your Spreadsheets

Perhaps most important—and certainly the most commonly used feature of the macro language—is the ability to automate your spreadsheets. You'll find many examples of task-automating macros throughout this book.

Consider a Data Entry macro that not only prompts you for what to enter and moves your cell pointer down a column, across a row, or directly to specific cells in the spreadsheet, but also checks your response to see if it falls in a certain range of values or dates, that it matches certain expected responses, or that it was entered as a value or label as appropriate.

How about an Automatic Tickler macro that warns you that *Today's the day* for some deadline or event as you load 1-2-3 each day? Or perhaps you'd like to have a Titles Toggle macro that automatically locks and unlocks horizontal titles, vertical titles, or both. Or you may be interested in having a macro that maintains an address database, searches for specific individuals by name, accomplishes a mail merge with pretyped form letters, and prints labels or envelopes automatically.

Add Menus to Your Spreadsheet

1-2-3 offers the ability to create custom menus and, as introduced in 1-2-3 for Windows, custom dialog boxes. This means you can add a list of menu choices to any macro, complete with clarifying descriptions and branches to subroutines that carry out your choices.

Horizontal custom menus have been used throughout the macros in this book. Some excellent examples are the Copy Command macro, the Enter Phrase macro, the Go with History macro, the File Directory macro, and the Case Conversion macro.

This book also offers techniques for creating special vertical menus you can scroll through with your arrow keys or mouse. These types of menus have the added advantage that you are not limited to the usual eight choices found in standard custom menus that show up horizontally on the screen.

Macros as a Learning Tool

Finally, macros are a great learning tool. Whether you're exploring the standard 1-2-3 commands and keystrokes used in a prewritten macro or working out the menus and command sequences required to write your own macro, a healthy by-product of the exercise will be a dramatic increase in your working knowledge of 1-2-3.

Summary

In its simplest form, a macro is a collection of saved keystrokes and commands that can be executed with a simple two-keystroke combination. However, macros can be much more, as summarized here:

- Macros can speed up your work with 1-2-3, saving you time, keystrokes, and a great deal of frustration.
- Macros can store information as well as keystrokes and commands.
- Macros can offer impressive new features, like word processing, not otherwise available in 1-2-3.
- You can use macros to completely automate your spreadsheet including automatic data entry, manipulation of data, cell pointer movement, and printing.

- With macros you can create custom menus designed to your own specifications.
- By learning 1-2-3 macros, you will inevitably learn a great deal more about 1-2-3.

In Chapter 2 you will be taken, step by step, through the creation of your first macro. You will also learn a few important macro conventions, such as how to stop a macro, where to locate your macros, and how to make the best use of uppercase and lowercase in your macro code.

Writing Your First Simple Macro

In the spirit of learning by doing, this chapter steps you through writing your first macro so you can see how it's done. The easiest type of macro to demonstrate is a macro that simply types a word in the cell occupied by your cell pointer. We'll use the word **Classic**.

Begin by moving to an unoccupied area of a blank spreadsheet—say, cell B2. Now type the word **Classic** and follow it with the character that looks like this: ~. This character, called a *tilde,* is read by 1-2-3 in its macro language as an Enter command. (You pronounce it like the last two syllables of the name Matilda.) You should now have the following typed in cell B2: **Classic~**.

Now move your cell pointer to the left (to cell A2) and type a label prefix (an apostrophe), a backslash, and the letter **A**, and press Enter. In the Edit Line you'll see '**\A**, while in cell A2 just **\A** displays, without the apostrophe.

NOTE: *We are using a backslash here, not a forward slash. This is very important.*

At this point, the **\A** entry provides identification only. It identifies the entry **Classic~** in cell B2 as a macro that we will want to be able to invoke later by pressing Alt+A in 1-2-3 for DOS or Ctrl+A in 1-2-3 for Windows. However, before the macro can be invoked in this way to process its keystrokes, you must take one more step.

Range Naming Your Macro

To be able to invoke your macro with a two-keystroke combination, you must assign a backslash-letter range name to the first cell of the macro. (So far, of course, the entire macro described here is only one cell long.) There are two ways to give a range name to that first cell:

Place the cell pointer on cell A2 (where we have previously typed \A), choose /Range Name Labels Right, and press Enter. (If you have 1-2-3 for Windows and you want to use the standard Windows menubar, choose Block | Names | Labels | Right and click OK.)

Alternatively, place the cell pointer on the cell to be named and choose /Range Name Create, type \A, and press Enter.

Note, however, the second method is not recommended and should *not* be used for the macros in this collection. Instead, use the first—/Range Name Labels Right command—for these reasons:

- It requires fewer keystrokes.
- It prompts you to take care of an important practice—that is, you first identify the macro by typing its name (\A in this case) in the cell to the left of the macro.
- You can use this technique to name more than one invoking or internal range name (names like JLOOP, JMENU, JCOUNTER, and so on) by choosing /Range Name Labels Right, pressing PgDn as required to highlight several names at once, and pressing Enter.

Titling the Macro

Strictly speaking, it isn't necessary to title your macros; but you'll find that adding a title to the top of each of your macros makes them much easier to locate and identify later. As a convention, all the macros in this book have been titled.

To title the simple, one-cell macro we've written here, move to C1 and type: **Amazing Macro**. If your title extends into cell D1 (as it will if C1 has the standard column width of 9), center it across both cells by choosing :Text Align Center, highlighting C1..D1, and pressing Enter. You can also add an outline around C1..D1 by choosing :Format Line Outline, highlighting C1..D1, and pressing Enter.

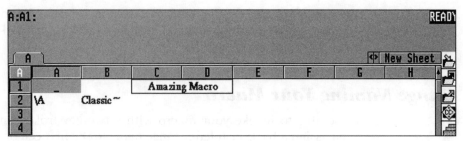

FIGURE 2.1 Your first simple macro.

Now you've written the macro, given it an invoking backslash-letter name, and identified just what the macro does—amazing us, of course, by typing the word **Classic**. At this point, your screen should look like the example in Figure 2.1.

Invoking Your Macro

Now we can invoke the macro. Move down several cells, to cell C5, for example, and while pressing the Alt key (or Ctrl in 1-2-3 for Windows), press the letter of the macro—in this case, the letter **A**. The word **Classic** will be typed immediately into that cell.

Now move to cell C8 and press Alt+A (or Ctrl+A in 1-2-3 for Windows) again. Once again you should see the word **Classic** typed into the current cell.

> **NOTE:** *Do not invoke this particular macro when the cell pointer is resting on any occupied cell—especially cells occupied by the macro itself. The macro's function is to type the word* **Classic,** *which means invoking the macro automatically causes it to type over any information that happens to reside in the current cell.*

What to Do if Nothing Happens

If the macro does not work at all, the reason probably has to do with improper naming of the macro's first cell. To check this, press the F5 Goto key, followed by \A. If you get a beep and an error message that reads *Invalid cell or range address,* this means that the macro has not been range-named. If the cell pointer jumps to another location, but it is not the location just to the right of the \A, the range-naming has been done incorrectly. If either of these problems occurs, go back to the instructions for range-naming your macro and repeat the steps for properly assigning a macro range name.

> **NOTE:** *You can always check for whether a range name exists by pressing the F5 Goto key, followed by the range name and Enter. If the cell pointer jumps to the desired location, the range has been named as you intended.*

Macros That Take up More Than One Row

Suppose you want your macro to type **Classic 123 Macro**? You can do this one of two ways:

 Change the first line of the macro to read:

```
Classic 123 Macro~
```

 Alternatively, you can delete the tilde from the end of the word **Classic** in cell B2, move your cell pointer to cell B3 and enter:

```
'123
```

and in cell B4 enter:

```
Macros~
```

The result in cell B3 will appear left-justified without the apostrophe, of course, so the range B2..B4 should look like this:

```
Classic
123
Macros~
```

This brings up an important point. Always remember that in a macro each line of code must be entered as a label. To enter a line of macro code that begins with a forward slash (/), a number (such as **4567**), or an arithmetic operator (such as + or @), you must first type a label prefix (typically, an apostrophe).

Refer to the macro shown in Figure 2.2. When you use this macro, pressing Alt+A (or Ctrl+A in 1-2-3 for Windows) plays back the contents of the cell named **\A** by typing the word **Classic**, then plays back the contents of the next cell down by typing **123**, and finally plays back the contents of the last cell in the series by typing **Macros** and pressing Enter. Unfortunately, it will be entered as **Classic123Macros** without the appropriate spaces between the words **Classic**, **123**, and **Macros**. To fix the problem, edit cells B2 and B3 by adding a space after the entries **Classic** and **123**. Once you've made that correction, invoking the macro will cause 1-2-3 to type the words **Classic 123 Macros** as intended.

A macro will always continue by playing back the next cell below until it comes to a cell that has no label (either a blank cell or a cell that displays a

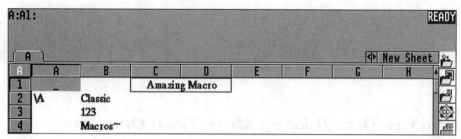

FIGURE 2.2 A macro consisting of more than one line.

numeric value), or until it comes to a branching command or a special {quit} command that tells 1-2-3 to "quit the macro and return to Ready mode."

Because every macro continues down to the next cell, two conventions have been used in this book to eliminate the possibility of having a macro continue past its intended end point. The first is to follow every macro with a blank cell. This works out nicely because the cell just to the right of that blank cell can easily be used as a title for the next macro.

The second convention is to end every macro with the {quit} command or one of the branching commands. This extra precaution protects against the possibility that you may delete a row in your spreadsheet that happens to coincide with the blank cell in your macro area that you depended on to stop a macro.

What the Macro Sees Is What You Get

Suppose instead of having your macro type **Classic 123 Macros**, you wanted it to type **123 Worksheet**? You might think that all you need to do is clear B2..B4, move to cell B2, type **'123 Worksheet~**, and press Enter.

If you do that, however, trying to run the macro will result in a beep and a shift to the Edit mode. This is because the macro tries to type the *visible* contents of cell B2 (no label prefix, just **123 Worksheet**). Just as manually typing the phrase **123 Worksheet** without first typing a label prefix will cause a beep, so setting up the macro to type those same characters for you makes 1-2-3 beep. What's the solution? Move to cell B2 and enter:

```
"123 Worksheet
```

which in cell B2 will show up as **'123 Worksheet** with only one apostrophe. Now move to cell C8 and press Alt+A (or Ctrl+A in 1-2-3 for Windows). The macro will type an apostrophe before it types **123 Worksheet**, and you get the entry **123 Worksheet** in cell C8.

How to Stop a Macro

Although a macro will always stop if it encounters a blank cell, a value, or a {quit} command, there will be times when you start the wrong macro and you want to stop it immediately before it does too much damage to your worksheet; or you may be running a macro designed with an endless loop that will continue until you stop it manually.

You should know about the two possible techniques for manually stopping a macro. The first is to press Ctrl+Break. If you do not have a key on your keyboard that reads "Break," try the Pause key—it should be the same thing.

Although pressing Ctrl+Break will stop your macro, it also causes a Break error message to appear. Simply press Esc at this point and you should be returned to Ready mode.

The second technique actually causes your macro to pause, after which you can resume the macro later. To pause any macro, press Ctrl+NumLock. Then, when you want to start up the macro again, press any key.

Where to Locate Your Macros

In this era of multiple spreadsheet pages, it makes most sense to store your macros on a separate page in the worksheet. If you have 1-2-3 for Windows or 1-2-3 Release 3.x or higher for DOS, it's no problem to place your macros on a separate page. In fact, as of Release 4.0 for DOS and Windows, you can even give that page a descriptive name like MACROS. Not only does this make it easy to get to your macros from any location in the spreadsheet file, but it places the macros in a safe location where work on other spreadsheet pages can't destroy important macro code.

If you have an earlier 1-2-3 version that supports only single page spreadsheets, it's critical that you place your macros in some out-of-the-way place where deleting columns and rows as you do your normal spreadsheet work won't coincidentally delete columns or rows containing your macros. Typically, this means placing your macros in an area some people call the "south forty"—a range far below any rows you might delete in spreadsheets you start at cell A1, and far to the right of any columns you might delete. For example, if you have spreadsheet tables in the range A1..X900, you might want to start your macros in AA1000 or, to be really safe, in AB2000. In that case, you would probably want to give a range name like ***MACROS** to the first cell in that area so you can quickly jump there from any other location in the spreadsheet by pressing the F5 Goto key, the F3 Name key, pointing to the ***MACROS** range name, and pressing Enter.

You should also be aware of the Macro Library capability found in Release 2.2 and higher. This feature allows you to place your macros in a separate Macro Library which does not reside in the current worksheet, but rather sits in the background available for your use across spreadsheets. This is covered in more detail in Chapter 7.

Uppercase versus Lowercase

You may have noticed the use of uppercase and lowercase in the creation of macros. Using uppercase and lowercase has become a standard convention to make macros easier to read and decipher, but there is some disagreement about which case should be used for macro commands and which for worksheet range names.

Some authors have opted for the use of uppercase for macro commands (using {GOTO} instead of {goto} for the macro equivalent of the F5 Goto key for example), and lowercase for range names. In fact, Lotus' own macro-recording features follow this convention.

On the other hand, most of the typing in a given macro usually consists of macro commands, which means that the standard macro-recording features result in more use of uppercase than lowercase. To a proficient typist, this approach seems counter-intuitive. In contract, using lowercase for commands and uppercase for range names tends to be easier to read, takes up less room on the screen, and seems a great deal less cumbersome to type. This latter convention, therefore, is the technique used and recommended here. Thus, instead of writing your macro code like this:

```
{GOTO}macros~{PGDN}{RIGHT}
```

we recommend you write it like this:

```
{goto}MACROS~{pgdn}{right}
```

Macro Range Names

Macros that you want to invoke with a simple, two-keystroke combination like Alt+A in 1-2-3 for DOS or Ctrl+A in 1-2-3 for Windows can be named with a backslash and any letter of the alphabet (\A, \B, \C, and so on). Lotus macros should not, however, be range-named with a backslash-*number* combination such as \1, \2, or \3, since such macros cannot be invoked by simultaneously pressing Alt or Ctrl and a number. The only exception to this is the \0 macro, a special Autoexecute macro, discussed in more detail in Chapter 3.

When it comes to backslash-character macros, then, you are limited to 27 macros in a given spreadsheet file. This is not the entire picture, however, since in Release 2.2 and higher, you can invoke any macro by giving it a multiletter name (like GRAPH or DATAENTRY or PRINT) and invoking the macro with the Alt+F3 Macro Run key. In fact, even in earlier releases you can invoke an unlimited number of macros by adding a Macro Launcher macro to your spreadsheet as described in Chapter 8. By being able to invoke your macros through descriptive range names instead of (or even in addition to) the backslash-letter types of invoking names already described, you can effectively break the 27-macro limitation.

So, for example, the Amazing Macro we created earlier could also be given the range name AMZ or AMAZE. It could be executed by first invoking the Macro Run key or Chapter 8's Macro Launcher and then entering the appropriate range name or pressing the F3 Name key and choosing the name from the list of range names that appears.

> **TIP:** *To the greatest extent possible, try to arrange your macros alphabetically and have the letter calling the macro correspond to the first letter of the macro name. Thus, the Amazing Macro is called by way of the \A invoking name, a Bold Font macro would be given the name \B, an Italic Font macro would be given the name \I, and so on, as shown in Figure 2.3.*

In addition to the range names used to call the macro, the range names *within* the macro (such as DLOOP or DCOUNTER) should always start with the letter of the macro. This is only a convention, not a rule, but you will find this technique invaluable. It not only enables multiple use of a much-needed word like LOOP, but it reduces the possibility of an accidental redundancy of range names within a single spreadsheet.

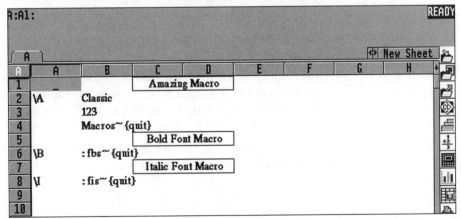

FIGURE 2.3 Examples of a convention for assigning macro backslash names.

Summary

In this chapter you have learned how to write your first simple macro. Some of the important points covered in this chapter are:

- It is better to use /Range Name Labels Right to name your macros than /Range Name Create.
- Range names are identified in the first column, the macro starts in the second column over, and the title of the macro identifying what it does goes in the third column, at the top of the macro.
- If nothing happens when you press the Alt+letter or Ctrl+letter combination, use the F5 Goto key to check whether your macro has been range-named properly.
- Macros always continue reading down to the next cell until they hit a blank cell, a cell containing a value, a {quit} command, or a branching command. Because of this feature, every macro should end with a {quit} or a branching command, even if it's followed by a blank cell.
- Every line of a macro is a label and must start with a label prefix like an apostrophe.
- You can stop a macro by pressing Ctrl+Break. You can pause a macro by pressing Ctrl+NumLock.
- Consistently locate your macros in an area where they are not likely to be written over or eliminated by work you do in standard spreadsheets. In the latest versions of 1-2-3, this means placing your macros on a separate page in the worksheet file. In earlier 1-2-3 versions, it means placing your macros in a separate behind-the-scenes macro library or off in the lower right area of the spreadsheet page, comfortably below and to the right of your spreadsheet areas.
- Use lowercase for macro commands and uppercase for range names.
- Macros can be named with a backslash and one of the 26 letters, with a backslash and a zero (for an autoexecute macro), or with a descriptive name to be invoked with the Alt+F3 Run key (Release 2.2 and higher) or a special Macro Launcher (described in Chapter 8).
- To the maximum extent possible, start all your internal macro range names with the same letter as the name of the macro itself.

In Chapter 3 we examine a few short but useful macros you can enter into any 1-2-3 worksheet file and start using immediately.

C H A P T E R | **3**

Adding a Few Short Macros

In this chapter we will start with a few simple one-liners—macros that are the easiest to grasp, quickest to write, and simplest to use immediately. You'll also learn how to combine keystrokes, macro commands, @functions, and menu-equivalent commands to create handy, timesaving macros; how to add new features to 1-2-3 like the ability to jump instantly to the lower left or upper right area of any spreadsheet; how to develop autoexecute macros that run automatically; and how to create an autoload file that opens at the start of any 1-2-3 session.

Getting Started

Our first macro in this chapter is designed to enter the current date in any cell. This macro is especially handy because you can use it in any spreadsheet and save over 20 keystrokes with each use.

Today's Date

Try creating it now. Starting with a blank worksheet, place your cell pointer in cell B2 and enter:

```
'@int(@now)~/rv~~/rfd4~~{quit}
```

Don't forget the apostrophe at the beginning. Remember, every line of a macro must be entered as a label. It should show up in cell B2 without the apostrophe as:

```
@int(@now)~/rv~~/rfd4~~{quit}
```

To title your macro, move to C1 and enter: **Today's Date Macro**. Then center it across two cells by choosing :Text Align Center, highlighting C1..D1, and pressing Enter. You may also want to add an outline around C1..D1 by choosing the WYSIWYG command :Format Line Outline, highlighting C1..D1, and pressing Enter.

To assign a range name to the macro, type '\T in cell A2. This will show up in the edit line at '\T with an apostrophe, but in cell A2 it will read simply \T. Now choose /Range Name Labels Right and press Enter. Your screen should look like Figure 3.1.

Move your cell pointer to cell C5 to try out your new macro. Press Alt+T (or Ctrl+T in 1-2-3 for Windows) and watch how the macro instantly places today's date in the current cell by entering the formula @int(@now), changes the date from a formula to a value with the /Range Value command, and uses /Range Format Date 4 to assign the date format *4* (*Long Int'l*) to the cell.

Keyboard-Equivalent Macro Commands

So far you've seen how a macro can execute slash-key commands, enter @functions, process special macro commands like {quit}, enter straight alphanumeric characters, and—as in the use of a tilde (~) for Enter—duplicate other keys on the keyboard. As it happens, 1-2-3 provides unique macro commands for most keys and keystroke combinations. Besides typing let-

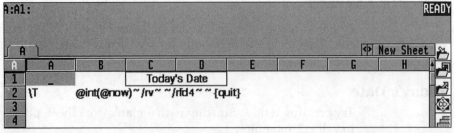

FIGURE 3.1 A macro to enter today's date from your computer's internal clock.

ters, numbers, and symbols found on your keyboard, macros can move as if you had pressed a directional key. They can also execute any of the function key operations and replicate the action of any of the special keys such as Del or Ins. Table 3.1 shows a complete list of keyboard-equivalent macro commands.

Table 3.1 Keyboard-Equivalent Macro Commands

Keyword Action	*Description*
Up Arrow	{up} or {u}
Down Arrow	{down} or {d}
Right Arrow	{right} or {r}
Left Arrow	{left} or {l}
PgUp	{pgup}
PgDn	{pgdn}
Ctrl+Right Arrow or Tab	{bigright}
Ctrl+Left Arrow or Shift+Tab	{bigleft}
Ins (in Edit mode)	{ins}
Del (in Edit mode)	{del}
Home	{home}
End	{end}
Slash (/)	/ or < (also see 1-2-3 for Windows list below)
Backspace	{backspace} or {bs}
Enter	~ (tilde)
Esc	{esc}
F1 Help	{help} (only in Release 2.2 and higher)
F2 Edit	{edit}
F3 Name	{name}
F4 Abs	{abs} (also see 1-2-3 for Windows list below)
F5 Goto	{goto}
F6 Pane	{window}
F7 Query	{query}
Alt+F7 Addin 1	{app1}
F8 Table	{table}
Alt+F8 Addin 2	{app2}
F9 Calc	{calc}
Alt+F9 Addin 3	{app3}
F10 Graph	{graph} (also see 1-2-3 for Windows list below)
Alt+F10 Addin Menu	{addin}

Table 3.1 *(Continued)*

Keyboard Equivalents for Release 3 and higher

Alt+F6 Zoom	{zoom}
Ctrl+PgUp	{nextsheet} or {ns}
Ctrl+PgDn	{prevsheet} or {ps}
Ctrl+End	{file}
Ctrl+End Ctrl+PgUp	{nextfile} or {nf} or {file}{ns}
Ctrl+End Ctrl+PgDn	{prevfile} or {pf} or {file}{ps}
Ctrl+End Home	{firstfile} or {ff} or {file}{home}
Ctrl+End End	{lastfile} or {lf} or {file}{end}
Ctrl+Home	{firstcell} or {fc}
End Ctrl+Home	{lastcell} or {lc}

Keyboard Equivalents for 1-2-3 for Windows

Ctrl+period	{anchor}
F4 Abs in Ready mode	{anchor}
F4 Abs in Edit mode	{abs}
F10 Menu or Alt	{menubar} or {mb} or {alt}
Slash (/) Menu	/ or < or {menu}
Ctrl+Right Arrow or Tab	{bigright} or {tab}
Ctrl+Left Arrow or Shift+Tab	{bigleft} or {backtab}

As Table 3.1 shows, you can use the {right} command to duplicate a press of the Right Arrow key. To move your cell pointer two cells to the right, you would use the macro command {right 2}. To create a macro that moves to the right eight times, move to cell C3 and enter the title **Right Macro**, center it across C3..D3 with the :Titles Align Center command, and use :Format Lines Outline to enclose the title in a box. Move to cell A4 and enter \R, choose /Range Name Labels Right and press Enter, and in cell B4, enter:

```
{right 6}{quit}
```

To try the macro, press Alt+R (Ctrl+R in for 1-2-3 for Windows). Your cell pointer should move six cells to the right.

To build a macro that moves to the left, enter **Left Macro** in cell C5, center it across C5..D5 with the :Titles Align Center command, and use :Format Lines Outline to enclose the title in a box. Enter \R in cell A6, choose /Range Name Labels Right and press Enter, and in cell B6 enter:

```
{left 6}{quit}
```

At this point, your screen should look like the example in Figure 3.2. Now you can use the Right Macro to move six cells to the right, and the Left Macro to move back where you started.

These macros can be altered, of course, to move any desired number of cells to the right or left, or they can be changed to prompt you for how many

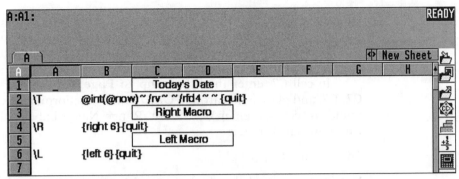

FIGURE 3.2 Adding macros to move right and left across the screen.

cells you want to move, or even offer you a customized menu of up to eight different sizes of jumps to the right or left. We will discuss this in more detail later.

These movement macros are so simple that you may wonder at their being included at all. You should know, however, that macros can also be activated in the middle of other standard 1-2-3 menu selections. Thus, if you want to use the /Copy command to copy from one cell to another location eight cells to the right, you can choose /Copy and, at the prompt for the range to copy from, press Enter. Then, at the prompt for a range to copy to, press Alt+R (Ctrl+R in 1-2-3 for Windows) and Enter. To copy to a cell *seven* columns to the right instead of six, choose /Copy and press Enter, then press Alt+R (Ctrl+R in 1-2-3 for Windows) to move six cells to the right, press the Right Arrow once for the seventh cell, and press Enter.

You can use these directional macros in any 1-2-3 menu selections involving range selection or cell movement, including /Range Format, /Range Erase, /Range Value, /Data Fill, and /Data Query, Input, Criterion, and Output. In fact, you can use them in any situation where the program prompts you to *Enter Range.* You can also use this technique with the F5 Goto key in response to the prompt to *Enter address to go to.*

Using this approach instead of simply pressing Ctrl+Right Arrow and Ctrl+Left Arrow has an advantage in that you can jump the cell pointer a designated number of cells every time. With Ctrl+Right Arrow and Ctrl+Left Arrow combinations, your pointer moves a variable number of cells depending on the width of the columns in the current screen.

Relocating the Cell Pointer

Here's another frustration-solver, as well as a real timesaver. Suppose you're moving down a typical worksheet, entering data or changing already existing data. You may have noticed that it can slow you down significantly to enter data at the bottom of the screen, while entering data at the top of the screen is much easier. (You can see what's coming up next, for one thing.)

If you've ever thought it would be nice to be able to jump both your pointer and the cell it occupies to the top of the screen, here's your solution:

In cell C7, enter the title **Jump to Page Top**, center the title across C7..D7, and place a box around C7..D7 with the :Format Lines Outline command. In cell A8, enter **\J**, choose /Range Name Labels Right, and press Enter. In cell B8 enter:

```
{d 18}{u 18}{quit}
```

Note how we used the single letter **d** instead of the word **down** in these directional macro commands. As you can see in Table 3.1, the **{left}**, **{right}**, **{up}**, and **{down}** commands can be entered as **{l}**, **{r}**, **{u}**, and **{d}**. You'll find that these shorter versions are easier to type and take up less room in a line of macro code.

To try out the macro, place your cell pointer at or near the bottom of the screen and press Alt+J (Ctrl+J in 1-2-3 for Windows). The macro quickly moves the cell pointer down 18 cells (scrolling the screen upwards at the same time), then up 18 cells to the original location. The effect will be to relocate the current cell to the top of the page. Try the macro from halfway down your screen and the effect is the same. In fact, from any point on your screen, the macro instantly relocates the current cell to the top.

This has become a classic macro—primarily because users find it simple to create and very useful. With a single two-keystroke combination, it always provides the user with an instant view of both the current cell and the page beneath it at once.

Jumping to the Outer Edges

Let's take a look at a couple of movement macros that actually add new features to 1-2-3. You are probably already familiar with 1-2-3's ability to jump your cell pointer to the lower right corner of the spreadsheet when you press the End and Home keys. However, 1-2-3 currently has no built-in shortcut for jumping you to the lower left or upper right corners—unless, of course, you use the following macros.

In cell C9, enter the title **Over from End Home**, center the title across C9..D9, and place a box around C9..D9 with the :Format Lines Outline command. In cell A10, enter **\O**. (**Note:** This is the letter **O**, not a zero.) Choose /Range Name Labels Right and press Enter. In cell B10 enter:

```
{end}{home}{d}{end}{l}{quit}
```

Now, in cell C11, enter the title **Up from End Home**, center the title across C11..D11, and place a box around C11..D11 with the :Format Lines Outline command. In cell A12, enter **\U**, choose /Range Name Labels Right, and press Enter. In cell B12 enter:

```
{end}{home}{r}{end}{u}{quit}
```

Once your macros are entered and range-named, you can jump to the lower left and upper right corners of any spreadsheet by pressing Alt+O and Alt+U. (In 1-2-3 for Windows, use Ctrl+O and Ctrl+U).

A Macro to Enter Month Headings

Suppose you want a macro to type the names of the first six months of the year horizontally across the spreadsheet page. In cell C13, enter the title **Month Entry Macro**, place a box around the two cells the title spans and center it, enter the name **\M** in A14, use the /Range Name Labels Right command, and in cell B14 enter:

```
Jan{r}Feb{r}Mar{r}Apr{r}May{r}Jun~{quit}
```

To invoke the macro, move the cell pointer to B18 and press Alt+M (Ctrl+M in 1-2-3 for Windows). The macro types Jan, moves to the right one cell, types Feb, moves to the right, and so on until it enters Jun and quits.

You can easily modify this macro to accomplish related tasks. For example, to enter the month titles vertically instead of horizontally, replace the **{r}** commands with **{d}**. To add a **Total** entry at the end of your list of months, edit the macro by typing in one more directional command and **Total~** just before the final {quit} command.

If you've followed the instructions for entering the macros described so far in this chapter, your screen should look something like the example in Figure 3.3.

Combining Menu Choices and Keyboard Equivalents

You've seen how to combine the typing of @functions with menu commands (as in the macro titled Today's Date), and how to combine straight typing with keyboard equivalents (as in the Month Entry macro). In this section, you'll get see how to combine slash-key menu commands with keyboard equivalents like directional commands. Later in the chapter, you'll see how you can use menubar-equivalent commands in 1-2-3 for Windows to replicate its Alt-key menubar commands.

Widen Column by One Space

Normally, in order to increase the width of a column to an exact value (as opposed to adjusting the column width with your mouse), you select

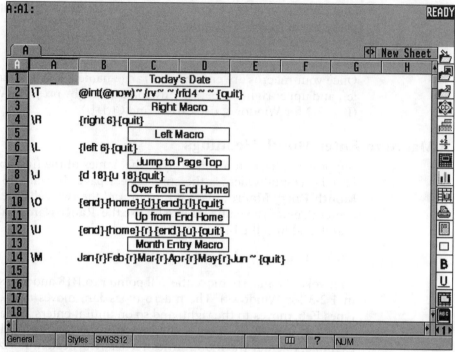

FIGURE 3.3 Examples of simple keystroke and movement macros.

/Worksheet Columnwidth Set and enter a new value or use your Right or Left Arrow keys to increase or decrease the column width.

To create a macro that widens the column automatically, start with a fresh spreadsheet page and in cell C1 enter **Widen Col 1 Space**. Create a box and center the title in C1..D1, give the macro the range name **\W**, and in cell C2 type an apostrophe and enter:

```
/wcs{r}~{quit}
```

Now try your macro. Move your cell pointer to column E, press Alt+W (Ctrl+W in 1-2-3 for Windows), and watch as the column width increases by one space. Invoke the macro three more times, and the column width increases by three more spaces.

Placing a Box around Two Cells

Although it's by no means required, we've been recommending here that you center and place an outline box around each macro title just to differentiate and visually separate the macros. Instead of repeatedly choosing the WYSIWYG commands :Format Lines Outline and :Text Align Center, enter in cell

C3 the title **Box Around 2 Cells**, but don't center it or enclose it in a box yet. Enter \B in A4, choose /Range Names Labels Right, press Enter, and in cell C4 enter:

```
:flo{r}~:tac{r}~{quit}
```

Now return to cell C3 and press Alt+B (Ctrl+B in 1-2-3 for Windows). The macro instantly creates an outline box across two cells and centers your new title within the box, saving you a total of 10 keystrokes with each use (the 12 keystrokes of the macro, minus the two-keystroke invoking combination).

Shortening the /Range Search Command

When you use the /Range Search command manually, you're required to:

1. Enter, accept, or change the default /Range Search range
2. Press Enter
3. Enter, accept, or change the default text to search for
4. Press Enter
5. Choose Formulas, Labels, or Both
6. Choose Find or Replace

What if you had a general, generic search macro that required only the search text to complete a typical search? Such a macro might set the /Range Search command to search through the entire worksheet page, clear the default search text for you, pause as you enter a new search string and press Enter, then automatically select Both (to cover the broader possibility that your string might be found in either formulas or labels) and the Find choice.

To create such a macro, enter **Find Data Macro** in cell C5 and press Alt+B (or Ctrl+B in 1-2-3 for Windows) to center and outline it. Enter \F in cell A6 and /Range Name the macro. Then, in cell B6, enter:

```
/rs{bs}{home}.{end}{home}~x{esc}{?}~bf{quit}
```

Your screen should look like Figure 3.4.

The macro starts by choosing /Range Search and then, to collapse the offered range to the current cell, presses the Backspace key. The Period key anchors the cell pointer and the macro uses End Home to highlight from cell A1 to the lower right corner of the spreadsheet. In response to 1-2-3's prompt for a search string, the macro types the letter **x** to enter a bogus string, and then uses Esc to clear the string. (Actually, this **x** could be any letter at all, and it's used to cover the contingencies that a search string may or may not be offered by default, so the Esc key will have a string to eliminate.)

The next command, **{?}**, is 1-2-3's way of pausing so you can enter a new search string. This is called an Interactive Command. You'll be seeing

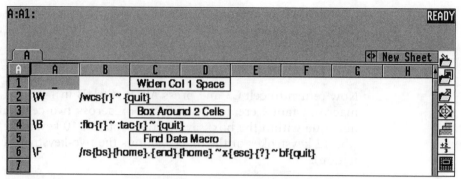

FIGURE 3.4 Macros that combine menu and keyboard-equivalent commands.

examples of this and other useful Interactive Commands as you go through subsequent chapters of this book. For now, you should know simply that the {?} pause command macro effectively waits for any and all keystrokes until the user presses Enter, at which time it continues as before.

Finally, the macro chooses Both and Find, and quits.

You can actually test the macro on strings found in the macro itself. Simply press Alt+F (Ctrl+F in 1-2-3 for Windows), enter the word **end**, and press Enter. Note how the macro finds the {end} command in the line of macro code you entered in cell B6.

Replacing All Zero Values with a Label

Now that you know one way to clear a default entry (by having the macro first type a bogus string, and then press Esc), let's look at a different macro that uses the same technique.

In cell C7, enter the title **Zero Display Change** and press Alt+B (Ctrl+B in 1-2-3 for Windows) to center and outline it across two cells. Enter \Z in cell A8 and /Range Name the macro. In cell B8, enter:

```
/wgzlx{esc}^-0-~{quit}
```

To test the macro, enter a zero in cells D12, D13, and D14. Press Alt+Z (Ctrl+Z in 1-2-3 for Windows) and watch how the macro uses the /Worksheet Global Zero Label command, enters a bogus label (the letter **x**), presses Esc to clear it, and enters the label **-0-** as a replacement for the usual 0 entry. When you're satisfied that the macro works as expected, erase the entries in D12..D14. To change back to the usual default setting for zeros, choose /Worksheet Global Zero No.

Speeding Up the Sort Feature

Here's another simple one-liner designed to save you six keystrokes as it chooses /Data Sort Reset, prompts you for a new sort range, pauses for your entry, chooses Primary, pauses for your choice of a primary sort field, and chooses Ascending Go.

To create the macro, enter the title **Sort Macro** in cell C9, press Alt+B (Ctrl+B in 1-2-3 for Windows) to center and outline it across two cells, enter **\S** in cell A10, /Range Name the macro, and in cell B10, enter:

```
/dsrd.{?}~p{?}~a~g{quit}
```

At this point, your worksheet should look like the example in Figure 3.5.

To test the macro, enter a small list of any type of sortable data in cells B12..D16 and press Alt+S (Ctrl+S in 1-2-3 for Windows). At the prompt for a range, type B12..D16 and press Enter. At the prompt for a Primary Field, press Enter to choose the first field in the database. The macro should instantly sort the data in B12..D16. (You may want to erase the database when you finish.)

Automating the @Date Function

Although you can enter any date in Release 3 and higher by entering it in the form mm/dd/yy and giving the cell a date format, Release 2 users must rely on the @date function. Unfortunately, typing the @date function can take up to 15 keystrokes, including the shift-key combinations required for @ and parentheses. Furthermore, the @date function requires that you enter the year first, then the month, then the day—which is not the most intuitive process. If you have Release 2, it's handy to have a macro that will start typing the @date formula for you and wait for you to enter the month, day, and year (in that order) before it completes the formula in the proper sequence.

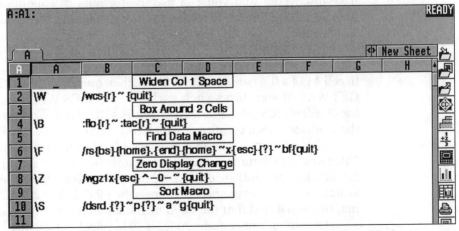

FIGURE 3.5 Adding more macros that use menu and keyboard-equivalent commands.

Begin by entering the title **Date Macro** in cell C11 and center and outline the title across two cells. Enter **\D** in cell A12, /Range Name the macro, and in cell B12, enter:

```
@date(,,){edit}{1 2}{?}{r}{?}{home}{r 6}{?}~/rfd4~~{quit}
```

When you invoke this macro in any blank cell, it begins by typing **@date(,,)** and then switches to Edit mode. At this point, the edit bar is at the end of the entry in the input line, so the macro moves it two characters to the left, just past the first comma, and pauses so you can type the month and press Enter. Then it moves to the right one cell, just past the second comma, and pauses so you can type the day and press Enter. It then uses Home to move to the front of the entry and right six characters to a point just past the opening parenthesis so you can type the year. When you press Enter, the macro uses /Range Format Date to give the cell a date format of 4 (*Long Int'l*).

Actually, this macro also can be useful for those with Release 3 or higher since, unlike a straight date entry, an @date formula can refer to values stored in other cells. For example, if the year 94 has been entered in a separate cell (say, cell F17) and you want to enter the date 5/1/94, you can use this macro to enter the formula **@date(F17,5,1)**. As you might guess, the macro pause {?} allows you to use a point-and-shoot method for entering a cell address just as you can manually. Thus, to refer to cell F17 when the macro pauses for the year, you can either type in the address of the cell containing that year value, or point to the cell with your mouse or cell pointer and press Enter.

Entering a Worksheet's Filename

If you're familiar with the @cell and @cellpointer functions, you may already have discovered that you can use the formula @cellpointer("filename") in Release 2.2 and higher to return the complete path, filename, and file extension for the current file. However, if you enter this particular @function in a worksheet file in Release 3 or higher and then open another file, you can get confusing results. For example, suppose you enter @cellpointer("filename") in cell A1 of a file named SALES.WK3, then open a separate file named BUDGET.WK3. If you then switch back to the SALES.WK3 file, you'll find that the @cellpointer("filename") entry returns BUDGET.WK3 until the next time the worksheet recalculates, at which time it changes to SALES.WK3.

The solution is to substitute @cell for @cellpointer when you use the "filename" attribute to identify your worksheets. For example, if you enter @cell("filename",A2) in cell A1 of one open worksheet file, then open or switch to another worksheet file, press the F9 Calc key, and return to the original file, you'll find that the @cell formula still returns the correct filename.

Of course, you can save at least 20 keystrokes by using a macro to enter the @cell formula for you. In cell C13, enter the title **Filename Macro** and center and outline the title across two cells. Enter \F in cell A14, /Range Name the macro, and in cell B14, enter:

```
@cell("filename",{d})~:ff5~~{quit}
```

If you've entered all the macros as described in these last sections, your screen should look like Figure 3.6.

To invoke the macro, move to any blank cell and press Alt+D (Ctrl+F in 1-2-3 for Windows). The macro begins by typing **@cell("filename"**, moves down one cell to enter the address of the cell below, closes the parentheses, enters the formula, and uses :Format Font 5 to give the cell an eight-point Dutch font (assuming default font configuration). Of course, you can change to any font by simply changing the font number 5 to any number from 1 through 8.

Naming Several Macros at Once

So far, you've been instructed to use the /Range Name Labels Right command on each macro as you create it. However, if you're creating several macros, one right after the other, you can save several keystrokes by waiting until the last macro is entered and then using /Range Name Labels Right on all the macro range names at once.

For example, you can easily range-name the macros in Figure 3.6 by placing your cell pointer on cell A2, choosing /Range Name Labels Right, highlighting down through cell A6, and pressing Enter. It's especially handy to know about this technique if you choose /Range Name Reset by mistake and need to rename your macros, or if you're writing a long macro with several internal range names (discussed in more detail in later chapters).

Format Macros

The format macros shown below are more examples of macros that call up 1-2-3's slash-key menu and step through the menu commands for you.

Examine Figure 3.7. You'll note that all four format macros are the same except for the fourth character. The purpose of the macros is to change the formats of a cell or a range with just a few keystrokes. Although you can accomplish the same tasks by clicking on format smarticons in 1-2-3 Release 2.4 and higher, those of you who prefer not to take your hands from the keyboard to add cell formatting will appreciate a macro that goes through the equivalent menu commands for you.

Thus, instead of choosing /Range Format Currency and pressing Enter twice to change a cell to a dollar format, you can press Alt+C. The macro chooses /Range Format Currency, presses Enter to choose two decimals,

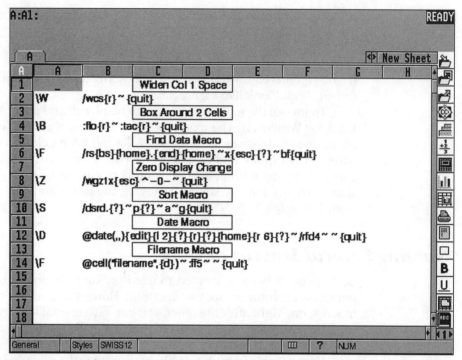

FIGURE 3.6 Adding macros that combine @functions with keyboard-equivalent commands.

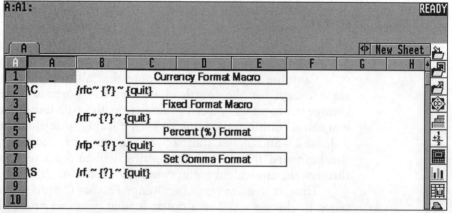

FIGURE 3.7 Four format macros (Currency, Fixed, Percent, Set Comma).

and pauses at the prompt to *Enter range to format:*, at which point you can either highlight a range or simply press Enter to accept the current cell.

These macros can be changed, of course, to choose other than the two decimals offered by 1-2-3 by default. As an example, you can change the Currency Format macro to reflect no decimals by having it read:

```
/rfc0~{?}~{quit}
```

This easy customizability means that macros have one distinct advantage over standard smarticons: They're much simpler to modify.

Using Menubar Commands in 1-2-3 for Windows

You've seen how to use macros to choose standard slash-key commands (also known as Classic Menu commands in 1-2-3 for Windows). In this section you'll learn how to write macros that choose the Menubar commands unique to 1-2-3 for Windows.

To activate the Menubar manually with your keyboard, you press the Alt key, followed by the underlined letter of the menu choice you want. For example, to assign the Currency format with no decimal points, you can press Alt, then the letter **r** (for Range), **f** (for Format), **c** (for Currency), the Tab key to move to the Decimals places box, 0 to change to zero decimal places, and Enter to choose OK.

Assuming you have 1-2-3 for Windows, you may want to go through these keystrokes manually just to remind yourself how it's done. In similar situations where you're writing a macro based on manual menu choices, you may even want to write down the steps you take on a piece of paper so you'll find it easy to duplicate them later with macro code.

Once you've gone through the process manually, enter the same keystrokes in cell B2 of a blank page or worksheet file, like this:

```
{alt}rfc{tab}0~
```

Give the macro the range name \C and include the title **Currency Format**. An example is shown in Figure 3.8.

As you can see in Figure 3.8, you can create formatting macros replicating the Menubar commands in 1-2-3 for Windows that will provide a Comma format with two decimal places (the Comma smarticon in 1-2-3 for Windows uses zero decimal places), a Percent format with one decimal (instead of the two decimal places used by the Percent smarticon), and a Date format macro that uses Date 1 (DD-MMM-YY).

As it happens, this technique for macro-writing in 1-2-3 for Windows is not as intuitive as the slash-key techniques already discussed. Will you

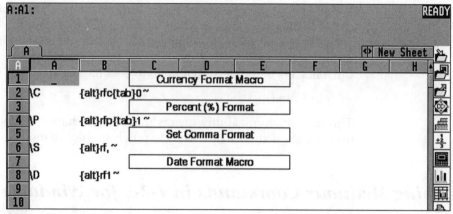

FIGURE 3.8 Four format macros using the 1-2-3 for Windows Menubar.

easily remember, for example, to include a {tab} command if you try to rewrite the Currency Format macro later?

Fortunately, 1-2-3 for Windows Release 4.0 and higher provides another method for accomplishing the same task without going through either the Classic Menu slash-key or Menubar commands. In these releases, special menu-equivalent commands are available for every menu action you can take. Since there are so many, they tend to be difficult to remember as well; but you can record keystrokes, menu choices, and mouse actions as a series of macro commands in the Transcript window, effectively letting 1-2-3 for Windows write your macro code for you and allowing you to copy the code to any location in a worksheet page. Instructions for recording your macros for 1-2-3 for DOS as well as for 1-2-3 for Windows are covered in detail in Chapter 4.

More Macros Combining @Functions and Keyboard Equivalents

You've seen several macros that combine @functions with keyboard equivalents. This section offers examples of macros using @sum, @round, @if, and @err.

The Add Macro

Without doubt, the most commonly typed formula in 1-2-3 is the @sum formula. Yet each @sum formula requires seven keystrokes, including the @ sign and parentheses shift-key combinations, in addition to the keystrokes or mouse actions required to establish the @sum range. It's no mystery, then, why 1-2-3 (Release 2.4 and higher) includes a smarticon to create the @sum formula for you.

If you prefer to keep your hands on the keyboard, however, you may be interested in a macro that will instantly sum a vertical range for you with the press of just two keys. Called the Add macro (see Figure 3.9), this short one-liner also makes for a handy subroutine that you can use in other, longer macros as you become more advanced with your macro-writing.

To create the macro, enter the title **Add Macro** in cell C1, give the macro the range name **\A**, and in cell B2 enter:

```
@sum({u}.{end}{u}{?}..)~{quit}
```

To try the macro, enter some values in F3, F4 and F5, then place your cell pointer in F6 and press Alt+A (Ctrl+A in 1-2-3 for Windows). Note how the macro types **@sum(,** moves up one cell, anchors the cell pointer, highlights to the last filled cell with End Up, and pauses so you can verify that it really selected the range you want to sum. (This is especially important if your range of values includes a blank cell, since End Up stops at the last cell below the first blank cell.) If you need to adjust the sum range, you can do so at this point. When you press Enter, the macro presses two periods (..) to convert the range to a top-to-bottom sequence (from F5..F3 to F3..F5 in this case), presses Enter, and quits.

Of course, you can easily modify this macro so that it adds a line at the top edge of the sum cell, or formats the cell for currency with two decimals, or changes the font, or moves to the left one cell and enters the word **Total**. You might want to experiment with these types of changes yourself, just for practice.

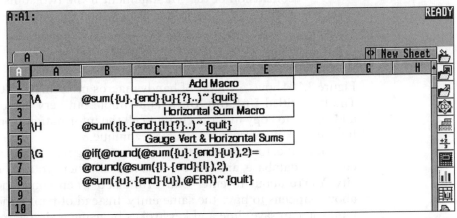

FIGURE 3.9 Three add macros (Add, Horizontal Sum, Gauge Vert . . .).

The Horizontal Sum Macro

If you want a macro that sums to the left, try the Horizontal Sum macro shown in Figure 3.9. As with the Add macro, this macro includes a macro Pause [?] command so you can verify and change the highlighted sum range if necessary before the macro completes the @sum formula. The macro reads:

```
@sum({l}.{end}{l}{?}..)~{quit}
```

The Gauge Vert & Horizontal Sums Macro

The Add macro and Horizontal Sum macro can be combined in a separate macro that compares the horizontal against the vertical sums of a matrix and provides an @sum formula if the two sums are equal, or an error message if they differ. Refer to the Gauge Vert & Horizontal Sums macro in Figure 3.9.

@if(@round(@sum({u}.{end}{u})),2)=   Begins with an @if statement to be used for the logic, *if the vertical equals the horizontal sum, insert the vertical sum, otherwise insert an Error message.* The @round formula is used to ensure that any differences in the two sums are not the result of rounding problems. This line includes the standard Add macro (minus a pause), followed by the number 2 for rounding to two decimal points, and an equals sign as part of the @if logic.

@round(@sum({l}.{end}{l})),2),   Types the rounded version of the Horizontal Sum macro (minus a pause), followed by a comma to continue the @if logic.

@sum({u}.{end}{u}),@ERR)~{quit}   Provides a vertical sum as the conclusion of the @if statement if the two sums are equal or an ERR entry if they differ, after which the macro quits.

Macros Using the /Copy Command

Figure 3.10 shows a couple of handy macros involving the /Copy command. The first, titled **Up/Copy Data**, is a simple but very useful one-liner that allows you to copy into the current cell the information from the cell above by using a kind of copy-in-reverse technique.

Imagine, for example, that you're entering names and addresses into a customer database, and you come to the cell where you enter the customer's city. You're about to enter **San Francisco** when you notice that the cell above happens to have the same entry. Instead of typing those thirteen letters, you can save time and keystrokes by using a simple macro that starts the copy command, presses Esc to free the cell pointer, moves up one cell, and presses Enter twice, like this:

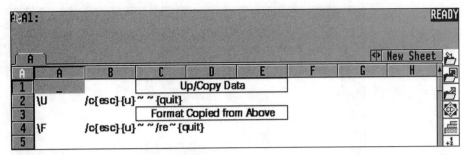

FIGURE 3.10 Two handy /Copy Macros.

```
/c{esc}{u}~~{quit}
```

Try it for yourself. After typing and range-naming the Up/Copy Data macro from Figure 3.10, enter some extraneous data in a blank cell. Move to the cell below it and press Alt+U (Ctrl+U in 1-2-3 for Windows). The macro instantly copies the data from above into the current cell.

To copy just the *format* of the cell above, try the macro titled, **Format Copied from Above**. This is simply a modification of the previous macro, using the commands:

```
/c{esc}{u}~~/re~{quit}
```

This macro instantly copies the data from the cell above and then /Range Erases the copied data, leaving just the format in the current cell.

Improving 1-2-3's Row Insert Feature

The same ideas can be included in a special macro to improve on 1-2-3's feature for inserting rows. Under normal conditions, inserting a row in a spreadsheet database leaves you with completely blank and unformatted cells. In this section we'll look at macros designed to insert a new row, and then copy both the data and formatting, or just the formatting without data, from the row above.

Insert Row with Data

Suppose you're working in a spreadsheet database, and you need to insert a new row to enter another record of data. If much of the data you plan to enter in that new row actually duplicates the data already entered in the row above, you'll save quite a bit of time by using the **Insert Row with Data** macro shown in Figure 3.11.

This macro inserts a row, then uses some some interesting techniques for copying the data above into the new row, as follows:

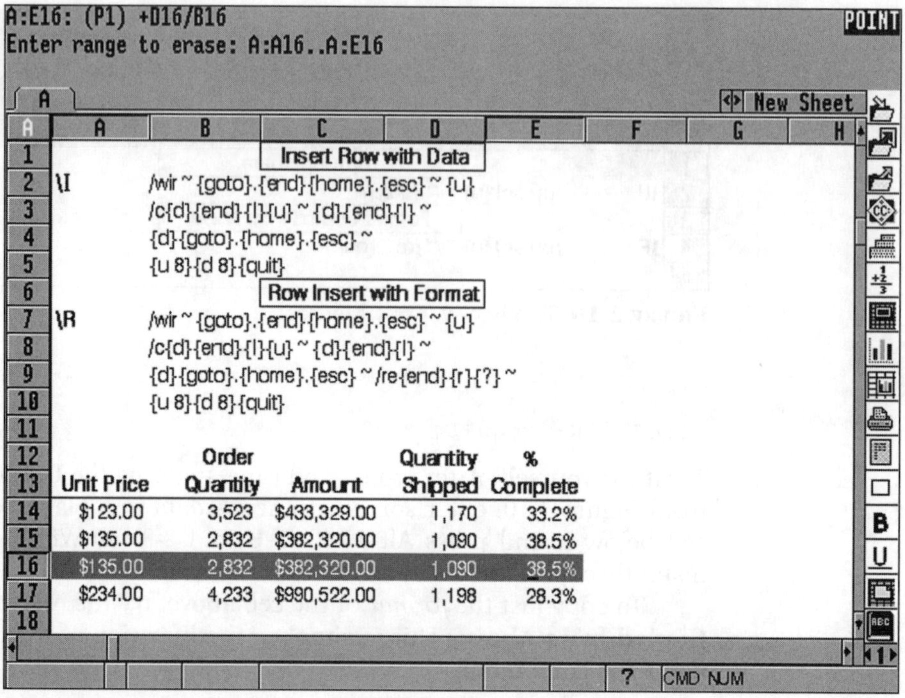

FIGURE 3.11 Macros to insert rows with data or formats.

/wir~{goto}.{end}{home}.{esc}~{u}   First inserts a new row, then uses the F5 Goto key in an unusual way to jump the cell pointer to the right-most cell of the current row. The macro does this by pressing Goto, then pressing the Period key (.) to anchor the cell pointer. Then it presses End Home, which highlights a range to the lower right of the active area of the worksheet. Another Period rotates the free corner of this range to the lower left. Then the macro presses Esc to collapse the range to the anchor cell. It's complicated, but the effect is to jump the cell pointer to the right-most active cell of the newly inserted row. Finally, the cell pointer is moved to the cell immediately below.

/c{d}{end}{l}{u}~{d}{end}{l}~   This line of the macro copies the row above into the newly inserted row. It starts with a /Copy command, copying the entire row by highlighting down one cell, then all the way to the left, then up one cell. For the copy destination, the cell pointer is moved down one cell to the new row and all the way to the left.

{d}{goto}.{home}.{esc}~   Moves the cell pointer back to the new row and jumps it to the left-most cell (typically column A) using the same Goto technique as above.

{u 8}{d 8}{quit}   Finally, the cell pointer position is adjusted more towards the center of the screen by moving down eight cells, then up eight cells.

Row Insert with Format

Take a look now at the macro titled **Row Insert with Format** in Figure 3.11. Instead of inserting a new row and leaving you with copied data, this macro leaves you with copied formats. Whereas most users format individual cells of a newly inserted row one-by-one, you'll find it much faster to use a macro that formats the entire row with the formats from the row above.

The trick is simple, really. The macro is a repeat of the **Insert Row with Data** macro, except that it also erases the copied data, leaving just the formats in the new row. Note the fourth line of the macro:

```
{d}{goto}.{home}.{esc}~/re{end}{r}{?}~
```

As you can see, this line ends with a /Range Erase command, then uses End RightArrow to highlight to the right. It also includes a Pause {?} command to wait for you to accept or extend the range to erase—an important addition in case your copied data includes gaps that would stop an End RightArrow sequence before the end of the row of data.

Creating Autoexecute Macros

An *autoexecute macro* runs automatically as soon as the file containing it is opened. You can create an autoexecute macro simply by naming it \0 (the number 0, not the uppercase letter "O"). However, since pressing the Alt (or Ctrl) key to start a macro only works with a letter, not a number, you'll find that you cannot manually invoke an autoexecute macro in 1-2-3 for DOS by pressing Alt+0 or in 1-2-3 for Windows by pressing Ctrl+0.

The trick for being able to manually invoke an autoexecute macro is to give it a second backslash range name that refers to a cell containing a pass-through *null command*. A null command is a set of empty braces {} that the macro reads, but for which it takes no action. The macro simply moves on to the next macro command. Figure 3.12 shows an example of this: an autoexecute macro with two invoking names. The first, which you invoke by pressing Alt+P (Ctrl+P in 1-2-3 for Windows), is a backslash-letter name and starts the macro with a null command. The second is the autoexecute \0 range name that invokes the second line of the macro when the worksheet file is opened.

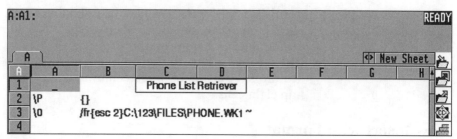

FIGURE 3.12 An autoexecute macro to retrieve a phone listing.

Suppose you have a phone listing in a worksheet file named PHONE.WK1 in the directory C:\123\FILES, and you want to be able to retrieve that file quickly from any directory. Instead of manually using the /File Retrieve command and laboriously searching for the appropriate subdirectory and the filename PHONE.WK1 from whatever subdirectory happens to be current, you can create a simple worksheet file with an autoexecute macro that retrieves the file for you. If you then save a copy of this relatively small worksheet file in every directory under C:\123, opening any copy of that file automatically causes 1-2-3 to retrieve the PHONE.WK1 file.

Note that, unlike the File Open command in Release 3 and higher, /File Retrieve closes the current file as it calls up a new file. This means that the autoexecute macro in Figure 3.12 actually closes down its own file when it has completed its task of retrieving PHONE.WK1.

Once you've created the autoexecute macro (including the important /Range Name Labels Right procedure), save it with a filename like 0GET-PHON.WK1 so it appears ahead of all other file names in the current directory when you /File Retrieve it. This will make the file very easy to access from anywhere in the 1-2-3 environment. After saving the file, you can test it by pressing Alt+P (Ctrl+P in 1-2-3 for Windows) or by closing the file and opening it again.

Understanding AUTO123 Worksheets

You might also want to consider saving your autoexecute macro with the name AUTO123.WK1 (or, in Release 3.0 or higher, AUTO123.WK3) in the default directory, so it becomes an autoloading file. In fact, any file named AUTO123 in the default directory is automatically opened each time you begin a 1-2-3 session. Since, in this case, the AUTO123 file contains an autoexecute macro, the macro also starts up by itself when you first load 1-2-3. (AUTO123 files and autoexecute macros are also discussed in Chapters 7 and 9.)

Summary

In this chapter we have introduced a collection of short macros that you can start using right away:

- A macro to insert today's date and assign a date format in the current cell.
- Left and Right macros to jump your cell pointer a designated number of cells left or right.
- The Jump macro to jump the screen view so the current cell shifts to the top of the page.
- Over from End Home and Up from End Home, macros that move your cell pointer to the lower left or upper right corners of the active spreadsheet area.
- A Month Entry macro to instantly enter Jan through Jun in a horizontal or vertical range.
- A macro that widens the current column by one space.
- A macro to place an outline around two cells and center the data across those two cells.
- The Find Data macro, designed as a shortcut for the /Range Search command.
- The Zero Display Change macro, which instantly converts all zero-entry cells in the current worksheet to display the label "-0-".
- An instant Sort macro that saves up to seven keystrokes as it prompts for a range and primary sort key before automatically sorting your data.
- A Date macro that allows you to enter month, day, and year while creating an @date formula in the current cell, then formats the cell for the short international date format.
- A Filename macro that labels the current worksheet with its complete path and filename.
- Format macros that use slash-key menu choices and 1-2-3 for Windows Menubar commands to assign formats to the current cell.
- Add macros that type the @sum formula for you, automatically setting the range to sum.
- The Gauge Vert & Horizontal Sums macro that creates a cross-checking @sum formula.

- Copy macros that copy the data and format, or just the format, from the cell above.
- Row Insert macros that insert a new row and copy the data and formats, or just the formats, from the row above.
- An autoexecute macro that, when you open the worksheet file containing it, automatically retrieves a separate file.

In addition to exploring these macros, this chapter covered the following concepts:

- As shown in Table 3.1, you can use keyboard-equivalent commands in a macro to duplicate pressing keys manually. You can even run macros with keyboard-equivalent commands while in the middle of manually accessing 1-2-3's menu commands.
- You can use a little-known feature of the F5 Goto feature to relocate your cell pointer to the opposite edge of a spreadsheet database.
- You can create an autoexecute macro by naming it \0. An autoexec macro runs automatically as soon as the file containing it is opened. To create an autoloading file, give your worksheet the filename AUTO123.

In Chapter 4 you'll learn about the Step mode for stepping through macros one command at a time, the Macro Debugger for watching your macro code as it executes in Step mode, and how to use the Macro Learn feature in Release 2.x and Macro Record feature in Release 3 and higher to get 1-2-3 to record your keystrokes for inclusion in custom macros.

4

Using Step, Record, and Learn Keys

In this chapter you'll learn how to debug your macros, how to step through a macro one keystroke or command at a time, and how to record your macros using the Macro Record and Macros Learn features.

Debugging Your Macros

The single most common error in writing macros occurs when you omit an important tilde (~). If your macro seems to operate incorrectly when you run it, or if it stops altogether, check first to see that all required tildes have been typed appropriately. Be careful, though. Depending on the resolution of your screen, a quotation mark can look like a tilde, and vice-versa. You may think the tilde is there, only to find after much searching and frustration that actually it was a quotation mark all along.

The second most common mistake is the omission of a parenthesis or braces, or the typing of braces where parentheses are required, or the inclusion of parentheses or square brackets where you need braces.

Another frustrating error occurs when you accidentally add one or more blank spaces where they shouldn't be, such as between the open brace and the keyword in a macro command, between macro arguments, in an

@function within a command, in a range name, or—the worst possible circumstance—at the end of a line of macro text. This last case can be maddening, since such spaces are not visible on the screen. However, pressing the F2 Edit key can reveal the intruding spaces in the upper panel. Just look for the location of the blinking cursor in the Edit mode. If the cursor rests immediately after the last letter, there are no extraneous spaces at the end of the macro line.

Another frequent error happens when your macro tries to refer to a misspelled range name, or a range name that has been deleted or that has not been named yet. Once you start writing macros with the liberal use of range names, this type of problem will arise from time to time. When your macro tries to operate on an incorrect or missing range name, 1-2-3 presents an error message warning you of an invalid cell or range address or an invalid range in a command like {branch}. To make it easier to find the problem, 1-2-3 also shows the cell address in the macro where the problem occurred.

If you're unsure about the location or existence of a range name as you type it into a new macro, press the F5 Goto key and enter the range name. If all is correct, your cell pointer should jump to the expected location in the worksheet. If the range name doesn't exist as entered in the macro, you must either correct the name in the macro (for example, it may be misspelled), or move to the proper location where the macro should exist and use /Range Name Labels Right or /Range Name Create to establish the missing range name.

Other common macro errors include:

- Spelling errors, including incorrect spelling of keywords, such as {WINDOWOFF} instead of {WINDOWSOFF}
- Missing arguments required by a macro command or @function
- Invalid argument separators
- Arguments of the wrong type; for example, a text argument when 1-2-3 expects a number
- Range names or subroutine names that inappropriately duplicate macro keywords such as Quit, Return, or Query
- A blank cell or a cell containing a value, which ends the macro before you intend it to end

Common errors specific to 1-2-3 for Windows include:

- Omitting a hyphen in a hyphenated macro keyword or putting in an extra hyphen in a hyphenated keyword
- Using an underscore instead of a hyphen in a macro keyword
- Omitting or misplacing an argument separator (typically a comma) when you intentionally left out an optional argument between two other arguments

- Using names or addresses without worksheet letters or file references when you need these to specify a location not in the current worksheet
- Omitting quotation marks required around some text arguments; for example, using {edit-goto RATES} instead of the required {edit-goto "RATES"}

The Step Command

If you cannot locate a macro error by scanning through the macro itself, try the Step key. In Release 2.x, you can shift to the macro Step Mode by pressing Alt+F2. In all other releases, press Alt+F2 and select Step. You should see the word STEP appear at the bottom of your screen. Once you switch to Step Mode, invoke your macro and then press any key several times (Lotus recommends you use the Spacebar). You can watch the macro play out a keystroke or command at a time at every press of a key and easily discover where the macro is hanging up.

In Step mode, you can also hold down any key and watch the macro step very quickly through its keystrokes and commands. If you have quick reactions, you may even be able to use this method of holding down a key until you are almost at the part of the macro where a problem occurred, then press the key several more times in succession to step more slowly through the next portion of the macro. This may take some practice, but it can be a real timesaver for long, complicated macros with a problem near the end.

In Release 2.x and 4.x, you get an additional bonus when you use Step: Each line of the macro and its cell address appear at the bottom of the screen as it is being played out. This is called the Macro Trace feature.

With Macro Trace, you can watch the macro code below your screen as the macro runs, allowing you to both read the macro itself and see its results at the same time. Figure 4.1 gives you an example of the Step mode Macro Trace feature in action. (In this example, the actual macro is also shown onscreen. However, this is done for clarity only; normally the macro would be out of sight.)

The macro in this example is the Row Insert with Format macro from Chapter 3, used to insert a row and give it the same format as the row above. As you can see, the cell pointer was placed at cell A10, the Step mode was activated, and the macro was started by pressing Alt+R (Ctrl+R in 1-2-3 for Windows). As the macro plays, the current line of macro code (the first line in this case) is displayed at the bottom of the screen. As you press any key, such as the Spacebar, each macro instruction is executed in turn and the next instruction is highlighted.

You can turn the Step mode OFF at any time during macro execution, and ON at any point where the macro is pausing for an interactive com-

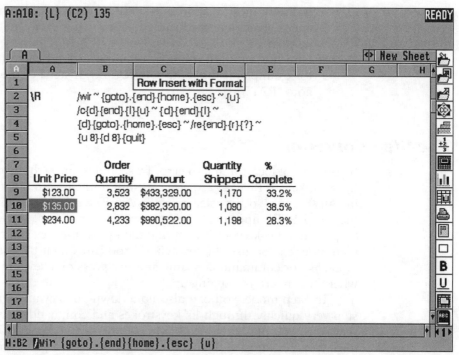

FIGURE 4.1 Using the Step mode Macro Trace feature in Release 2.x. (Note the macro code at the bottom of the screen.)

mand such as a bracketed question mark {?} pause. If your macro is running in Step mode, use the Alt+F2 keystroke combination to return to normal speed. If you are running at normal mode and the macro has paused for your input, use Alt+F2 to switch to Step mode.

If the macro produces an Error message in the Step mode, press Ctrl+Break to break out of the macro. (You may have to press Esc at this point as well.) Then use the F2 Edit key to modify the macro.

After you have finished debugging your macro, be sure to leave the Step mode by pressing Alt+F2 again.

Using the Alt+F2 Record Key in Release 3 and Higher

With the advent of Release 3, Lotus added new features to the Alt+F2 key, based on its new Record Buffer. The Record Buffer is a 512-byte area of computer memory in which 1-2-3 records all your keystrokes in the background as you type them, always saving your most recent keystrokes. As the buffer fills up, 1-2-3 discards keystrokes from the beginning of the buffer (your earliest keystrokes) to make room for your most recent keyboard input.

The Record Buffer is completely unobtrusive; for the most part, you will not be aware of the buffer at all until you press Alt+F2 and choose Playback or Copy from the menu choices **Playback**, **Copy**, **Erase**, and **Step**.

The Record key menu choices are described as follows:

Playback   Gives you access to the Record Buffer where you can view your latest keystrokes, edit the keystrokes, and highlight any portion of the keystrokes you wish to play back starting from your current cell. This allows you to play back your keystrokes without having to create a macro in your worksheet.

Copy   Allows you to view your latest keystrokes in the Record Buffer, edit the keystrokes, and highlight any portion of the keystrokes you wish to copy in macro format into your spreadsheet.

Erase   Erases the entire Record Buffer so the keystrokes you type from that point on are recorded starting at the beginning of the buffer.

Step   Exactly duplicates the Step key in Release 2.x, permitting you to step through a given macro one keystroke at a time. In Release 3.x, this option does *not* include the Macro Trace feature found in Release 2.x.

An Example of the Alt+F2 Record Feature

The simple spreadsheet in Figure 4.2 was created by starting with a blank worksheet and entering the numbers 123, 234, 345, 456, and 567 in cells D4..D8. Then the cell pointer was moved to D9 and the @sum formula was typed. To establish the @sum range, the UpArrow was pressed, then a period, then End UpArrow, and finally a closing parenthesis and Enter. Alt+F2 was pressed to demonstrate the menu you get when you use the Alt+F2 Record key in Release 4 for DOS.

The reason for going through all that was to show you how those keystrokes are recorded in the Record Buffer of Release 3 and higher. Refer now to Figure 4.3. This view of the worksheet was created by pressing the Alt+F2 key and selecting PLAYBACK. Notice that the spreadsheet drops down to display the entire 512-byte buffer, just as it drops when you use the F2 Edit key on any cell entry that exceeds 80 characters in Release 3 and higher.

As you can see, as each element of the spreadsheet was created, the keystrokes used were automatically saved in the Record Buffer. The format that the Record Buffer uses is the macro command language.

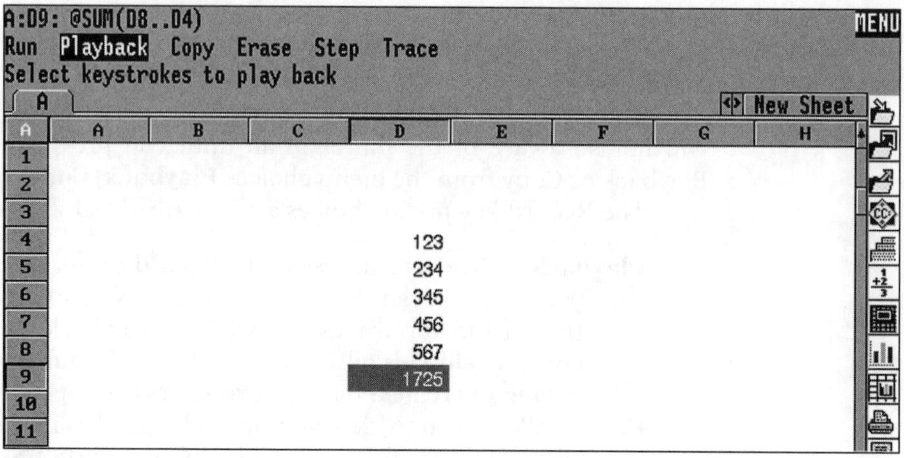

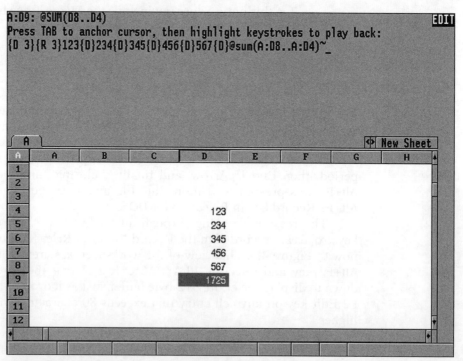

FIGURE 4.2 A simple spreadsheet created in Release 4.

FIGURE 4.3 Invoking Record Playback in Release 3 and higher.

You may have noted that 1-2-3 did not record the arrow keys used to highlight the @sum range, but recorded the result of those keystrokes instead. In some instances, this can be unfortunate. In this case, for example, playing back these keystrokes will correctly sum the specific column originally summed, but you will not be able to copy these keystrokes into the worksheet and use them as a general, generic macro that will sum a column of numbers in any location in the worksheet.

If you want to play back any portion of the recorded keystrokes, press TAB to anchor the cursor, then highlight the keystrokes to play back. In this same way, if you select COPY, you can press TAB to anchor the cursor, then highlight the keystrokes to copy into your worksheet. You will be prompted for the destination range. Respond by pointing to and highlighting the cells spanning the first row where you want the macro to appear. The keystrokes will appear starting at the first cell of the destination range and continuing downward from there.

TIP: *Since we're talking about Release 3 or higher, it's a good idea to insert a new sheet where you can copy your recorded macro code. Furthermore, since the Alt+F2 COPY feature fits the transferred macro code to the width of the destination column you specify, you may want to widen the column from the usual default width of 9 before you press Alt+F2. (A column width of 30 to 50 usually works well to accommodate typical lines of macro code.)*

At that point all you need to do is range name the first cell of the macro with a backslash-letter combination (\A, \B, etc.), move your cell pointer to the location where you want your macro to start, and press the appropriate Alt+*letter* combination (Ctrl+*letter* in 1-2-3 for Windows).

In addition to recording standard keystrokes and macro keywords, the Record Buffer will also record composed characters you can create using the Compose key. It will not, however, record Alt+F1 Compose, Alt+F2 Record, Alt+F3 Run, or Alt+F4 Undo. Neither will it record Ins, Scroll Lock, Caps Lock, Num Lock, Print Screen, or Ctrl+Break. When you use Ctrl+Break to leave a menu, 1-2-3 records the equivalent number of {esc} keystrokes.

As a final note on this feature, you may find the Record Buffer both intriguing and frustrating. It can be intriguing because it offers a new functionality and a new way to reenter recent data that in some way has been written over or erased. Unfortunately, you may experience some frustration at realizing that the keystrokes you want to play back have been shoved out of the Record Buffer by more recent keystrokes; or at finding that some of your keystrokes cannot be recorded in the buffer at all; or at having to do more editing than you might have expected after copying the keystrokes into a macro area.

Using the Alt+F5 Learn Key in Release 2.x

If you have Release 2.x, you may find the Alt+F5 Learn Key more to your liking—though it has limitations of its own. Although only available as a separate add-in for Release 2 and 2.01, the Alt+F5 Learn key is a welcome addition to the function keys of the later releases of the 2.x family. Instead of manually typing your own macros, you can use the Release 2.x Learn feature to record your keystrokes as you work, so that later 1-2-3 can automatically and instantly perform those same repetitive tasks for you.

Creating the Learn Range in Release 2.x

Before the Alt+F5 Learn key can be used in Release 2.x, you must call up the main command menu and create a Learn Range—a location in the worksheet where 1-2-3 can record your keystrokes. Try this:

1. Move to an area where your keystrokes can be recorded without interfering with the function or appearance of your worksheet. (One convenient way to do this is by pressing End Home PgDn RightArrow—an area guaranteed to be blank and a place where inserting or deleting rows will not destroy your input.)
2. Increase the column width (30 to 50 works well), then choose /Worksheet Learn Range. You will see a prompt, "Enter Learn range:", in the upper control panel.
3. At the prompt, lock in your cell pointer with the period (.) key and highlight a single-column range. Trying to highlight a multicolumn range also works, but only because 1-2-3 is programmed to automatically reduce it to a single-column range in any case. See the example in Figure 4.4.

> **NOTE:** *It's best to highlight a range that is much larger than you think you'll need, so 1-2-3 doesn't run out of space while recording your keystrokes. You will typically run out of learn range space long before you ever thought you would, so try making the range four times larger than you think you need. If 1-2-3 does run out of space while recording your keystrokes, it interrupts you with the error message, "Learn range is full." Instructions for what to do in that case are covered later in this section.*

4. Move to the area of the worksheet where you want to start performing the task to be recorded. Typically, the learn range is not visible as you perform this task.

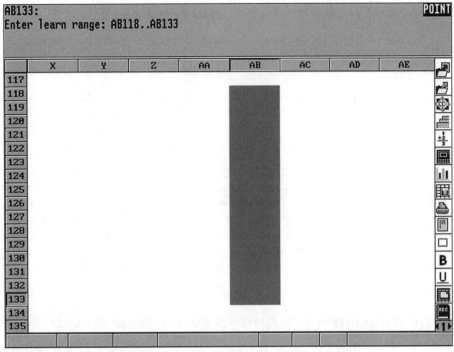

FIGURE 4.4 Creating a Learn Range in Release 2.x.

5. Press the Alt+F5 Learn key to start the recording. You will see a LEARN indicator appear in the lower part of your screen.

6. Perform the task you want to automate. Don't worry if you make a mistake; you can always go back and edit the recorded keystrokes later.

7. At the end of the task, press the Alt+F5 Learn key again to turn off the recording feature. The LEARN Indicator disappears.

8. Move to the Learn range. If you pressed End Home PgDn Right-Arrow to go there originally, press End Home End UpArrow now to return.

9. Review the recorded keystrokes and make any changes that seem appropriate. As you edit the recorded keystrokes, be sure not to leave any empty cells in the middle of the macro, or 1-2-3 will interpret the blank cell as the end of the macro. If you made more mistakes than you care to change, erase the learn range using /Worksheet Learn Erase and start again at Step 1.

10. Once you are satisfied that the macro has no errors, type an apostrophe and a backslash-letter combination (type '\A, for example) in the cell to the left of the first cell of the Learn range, and press Enter. Finally, select /Range Name Labels Right and press Enter.

How to Handle an Error during Learn

If, while the LEARN feature is recording your keystrokes, you suddenly get an error message indicating that you have run out of space in your Learn range, do one of the following:

 Erase the learn range by selecting /Worksheet Learn Erase, then make the learn range larger by selecting /Worksheet Learn Range and pressing PgDn several times, and Enter. At this point you can start the entire process over again at Step 1.

 Alternatively, you can leave the recorded keystrokes in place and establish a second learn range below the previous range. Do this by selecting /Worksheet Learn Range and pressing the period key (.) twice, then End, DownArrow, PgDn several times, period (.) twice again, DownArrow, and Enter. When you press Enter, your cell pointer will jump back to the location where you were interrupted, and you can proceed with your task where you left off.

How the Learn Feature Records Your Keystrokes

As with the Alt+F2 Record key in Release 3 and higher, the Alt+F5 Learn feature in Release 2.x records your keystrokes in the 1-2-3 macro language. For example, when you press the F2 Edit key, the Home key, the Delete key, and Enter, the macro commands recorded by 1-2-3 will be **{edit}{home} {del}~**.

In addition to recording standard keystrokes and macro keywords, the Learn feature will also record composed characters you can create using the Compose key. It will not, however, record Alt+F1 Compose, Alt+F2 Record, Alt+F3 Run, or Alt+F4 Undo. Neither will it record Ins, Scroll Lock, Caps Lock, Num Lock, or Print Screen. Unlike the Alt+F2 Record key in Release 3 and higher, when you use Ctrl+Break to leave a menu, Release 2.x records the macro keyword {break} instead of using the equivalent number of {esc} keystrokes.

There is another, more significant difference in the way the Alt+F5 Learn feature in Release 2.x records your keystrokes as compared with the Alt+F2 Record feature of Release 3 and higher. As we pointed out in Figure 4.3, you will not be able to create a general, generic macro using the Record feature in Release 3 and higher without some extensive editing.

If you will refer now to Figure 4.5, however, you can see that the Learn range in Release 2.x correctly captured exactly the keystrokes typed. Unfortunately, some of the keystrokes are isolated in single cells, but that can be easily rectified through use of the /Range Justify command at cell AB418. The important thing to note here is that creation of the @sum range

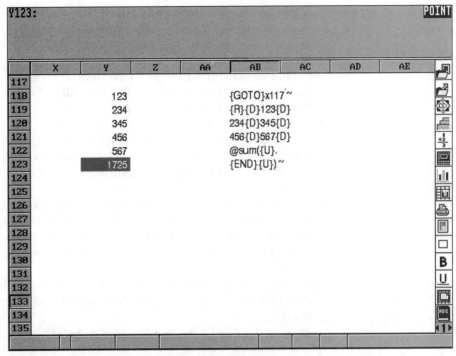

FIGURE 4.5 Using the Learn Range in Release 2.x.

in the macro consists of the abbreviated version of {up}.{end}{up}. This is written in such a way as to be useful for a summing macro that you can use anywhere in the spreadsheet.

Summary

In this chapter we looked at techniques for debugging your macros using the Step key and at methods for recording your keystrokes using the Record key in Release 3 and higher and the Learn key in Release 2.x. The following items were covered:

- The most common errors in your macros will be omission of a tilde where required, omission of a parenthesis or bracket, accidental inclusion of blank spaces, and reference to range names that do not exist as called out.
- To check the location or existence of a range name, press the F5 Goto key and enter the range name. If all is correct, your cell pointer should jump to the expected location in the worksheet.

- If you are not able to locate a macro error by scanning through the macro itself, use the Step key to run the macro a keystroke at a time at every press of the Enter key.
- The Record Buffer of Release 3 and higher is a 512-byte area of computer memory in which 1-2-3 records all your keystrokes in the background as you type them. Pressing Alt+F2 will offer the choices **Playback**, **Copy**, **Erase**, and **Step**.
- If you want to play back any portion of the recorded keystrokes, press TAB to anchor the cursor, then highlight the keystrokes to play back. In this same way, if you select COPY, you can press TAB to anchor the cursor, then highlight the keystrokes to copy into your worksheet.
- The Alt+F5 Learn feature of Release 2.x will record your keystrokes as you work, so that later 1-2-3 can automatically and instantly perform those same repetitive tasks for you. However, before the Alt+F5 Learn key can be used, you must call up the main command menu and create a Learn Range.
- If you get an error message during Learn, erase the learn range and start over, or establish a second learn range and continue where you left off.
- As with the Alt+F2 Record key in Release 3 and higher, the Alt+F5 Learn feature records your keystrokes in the 1-2-3 macro language.

In the next chapter we will explore some of the advanced macro programming commands such as {branch}, {menubranch}, {indicate}, and {break}.

The Macro Programming Commands

Beyond Macro Keywords

In addition to the macro keywords that serve as macro equivalents for function keys, directional keys, and task keys on your keyboard, 1-2-3 has a strong collection of advanced macro programming commands in braces, as shown in Table 5.1.

These advanced programming commands can be divided into seven categories. They include commands to control the screen, allow user input, control the program flow, interrupt the program flow, manipulate data, manipulate files, and access add-ins, as listed in Table 5.2.

Macro Commands in 1-2-3 for Windows

If you have 1-2-3 for Windows, you have the ability to use hundreds of extra macro commands beyond those listed in Tables 5.1 and 5.2. This is because Lotus has created command-equivalent macro keywords for every option you can access manually through the MenuBar. For example, the Edit Copy command in the MenuBar has an equivalent macro command: {Edit-Copy}. For more on 1-2-3 for Windows commands, refer to Appendix A.

Table 5.1 Advanced Macro Programming Commands*

Programming Command	Description
{}	Null subroutine
{?}	Pauses for input until Enter is pressed
{app1} - {app4}	Invokes add-ins, same as Alt+F7 through Alt+F10
{appendbelow}	Copies data to row below database (Rel. 3+)
{appendright}	Copies data to column right of database (Rel. 3+)
{beep}	Plays one of four tones
{blank}	Erases the cell or range designated
{bordersoff}	Turns borders off, same as {frameoff} (Rel. 2.2+)
{borderson}	Turns borders on, same as {frameon} (Rel. 2.2+)
{branch}	Continues the macro at another location
{break}	Backs out of all menu levels (Rel. 2.2+)
{breakoff}	Disables the use of Ctrl+Break
{breakon}	Enables the use of Ctrl+Break
{clearentry} or {ce}	Clears display such as default filename (Rel. 3+)
{close}	Closes a file opened with {open}
{contents}	Copies a cell's displayed value to a location
{define}	Designates a cell to store subroutine parameters
{dispatch}	Branches to the address shown in the dispatch cell
{extend}	Same as Alt+F10, calls Add-in Manager
{filesize}	Returns the size of the file designated
{for}	Runs a macro subroutine a specific number of times
{forbreak}	Ends the execution of a {for} loop prematurely
{form}	Pauses for input, similar to /Range Input (Rel. 3+)
{formbreak}	Ends a {form} command (Rel. 3+)
{frameoff}	Turns frame off, same as {bordersoff} (Rel. 2.2+)
{frameon}	Turns frame on, same as {borderson} (Rel. 2.2+)
{get}	Stores the next keystroke in the designated cell
{getlabel}	Stores the prompted label in the designated cell
{getnumber}	Stores the prompted number in the designated cell
{getpos}	Finds the current byte pointer position of a file

Table 5.1 (*Continued*)

Programming Command	Description
{graphoff}	Turns graph view off (Rel. 2.2+)
{graphon}	Turns graph view on (Rel. 2.2+)
{if}	Tests a condition and branch accordingly
{ifkey}	Tests whether a key name is currently valid
{indicate}	Replaces the Ready mode indicator with a message
{let}	Copies the value of a cell or label to a cell
{look}	Looks to see if the user has typed a keystroke
{menubranch}	Displays a designated menu of up to eight choices
{menucall}	Calls up to eight menu choices as subroutines
{onerror}	Branches to a routine if the macro sees an error
{open}	Opens a file before reading, writing, or sizing it
{paneloff}	Freezes the upper control panel
{panelon}	Unfreezes the upper control panel
{put}	Enters a value or string into a table
{quit}	Quits the macro, returns to Ready mode
{read}	Reads a portion of text or sequential data file
{readln}	Copies a line from an ASCII file to the worksheet
{recalc}	Recalculates the designated range rowwise
{recalccol}	Recalculates the designated range columnwise
{restart}	Stops subroutine from returning to the main routine
{return}	Returns control from subroutine to the main routine
{setpos}	Changes the byte pointer position in an ASCII file
{wait}	Causes the macro to pause for a designated time
{system}	Suspends 1-2-3 and runs command at the DOS command
{windowsoff}	Freezes the worksheet portion of the screen
{windowson}	Unfreezes the worksheet portion of the screen
{write}	Writes a string of characters to an ASCII file
{writeln}	Writes a complete line to an ASCII file
{[*rangename*]}	Branches to a subroutine

*The designation Rel. 2.2+ means "Release 2.2 and higher," and Rel. 3+ means "Release 3 and higher."

Table 5.2 Advanced Macro Programming Command Groups

Command Groups	*Programming Commands*
Screen Control Commands	{bordersoff}, {borderson}, {clearentry} or {ce}, {frameoff}, {frameon}, {graphoff}, {graphon}, {indicate}, {paneloff}, {panelon}, {windowsoff}, {windowson}
User Input Commands	{?}, {get}, {getlabel}, {getnumber}, {look}, {menubranch}, {menucall}
Program Flow Commands	{}, {[*rangename*]}, {branch}, {define}, {dispatch}, {for}, {forbreak}, {if}, {ifkey}, {onerror}, {return}, {restart}, {system}
Program Interrupt Commands	{beep}, {break}, {breakoff}, {breakon}, {quit}, {wait}
Data Manipulation Commands	{appendbelow}, {appendright}, {blank}, {contents}, {form}, {formbreak}, {let}, {put}, {recalc}, {recalcol}
File Manipulation Commands	{close}, {filesize}, {getpos}, {open}, {read}, {readln}, {setpos}, {write}, {writeln}
Add-in Commands	{app1}, {app2}, {app3}, {app4} or {extend}

TIP: *In every version of 1-2-3 after Release 2.01, you can quickly call up a help screen that lists all the macro commands. Simply type an opening brace in the Input Line and, without pressing Enter, press the F1 Help key.*

What's more, you can get detailed information about individual macro commands whose keyword you already know by simply typing the opening brace and keyword and (again, without pressing Enter) using the F1 Help key. You'll be taken automatically to the specific page in the Help system that explains and provides examples for the macro command you typed. (You can also type an @ sign and press F1 to get help on @functions, or type the name of a specific @function to jump right to the Help system page that tells you about that @function.)

Macro Range Names

Most 1-2-3 users tend to overlook the power of range-naming in everyday spreadsheet work. Once you start writing macros, however, range-naming typically becomes second nature. Not only are you more likely to name specific areas of your spreadsheets more often, but soon you'll start assigning internal macro names to individual lines of your macros to identify custom menus, loops, counters, and so on.

In keeping with the convention of entering the macro-invoking range names (such as **\A**, **\B**, and so on) in the column to the left of the macro, internal macro range names such as JLOOP or ZMENU are also best displayed to the left of the lines of the macro they refer to. As noted earlier, this facilitates both naming of the ranges as well as later identification of the macro range names.

From time to time your macros will refer to a cell location in the spreadsheet. In such cases it is *strongly* recommended that you identify those cell locations by range names rather than by cell coordinates. You will also find it best to use this convention for the branching commands, such as {branch} or {menubranch}. For example, you're almost always better off writing {branch JLOOP} rather than {branch A32} or {menubranch ZMENU} rather than {menubranch A59}. There are several reasons for this:

 Referring to range-named cells will make your macros more general and usable across more than one spreadsheet. So if you decide you want to transfer the macro to another spreadsheet, you can use it right away without having to change row and column cell references.

 Cell references typed in a macro do not change automatically if you delete or insert rows or columns as they do in spreadsheet formulas. Macros are commands entered as labels, you'll remember, and labels do not change when you calculate the spreadsheet. So a macro's reference to cell J234 would remain unchanged if you later deleted row 233; this can cause your macro to use the wrong location in its operation.

 You will want to be able to move your entire macro or macro subroutine to a different location within the worksheet without having to worry that it may branch to an incorrect line in the macro itself. By giving range names to your branching destinations, you can move your macros with impunity.

Although range names can be either upper- or lowercase, all range names in this book are shown in uppercase for better legibility.

Range names can also include dashes, commas, dollar signs, and so on; but Lotus does not encourage use of these symbols. Rather, the standard conventions you already use in creating your filenames have been adopted here in the creation of range names, including an attempt to keep to eight letters or less (not always achieved, but recommended) and the use of the underline symbol to separate words in a range name (not required since spaces are acceptable, but recommended).

The internal range names you will use most often in your macros are likely to end in the words MENU, LOOP, or COUNTER. This is because the most useful and typical kinds of programming techniques available in the 1-2-3 macro language include calling up a custom-made menu, looping back to an earlier part of the macro, or counting the number of times a particular loop or subroutine has been run.

As stated in Chapter 2, we recommend that all range names shown to the left of a particular macro start with the letter of that macro. Since there will usually only be one **A** macro, one **B** macro, and one **C** macro, this convention reduces the possibility of accidentally reusing an internal range name like LOOP in more than one macro.

Data Entry Down

In this section you'll learn about one of the most important macro tools: the {branch} command that instructs 1-2-3 to continue a macro at a different location. You'll find a perfect example of this command in a macro designed to aid typical data entry in a column. Instead of entering information by typing the entry, pressing the DownArrow key, typing the second entry, pressing the DownArrow key again, and so on, try the macro shown in Figure 5.1.

This macro starts with a pause, waiting for your entry. Once you type it and press Enter, the macro continues by moving down one cell. The {branch} tells 1-2-3 to continue the macro at the cell location range-named **\D**. In other words, the macro loops back to the beginning and starts over again.

Understand that the {branch} command is not an instruction to the *cell pointer* to move to a range name or cell designation. We have the F5 Goto key for that, written in 1-2-3's macro language as {goto}. Instead, this com-

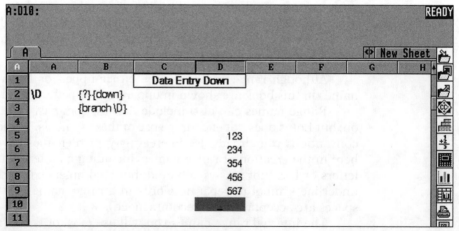

FIGURE 5.1 Data Entry macro moving down.

mand is an instruction to 1-2-3 to continue processing the macro code found at a specified location, regardless of what the cell pointer is doing.

Using the Data Entry Macro

Suppose you start this macro, enter a few dozen numbers in a column, and suddenly realize that the entry you made five cells ago is incorrect? You could press Ctrl+Break to leave the macro, of course, then move up five cells, correct the entry, move back down again, and finally resume the macro. But there's a better way.

The {?} pause is waiting for a press of the Enter key before it can continue. This means that you can enter data at this point, or you can move the cell pointer. In fact, you can move the cursor up five cells, type the correct input, then enter the input by using the DownArrow key instead of the Enter key. Since you haven't pressed Enter, the macro is still in the Pause mode.

You could actually change several cells in this way: typing the entry, entering it with the DownArrow key instead of the Enter key, typing more data and entering it with the DownArrow key, and so on. When you're ready to resume the use of the Data Entry macro, place your cell pointer on the last item you typed at the bottom of the column and press Enter. To quit this macro at any time, press Ctrl+Break.

Changing the Data Entry Macro

What if you want your entry centered as you move down the column? You could type the caret symbol [^] before each entry or you could center the entire column after the fact by selecting /Range Label-Prefix Center and highlighting the column you want to center; but why not have the macro take care of all that for you?

It's easy enough to make the change. Just include a caret [^] in front of the bracketed question mark in your macro code. That way, the macro will type the centering symbol first, pause for your entry, insert the entry, move down one cell, and loop back to the beginning of the macro.

NOTE: *To type this line of the macro, you must actually type '^{?}{down} with an apostrophe. Of course, all that will appear on the screen is ^{?}{down}. This is an important distinction, because without the beginning apostrophe, 1-2-3 will take the caret to be an instruction to center the entry {?}{down} rather than including the caret as a visible part of the working macro.*

In this same way, you can modify the Data Entry macro to right-justify each entry by first typing quotation marks. Remember, though, that you must actually type '"{?}{down} so that it will appear as "{?}{down}.

You may also want a Data Entry macro that will make entries moving in a row to the right rather than down. This is an easy modification: Change the word {down} to the word {right}.

Given these choices of all of the possible ways you might want your Data Entry macro to operate, it might make more sense to put the choices into a menu. That way, rather than modify your macro or write several different macros to automate all kinds of data entry, you could have one menu-driven macro that covers all possibilities. Just such a Data Entry macro is presented in Chapter 9.

Calling a Subroutine

A subroutine is actually another macro—a kind of submacro where the main macro temporarily branches, after which it returns to the place where it left off. To create a command that tells 1-2-3 to branch to a subroutine and return, you simply enter the range name of the subroutine enclosed in braces.

The Save and Print macro in Figure 5.2 provides a simple example with a subroutine called SOUND. The purpose of the macro is to calculate the worksheet and sound four tones to indicate the calculation is complete, save the file, sound four more tones to indicate the /File Save is complete, and finally print the worksheet, sounding four more tones to tell the user that the printing is complete.

To create this example, it is important that you give the subroutine the range name SOUND. Remember, you can create both the \S and SOUND

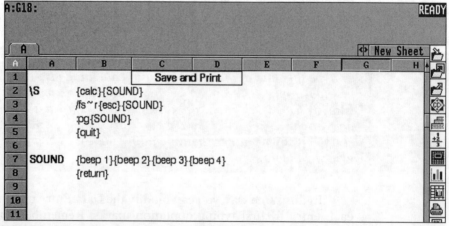

FIGURE 5.2 Save and Print macro with subroutine.

range names at the same time by placing your cell pointer on the \S, selecting /Range Name Labels Right, and pressing PgDn and Enter.

The subroutine SOUND consists of the four {beep} commands and a {return} command. By including in the {beep} commands any number 1 through 4, you can create four different tones. The {return} command tells 1-2-3 to return to the place in the main macro where it left off. As you can see, using this subroutine saves you from having to type the four {beep} commands at the end of the first three lines of the macro. And by using the range name SOUND, you provide a short description telling what the subroutine does.

You can easily interpret the third line of the macro by pressing the indicated keystrokes. You will see that they equate to :Print Go Quit.

However, you may have a question about the second line. It accomplishes a /File Save of the current file and selects Replace; but you may wonder why we have included an Esc command. This is a convention that you will see often in this book. The Esc covers the possibility that you will be using the macro in a file that has not yet been saved. If the file is new, 1-2-3 offers no Replace choice when you choose /File Save, so the macro presses the Esc key to undo the R just typed. If it is needed, of course, the Esc command that follows has no effect.

Writing Your First Menu Macro

In the following pages you can step through your own first creation of a few more utilitarian macros that depend very much on the use of custom-made menus. Let's start with the Combine Files Macro. This macro is used to quickly combine several files into the current worksheet. Normally this would require at least 11 keystrokes per file, not including the filename selections. Instead, 1-2-3 can do the same task after just one keystroke per file (not including the filename selections). If you have 10 files to combine, this means a savings of 100 keystrokes.

To type this macro, refer to Figure 5.3. To range name the macro, place your cell pointer on the \C cell, select /Range Name Labels Right, and press End DownArrow and Enter. Here's how the macro works:

{end}{home}{d}{end}{l}   The macro starts by moving the cell pointer to the lower right corner of the worksheet, then down one cell, and End Left to column A. This places your cell pointer just below the lower left corner of the current worksheet, which is the appropriate place to /File Combine a new file into the worksheet.

/fcce{?}~   The macro selects /File Combine Copy Entire, then pauses so you can select or type the file name you want to combine. When you press Enter, the tilde completes the command.

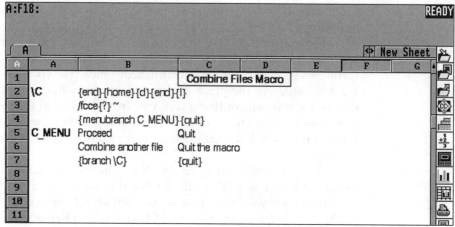

FIGURE 5.3 The Combine Files macro with menu.

{menubranch C_MENU}{quit}   Tells the macro to look for a custom menu where the first cell of the menu is named C_MENU. It then calls up all the menu items and pauses for the user's menu choice. The macro does not process the {quit} command at this point—in fact, this command is only included so the macro quits if you press Esc instead of selecting one of the menu choices.

In fact, pressing Esc once your custom menu appears in the upper panel always causes 1-2-3 to continue processing the macro code just after the end of the {menubranch} command. If there is no {quit} command after a {menubranch}, pressing Esc causes the macro to type whatever happens to reside in the next cell down. In this case, it would cause the macro to type the word PROCEED, then continue down to type the next cell, and so on until the macro reaches some inconsistency that prevents it from continuing.

Because of this potentially dangerous feature of the {menubranch} command, every use of {menubranch} presented in this book is followed by a {quit} command, or by another menubranch command that allows the macro to continue at a different menu level. This is an important convention that also permits the ability to back out of menus level-by-level just as you can back out of standard menus already available in 1-2-3.

Proceed Quit   These are the menu choices that appear after 1-2-3 reads the command {menubranch C_MENU}. Note that the range name C_MENU in cell A4 is shown just to the left of the word *Proceed*, indicating that cell B5 has been given the range name C_MENU. In other words, only the first cell of the menu choices requires a range name. The {menubranch} command causes the macro to automatically look for other menu choices to the right of this first choice—up to a total of eight choices.

A few things can go wrong even at this early stage in the creation of menus and it seems appropriate to mention them here. First of all, you must use the {menubranch} command to call up menus, not the {branch} command. While this seems a simple instruction, it's surprising how often you are likely to type {branch} by mistake.

Because the menu command looks for all menu choices to the right of the first choice, you can accidentally include data not intended as menu choices if you overlook data in the cells immediately to the right of your menu choices. In 1-2-3 Release 2.x, this can even result in the error message: *Invalid use of menu macro command* if the total space taken up by the extraneous menu choices exceeds the space provided for menu choices in the upper panel. For that matter, even intended menu choices can result in the error message in Release 2.x if the choices take up too much space. In that case, you must edit your menu choices to shorten them down to a total of 80 characters, including spaces.

Another obvious mistake that occurs all too often when you create menus is forgetting to give your menu a range name. If you try to run the macro without first assigning the required range name, 1-2-3 gives you an error message that warns you: "Invalid range name in MENUBRANCH."

Combine Another File   Quit the Macro   These second lines of the macro menu are the entries that explain the menu choices. As with standard Lotus menus, when the user points to either of these choices, the explanation for that choice appears in the upper panel. This line of the macro can accommodate explanations exceeding 80 characters (the macro will still run), but the user won't be able to read more than the first 80 characters.

{branch \C}   If the user selects *Proceed*, the macro branches back to the beginning and starts over.

{quit}   Of course, if the user selects *Quit*, the macro reads the {quit} command and returns to Ready mode.

> **NOTE:** *If you have the latest release of 1-2-3 for Windows, you will want to explore the menu commands listed under User Environment in Appendix A.*

A Menu Macro to Change Directories

Let's look at another menu macro offering a few more choices. The File Directory/Retrieve macro is designed to change your file directory and start a /File Retrieve operation, offering a full-screen view of all of the files in that directory. Since opening a worksheet file with this macro automatically changes the current directory, you can manually open another file in the same directory later by simply choosing /File Retrieve or—in Release 3.x and higher—/File Open.

This type of macro is especially handy if you work on a network where worksheet files are located in any one of several long, complicated subdirectories. Instead of manually typing or selecting the subdirectory of a separate subdirectory of a main directory where your files are located, you can use this macro to do the work for you. An example of this is Figure 5.4 below.

{menubranch FMENU}{quit}   Tells the macro to call up the menu named FMENU. This is another example where the {quit} command is included merely to cover the possibility that you might press Esc after you see the menu choices *Budgets, Sales, Default,* and *Quit* in the upper panel.

The first menu choice, *Budgets,* is only an example of the type of files you might have in your own 1-2-3 subdirectory. After you start the macro and choose *Budgets,* the macro branches to the following commands:

/fdC:\123\BUDGETS~   Chooses /File Directory and switches to the subdirectory C:\123\BUDGETS. You will want to substitute the drive and path of your own favorite subdirectory in place of this entry. In that case, don't forget to replace the *Budgets* menu choice with an appropriate menu choice that works for you.

/fr{name}   Selects /File Retrieve and presses the F3 Name key to display a full-screen view of all the files in the directory. At this point,

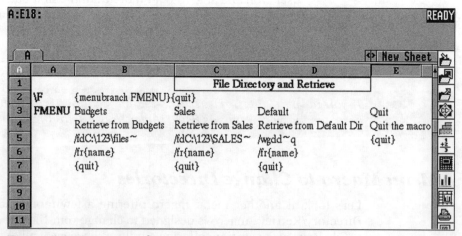

FIGURE 5.4 Menu macro for Instant File Directory and Retrieve.

the user can choose the name of the worksheet file to open and press Enter.

> **NOTE:** If you have 1-2-3 Release 3 or higher, you might want to substitute the command for opening a file, /FO.

{quit}   After the user makes a file selection and presses Enter, the macro quits.

Strictly speaking, the {quit} command is not necessary here, since retrieving another file causes the macro to quit as the current worksheet file is dropped. We have included it here, however, to encourage the habit of always ending a macro with a {quit} or branching command; to provide a visible signal as you read the macro that this is the end of the macro; and to cover the possibility that you may be using this macro in a Macro Library that operates from outside the current worksheet. (More on that subject later.)

> **NOTE:** *When you choose /File Retrieve manually in a worksheet you've modified since last saving it, 1-2-3 Release 2.2 and higher will prompt you with a No Yes menu and the instruction, "Worksheet changes not saved! Retrieve file anyway?" However, when you include the /FR command in a macro, 1-2-3 bypasses that warning and proceeds with the /File Retrieve process.*

If you run this macro and choose the second menu option (*Sales* in our example), the macro operates the same way as it does for the *Budgets* selection, switching to the appropriate subdirectory and starting the /File Retrieve command.

The third menu option, *Default*, includes an interesting trick for switching to your default directory.

/wgdd~q   This line chooses the menu options /Worksheet Global Default Directory, presses Enter to accept the default directory offered, and quits out of the /Worksheet menu tree. Here's the trick: When you use the /Worksheet Global Default Directory command, even manually, it also changes the current file directory just as if you had accessed the /File Directory command.

To include an additional menu choice for another 1-2-3 subdirectory, move the *Default* and *Quit* menubranch choices to the right and write the new menu choice in the space you created. Just give the menu choice a title that corresponds to the particular subdirectory you want to switch to (such as *Sales, Cash, Inventory,* and so on) and add to the line that begins **/fd** the drive and path for the subdirectory you want the user to be able to choose.

Slide to Left Side or Top

In Chapter 3, you learned about macros that add two new features to 1-2-3: the ability to jump instantly to the lower left and upper right corners of the active spreadsheet area. Another feature which is not already available directly from the keyboard is the ability to jump to the left edge of the worksheet (staying in the same row) or to the top line of the worksheet (staying in the same column). Normally, to jump to the left edge using the mouse, you must drag the horizontal scroll box to the far left. Using the keyboard you must typically use Ctrl+LeftArrow or End LeftArrow repeatedly. These techniques can be tedious, especially if you dislike repetitive keystrokes and prefer not to take your hands from the keyboard to use the mouse.

Fortunately, you can create a macro like the one in Figure 5.5 to handle this for you. The Left Side or Top macro uses an interesting trick: It works by locking in your titles and pressing the Home key. If you lock in vertical titles at any location in the spreadsheet, pressing Home takes you to the top cell in your current column just to the right of the titles. With horizontal titles, pressing Home takes you to the leftmost cell just below the titles in your current row. Try this manually and you'll see how the macro works.

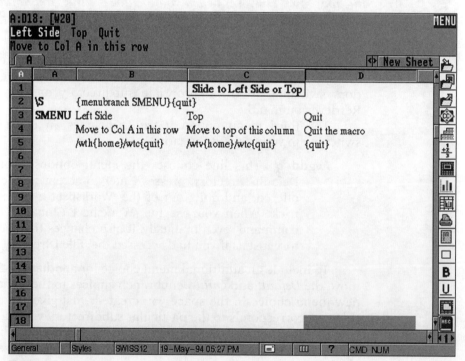

FIGURE 5.5 A Menu macro to slide to left side or top

{menubranch SMENU}{quit}   Pressing Alt+F (Ctrl+F in 1-2-3 for Windows) will cause the menu choices *Left Side* and *Top* to appear. Press L to jump to Column A, or press T to jump to Row 1.

/wth{home}/wtc{quit}   When you select *Left Side,* the macro causes a /Worksheet Titles Horizontal sequence, and a press of the Home key to jump your cell pointer to the leftmost cell under the newly created horizontal titles. This is followed by a /Worksheet Titles Clear and a Quit command.

/wtv{home}/wtc{quit}   If you select *Top,* the macro causes a /Worksheet Titles Vertical sequence, and a press of the Home key to jump your cell pointer to the uppermost cell to the right of the newly created vertical titles. This is followed by a /Worksheet Titles Clear and a Quit command.

You'll be impressed by how quickly this macro executes to create the titles, move the cell pointer, delete the titles, and quit. Take note, however: This macro will not work properly if you have already locked in your titles on the current worksheet. In fact, it will instantly clear away any titles you may have locked in, so use the macro judiciously.

If you tend to use titles often, you can precede this macro with another toggle macro to turn your titles off and back on automatically. See the Titles Toggle macro in Chapter 7.

Row or Column Delete with Unprotect

Sometimes the potential danger that a macro can do is so great that it becomes important to provide a safeguard against its accidental use. Menus, in addition to offering choices, can also offer safeguards; and the macro in Figure 5.6 provides an excellent example of this. The purpose of the macro is to facilitate the deletion of a column or row when the entire worksheet is protected.

{menubranch RMENU}{quit}   Branches to the menu offering the choices *Cancel, Row Delete,* or *Delete Column.* (We did not use *Column Delete* because the word Cancel and the word Column both start with the letter C.)

The *Cancel* choice simply leads to a {quit} command. It has been used as the first choice so that an accidental pressing of the Enter key will not delete a row or column in error—and to require that the operator make a conscious decision to press R or D before actually deleting a row or a column. You will notice that the explanation line below these two choices both say *Proceed at Risk.* Rather than using this line to explain what is about to happen, the line has been used to provide a warning for what is otherwise an obvious menu choice.

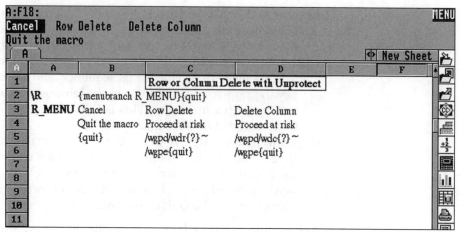

FIGURE 5.6 Row or Column Delete macro with Unprotect.

/wgpd/wdr{?}~ Selects /Worksheet Global Protect Disable, then /Worksheet Delete Row, and pauses for painting in of the number of rows you want to delete.

/wgpe{quit} Selects /Worksheet Global Protect Enable and quits, thus turning the global protection back on again. Of course, this macro would never be used in a worksheet which is not globally protected. Such use would result in a row or column delete as expected, but it would lock in global protection, resulting in the inability to make further entries until the global protection has been turned off or selected areas of the worksheet have received a /Range Unprotect.

Prune Number of Files

The macro in Figure 5.7 is an example of a menu macro that loops back on itself. This provides a handy way of getting your macro to repeat a series of keystrokes with just one manual keystroke on your part.

The purpose of the macro is to eliminate unwanted worksheet, graph, or print files to reduce the amount of memory they take up on your hard disk or floppies. Without a macro, this exercise can take from 7 to 12 keystrokes per file. That means 70 to 120 keystrokes to eliminate 10 files.

{menubranch PMENU1}{quit} Branches to the menu choices *Worksheet, Graph, Print,* or *Quit.* Under each of the first three choices is the explanation line, Check Memory and List Files.

/flw~ Types the /File List command and selects Worksheet. This causes the screen to be replaced with a complete list of all of the

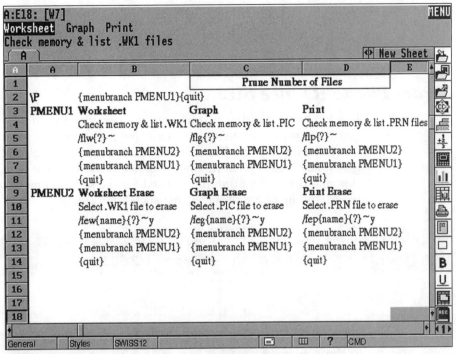

FIGURE 5.7 Looping macro to prune number of files.

worksheet files available for deletion. At this point you can scroll through the files to determine the amount of memory each file occupies. When you press Enter, the screen will revert to its original view of the worksheet.

{menubranch PMENU2} Branches to the second menu choices, *Worksheet Erase, Graph Erase, Print Erase,* and *Quit.* You are prompted to select the .WK* file, .PIC file or .PRN file you want to erase.

/few{name}{?}~y Types /File Erase Worksheet, replaces the screen with a list of all of your .WK1 files, then pauses for your selection. When you press Enter, the file you select will be erased.

{menubranch PMENU2} Branches again to the second menu. If you want to erase another worksheet file, you can press the letter W or Enter at this point. You can repeat this looping exercise of pointing to the file to erase, pressing Enter twice, then pointing to the next file to erase, pressing Enter twice, and so on until all of your unwanted files are eliminated.

If you want to return to the first menu, press Esc. The macro will process the very last line, causing it to branch to the higher menu level. If instead you want to quit the macro, press the letter Q twice. The first Q causes a menubranch to the first menu and the second Q returns you to Ready mode.

Xtract File to Reduce Size

In addition to creating custom menus to provide for choices or to give safeguard warning statements, you can also use the menu structure to create a two-lined instruction. This is done by having the menubranch call up a single-choice menu. Then the menu choice is used for the first line of instruction and the explanation line is used for the second line of instruction. The macro in Figure 5.8 provides just such an example.

NOTE: *If you have the latest version of 1-2-3 for Windows, check out the {Alert} command under User Environment in Appendix A.*

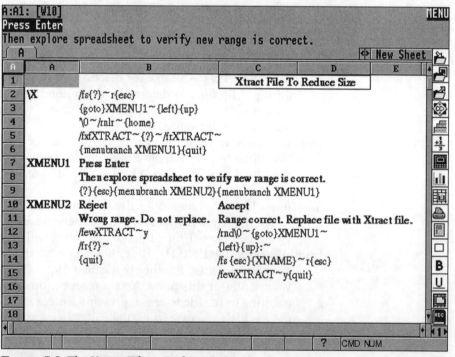

FIGURE 5.8 The Xtract File to Reduce Size macro.

This example also offers an excellent technique to enable your macro to leave the current worksheet file and continue processing in a separate file. Unless you have the advantage of a Macro Library capability as provided by Release 2.2 and higher, leaving the file that contains a processing macro will usually cause the processing macro to quit. Here we have a technique for continuing such a macro in a separate file.

The purpose of the macro is to prompt you through a /File Xtract to reduce the size of your worksheet. You may have had this situation: For no apparent reason, it seems that your file takes much longer to save or retrieve than expected or you suddenly receive a Memory Full message when you were sure that your file didn't take up that much memory. You press End Home to jump to the lower right corner of your spreadsheet and find that an extraneous entry has been inserted in a faraway cell of your worksheet. You would imagine, of course, that simply erasing the offending data and resaving the file would fix the problem, but if the file has been saved at this size it cannot be reduced in this way. The fact that the file has been saved just once as a large file ensures that it will always be a large file, no matter how much you try to reduce it by erasing cells or deleting rows or columns.

In Release 3 Lotus corrected the problem, so that erasing the extraneous entry reduces the worksheet size. This doesn't eliminate the need for /File Xtract in that Release, though, since doing a /File Xtract is still the best way to eliminate all of the unwanted data of a large file to reduce it to a new size.

Unfortunately, reducing the size of a file by extracting a portion of the file can be a dangerous undertaking that has caused many a Lotus expert to lose an important spreadsheet. The Xtract File macro not only steps you through the ticklish task of extracting a file from a worksheet, but it includes pauses and prompts to allow for double-checking to see that your extracted range is the range you intend.

/fs{?}~r{esc}   Saves the file first, just in case the extract portion is not acceptable and you want to return to the original file. Note we have repeated the convention of having the macro type the letter r for replace, followed by {esc} for nonreplacing files.

{goto}XMENU1~{left}{up}   This may look like an instruction to the macro to call up the menu named XMENU1, but look again. It is actually an instruction to the cell pointer to move to the cell with the range name XMENU1, then to move one cell to the left, then one cell up. In our example in Figure 5.8, this means the cell pointer will move to cell A6.

\0~/rnlr~{home}   After the cursor has moved to this location, the macro types an apostrophe, a backslash, a zero (not an O), and presses Enter. In other words, it types the backslash-zero \0 name for an autoexecuting macro. Then, at that same cell, it selects /Range Name Labels Right and presses Enter, which effectively turns on the autoexecuting macro for the next time the file with this new macro starting at cell B6 is retrieved. The {home} command moves the cursor to the Home location.

/fxfXTRACT~{?}~/frXTRACT~   Starts the /File Xtract of the file, giving it the temporary filename XTRACT. The question-mark pause allows you to paint in the area you want to extract. Make sure that the extract area includes this macro. This is very important. The file named XTRACT is then retrieved.

At this point, you would normally expect the macro to quit. But since the new XTRACT file includes the \0 autoexecuting macro just created, the macro actually picks up where it left off in the original file and continues.

{menubranch XMENU1}{quit}   Calls up a single-choice menu which reads *Press Enter,* followed by the direction to *Then Explore Spreadsheet to Verify New Range Is Correct.* This technique offers a long, two-part instruction that can only be done in this way through the use of a single-choice menu.

{?}{esc}{menubranch XMENU2}{menubranch XMENU1}   Pauses to allow you to move around the extracted file to see that it contains everything you need. The Esc command is included to nullify any accidental typing you may do in one of the cells that might destroy an important formula or piece of data. The macro then calls up the menu choices *Reject* and *Accept.*

/fewXTRACT~y/fr{?}~{quit}   If you reject the extracted file, the macro erases that file and does a /File Retrieve, pausing for you to type in the original filename. Note the {quit} command is not really required, since the macro stops as soon as it leaves the present file to retrieve the original file.

/rnd\0~{goto}XMENU1~{left}{up}:~   If you choose *Accept,* the macro will do a /Range Name Delete of the range name \0 so that the autoexec macro won't activate the next time you retrieve this file. Then the cursor moves to the cell called XMENU1, moves left one cell, and moves one cell up. At this point it replaces the \0 with a colon so it is not accidentally range-named in the future.

/fs{esc}{?}r   Does a /File Save sequence, cancels out the XTRACT name offered, pauses for your entry of the original filename (or another filename if you'd like to keep the original file intact), chooses Replace, and presses Esc.

/fewXTRACT~y{quit}   Finally, the macro erases the temporary file named XTRACT and quits. Now if you press End Home, you should find that your file has been reduced to the new size you require.

Summary

This chapter provides an overview of the macro programming commands. You were introduced to macro commands that pause for an entry as well as custom menus that pause for a menu choice. The macros in this chapter are summarized as follows:

- The Data Entry Macro which automates input of data moving down a column.
- The Save and Print macro which includes a simple example of a subroutine.
- A menu macro to facilitate the combining of several files into the current worksheet.
- A macro to jump your cursor to the leftmost column or the topmost row, regardless of where you are in your worksheet.
- A menu macro to delete a row or column when Global Protection is on.
- A looping macro to prune the number of files you have in order to save space on your floppy or hard disk.
- A way to reduce the size of your worksheet with an Xtract File macro.

In the next chapter we explore several techniques involved in the art of range naming.

The Art of Range-Naming

In the last chapter we introduced a few conventions and recommendations on the use of named ranges. In this chapter we review ways to get more out of range-naming, different kinds of macros available through the use of range names, and ways to give your current cell a temporary place-marker.

Jump to Upper Right Corner and Return

In Chapter 3, you learned how to use macro commands to jump to the upper right corner of your worksheet. The macro in Figure 6.1 uses the same technique, but it also offers a method for marking your place in the worksheet. That way, after you jump to the upper right corner, you can either return to your original location or remain at the destination cell. This is one example of a macro that uses a place-marker.

/rncJHERE~~/rndJHERE~/rncJHERE~~ This series of commands may appear a little redundant. First the macro types /Range Name Create JHERE Enter and accepts the location offered by pressing Enter. So if the range name already exists, this command simply renames the range name at the already established

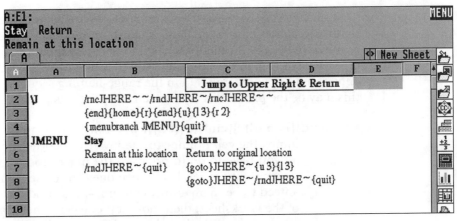

FIGURE 6.1 A macro to jump to the upper right corner.

location. (If the range name does not exist, the range name is then established at the current cell.) Then the macro executes a /Range Name Delete of the same JHERE range name. And in the third use of /Range Name, the macro once again does a /Range Name Create of JHERE, this time definitely establishing the location of the range name at the current cell.

This may seem like a lot to go through to get the name JHERE assigned to the current cell, but it is an important convention that should be used in 1-2-3 Release 2.x whenever you are having your macro do any range-naming.

You may wonder why we bother with the first step. After all, the second step will delete any pre-established use of the range name, so why not start with a /Range Name Delete before the final /Range Name Create? This would be a great idea, except that the range name may *not* already exist, and trying to delete a range name that does not exist causes an error and your macro stops. So to cover all contingencies, create (or recreate) the range name, delete the range name, and finally create the range name in the desired location.

Some 1-2-3 users have suggested that the same effect could be achieved by following a /Range Name Create command with a Backspace, then entering the new cell coordinates. This works in every 1-2-3 release 3.0 and higher, but in Release 2.x it can create problems. In every 2.x release, if the range name you are trying to relocate happens to share the same cell coordinates with another range name, moving one range name inadvertently moves the other range name as well. This "tagalong" move of range names can wreak havoc with your worksheet, so it is not recommended.

Incidentally, when typing the **/rnc~~ /rnd~ /rnc~~** sequence, notice that the creation of a range name requires two tildes, whereas the deletion requires only one. As mentioned in an earlier chapter, the most common error in writing macros is the tendency to leave out required tildes. This tendency seems to come up often in the range-naming sequence, so expect that this may be the problem if your macro stops at this point.

{end}{home}{r}{end}{u}{l 3}{r 2}   Since pressing End Home always jumps the cell pointer to the lower left corner of the worksheet, all you have to do to program the macro to jump farther, to the upper right corner, is to move one cell to the right—this is guaranteed to be in an empty column—press End Up to go to the top of the worksheet, then move left one cell. The final {l 3} and {r 2} commands are included to position the cell pointer more towards the center of the screen.

{menubranch JMENU}{quit}   Calls up the menu choices *Stay* and *Return*. If you select *Stay*, the macro deletes the temporary placemarker named JHERE and quits. If you select RETURN, the macro processes a {goto} command to go back to your original location JHERE, moves up three cells and left 3 cells to adjust the cell pointer more towards the center of the screen, then uses {goto}JHERE~ to return again to your original place-marker. Finally, the macro deletes the range name JHERE and quits.

Using {windowsoff} and {paneloff}

This is a good place to explore the {windowsoff} and {paneloff} commands. The {windowsoff} command is used to suppress refreshing of the worksheet during operation of a macro, and the {paneloff} command is used to suppress changes in the display of instructions in the upper panel. Both of these commands can be thought of as instructions to freeze an area of the screen in its current state.

Refer now to a modified version of the Jump to Upper-Right Corner macro in Figure 6.2. The {windowsoff} and {paneloff} commands have been added to the first line of the macro and to the first line under the *Return* choice of the menu. The {panelon} and {windowson} commands have been added as a new fourth line of the macro. Here's why:

{windowsoff}{paneloff}   These commands accomplish three things: The annoying flicker of a typical macro can be completely eliminated, the macro will operate faster, and you will be less likely to become disoriented because the screen stays unchanged while it is processing commands.

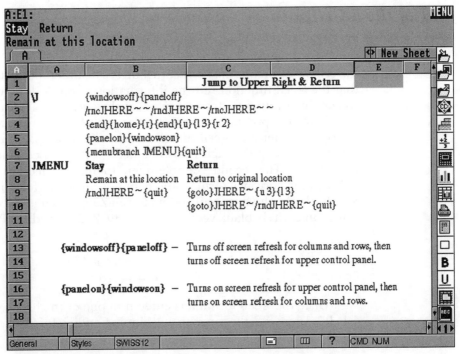

FIGURE 6.2 Modified macro to jump to upper right corner.

> **{panelon}{windowson}** Although turning on the windows and panels can be done in any order you like, typing {panelon} before {windowson} is recommended to suppress one last flicker of the window which would occur if the command read {windowson}{panelon} instead. The upper panel is turned back on just before the {menubranch} command so you can see the menu choices, *Stay* and *Return*. The windows are turned back on at this point so you can see the upper left corner of the worksheet where the previous line of the macro sent your cell pointer.

> **{windowsoff}{paneloff}** If you select *Return*, the first command once again turns off changes to the main screen, and {paneloff} turns off changes to the upper panel. You may wonder, then, how you are able to watch your cell pointer jump instantly back to the original cell—especially since if you glance farther down the macro, you'll notice that the macro ends without a corresponding {windowson}{panelon}. This is because when a macro ends, it automatically returns the windows and panel to an "on" condition; and {windowson}, whether spelled out or automatic, always causes the screen to display the end result of any instructions given to the cell pointer while the windows were off.

Using the @Cellpointer Command

The @cell and @cellpointer functions are two of the most important @functions you'll be using in macros. Both @functions return information about the cell based on one of several attributes. The difference between the two is that the @cell function returns information about a designated cell, while @cellpointer returns information about the current cell location.

Table 6.1 provides three examples each for all of the attributes using the @cellpointer and @cell functions. The first example refers to protected cell Z37 (width 12) which is also named HERE and contains the centered label ^Total. The second example refers to unprotected cell Z38, is formatted with the currency format, and contains an @sum formula that totals to $1230.67. The third example refers to cell Z39, which is also the first empty cell of an entirely blank vertical range Z39..Z42 named EMPTY.

```
Cell Z37:      Total          ←←←^Total
Cell Z38:      $1,230.67      ←←←@sum(Z30..Z36)
Cell Z39:                     ←←←(blank cell)
```

Once the @cell formula is entered in one of the forms shown in Table 6.1, 1-2-3 converts the range to a beginning-ending form, like this: Z38..Z38.

Using the {let} Command

The @cell and @cellpointer functions are most useful in macros when combined with the {let} function. The {let} command is like saying "Let this cell *become like* this cell." Some examples of the {let} command are as follows:

{let J27,Z39}	Gives J27 the same contents as Z39
{let J27,999}	Gives J27 the value 999
{let J27,"Sales"}	Gives J27 the word Sales
{let J27,"Sales"&"man"}	Gives J27 the word Salesman
{let J27,@cell("width",Z39)}	Gives J27 a value equal to Z39's width
{let J27,J27+1}	Increments the value in J27 by 1

As you can see, the first example, {let J27,Z39}, can be used to accomplish the same thing as the /Copy command, except that with a copy command you specify the source cell first, followed by the destination cell, like this: /cZ39~J27~. On the other hand, using the {let} command, you specify the destination cell first, followed by what you want to go into the destination cell. The {let} command is also visibly faster than the copy command. Unfortunately, the {let} command only returns a label or a value to the destination cell. If your macro requires that either the formula or the cell format of the Source cell be copied, it's best to revert back to the standard copy command.

Table 6.1 Use of the @Cell and @Cellpointer Functions

@cellpointer(string)	*@cell(string,range)*	*Returns*
@cellpointer("address")	@cell("address",HERE)	$Z$37
	@cell("address",Z38)	$Z$38
	@cell("address",EMPTY)	$Z$39
@cellpointer("col")	@cell("col",Z37)	26
	@cell("col",Z38)	26
	@cell("col",Z39)	26
@cellpointer("contents")	@cell("contents",Z37)	Total
	@cell("contents",Z38)	$1,230.67
	@cell("contents",Z39)	0
@cellpointer("coord")	@cell("coord",Z37)	$A:$Z$37
(Release 3 and higher)	@cell("coord",Z38)	$A:$Z$38
	@cell("coord",Z39)	$A;$Z$39
@cellpointer("filename")	@cell("filename",Z37)	C:\123\FILES\COST.WK3
(Release 2.2 and higher)	@cell("filename",Z38)	C:\123\FILES\COST.WK3
	@cell("filename",Z39)	C:\123\FILES\COST.WK3
@cellpointer("format")	@cell("format",Z37)	G (default)
(Returns "A" in Rel 3	@cell("format",Z38)	C2 ($, 2 dec)
if format is automatic)	@cell("format",Z39)	(blank)
@cellpointer("protect")	@cell("protect",Z37)	1 (protected)
	@cell("protect",Z38)	0 (unprotected)
	@cell("protect",Z39)	1 (protected)
@cellpointer("prefix")	@cell("prefix",Z37)	^
	@cell("prefix",Z38)	(blank)
	@cell("prefix",Z39)	(blank)
@cellpointer("row")	@cell("row",Z37)	37
	@cell("row",Z38)	38
	@cell("row",Z39)	39
@cellpointer("sheet")	@cell("sheet",Z37)	1
(Release 3 only)	@cell("sheet",Z38)	1
	@cell("sheet",Z39)	1
@cellpointer("type")	@cell("type",Z37)	v (for value)
	@cell("type",Z38)	l (for label)
	@cell("type",Z39)	b (for blank)
@cellpointer("width")	@cell("width",Z37)	12
	@cell("width",Z38)	12
	@cell("width",Z39)	12

A Self-Modifying File Retrieve Macro

You can do quite a bit more with the {let} command than you can with the copy command, however, especially when used with @cell or @cellpointer. The /File Retrieve macro in Figure 6.3 shows how the @cellpointer formula works in conjunction with the {let} command.

The purpose of the macro is to allow you to accomplish a /File Retrieve of a file by pointing to a cell containing the filename. This is also our first example that uses the principle of the *self-modifying macro*.

A self-modifying macro is a macro that rewrites its later lines before it runs them. In this case, the first line of the macro rewrites its third line based on the location of the cell pointer when you press Alt+F (Ctrl+F in 1-2-3 for Windows). The macro then selects /File Retrieve, types the contents of the modified line, then enters it with the tilde in the last line.

Figure 6.3 includes a simple table of filenames in the current directory. Of course, as you recreate this macro, you will want to change the table to reflect files from your own current directory.

This macro is most effective in an AUTO123 file that opens automatically when you first start your 1-2-3 session. The idea here is to list only the files you visit most often, thereby facilitating your /File Retrieve of specific worksheets at start-up.

{let FNAME,@cellpointer("contents")}~ Causes the cell named FNAME to display the contents of the current cell. If, for example, you point to the cell containing the filename CASHFLOW before pressing Alt+F (or Ctrl+F in 1-2-3 for Windows), this com-

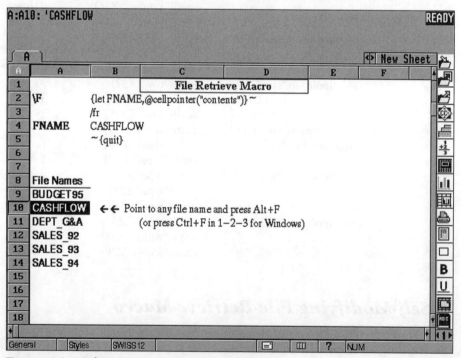

FIGURE 6.3 A File Retrieve macro using @cellpointer.

mand causes the word CASHFLOW to be entered into the cell of the macro itself named FNAME.

/fr   Selects /File Retrieve. If you want to have this macro designate a specific directory path, you can modify it by adding an asterisk and {esc} command, followed by the file directory. For example, you may change the line to read: **/fr*{esc}c:\123\files**. If you have Release 3.0 or higher, you might consider changing this line to /fo for /File Open instead of /fr for /File Retrieve.

SALES   Although we have entered a filename in this cell named FNAME, the macro will work just as well if FNAME is blank, since the macro fills it in with the first {let} command.

~{quit}   The tilde completes the command, whereupon the new file is retrieved. Unless you are working with a Macro Library macro that operates from outside the current worksheet file, the macro quits at this point even without the {quit} command. We have included it here as a convention and to cover the possibility that you may have used /File Open instead of /File Retrieve or plan to add this macro to a Macro Library (discussed in detail in Chapter 7).

Using @Cellpointer to Create a Place-marker

The @cellpointer formula can also be used in conjunction with {let} to create a place-marker. Instead of using the /Range Name Create method to give a range name to the current cell as described above, you can use @cellpointer("address") to store the absolute address of the current cell in another named cell, then use the {goto} command to return to the stored location.

For example, having your macro run the command **{let UHERE, @cellpointer("address")}** at cell AB237 causes the cell named UHERE to display the absolute address of the current cell like this: $AB$237. Once that information is stored in UHERE, your macro can move you around the spreadsheet and return to your original location by executing a {goto} command, then doing a subroutine branch to UHERE to read the cell address $AB$237, and finally continuing after the subroutine call with a tilde that completes the {goto} sequence.

Figure 6.4 shows two simple examples using place-markers. In the first example, written for Release 2.x, the current cell is range-named FHERE using /Range Name Create, /Range Name Delete, and /Range Name Create again. After a pause command {?} that allows you to move anywhere in the worksheet, the macro executes a {goto} command to go to FHERE, the originally range-named location. In the second example, the current cell is not range-named. Rather, the cell that was prenamed UHERE is made to display the current cell pointer address. After a macro pause, the macro exe-

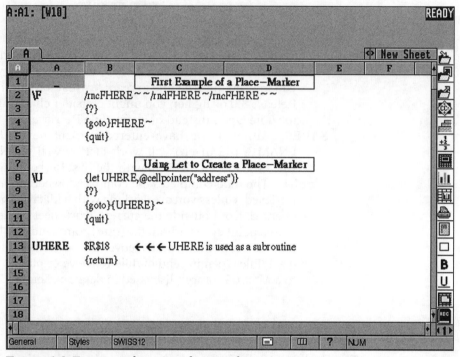

FIGURE 6.4 Two examples using place-markers.

cutes a {goto} command, followed by a *subroutine* call to UHERE, where the macro reads the original cell address before it returns to execute a tilde, jumping you to your starting point.

Note that in the first example, the final {goto} command is followed by the range name FHERE, while in the second example, the {goto} command is followed by a subroutine call to the range name UHERE in braces, like this: {UHERE}. If you neglect to enclose UHERE in braces in the second example, the macro will not return to your original location, but instead will jump to B9, the cell which was prenamed UHERE.

A Place-Marker Macro to List and Print a Range Name Table

The macro in Figure 6.5 provides a good example of the {let} command used with @cellpointer("address") to create a place-marker. This macro stores the current cell address, creates a table of all your range names beyond the End Home position, prints the table, and returns to your original cell location.

{windowsoff}{paneloff}   Turns off changes to the main worksheet area and the upper panel, suppressing screen flicker and speeding up the macro.

{let LHERE,@cellpointer("address")}   Stores in cell B13 (named LHERE) the address of the current cell pointer location.

{end}{home}{right}{end}{up}/rnt~   Moves to the End Home location and to the right one column, then jumps to the topmost cell (row 1) of that column where the macro executes a /Range Name Table command.

/wccs{right}~12~   Selects /Worksheet Column Column-range Set-width, highlights the current cell and one cell to the right, presses Enter, and enters a column width of 12.

:prs{bs}.{end}{down}{panelon}{windowson}{right}{?}~   Selects :Print Range Set, presses Backspace to free the cell pointer, presses the Period (.) key to lock in the pointer, highlights the range name table, turns on the panel and windows, and pauses so you can view the table before printing. If you decide to keep the table in place without printing, you can press Ctrl-Break at this point.

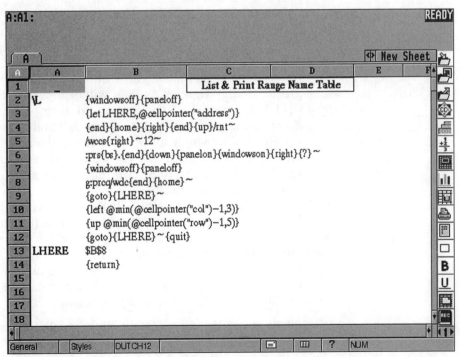

FIGURE 6.5 Macro to list and print range name table.

{windowsoff}{paneloff}   Turns off the windows and panel to complete the macro without screen flicker.

g:prcq/wdc{end}{home}~   Selects the Go command to print the range table, chooses :Print Range Clear Quit, then selects /Worksheet Delete Column, and presses End Home to delete the range table.

{goto}{LHERE}~   Presses the F5 Goto key, does a subroutine branch to read the address in LHERE, and then enters that address with the tilde.

{left @min(@cellpointer("col")-1,3)}   This is an interesting command designed to reposition your current cell more towards the center of the screen. In addition to the ability to add values to the directional commands as in {left 19} or {up 7}, you can also add @functions which equate to values. Using the @min function in combination with @cellpointer("col"), you can cause your cell pointer to be moved either to the left one cell less than the number of the current column or to the left three cells, whichever is less. In other words, if you are in the second column (Column B), this command will move you 2 minus 1 = 1 cell to the left. If you are in the third column (Column C), you will be moved 3 minus 1 = 2 cells to the left. In any column greater than C, you will be moved three cells to the left.

{up @min(@cellpointer("row")-1,3)}   Moves your cell pointer either up one cell less than the number of the current row or up five cells, whichever is less. In other words, if you are in Row 4, this command will move you 4 minus 1 = 3 cells up. In any row greater than 5, your cell pointer will be moved five cells up.

{goto}{LHERE}~{quit}   Returns you to your original cell again. Since moving your cell pointer to the left and up several cells had the effect of moving your original cell to the right and down several cells, your original cell was positioned more towards the center of the screen. This line of the macro returns you to the original cell and the macro quits.

$B$8   This cell, range-named LHERE, is used as a subroutine in the line above. It can be blank before you run the macro, since the macro writes to it with the {let} command in the second line.

{return}   The {return} command is usually added at the end of a subroutine. It tells the macro to return to the place where it left off before it ran the subroutine, which in this case happens to be at the tilde before the final {quit} command.

We will be using the @min(@cellpointer) technique often in placemarker macros throughout this book to keep the cell pointer from being relocated to the upper left corner of the screen after the macro returns you to your original cell.

Viewing a Named Range

A place-marker is not always required to leave your present location and return with a single keystroke. In some cases, the built-in features of 1-2-3 can allow a kind of View-and-Enter operation. For example, you can visit cell A1 by pressing the F5 Goto key, then the Home key. When you want to return, press Esc. You can visit the End Home location in the same way by pressing the F5 Goto key, then End Home, and finally Esc.

Here's a little trick to view a named range and return. Press /Range Name Create, press the F3 Name key twice to get a full-screen view of all your range names, select or type in an existing range name, and press Enter. The cell pointer will jump to the range name and highlight it. You can then view all four corners of the range by pressing the period [.] key. When you want to return to your original location, press Enter. This completes the /Range Name Create sequence, recreating the range name in its previously established location, at which point your cell pointer automatically jumps back to the original cell.

Explore Four Corners of the Worksheet

The macro in Figure 6.6 allows you to view all four corners of your entire worksheet, then returns to your original cell when you press Enter. In the process, it makes clever use of the /Range Name Create sequence to highlight a range (from Home to End Home) while providing you with an instructional prompt.

We have covered another way of creating an instructional prompt by doing a {menubranch} to a single-choice menu. For example, your macro may have the instruction **{menubranch CMENU}** where CMENU looks like this:

```
CMENU    PRESS RETURN.
         THEN HIGHLIGHT THE RANGE.
```

The drawback of this type of instructional prompt, however, is that it requires you to press Enter before you can proceed with any other activity in the macro.

The Xplore 4 Corners macro in Figure 6.6 allows you to press the period key, the pointer keys, or the Enter key in response to what looks like an instructional prompt, though it is actually a range name being created.

> **{paneloff}** Suppresses screen flicker and, in Release 2.x, the "Enter name" prompt that would otherwise appear at the next macro instruction.
>
> **/rnc{panelon}Type. or Enter~{bs}{home}.{end}{home}** Selects /Range Name Create. In Release 2.x, this is done without display-

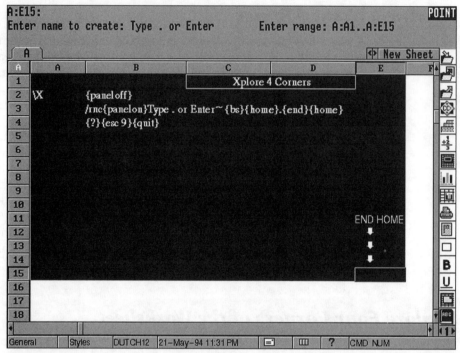

FIGURE 6.6 Macro to explore four corners of the worksheet.

ing the "Enter name" prompt. The macro then turns on the upper panel to type the range name *"TYPE . OR ENTER"*.

For example, if you have a worksheet with an End Home position of G147, the upper panel will look something like this in Release 2.x:

```
TYPE . OR ENTER    Enter Range: A1..G147
```

In Release 3 and higher, the {panelon} command restores the /Range Name Create prompt, so the upper panel will look like this:

```
Enter name to create: TYPE . OR ENTER    Enter Range:
A:A1..A:G147
```

This is a unique use of a 15-character range name (the maximum length), which even in Release 3 will not look like a range name at all, but rather like an instruction.

For the range, the macro presses Backspace to free the pointer, Home to jump to cell A1, the period (.) key to lock in the pointer, and End Home to highlight to the lower right corner of the worksheet.

{?}{esc 9}{quit}   The macro pauses so the user can either type the period (.) key to explore the four corners of the worksheet or press Enter to end the macro. If the user presses Enter, the macro escapes from the /Range Name Create menu without input, and returns to Ready.

Quick Range Recalculate

The Quick Range Recalc Macro in Figure 6.7 is another example of a macro that imbeds an instruction right into the name of the range during a /Range Name Create sequence.

> **TIP:** *If you'd like to calculate a single cell in your spreadsheet, try moving your cell pointer there and pressing the F2 Edit key and Enter. Assuming the cell doesn't depend on serial calculation of several other cells, you'll see the cell recalculate instantly. In a complex spreadsheet, this little trick is much faster than pressing F9 Calc to calculate the entire spreadsheet when all you care about for the moment is one cell. It works because pressing F2 and Enter creates the same effect as entering the formula in the cell for the first time. Since typing a formula for the first time returns current information, pressing F2 and Enter effectively updates, or recalculates, the current cell.*

In that same way, copying a range to itself creates the effect of entering the formulas in that range as if for the first time. Therefore, copying a range to itself will update, or recalculate, that range. Unfortunately, there is no easy way to copy a range to itself from the bottom of the range—which is usually where your pointer is located when you decide you want it recalculated. From that position you will have to move to the top of the range, execute the /Copy command, paint in the range to copy from the top down, then move back to your original location at the bottom of the range.

Instead of copying a range to itself, you may want to use the macro {recalc} command as presented in the Quick Range Recalc macro in Figure 6.7. This is an especially handy macro in a spreadsheet that contains dozens of @d functions like @dsum, @dcount, @davg, and so on, since these types of @ functions tend to take the longest to recalculate.

{windowsoff}{paneloff}   Suppresses screen flicker and the "Enter name" prompt that would otherwise appear at the /Range Name Create sequence.

/rncRANGE TO CALC?~~/rndRANGE TO CALC?~   Creates a range name called "*RANGE TO CALC?*", then deletes that same range name.

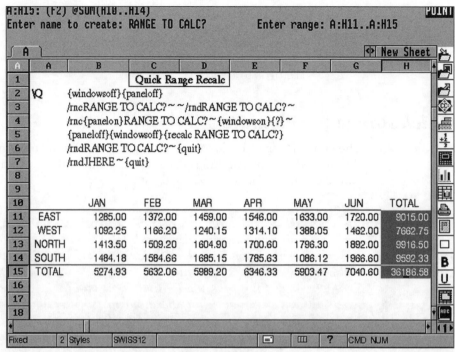

FIGURE 6.7 The Quick Range Recalc macro.

/rnc{panelon}RANGE TO CALC?~{windowson}{?}~ Starts by doing a /Range Name Create, then turns on the panel in mid-command to type "*RANGE TO CALC?.*" The macro then turns on the main screen and pauses so you can highlight the range you want calculated. In Release 2.x, the upper panel will look like this:

```
RANGE TO CALC?    Enter Range:
```

In Release 3 and higher, the {panelon} command restores the /Range Name Create prompt, so the upper panel looks like this:

```
Enter name to create: RANGE TO CALC?  Enter Range:
```

In other words, it looks as if you are being prompted to enter the range you want to calculate, when in fact you are being prompted to enter the range of the area to be named "*RANGE TO CALC?.*" The main advantage here is that you can highlight the range from the bottom up if that is more convenient.

{paneloff}{windowsoff}{recalc RANGE TO CALC?} turns off the upper panel and main screen, then recalculates the range named "*RANGE TO CALC?.*"

/rndRANGE TO CALC?~{quit} The macro ends by deleting the range name and processing a {quit} command. This is done primarily so that your worksheet is not cluttered with unnecessary range names.

You will probably be surprised at how quickly this macro runs, considering all that it has to do. Immediately after you press Alt-Q, you will be prompted for the range to calculate, and the recalculation seems instantaneous.

You can also add conditions and number of iterations to the {recalc} command if you like. You could, for example, instruct your macro to recalculate a range until the first cell of the range is greater than 100 or until 20 iterations have been performed—whichever comes sooner. That command might look like this:

```
{recalc RANGE TO CALC?,@cellpointer("contents")>100,20}
```

Although this kind of additional magic is fairly advanced and the average 1-2-3 user will not have occasion to use it, it gives you some idea of the kind of power you can have using the {recalc} command. In the meantime, you can start using the Quick Range Recalc macro right away.

There is one **very important** caveat, however, which must be taken into consideration in your use of this macro. It is critical that you keep in mind that this macro assumes there are no serial calculations outside the range which must be recalculated before the formulas in the range will calculate properly. If you are not sure about this, or if the calculation involves something more that just a quick look at a range, you should revert to the F9 Calc key to calculate the entire file. In any case, it is always a good idea to do a final F9 Calc of your worksheet before you either save it or print it out for others.

Improving on the /Range Transpose Command

The /Range Name Create method of establishing an instructional prompt as seen in the Xplore 4 Corners macro and Quick Range Recalc macro can also be used in a macro designed to improve on the /Range Transpose command.

The /Range Transpose command is used to copy columns to rows or rows to columns. This can be especially handy if you decide after creating a matrix of headings and data that you want to transpose the entire matrix. An example of this is seen in Figure 6.8.

Unfortunately, this operation returns you to your original location and leaves the original matrix intact. You may prefer to use a macro that accomplishes the /Range Transpose, erases the original matrix, and leaves the cell pointer at your new matrix. Such a macro is shown in Figure 6.9.

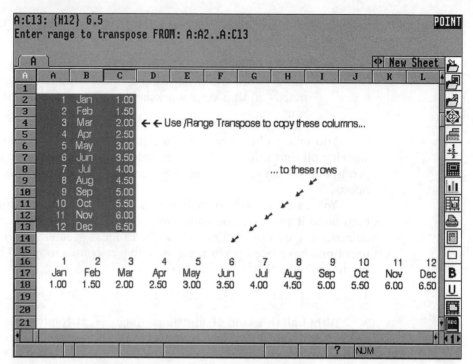

FIGURE 6.8 Transposing a matrix of columns to rows.

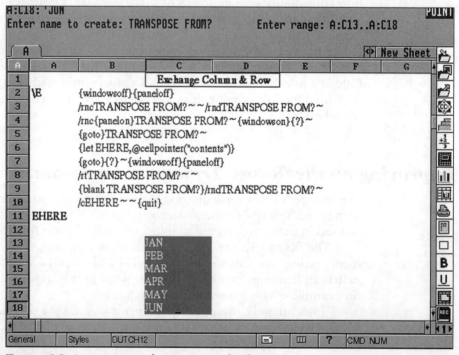

FIGURE 6.9 A macro to exchange row and column.

88

Here's how the macro works:

{windowsoff}{paneloff}   Suppresses screen flicker and, in Release 2.x, the "Enter name" prompt that would otherwise appear at the /Range Name Create sequence.

/rncTRANSPOSE FROM?~~/rndTRANSPOSE FROM?~   Creates a range name called *"TRANSPOSE FROM?"*, then deletes that same range name.

/rnc{panelon}TRANSPOSE FROM?~{windowson}{?}~   Starts by doing a /Range Name Create, then turns on the panel in mid-command to type *"TRANSPOSE FROM?."* The main screen is then turned on and the macro pauses so you can highlight the range you want to transpose.

{let EHERE,@cellpointer("contents")}   Although this may look like a use of the {let} command with @cellpointer as a place-marker to store the current address in EHERE, it is actually a way of storing the value of the current cell in EHERE for later use. It is exactly the same as selecting /Range Value and pressing Enter for the source prompt and entering EHERE for the destination prompt (/rv~EHERE~).

{goto}{?}~{windowsoff}{paneloff}   Prompts you for the location to transpose the range to, moves to that location, and turns off the windows and panel to suppress screen flicker.

/rtTRANSPOSE FROM?~~   Selects Range Transpose, then uses the range name *TRANSPOSE FROM?* as the range to transpose. The second tilde tells 1-2-3 to transpose to the current location you have just moved to.

{blank TRANSPOSE FROM?)/rndTRANSPOSE FROM?~   This is the first example using the {blank} command. It is the exact macro equivalent to /Range Erase and will accept a single cell address, a range, or a range name. In this case, we are blanking (erasing) the range-named *TRANSPOSE FROM?*. The macro then selects /Range Name Delete to eliminate the range name *TRANSPOSE FROM?*.

/cEHERE~~{quit}   Copies the value stored in EHERE to the current cell. This is necessary in case the starting cell of the source range you are transposing from is the same as the starting cell of the destination range. If they are the same and the {blank} command erased that cell, copying the value stored in EHERE will restore it. The macro quits at this point.

The last cell of the macro has been range-named EHERE and it is used as the place to store the value of the starting cell of the Source range.

The Copy Macros

If you're working with 1-2-3 for DOS, you may have experienced this frustration. You want to copy data from cell B2 to cells B4, B6, B8, and B10. In other words, you want to copy to every other cell. So you select /Copy and press Enter, then move down two cells to A6 and again press Enter. So far, so good. But the cell pointer has jumped back up to cell B2, so you press DownArrow twice again, then select /Copy and press Enter, press two more DownArrows to cell B6, and again press Enter. That works, but now the cell pointer jumps back up to cell B4. So you press DownArrow twice again and wonder why Lotus didn't include a Copy-and-Stay-Put capability.

Actually, there is such a feature, known as Copy-and-Paste, in every Windows spreadsheet. For example, in 1-2-3 for Windows, you can copy a cell or block to the Windows Clipboard, move to your destination, and paste the data from the Clipboard to the worksheet, while your cell pointer remains at the destination.

If you're still working with 1-2-3 for DOS, you may be interested in the four unique approaches to the Copy command described below—two manual and two macro-driven.

Copying to Every Other Cell

The first approach doesn't involve a macro at all, but is a strange twist of the standard copy command. By now you are used to the typical method of copying from one cell to a vertical range by pressing Enter at the prompt for a source range and highlighting the vertical range at prompt for a destination. This fills every cell in the column with the source data.

However, when you want to copy to every other cell, instead of copying from a single cell to a highlighted column, try copying from a highlighted column (blank except for the first cell) to a single cell. This may seem counterintuitive at first, but it works. For example, if you want to copy the number **123** from cell B2 to every other cell through B10 as shown in Figure 6.10, select /Copy and at the prompt for a source range, point in the range B2..B8 and press Enter. Note that most of the source range at this point is actually blank.

At the prompt for a destination range, move the pointer down two cells to B4 and press Enter. That's all there is to it. The results are shown in Figure 6.11. The information in B4 is instantly copied into alternate cells B4, B6, B8, and B10, using only 12 keystrokes (including the highlighting keystrokes).

If you want two different entries to be duplicated in alternate cells down a vertical range, use the same technique. For example, if you have the word **LOTUS** in cell B2 and the number **123** in cell B3, going through the same steps will result in dual entries copied to alternate cells as shown in Figure 6.12.

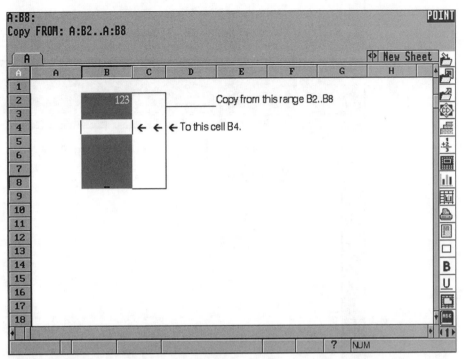

FIGURE 6.10 A technique to copy to alternate cells.

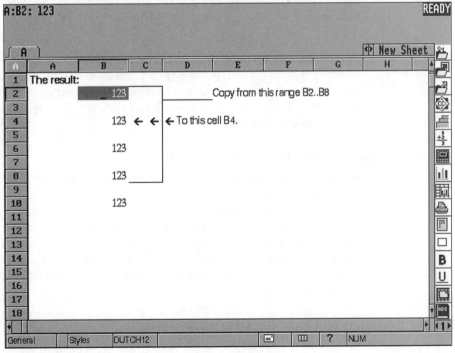

FIGURE 6.11 Result of copying to alternate cells.

91

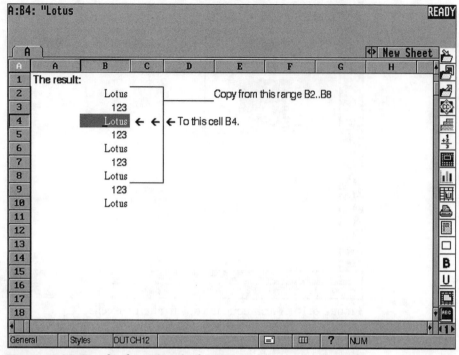

FIGURE 6.12 Result of copying dual entries to alternate cells.

Unfortunately, this method only works when you're copying from one or more cells in an otherwise empty column or row, to that same empty column or row. So, if you're trying to copy to every other cell (B4, B6, B8, etc.) where the alternate cells in the column (B4, B6, B8, etc.) already have data, this method will not work.

Repeated Copying from a Named Cell

Here's another manual method you may want to try. Place your cell pointer on cell B2, select /Range Name Create, name the current cell with just the letter C, and press Enter. By naming the cell to be copied with the letter C, you make it easier to accomplish the /Copy command in another cell. Move your pointer now to C4 and select /Copy, type C, and press Enter twice. Go through the same sequence at cells C6, C8, and C10; in each cell type /cc and Enter twice. Each copy only takes seven keystrokes, including keystrokes for pointer movement.

Using a Macro to Copy to Alternate Cells

Fortunately, you can create a macro to get around the limitations of the manual techniques of copying to alternate cells. Refer to the macro in Figure 6.13.

Here's how the macro works:

{menubranch CMENU1}{quit} Calls up the menu choices *Down, Right,* and *Quit.* If you want to copy to alternate cells in a column, choose *Down.* To copy to alternate cells in a row, choose *Right.*

{let EDIR,"{down 2}'} or **{let EDIR,"{right 2}"}** This is a good example of the use of {let} in a self-modifying macro. In this case, the {let} command changes the subroutine cell of the macro named EDIR to either {down 2} or {right 2}, depending on your menu selection.

{branch E_MORE} Branches to the looping cell of the macro named E_MORE.

/c~{EDIR}~{EDIR} This line copies from the current cell, then branches to the subroutine at EDIR for the copy destination. If you selected DOWN at the first menu, EDIR reads {down 2}. If you selected RIGHT, EDIR reads {right 2}. After the copying, the cell pointer jumps back to the current cell. A second subroutine call to EDIR moves the cell pointer back to the destination cell.

{menubranch CMENU2}{quit} Calls up the menu choices *Continue* or *Quit.*

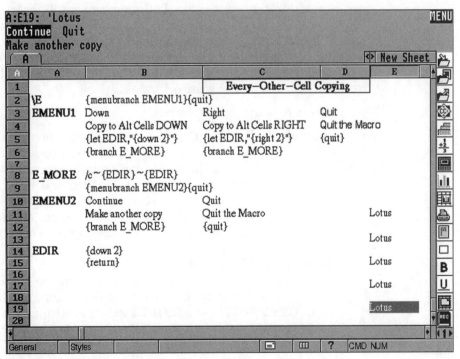

FIGURE 6.13 Macro to copy to alternate cells.

{branch E_MORE}   If you select *Continue,* this command will cause the macro to loop back to the copy command at E_MORE. At each press of the CONTINUE selection, the macro makes another copy in the next alternate cell of the column, then moves the cell pointer to that location.

The last two lines of the macro consist of the subroutine at EDIR. Notice the {return} command that instructs the macro to continue at the point where it left the main macro.

Although it takes a while to step through how the macro works, the actual performance of the macro is surprisingly quick. Almost as fast as you can press Enter to select the word *Continue,* the macro will copy to one more alternate cell.

The macro in the next section offers a more general solution to the problem of a copy command that is not designed to stay at the destination cell. In fact, it offers more features than just the copying of data to alternate cells.

Copy-and-Stay Macro

Imagine a situation where you want to copy from one area in your spreadsheet to a remote location. You press /Copy and highlight the source range you want to copy, then press Enter. You move to the remote location, which requires a dozen presses of the PgDn key, several RightArrows, and a few UpArrows. You're finally there, so you press Enter. But now the cell pointer jumps back to the source location, so you have to go through the same keystrokes to get back to the destination location to continue your work. It seems redundant and frustrating, and the type of problem that can best be solved by a macro. See Figure 6.14.

Here's how the macro works:

{menubranch CMENU}{quit}   Calls up the menu choices *Standard, Copy-and-Stay, Reverse Copy,* and *Xtra-Copy-Here.* The *Standard* choice is included so you can replace a manual selection of the /Copy command with a press of Alt-C and Enter. So by adding only one keystroke to achieve a standard copy, you gain the advantage of three more ways to copy data. The *Standard* choice also "remembers" the cell or range copied, which comes in handy when you want to make extra copies.

{windowsoff}{paneloff}   If you select *Standard,* the macro begins by turning off the windows and panel to suppress screen flicker during the /Range Name Create and Delete commands to come.

/rncCOPY FROM?~~/rndCOPY FROM?~   Using the same technique we demonstrated in the Quick Range Recalc macro, these commands create the range name *"COPY FROM?,"* then delete it again.

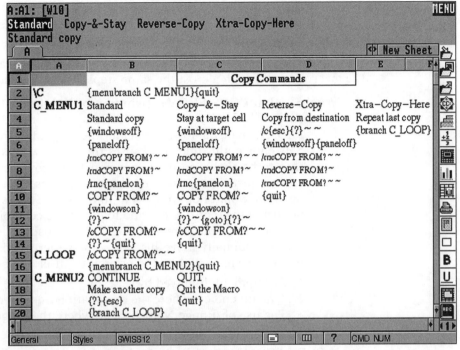

FIGURE 6.14 The Copy-and-Stay macro.

/rnc{panelon}COPY FROM?~{windowson}{?}~ Recreates the range name *"COPY FROM?,"* pausing for you to enter the range. Since the upper panel is off until the macro starts to type the words *"COPY FROM?,"* it will look like this in Release 2.x:

```
COPY FROM? Enter range:
```

In Release 3 and higher, the upper panel will look like this:

```
Enter name to create: COPY FROM?    Enter range:
```

In either case, you are being prompted to highlight the range you want to copy from. The advantage of the first example, of course, is that it looks more like a real Lotus command. You may also notice that the {windowson} command is issued just prior to the question-mark pause. This is required because without this command you would not be able to see your cell pointer move to highlight the range you want to copy.

/cCOPY FROM?~{?}~{quit} Starts the /Copy command to copy the range named *"COPY FROM?"* to another location. The macro pauses at the prompt, "Range to copy TO:" so you can point to the cell where you want your copy to appear. When you press Enter, the macro quits. Notice that we did not delete the range name *COPY FROM?* before the macro quits. The reason for this becomes clear with the *Xtra-Copy-Here* choice.

If you invoke the macro and select *Copy-and-Stay* instead of *Standard*, the macro goes through almost the same steps, with two exceptions:

/rnc{panelon}COPY FROM?~{windowson}{?}~{goto}{?}~   As in the *Standard* choice, the macro recreates the range name *"COPY FROM?,"* pausing for you to enter the range. But in the *Copy-and-Stay* choice, this line also causes the *Enter address to go to:* message to be shown in the upper panel. We could, of course, have entered just the question-mark pause at this point, but then the operator would not know what to do next. That is to say, we are not using the {goto} command to direct the cell pointer to go to a cell location, but more accurately we are using it to instruct the user to manually move his cell pointer there. This is the fourth method we have explored to prompt the user; the other three are:

1. A statement, followed by {?}{esc}.
2. A menu choice, where the explanation line directs the user.
3. The use of /Range Name Create where the range name is also an instructional prompt.

/cCOPY FROM?~~{quit}   As in the *Standard* choice, the macro starts the /Copy command to copy the range-named *"COPY FROM?,"* but in this case the copy is made at the cell where you've just moved your cell pointer. And since you moved your cell pointer to the new location *before* starting the copy command and simply made the copy at the current cell, the cell pointer stays at the destination cell.

Using the Reverse Copy Option

The *Reverse Copy* option uses the same concept, starting the copy command from the destination cell. You can do this yourself manually by selecting /Copy and pressing Esc, which frees your cell pointer to move to the source area. After designating the cell or range you want to copy, press Enter. The cell pointer will jump back to your original location, which presumably is where you want the copied data to go; so at this point you press Enter once again. Your copying is complete and your cell pointer remains at the destination cell. Not counting moving to the area to copy from and painting in the range, this is all done manually in five keystrokes and automatically by the *Reverse Copy* option in three keystrokes.

Using the Xtra-Copy-Here Option

The purpose of the *Xtra-Copy-Here* choice is to allow you to make additional copies of a cell or range already copied once using this macro. To make an

additional copy, move to a new location, invoke the macro, and press the letter X for *Xtra-Copy-Here*.

> **{branch C_LOOP}**   Branches to the subroutine at C_LOOP.
>
> **/cCOPY FROM?~~**   Assuming you have already moved to the loca-
> tion where you want the extra copy to appear, the macro starts
> the /Copy command and responds to the prompt for a source
> range by entering the range name *COPY FROM?*. At the prompt
> for a destination range, the macro simply presses enter, selecting
> the current cell.
>
> **{menubranch C_MENU2}{quit}**   Branches to the menu choices
> *Continue* and *Quit*. If you select *Continue*, the macro pauses so
> you can point to the location where you want the new copy to
> appear. The {esc} command just after the question mark in braces
> {?} is included to ensure you don't type an erroneous entry at your
> new location before the copy is complete. When you press Enter,
> the macro branches back to the cell named C_LOOP and executes
> another copy of the range name *COPY FROM?* at the current cell.

Copying a Relative Formula as Absolute

When you move a formula from one cell to another, all of the cell references
in the formula stay unchanged. On the other hand, when you use the copy
command instead of the move command, the cell references change in relative terms. This "relative copy" aspect of 1-2-3 is an important feature of the
spreadsheet environment, since 90 percent of the time you want exactly
that—a relative copy of the original formula.

Occasionally, however, you want to make an exact duplicate of a formula to be entered in another cell. The way you handled this initially was
probably to copy the formula from one cell to the other, move your cell
pointer to the new copy, press F2 Edit and change the cell references so that
they exactly match the cell references in the original.

At some point you may have learned another trick: Before making
the copy, you change the formula to a label by pressing F2 Edit, then
Home to move the blinking cell pointer to the beginning of the word; then
press apostrophe and Enter. Once the original is a label, you can copy it to
another cell as an exact duplicate. Then all you have to do is eliminate the
apostrophes from both the original and the copy and presto—you have two
versions of the same formula.

It's handy; and as a single exercise it can save you a great deal of time—
especially for a long, complicated formula. If you find yourself having to do
this kind of absolute (as opposed to relative) copying often, however, you
may want to have the macro in Figure 6.15 handle it for you.

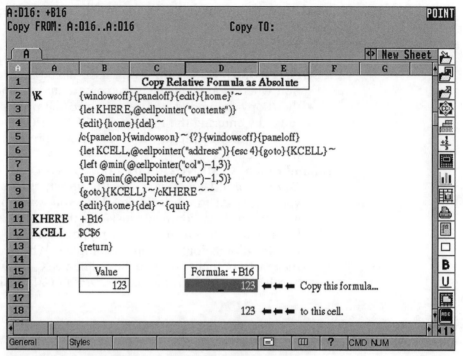

FIGURE 6.15 Macro to copy relative formula as absolute.

{windowsoff}{paneloff}{edit}{home}'~ Suppresses screen and panel flicker and avoids unnecessary update to the screen as 1-2-3 shifts to the Edit mode, presses Home to move to the beginning of the formula, enters an apostrophe to turn the formula into a label, and presses Enter.

{let KHERE,@cellpointer("contents")} Copies the label form of the current cell's formula to the cell named KHERE. This use of the {let} command achieves the same result you would get using the /Copy command, but it does it slightly faster.

{edit}{home}{del}~ Deletes the apostrophe from the original cell to change it back to a formula.

/c~{panelon}{windowson}~{?}{windowsoff}{paneloff} Begins the copy command, copying the current cell; but, at the prompt for a destination range, the macro pauses so you can move to the location where you want to copy the formula. The screen and panel are turned off again before the command is completed. (Although this looks like the beginning of the copying you might expect in a macro designed to copy a relative formula as absolute, it is actually only included so you will see 1-2-3's prompt for a source range.)

{let KCELL,@cellpointer("address")}{esc 4}{goto}{KCELL}~   While you are still in the middle of the /Copy command, the macro records your destination cell, storing the cell address in the cell named KCELL, then escapes from the /Copy command without completing it. The cell pointer is then sent to the cell address stored in KCELL—in other words, to the cell you pointed to in response to the prompt from the last line.

{left @min(@cellpointer("col")-1,3)}   Moves your cell pointer either left one cell less than the number of the current column or left three cells, whichever is less. In other words, it repositions your current cell horizontally towards the center of the screen as shown in an earlier macro in Figure 6.5.

{up @min(@cellpointer("row")-1,5)}   Moves your cell pointer either up one cell less than the number of the current row or up five cells, whichever is less. This repositions your current cell vertically towards the center of the screen.

{goto}{KCELL}~/cKHERE~~   Returns the cell pointer to the target cell, then copies the label form of the original formula from KHERE to the current cell.

{edit}{home}{del}~{quit}   Deletes the apostrophe to return the label to a formula matching the original formula and quits.

You will notice as you use this macro that instead of moving back to the source cell, this example leaves the cell pointer at the destination cell, assuming that location is your probable destination when doing absolute copies of this type. You will also find that the {up @min} and {left @min} commands added to move the cell pointer more to the center of the screen only become necessary when the destination cell is not in the same screen as the original cell.

Absolute Value Macro

There is one drawback to the macro just reviewed: If you want to copy the original formula as an absolute formula to several different cells, it can be tiresome to run the macro over and over again to achieve that result. You could, of course, edit the original formula to put dollar signs ($) in front of all of the cell addresses, thus changing all of the cell addresses to absolute rather than relative references; but that can be more tedious than running our macro repeatedly and you may not want to leave the original formula with absolute references—which means having to delete the dollar signs after your copying is done.

Here's another technique. Move your cell pointer to the first destination cell and press the plus key (+), then move to the source cell you want to copy from and press the F4 Abs key. This will cause the destination cell to contain a plus sign and the absolute cell address of the original cell, something like this: $C$14. Not only will the results of that formula give you the same results as the original formula, but you can also then copy the absolute-cell formula to other cells. Therefore, all of your copy cells will give the same result.

There's more. At the point where you press the F4 Abs key, try pressing it twice. In Release 2.x, the formula will show a relative column and an absolute row, something like this: +C$14. In Release 3.x and higher, the formula includes a sheet letter, like this: +A:C$14. Try pressing the F4 Abs key three times and you'll get an absolute column and relative row, like +$C14 in Release 2.x or +A:$C14 in Release 3.x and higher. Continue pressing the F4 Abs key to get different combinations of absolute and relative coordinates.

Of course, we have a macro that will copy an entire range in absolute terms without these presses of the F4 Abs key. Refer to the macro in Figure 6.16 called "Xtract to Absolute-Copy a Range."

This macro uses two facts about 1-2-3 you probably know:

- 1-2-3 has the ability to extract a range to file with formulas intact.
- Moving (as opposed to copying) a range of formulas makes no relative changes to the formulas.

The macro works by naming the range of formulas you want to copy, extracting a copy to another file, moving the range itself to a new location,

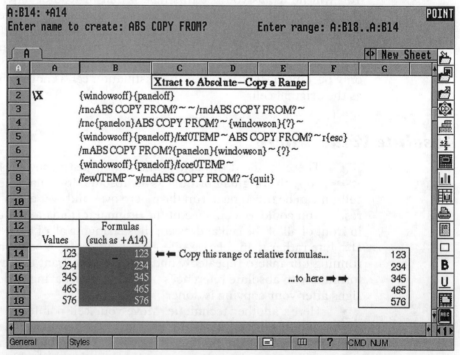

FIGURE 6.16 Using /File Xtract to absolute-copy a range.

and finally /File Combining the extracted copy of the range to the original location. The first three lines of the macro are by now familiar: turning off the windows and panels, creating a range name called *ABS COPY FROM?*, turning the windows and panels back on, and pausing for you to highlight the range you want to copy.

{windowsoff}{paneloff}/fxf0TEMP~ABS COPY FROM?~r{esc}
Turns off the windows and panel, selects /File Xtract Formulas and designates the Xtract File name to be 0TEMP. Note the Xtract File name starts with a zero, not the letter O, so that the file will be among the first to be listed during later /File Retrieve operations in the unlikely event that the macro is interrupted and the file name remains in your current directory in error. The range that the macro extracts is the range named *ABS COPY FROM?*. The macro selects Replace, then presses Esc to cover two possibilities: that the file exists (and requires a Replace to continue with the /File Xtract), or that it does not exist (and requires an Esc to eliminate the pressing of the letter R for Replace).

/mABS COPY FROM?{panelon}{windowson}~{?}~ Uses the /Move command to move the range named *ABS COPY FROM?*, then turns on the windows and panel to allow you to designate your destination range.

{windowsoff}{paneloff}/fcce0TEMP~ After a /Move, the cell pointer jumps back to the original location. At this point, the macro turns off the windows and panel and selects /File Combine Copy Entire, and enters the filename 0TEMP, which contains the original range to copy.

/few0TEMP~y/rndABS COPY FROM?~{quit} Finally, the macro selects /File Erase Worksheet to erase 0TEMP, types Y for Yes at the warning prompt, deletes the range named *ABS COPY FROM?*, and quits.

The result will be two ranges with identical formulas: the original range moved to a new location and a copy of the original range extracted and /File Combined back to the original location.

Moving Macros to Stay or Return

The Move-and-Stay macro in Figure 6.17 is similar in concept to the Copy-and-Stay macro in Figure 6.14, offering the same kind of choice between *Standard*, a *Move-&-Stay* command, and a *Reverse Move*. (Of course, there is no *Xtra-Move-Here* command.) Like the Copy-and-Stay macro, this macro will take a little getting used to, but it will save much of the frustration connected with doing a standard move in 1-2-3 for DOS.

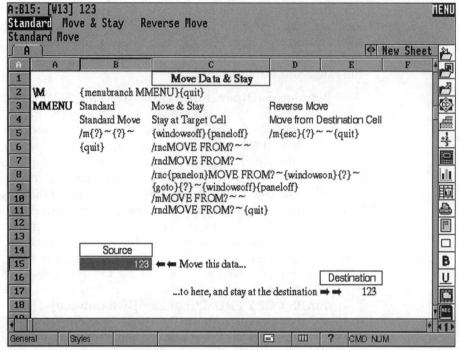

FIGURE 6.17 The Move-and-Stay macro.

If you select the *Standard* choice, the macro simply steps you through the selection of the /Move command, pausing after the /Move prompts for your entry.

If you select *Move-&-Stay*, the macro creates the range name *MOVE FROM?*, pauses for your designation of the range, prompts you for the location to go to, and moves the range from that location, leaving you at the destination cell at the completion of the /Move sequence.

If you select *Reverse Move*, the macro simply prompts you for the range you want to move (assuming you are already at the destination range) and moves that range to your destination location.

Summary

In this chapter you were introduced to the following new concepts:

- Two ways of creating a place-marker: using /Range Name Create-Delete-Create and using the {let} command with @cellpointer ("address").
- Use of the {windowsoff} and {paneloff} commands.

- Use of the @cell and @cellpointer functions
- The use of the {let} command and subroutines to create place-markers.
- The concept of self-modifying macros.
- Some techniques for moving quickly and easily around your spreadsheet.
- Ways to reposition your current cell to the center of the screen.
- A new macro technique to create a range prompter out of a /Range Name Create command.
- Tips on how to copy to alternate cells or copy formulas in an absolute rather than relative way, without the use of macros.

Macros covered in this chapter which use these techniques are summarized as follows:

- A macro to jump the cell pointer to the upper right corner of your worksheet and back again.
- A self-modifying file-retrieve macro.
- A place-marker macro to list and print a range-name table.
- A macro to explore four corners of the worksheet.
- A Quick Range Recalc macro to calculate just a range of your spreadsheet.
- A macro to transpose a matrix of columns to rows.
- A macro to copy to alternate cells.
- Macros to copy a relative formula as absolute or a range of formulas as if they were absolute.
- Copy-and-Stay and Move-and-Stay macros that leave your cell pointer at the destination cell.

In the next chapter we will look at ways to create a background library of macros using one technique in Release 2.x and a different approach in Release 3 and higher. You'll learn techniques for running these background macros from within the current worksheet, though they actually reside in a location other than the current worksheet.

7

Creating a Background Macro Library

A background Macro Library is a collection of macros that you can store in a file outside the currently open worksheet. In this chapter, you'll learn how to store and run such macros in the background in 1-2-3 Release 2.2 and higher without leaving the current worksheet.

If you have an earlier release of 1-2-3, such as 2.0 or 2.01, you have no facility for running macros stored outside the current worksheet. (That feature was not introduced until Release 2.2.) However, you can always keep your macros in a separate saved .WK1 file; and if you give them range names, you can easily import the macros individually into your worksheet. Even if you have Release 2.2 or higher, you can use the techniques in the following section to quickly transfer stored macros from one worksheet file to another.

Transferring Macros between Worksheet Files

Let's assume you have a worksheet file with a dozen or so of your favorite macros. For argument's sake, we'll call this macro worksheet FAVORITE.WK1. In that worksheet, move your cell pointer to the upper left corner of the first macro (typically cell A1).

Now give a two-letter range name to the macro. To make it simple and easy to remember, make the first letter M for Macro and the second letter the same as the letter you use with Alt (or Ctrl in 1-2-3 for Windows) to invoke the macro. Thus, if your first macro is the Add Macro that you invoke by pressing Alt+A or Ctrl+A, you'll be giving that macro the range name MA. If your second macro is the Box Macro that you invoke by pressing Alt+B or Ctrl+B, you'll be assigning it the range name MB.

Name each separate macro in this way, by selecting /Range Name Create, and at the prompt for a range name, entering MA, MB, and so on. At the prompt for a range, highlight the entire macro, including the title at the top and the range names on the left side (a minimum of three columns and two rows, if you followed our recommended macro structure). The example in Figure 7.1 shows a /Range Name Create sequence for the first macro in a typical collection of favorites.

Once you have assigned specific two-letter names such as MA, MB, and so on to each of your macros, be sure to save the file. *The following instructions will not work unless you remember to save the file after the macros have been range-named in this way.*

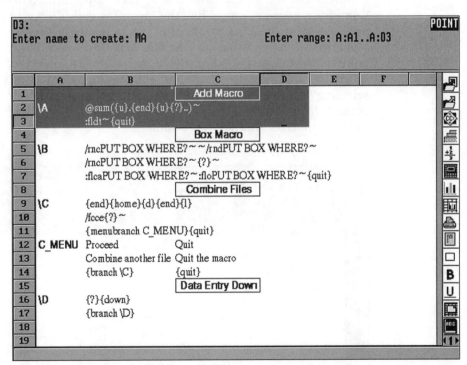

FIGURE 7.1 Giving range names to each macro in a collection.

Now start a blank worksheet or open an existing worksheet and move to a blank area where you want one of your favorite macros to appear. At this point you can either select /File Combine Copy Entire and at the prompt, "Name of File to Combine", select the entire file containing your favorite macros; or you can select /File Combine Copy Named-range and at the prompt, "Enter range name or address:", type the two-letter combination you used to name one of your macros. In the example in Figure 7.2, the MA macro was already /File Combined into the worksheet in this way, and the cell pointer was moved to C3 where the MB macro is about to be /File Combined.

It may seem like a lot to go through to create an on-disk library of your favorite macros and /Range Name them so you can easily import specific macros, but after the initial setup and range naming you'll find that the keystrokes to /File Combine the macros into your current worksheet can become second nature. As you will see, it only takes seven keystrokes (/fccnMA, for example) to identify the macro and a few more cell pointer movements and presses of the Enter key to get the macro into your current worksheet.

There is only one other action to take before the macro will work in your current worksheet—and this is very important. Whenever you /File Combine a range or entire file, the incoming cells do *not* bring their range names with them. This means that not only will a given macro *not* bring along its two-letter name such as MA, MB, and so on; but it will also leave behind its backslash-letter range name and any internal range names it needs to run. You must therefore range-name all your macros again by selecting /Range Name Labels Right in the column to the left of your macro code. At the prompt for a range, be sure to press PgDn enough times to highlight the macro's internal range names.

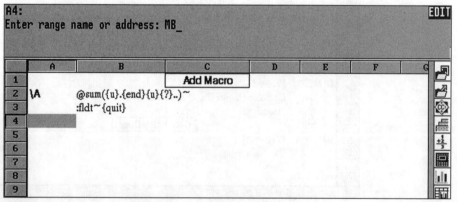

FIGURE 7.2 Importing individual macros from disk.

The Macro Library Manager for Release 2.2 through 2.4

With the advent of 1-2-3 Release 2.2, Lotus introduced an add-in called the Macro Library Manager. With this add-in you can keep your commonly used macros hidden in the background (sometimes called hyperspace), rather than in your current worksheet. The Macro Library Manager does this by storing your macros in separate background files with an .MLB extension.

> **NOTE:** *Creating a Macro Library to work in the background in Release 3 or higher is quite different. Since you can have several files open and active in a 1-2-3 session using Release 3 or higher, there is no need for a special add-in like the Macro Library Manager in Release 2.2. If you have Release 3 or higher, you may want to skip ahead to the section on Release 3 Macro Libraries that describes how background macros can be kept in separate active worksheet files.*

Installing the Release 2.2 Macro Library Manager

As an add-in, the Macro Library Manager introduced in Release 2.2 takes up extra RAM, whether or not you have created and saved macros to the Macro Library. If memory is not a consideration, you may choose to have 1-2-3 attach this add-in automatically each time you start a 1-2-3 session. This is done by selecting /Worksheet Global Default Other Add-in Set as shown in Figure 7.3. A menu prompts you to assign a number (1 to 8) to the add-in, after which all add-ins and subdirectories in your main 1-2-3 directory appear.

The Macro Library Manager is in a file called MACROMGR.ADN on the Install Disk that comes with your Release 2.2, 2.3, or 2.4 package. If you have a hard disk system, the file should already be in the directory that contains your 1-2-3 System files. MACROMGR.ADN should appear as one of the choices of add-ins you can select at this point, as shown in Figure 7.4.

You will be prompted to assign Alt+7, Alt+8, Alt+9, or Alt+10 to the add-in to make it easier to invoke later. Alternatively, you can select "No-key."

In addition to automatically *attaching* the add-in, you can have 1-2-3 automatically *invoke* the add-in when you start your 1-2-3 session. To do that, select Yes at the Invoke prompt. The settings sheet shown in Figure 7.5 demonstrates the results.

If you select Yes, 1-2-3 looks for your individual Macro Libraries in the same directory as the MACROMGR.ADN—in other words, in your main

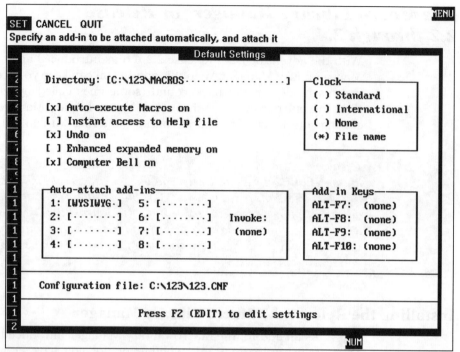

FIGURE 7.3 Setting an add-in to automatically attach.

1-2-3 directory—regardless of the default directory you have established. This differs from manually invoking MACROMGR.ADN, which causes 1-2-3 to search the default (or current) directory for your individual Macro Libraries.

Select Quit and choose Update Quit to change the configuration of your 1-2-3. After this, whenever you start up a 1-2-3 session, the Macro Library Manager add-in will be attached automatically.

If you prefer not to change your 1-2-3 configuration, you can always attach the MACROMGR.ADN manually by selecting /Add-in from the command menu or pressing the Alt-F10 Add-in key (if it has not been assigned to another add-in application). You will see the menu choices *Attach, Detach, Invoke, Clear,* and *Quit.* The first selection you must make for the Macro Library Manager add-in is *Attach,* since you cannot invoke an add-in before you attach it. At the choice of add-ins to attach, highlight MACROMGR.ADN and press Enter. As with automatic global attachment, you will be prompted for an Alt+Function Key combination to assign to the add-in, though you may select No-Key.

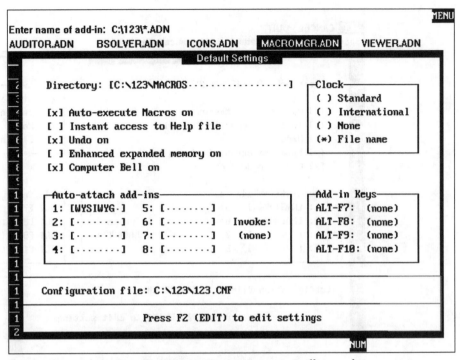

FIGURE 7.4 Selecting MACROMGR.ADN to automatically attach.

Invoking the Release 2.2 Macro Library Manager

Once the MACROMGR.ADN is attached, you can invoke it by pressing the appropriate Alt+Function Key combination (if you assigned one), or by selecting /Add-in Invoke. If you use /Add-in Invoke, 1-2-3 presents you with the names of all add-in applications you may have attached. Select MACROMGR and press Enter.

The menu choices *Load, Save, Edit, Remove, Name-list,* and *Quit* will appear. Do not select *Load, Remove,* or *Name-list* unless you already have .MLB files on disk ready to be loaded, removed, or listed. And as you might guess, you cannot Edit an .MLB Macro Library file unless it has first been Saved or Loaded.

Creating a New .MLB File in Release 2.2

If you have no .MLB Macro Library files, you can create one from macros in the current worksheet (assuming you have macros in the current worksheet) by selecting *Save.* 1-2-3 prompts you for the Macro Library filename

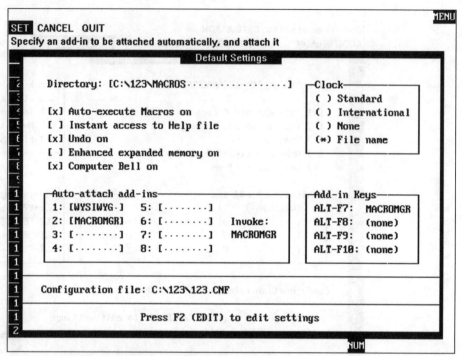

FIGURE 7.5 Setting the MACROMGR.ADN to automatically invoke.

under which to save the macros. You might use the filename MACRO_1, for example. 1-2-3 automatically adds the file extension .MLB to your new Macro Library file.

If you want your .MLB file to be loaded into memory automatically whenever the Macro Library Manager is attached, save it with the name AUTOLOAD.MLB. No macros in the library will execute automatically, not even \0 autoexecute macros, but they will be ready for you to use manually.

After you establish the Macro Library filename, 1-2-3 prompts you to "Enter Macro Library Range." You can respond by typing in the coordinates for a range which includes your macro titles, range names, and macro code, but it is usually better to highlight the range with your cell pointer so you can be sure you covered the entire macro area. An example is shown in Figure 7.6.

Then 1-2-3 prompts you for whether to use a password to lock the library file. If you do decide to lock the file, you must be sure to remember the exact combination of uppercase or lowercase letters you typed for the password. When you save data in a library with a password, you can only edit the library if you enter the password again exactly as it was first entered, including case.

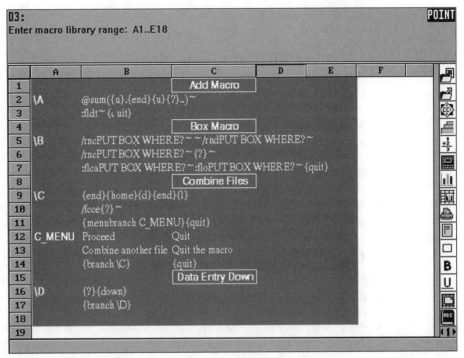

FIGURE 7.6 Saving macros to a macro library file.

As the macros are saved in their own Macro Library file, 1-2-3 simultaneously erases them from the current worksheet. Don't let this bother you; they aren't lost, but only moved to another file. To place a copy of the saved macros back in the worksheet as before, press the Alt+ Function Key combination for your Macro Library Manager (if any) or select /Add-in Invoke MACROMGR and press Enter. From the menu choices, select *Edit.*

Editing an .MLB File in Release 2.2

If you choose *Edit* from the /Add-in Invoke menu, 1-2-3 prompts you for the Macro Library file to edit and a location in your worksheet to place the library macros. You can indicate any unprotected area of the worksheet, but you should make sure that the area is blank or contains unimportant data because the Macro Library Manager writes over existing data when it copies the .MLB file into the worksheet.

When you bring library macros back into a worksheet by selecting *Edit,* any of its range names that happen to match range names in your worksheet set up a potential conflict. 1-2-3 prompts you for whether to ignore or write over existing range names in the worksheet. For this reason, you should try to make all range names in any macro you write unique to that macro.

After editing .MLB macros, you can save any changes that you make by selecting /Add-in Invoke MACROMGR Save. This saves the macros back into their same Macro Library file with its .MLB extension.

As for the other menu choices 1-2-3 offers when you invoke the MACROMGR add-in, the *Remove* command allows you to erase a Macro Library file from RAM memory, although the Macro Library Manager leaves a copy of the library file on disk. To use the library file again, use the /Add-in Invoke MACROMGR Load command. The *Name-List* command places in your worksheet a list of all the range names in any Macro Library files you have loaded. As with *Edit*, however, make sure that the area is blank or contains unimportant data, because the Name-List writes over existing data.

Loading Release 2.2 .MLB Macros with AUTO.123

Having 1-2-3 automatically attach and invoke your MACROMGR.ADN program (via the /Worksheet Global Default Other Add-in Set sequence as described above) causes 1-2-3 to look for your individual .MLB files in the same directory as the MACROMGR.ADN file—in other words, in your main 1-2-3 directory—regardless of the default directory you have established.

You can use another technique, however, which allows you to keep all your .MLB files in a separate macro subdirectory. (You may have decided to create a subdirectory for your macro files, such as C:\123\MACROS, for example.)

When you call up 1-2-3, it searches the default directory and retrieves any file named AUTO123.WK1. If the AUTO123.WK1 file includes an auto-executing macro (a macro that begins with a backslash-zero \0), that macro runs automatically as soon as the AUTO123.WK1 file is retrieved.

Imagine, then, an AUTO123.WK1 file with an autoexec macro that attaches and invokes your MACROMGR.ADN, loads your favorite .MLB Macro Library file, and finally does a /Worksheet Erase Yes to clear the screen. You have the advantage of having the macro in this file load your .MLB files from any subdirectory where you choose to store them.

Such an AUTO123.WK1 file is shown in Figure 7.7. However, you must save this AUTO123.WK1 file to the 1-2-3 default directory before it will be automatically retrieved by 1-2-3 when you begin your 1-2-3 session.

{} The macro begins with a null pass-through command. This is done to allow the macro to have two starting names: the \A name included for testing purposes only and the autoexecuting \0 name that will start the macro automatically as soon as the AUTO123. WK1 file is loaded by 1-2-3 at start-up.

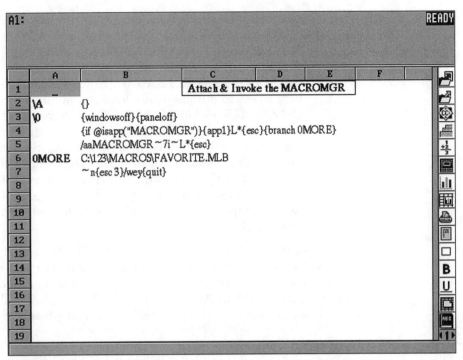

FIGURE 7.7 AUTO123 file to attach and invoke the MACROMGR.ADN.

{windowsoff}{paneloff}   Suppresses screen flicker and speeds the macro.

{if @isapp("MACROMGR")}{app1}L*{esc}{branch OMORE}   This line introduces a new concept covered in more detail later: the macro {if} command. For now, suffice it to say that if the statement included in the argument is true, the macro continues reading the rest of the line. If it is false, the macro skips down to the next line. In this case, the macro uses the {if} command with the @isapp function to test for whether the MACROMGR.ADN file has been attached. If so, the macro continues on this same line, running the {app1} command which invokes the MACROMGR application. (Note, this assumes that the MACROMGR add-in, if attached, was assigned the Alt+F7 combination for invoking.) The L is for Load and the asterisk and Esc are included to eliminate any default prompts which may appear when Load is selected. Finally, the macro branches to the line of the macro specifying your file of favorite macros.

/aaMACROMGR~7i~L*{esc}   If the @isapp function comes up false when checking for whether the MACROMGR add-in has been attached, the macro skips the rest of the last line and continues at this one. Its purpose is to select /Add-in Attach, enter MACROMGR, assign the Alt+F7 key, and finally eliminate any default prompts which may appear when Load is selected.

C:\123\MACROS\FAVORITE.MLB   Note, the example we are using here is set to automatically load the Macro Library file named C:\123\MACROS\FAVORITE.MLB. To change either the directory path or filename listed in that macro to match your own directory path or to specify another .MLB file to load automatically, modify this line of the macro as you type in the macro initially.

~n{esc 3}/wey{quit}   Enters the directory path and filename of your favorite .MLB macros, selects N for No at the prompt for a password, escapes from the /Add-in Attach menu, erases the worksheet, and quits.

To use this macro in an AUTO123.WK1 file, start with a blank worksheet, type in the macro lines, /Range Name the macro, and save the file. It is very important to save the file before you test the macro to ensure that it works properly, since the /WEY command in the last line will erase the current worksheet to start your 1-2-3 session off with a blank worksheet.

Rules and Conventions for the Release 2.2 Macro Library

Note the following 12 rules and conventions when you use the Macro Library Manager:

1. 1-2-3 brings a Macro Library file into active RAM when you select either the Load or the Save command from the Macro Library Manager menu. You can have up to 10 libraries in memory at the same time, each library containing up to 16,376 cells, or the equivalent of two columns wide by 8,188 rows long.

2. When you specify a range of macros you want to save into a Macro Library file, a cell will be allocated in conventional memory in the library file for each cell in the range, even if it is empty. To save memory, make your macros as compact as possible.

3. A Macro Library has no cell coordinates, so you cannot refer to cells or ranges in a library with cell or range coordinates, though you can refer to either by using range names.

4. You will not be able to use the /Copy or /Move commands to manipulate cell coordinates, range coordinates, or even range names in an .MLB Macro Library file (unless, of course, you count those instances where you bring the file into the current worksheet for editing with the /Add-in Invoke MACROMGR Edit command).

5. You can, however, use advanced macro commands, such as the {let} command, to move data between libraries or between the

worksheet and a library. For example, you can use the macro line **{let MACRO_CELL,+A4}**, where **MACRO_CELL** is a named range in a Macro Library file. The macro keywords which can be used for this type of manipulation of named ranges in a Macro Library file are:

{blank}	{get}	{if}	{put}	{recalccol}
{contents}	{getlabel}	{let}	{read}	{setpos}
{define}	{getnumber}	{look}	{readln}	{wait}
{filesize}	{getpos}	{open}	{recalc}	{writeln}

6. As with worksheet files, you cannot save more than one Macro Library file with the same name. If you try, 1-2-3 prompts you for whether to write over the previous library file.

7. You will not be able to save a range of macros in a Macro Library file if the range includes a link to another file. Trying this will cause an error message.

8. When you save a formula into a Macro Library, any ranges or cells that the formula references must also be saved into the same Macro Library or the formula will not display the correct results. Even though there are no cell addresses in a Macro Library, you can have cell references within a formula. The Macro Library version simply maintains the relative position of the referenced cell to the formula.

9. When you save a range in your worksheet to a Macro Library file, any formulas still remaining in your worksheet that refer to cells within that range will continue to refer to the same cells, even though they will be empty after the /Add-in Invoke MACROMGR Save command.

10. When you edit a Macro Library file, any range names in its macros that match range names in your worksheet set up a potential conflict. 1-2-3 will prompt you for whether to ignore or write over existing range names in the worksheet. For this reason, you should try to make all range names in any macro you write unique to that macro.

11. When you specify a range name to start a macro or as an argument in a macro command, 1-2-3 searches for the range name in this order: 1) the current worksheet; 2) the first Macro Library placed in active RAM by the Save or Load command; 3) the second library placed in active RAM by the Save or Load command; and so on. This is another strong reason for making sure that the range names in each macro are unique to that macro.

12. An .MLB library macro can do a /File Retrieve of any file and continue to operate, with one exception. If the retrieved file contains an autoexecute macro, the autoexecute macro will run instead of the library macro.

Running Macros from the Release 2.2 Macro Library

With the background capability of a Macro Library you can run all types of macros. What's more, you can create a macro that works across worksheet files. For example, you can have a macro that will take you from your current file by erasing the worksheet or retrieving another file, then return to the original file and cell pointer position to continue where you left off.

The macro in Figure 7.8 shows an example of such a Macro Library macro. This is a type of place-marker macro that stores the current filename, erases the worksheet, then does a /File Retrieve to return to the original worksheet file.

Be aware, however, that this macro will not work if you run it as a worksheet macro instead of as a Macro Library macro. It is important to have this macro run in the background. Otherwise, as soon as the macro comes to the second line erasing the worksheet, the disappearing worksheet will also mean a disappearing macro, and the macro will stop. So long as you save this macro into a Macro Library, however, and provided it does not also exist in the current worksheet, pressing Alt+P (Ctrl+P in 1-2-3 for Windows) will cause the effect described.

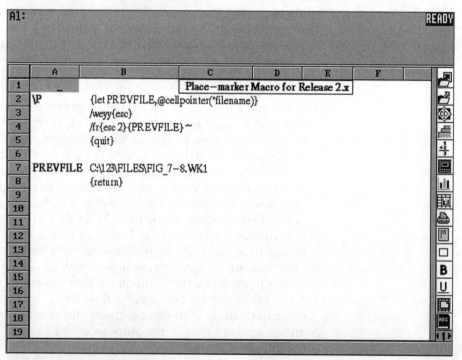

FIGURE 7.8 Place-Marker macro to return to the previous file.

Here's how the macro works:

{let PREVFILE,@cellpointer("filename")}   Causes the filename of the current worksheet to be stored in the cell named PREVFILE.

> **NOTE:** *The attribute "filename" was introduced with Release 2.2, and is not available in earlier releases of 1-2-3.*

/weyy{esc}   Selects /Worksheet Erase Yes. In Release 2.2, if any changes have been made to the worksheet, an additional prompt asks whether you really want to erase the worksheet. If so, the Y for Yes completes the command sequence and the {escape} command has no effect. If there have been no changes, the prompt will not appear and the Y that the macro types will be eliminated by the {esc} command.

/fr{esc 2}{PREVFILE}~   Selects /File Retrieve, then presses Escape twice to eliminate the file directory path. The macro then does a subroutine branch to PREVFILE. At PREVFILE, the filename which was stored there by the {let} command is typed for you (including the directory path) and the {return} command returns the flow of the macro to the tilde at the end of the third line where the /File Retrieve sequence is completed. The macro quits in the last line.

By itself, this macro is completely useless, since it records your current filename, erases the file, then /File Retrieves that file again, putting you back where you started. It is not intended as a standalone macro, however, but as an example of how to leave a file and return using a Macro Library macro. You can use the first line's {let} command in other macros, then use the /File Retrieve that continues at a subroutine (like the PREVFILE subroutine shown) to jump you back to the file where you started.

Summarizing the Use of the 2.2 Macro Library

The preceding few pages covered quite a scope of information, which may seem like a lot to contemplate at this time. Fortunately, you won't have to bother with any of this to explore the world of macros. You may prefer to simply work with the macros in your current worksheets for the time being; then when you are ready for Macro Library information, you will find that these pages provide you with everything you need to know.

Using a Background Macro Library in Release 3 and Higher

Although 1-2-3 versions found in Release 3 and higher do not have the Macro Library Manager add-in that shipped with Release 2.2 through 2.4, you can store and use background macros in these higher versions in two ways: either on a separate sheet in the same worksheet file, or in a separate active .WK3, or (in the latest 1-2-3 for Windows) .WK4 file.

Storing .WK3 Macros on a New Sheet

Suppose, for example, that you want some background macros to operate within a multiple-sheet file, though not on the current sheet. Simply create a separate sheet by selecting /Worksheet Insert Sheet After, and then /File Combine the required macros into that separate sheet. After range-naming the macros as described earlier, move back to the previous sheet and access the macros from there.

When you save the worksheet file, the new sheet of macros is saved with that file and you can easily invoke the macros whenever the file is open. Assuming there's no range-name conflict between the macros and the rest of the worksheet file, you can leave the macros on their separate sheet in the background and run them as if they were stored on the current sheet.

Storing .WK3 Macros in a Separate File

However, if you want your macros to work across files, you may find a second method more appealing. Select /File Open After and call up another .WK3 (or, in the latest 1-2-3 for Windows, .WK4) file that contains macros. So long as those macros do not contain references to range names which are specific to the macro file, the macros will work just as if they were in the current worksheet.

Fortunately, 1-2-3 even provides a way to get these macros to work across files when they *do* contain references to range names in the macro file. The technique is to provide a filename identifier before each such range name, enclosed in double angled brackets. Thus, a macro in the 3PRINT.WK3 file that refers to a cell named STOREVALUE would be changed to refer instead to: <<3PRINT>>STOREVALUE.

However, if you change the name of the 3PRINT.WK3 worksheet to another filename, or if you have just /File Combined the macros in 3PRINT.WK3 from another worksheet, you must be sure to change all <<*filename*>> references in your macros. Since this can be problematic, Lotus has provided a wildcard filename reference that you can use in any macro in Release 3 or higher. The wild card filename is a set of angled brackets surrounding a question mark. Thus, in our example using STOREVALUE you can substitute the following: <<?>>STOREVALUE.

In order to make the .WK3 macros we will be exploring as generic and portable as possible, most of the remaining macros in this book are shown in two ways: in the standard Release 2.x form and in a modified form for Release 3 and higher which includes the wildcard filename <<?>> prefix where necessary. With rare exception these macros will work across files perfectly well from the background, from separate active files, and whether brought in using /File Retrieve, /File Open, or /File Combine.

> **NOTE:** *The one disadvantage when using a wildcard filename is the possibility of an error message if you mistakenly duplicate your macro range names in two separate active files. For example, suppose you have a macro in one open Macro Library file that changes the value of <<?>>MTOGGLE, and you create another macro that includes a reference to <<?>>MTOGGLE. When you try to run either macro in that case, it will halt and an error message will appear at the bottom of your screen.*

Actually, the importance of keeping your macro range names unique has always been an issue for single worksheets; but now you should extend to all of your files the care you give to making range names unique in a single file.

Starting Your .WK3 Macro Library with AUTO123

Instead of retrieving the worksheet you want to work on, then selecting /File Open After to open a separate worksheet file of your favorite background macros, you may want to do the reverse. In other words, you start by retrieving your favorite macro file, then do a /File Open Before or /File New Before to get to the worksheet you want to work on.

This approach is accomplished for you automatically with the auto-exec \0 macro in Figure 7.9. This autoexec macro is designed for use in an AUTO123.WK3 file filled with your favorite macros. As an AUTO123 file, it will be loaded automatically when you start your 1-2-3 session, provided the file is kept in your default directory. And with its autoexecuting macro (a macro that begins with a backslash-zero \0) the macro runs automatically as soon as the AUTO123.WK1 file is retrieved.

{}   The macro begins with a null pass-through command. This is done to allow the macro to have alternate starting names: the \A name for use in starting the macro manually (usually for testing purposes) and the \0 name to start the macro automatically.

{menubranch AMENU}{quit}   Calls up the menu choices *Yes* and *No*, prompting you for whether you want to include this Macro Library in this session.

If you select *No* at the first menu, the macro will branch to AMENU3 and offer the choices *File_Retrieve*, *Blank_Worksheet*, and *Quit*. The first choice starts the /File Retrieve command and presses the F3 Name key, displaying all the files of the current directory. If you select *Blank_Worksheet*,

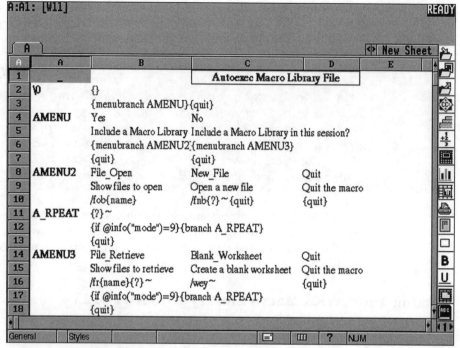

FIGURE 7.9 Autoexecuting Macro Library in AUTO123.

the macro does a /Worksheet Erase Yes to provide you with a new, blank worksheet. Either way, the AUTO123 file will be replaced and you will be operating without this Macro Library file. If you select Yes, the macro branches to AMENU2 and offers the choices *File_Open*, *New_File*, and *Quit*.

/fob{name}{?}~ The *File_Open* choice starts /File Open Before, presses F3 Name to show a list of all available files to open, and pauses for your choice.

{if @info("mode")=9}{branch A_REPEAT} The {if} command is similar to the @if function, except that the truth of the {if} condition affects macro flow rather than returning a 1 or 0 as with the @if function. If the condition is true, the macro continues to read along the same line. If the condition is false, the macro skips to the next line down. In this case, the macro is testing for whether you are still in the "file" mode.

Lotus introduced the @info function with the advent of Release 3. It does not exist in Release 2.x. Its attributes are as shown in Table 7.1.

By checking for whether the @info("mode") equals 9, your macro is testing for whether you pressed Enter (ending the bracketed question mark

Table 7.1 The @Info Attributes in Release 3

@Info Attributes:	*Example:*	*Description:*
@info("directory")	C:\123\FILES\	The current directory
@info("memavail")	420306	Current available memory
@info("mode")	0 Wait	The current mode
	1 Ready	
	2 Label	
	3 Menu	
	4 Value	
	5 Point	
	6 Edit	
	7 Error	
	8 Find	
	9 Files	
	10 Help	
	11 Stat	
	13 Names	
	99 All Other	
@info("numfile")	1	Number of Active Files
@info("origin")	$A:$A$1	First cell pointer location at the start of the 1-2-3 session
@info("osreturncode")	0	Value returned by the most recent /System command
@info("osversion")	DOS Version 3.10	Operating System version
@info("recalc")	Automatic	Current Recalc Mode
@info("release")	3.00.00	1-2-3 Release number
@info("system")	pcdos	Operating System
@info("totmem")	432898	Total available memory

pause) because you selected a file or another directory. If you selected another directory, the macro branches back to the bracketed question mark pause to await your selection of a file. Once you select a file, you are returned to READY mode from the FILE mode, and @info("mode") no longer equals 9. The file you selected is retrieved, and the macro quits.

/fnb(?}~{quit}   The NEW_FILE choice causes the selection /File New Before and pauses for your selection of a new filename.

Whether you select FILE_OPEN or NEW_FILE, the result will feel the same as having retrieved a file or having started with a blank worksheet, except that you now have your AUTO123 file containing your favorite macros in the background. You can access those macros from the current file or from any worksheet file you open during the current 1-2-3 session.

None of this will make any sense, however, unless you add your favorite macros to the AUTO123.WK3 file. Only after you have added the macros does the AUTO123.WK3 file become an effective and automatically loading Macro Library file.

Placing AUTO123.WK3 in the Default Directory

AUTO123 files will not load automatically unless they reside in your default directory. This means that you will want to either use /Worksheet Default Directory (don't forget to select Update) to change your default directory to the directory where you keep your other macro files or save or copy your AUTO123 file to your default directory. That way, the next time you load 1-2-3, the program will automatically retrieve the AUTO123 file and run its autoexec \0 macro.

Summary

In this chapter we explored the use of Macro Libraries. You can simplify the transfer of macros from worksheet files on disk to the current worksheet by giving the macros range names such as MA, MB, and so on, /File Combining the named macros into the current worksheet, and assigning the required operating range names to the imported macros.

In Release 2.2, you can use the MACROMGR.ADN application to hold macros in a type of hyperspace outside the current worksheet. To have 1-2-3 attach this add-in automatically each time you start a 1-2-3 session, select /Worksheet Global Default Other Add-in Set. You also have the option of having 1-2-3 automatically invoke or run the add-in when you start your 1-2-3 session. If you prefer not to change your 1-2-3 configuration, you can always elect to attach the MACROMGR.ADN manually by selecting /Add-in from the command menu or pressing the Alt-F10 Add-in key.

If you have no .MLB Macro Library files, you can create one from macros in the current worksheet by selecting Save. If you want your .MLB file automatically loaded into memory whenever the Macro Library Manager is attached, save it with the name AUTOLOAD.MLB. To edit an .MLB Macro Library file, choose /Add-in Invoke MACROMGR Edit. After editing .MLB macros, you can save any changes that you make by selecting /Add-in Invoke MACROMGR Save.

You can create an AUTO123.WK1 file with an autoexec macro that attaches and invokes your MACROMGR.ADN, loads your favorite .MLB

Macro Library file from any subdirectory where you choose to store it, and clears the screen.

With the background capability of a Macro Library, you can also create a place-marker macro that will take you from your current file by erasing the worksheet or retrieving another file, then return to the original file and cell pointer position to continue where you left off.

Although Release 3 and higher do not have a Macro Library Manager add-in as found in Release 2.2, these releases allow background macros in a separate sheet of the same worksheet file or in a separate active file. To create background macros to operate across files, select /File Open After and designate another .WK3 file that contains macros. So long as those macros do not contain references to range names which are specific to the macro file, the macros will work just as if they were in the current worksheet.

If your .WK3 macros contain references to range names in the macro file, provide a filename identifier or wildcard filename before each such range name, enclosed in double angled brackets. Because you can mistakenly duplicate macro range names in two separate active files, try to make each of your macro range names unique to a single file.

In Release 3 and higher, you can open a file of your favorite macros automatically with the \0 autoexec macro in an AUTO123.WK3 file as shown in Figure 7.8. If you save or copy your AUTO123 file to your default directory, the program will automatically retrieve the AUTO123 file and run its autoexec \0 macro when you start your 1-2-3 session; your background macros will run from the current file or from any worksheet file you open during the session.

In the next chapter we will explore the concept of toggle-switch macros, including macros to toggle between alternate locations, to toggle your titles on and off, to toggle Recalculation between automatic and manual, to toggle between file directories, and so on.

8

Toggles and the Macro Run Key

In this chapter we introduce the use of toggles in your macros, including a toggle to jump to often-visited areas of your spreadsheet. This chapter also covers the Alt+F3 Macro Run key in Release 2.2 and higher, a simulation of the Alt+F3 Macro Run key in Release 2 and 2.01, and ways to jump your cell pointer to special areas such as a notepad area, appointment calendar area, pop-up calculator window, and a custom help screen.

The Order of Range Names

Since we are reviewing ways of moving quickly and easily around the work-sheet, this is a good place to introduce a little trick involving the use of range names to jump to often-visited areas of your spreadsheet. As already men-tioned, pressing the F5 Goto key and the F3 Name key shows range names in the upper panel as possible Goto locations. This means that pressing F5 Goto, then F3 Name, then Enter, causes your cell pointer to jump to the first range name in the list.

Here's the trick. Since the range names are listed alphabetically, you can create a special range name that will always appear first in the upper panel. So if there's some prime area in your spreadsheet you'd like to visit often, simply name the upper left corner of that area with the special name. Then when you press F5 Goto, F3 Name, Enter, your cell pointer jumps there instantly.

 You might think that using the range name AAA would work for this, but it turns out that numbers are listed ahead of letters. Then how about 000? That would be a good idea, except that certain symbols come ahead of numbers. All things considered, the best choice seems to be the number sign (#). Actually, this is especially handy because you can establish several range names throughout your spreadsheets that you think you might want to visit often and give them names like #1, #2, #3, and so on. Then when you want to visit the first area you press F5 F3 Enter, for the second area press F5 F3 RightArrow Enter, for the third area press F5 F3 RightArrow RightArrow Enter, and so on.

Using the Alt+F3 Macro RUN Key in Release 2.2 and Higher

The Alt+F3 Run key is used to provide another way to run macros beyond the Alt+letter method we have used so far. When you press Alt+F3, you will be able to access macros by:

 Pointing in a single-line or full-screen listing of range names to one of the backslash-letter macro names (such as \A, \B, \C, etc.);

 Pointing in a range-name listing to any of the nonbackslash range names that identifies the first cell of a macro;

 Entering any of the nonbackslash range names that identifies the first cell of a macro;

 Entering the cell address of the first cell of any macro;

 Pointing in your spreadsheet to the first cell of any macro.

Of course, to use the Alt+F3 Run key, you must have macros already written and in place. When you press Alt+F3, you will see the prompt, "Select the macro to run," and a single-line listing of range names. If you then press the F3 Name key, the screen is replaced with a full-screen listing of range names from which you can choose your macro invoking name. An example of such a listing is shown in Figure 8.1.

Using a Separate Macro-Launcher Name

You will notice that Figure 8.1 shows several range names that start with the underline symbol. These are macro range names that can be used

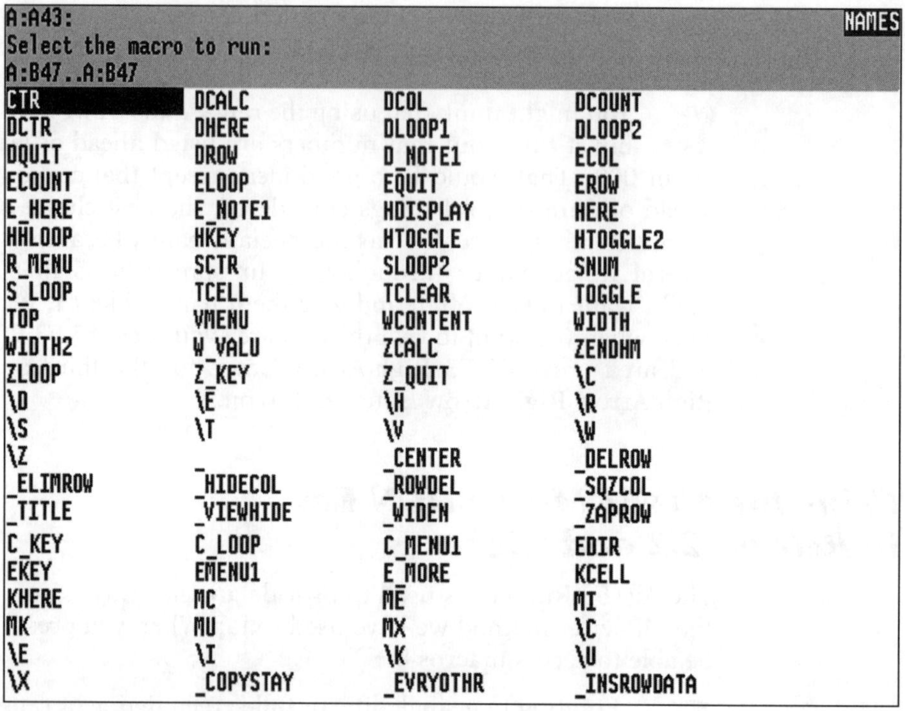

```
A:A43:                                                              NAMES
Select the macro to run:
A:B47..A:B47
CTR            DCALC          DCOL           DCOUNT
DCTR           DHERE          DLOOP1         DLOOP2
DQUIT          DROW           D_NOTE1        ECOL
ECOUNT         ELOOP          EQUIT          EROW
E_HERE         E_NOTE1        HDISPLAY       HERE
HHLOOP         HKEY           HTOGGLE        HTOGGLE2
R_MENU         SCTR           SLOOP2         SNUM
S_LOOP         TCELL          TCLEAR         TOGGLE
TOP            VMENU          WCONTENT       WIDTH
WIDTH2         W_VALU         ZCALC          ZENDHM
ZLOOP          Z_KEY          Z_QUIT         \C
\D             \E             \H             \R
\S             \T             \V             \W
\Z                            _CENTER        _DELROW
_ELIMROW       _HIDECOL       _ROWDEL        _SQZCOL
_TITLE         _VIEWHIDE      _WIDEN         _ZAPROW
C_KEY          C_LOOP         C_MENU1        EDIR
EKEY           EMENU1         E_MORE         KCELL
KHERE          MC             ME             MI
MK             MU             MX             \C
\E             \I             \K             \U
\X             _COPYSTAY      _EVRYOTHR      _INSROWDATA
```

FIGURE 8.1 Using the Alt+F3 Run key in Release 2.2.

to invoke (run) specific macros through use of the Alt+F3 Run key. Throughout the rest of this book we have given every macro two starting names: the backslash-letter name you are familiar with and a macro-launcher name that can be invoked through the use of the Alt+F3 Macro Run key. These macro-launcher names have been created starting with an underline so they will appear grouped together, making them easy to identify when you press the Alt+F3 Run and F3 Name keys. (Note, under *no* conditions should you point to a non-macro range name in this screen and press Enter.)

Thus, to run any specific macro after pressing Alt+F3 and F3, you can point to either its backslash-letter macro name, or to its macro-launcher range name that represents the first cell of the macro, and press Enter. The advantage here is that instead of being limited to the usual 26 macros that you invoke by pressing the Alt (or Ctrl) key and the letters A to Z, you can invoke your macros by way of an almost unlimited number of macro-launcher range names.

Other Uses of the Alt+F3 Macro Run Key

In addition to using the point-and-shoot method of selecting a macro name after you press Alt+F3, you have the option of invoking a macro by pressing Alt+F3 and Esc (to free the pointer), pointing to the first cell of the actual macro in the worksheet, and pressing Enter. This gives you the extra advantage of seeing what the macro looks like just before you run it. Figure 8.2 shows an example of this, where the user pressed Alt+F3 and Esc, then pointed to the first cell of a macro called "Today's Date in Words."

Of course, you could also type one of the macro-invoking names at this point or the cell address that corresponds to the first cell of the desired macro.

You may have noticed that the macro-invoking range names shown in cells A5 and A14 in Figure 8.2 actually represent the second lines of the macros shown. The first lines of these macros have backslash-letter range names, and consist of nothing but the pass-through null command {}. As mentioned in earlier chapters, this is the technique that permits dual naming of a macro. The macros shown can be invoked by pressing Alt+T and Alt+U (Ctrl+T and Ctrl+U in 1-2-3 for Windows) or by pointing to the range names _TODAY and _UPDATE in the Alt+F3 Run key range-name screen.

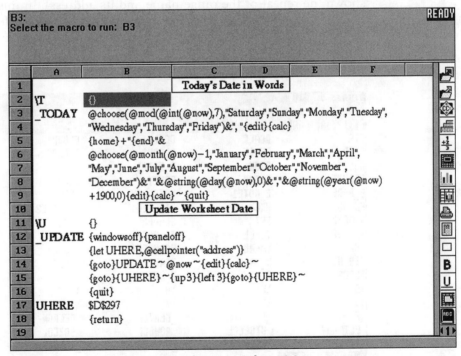

FIGURE 8.2 Alt+F3 Run used with Esc in Release 2.2.

```
A:A37: U [W10] '\C                                                      NAMES
Select the macro to run:
C:\123\AUTOMACR\FIG8-4.WK3
C_KEY           C_LOOP          C_MENU1          EDIR
EKEY            EMENU1          E_MORE           KCELL
KHERE           MC              ME               MI
MK              MU              MX               \C
\E              \I              \K               \U
\X              _COPYSTAY       _EVRYOTHR        _INSROWDATA
_KOPYABS        _UPCOPY         _XTRAABS         <<FIG8-4.WK3>>
```

FIGURE 8.3 Using the Alt+F3 Run key in Release 3 and higher.

Using the Alt+F3 Run Key in Release 3

So far we have shown two Alt+F3 screens from Release 2.2. The same types of screens and accessibility are available in Release 3 and higher, with a few minor differences. Figure 8.3 shows the screen you will see when you press the Alt+F3 Run key followed by the F3 Name key in Release 3 and higher.

In Release 3 and higher, the screen shows range names only four across, and a filename just below the prompt (where Release 2.2 would have shown the repeat of the range name and its address). In this case, the cell pointer is pointing to another open file and the filename refers to that file. If you press Enter on that file, you will see another set of range names, as shown in Figure 8.4.

```
A:A43: U [W10] '\C                                                      NAMES
Select the macro to run:
C:\123\AUTOMACR\FIG8-3.WK3
CTR             DCALC           DCOL             DCOUNT
DCTR            DHERE           DLOOP1           DLOOP2
DQUIT           DROW            D_NOTE1          ECOL
ECOUNT          ELOOP           EQUIT            EROW
E_HERE          E_NOTE1         HDISPLAY         HERE
HHLOOP          HKEY            HTOGGLE          HTOGGLE2
R_MENU          SCTR            SLOOP2           SNUM
S_LOOP          TCELL           TCLEAR           TOGGLE
TOP             VMENU           WCONTENT         WIDTH
WIDTH2          W_VALU          ZCALC            ZENDHM
ZLOOP           Z_KEY           Z_QUIT           \C
\D              \E              \H               \R
\S              \T              \V               \W
\Z                              _CENTER          _DELROW
_ELIMROW        _HIDECOL        _ROWDEL          _SQZCOL
_TITLE          _VIEWHIDE       _WIDEN           _ZAPROW
<<FIG8-3.WK3>>
```

FIGURE 8.4 Using the Alt+F3 Run key to point to another file.

Simulating the Alt+F3 Run Key in Release 2.0/2.01

In case those of you with the earlier Release 2.0 and 2.01 of 1-2-3 are feeling left out, you'll be glad to know you can simulate the Alt+F3 Run key with a simple macro as shown in Figure 8.5.

You will need to /File Combine or create this macro in the current worksheet before you use it. Don't forget to select/Range Name Labels Right to range name the macro before using it.

When you invoke this macro by pressing Alt+Z (Ctrl+Z in 1-2-3 for Windows), you won't see a prompt, but you will see a list of your range names—an indication that you should now point to one of the macro-invoking names and press Enter to run the macro. Alternatively, you can press Esc, point to the first cell of the macro you want to run, and press Enter. The macro will run as if you had invoked it through the Alt+letter combination.

CAUTION: Using either the Alt+F3 Run key or the Macro Launcher can be useful, but only if you handle them correctly. In addition to using the extra techniques and tips included here, it is strongly suggested that you pay particular attention to the location where your macro will run.

More importantly, you must be careful while using the spreadsheet-pointing method that you actually point to the first cell of the macro. The tendency will be to point to the range name identifier to the left of the actual range name; if you do that you will get unexpected, and sometimes catastrophic, results.

The Home-Alternate Toggle

Now that we have discussed alternate ways to start a macro using range names, let's look at another use of range names. By including instructions in your macro to modify the information in one of its named cells, you can create a macro toggle-switch.

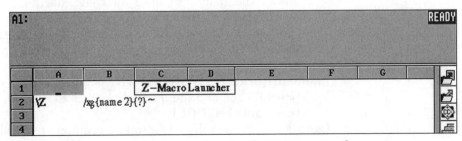

FIGURE 8.5 Macro Launcher to simulate the Alt+F3 Macro Run key.

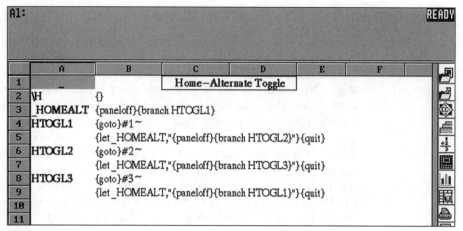

FIGURE 8.6 First example of a toggle macro.

The Home-Alternate Toggle in Figure 8.6 includes such a toggle-switch. This macro is designed to jump your cell pointer to one of three often-visited areas of your worksheet when you press Alt+H (Ctrl+H in 1-2-3 for Windows). And as a toggle macro, it actually changes what it does each time you run it. One press of Alt+H (or Ctrl+H) jumps your cell pointer to the first pre-established range (we'll call it #1); running the macro a second time jumps your cell pointer to the second range (#2); running it again jumps your cell pointer to the third range (#3); running it a fourth time jumps you back to #1 again, and so on.

Before starting the macro it is necessary to find three areas in your worksheet that you think you might be visiting often. Then using /Range Name Create, name the upper left corner of the first area using the range name **#1**, the second area using the range name **#2**, and the third area using the range name **#3**.

{} The macro begins with a null pass-through command, which allows the macro to have alternate starting names: You can invoke the \H starting name by pressing Alt+H (or Ctrl+H) and the _HOMEALT starting name by pressing the Alt+F3 Run key in Release 2.2 and higher or with the Macro Launcher shown in Figure 8.5.

{paneloff}{branch HTOGL1} The panel is turned off to suppress panel flicker, and the macro branches to the first toggle subroutine, named HTOGL1.

{goto}#1~ Presses the F5 Goto key, sending your cell pointer to the upper left corner of the first area you have range-named **#1**.

{let _HOMEALT,"{paneloff}{branch HTOGL2}"){quit} Copies the commands {paneloff}{branch HTOGL2} to the beginning of the macro, so the next time you use the macro it will begin by branching to the second subroutine that starts at HTOGL2 rather than HTOGL1.

The macro quits at this point, self-modified and prepared to go to location #2. In this same way, pressing Alt+H again will cause it to self-modify to go to location #3, and pressing Alt-H again will cause it to return to location #1.

> **NOTE:** *Although we turned the panel off at the beginning of the macro, issuing a {panelon} command is not required since quitting the macro causes any {paneloff} or {windowsoff} commands to be canceled.*

Using the Home-Alternate Toggle in Release 3

The Release 3 version of this macro is shown in Figure 8.7. As you can see, this macro is almost identical to the .WK1 version in Figure 8.6, except that a <<?>> wildcard filename (double angle brackets surrounding question marks) has been added to the front of references to the range name _HOMEALT.

Of course, the .WK1 version of the Home-Alternate Toggle without the wildcard filename <<?>> will work perfectly well in Release 3, but if you want to modify the macro to work in the background in a separate active file, the macro needs some way of finding the _HOMEALT range name referred to in the {let} commands in the fourth, sixth, and eighth lines. By

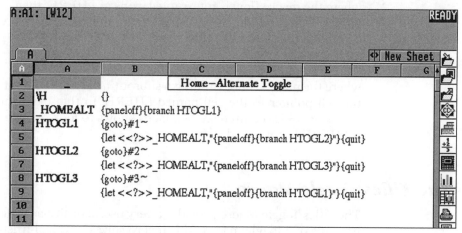

FIGURE 8.7 A Release 3 Macro Library version of a toggle.

supplying a wildcard filename, you let the macro know to check all other active files if the _HOMEALT filename is not found in the current worksheet file.

You may be wondering why the wildcard filename <<?>> is not required in front of the HTOGL1, HTOGL2, and HTOGL3 range names shown in the {branch} commands of the macro. The reason has to do with a distinction between macro flow and range-name locations.

When a macro starts in a separate file, any flow commands such as {branch}, {menubranch}, {menucall}, or the subroutine calling command {*rangename*} automatically assume that the macro flow continues in the same file as the main macro itself. On the other hand, commands with range names which affect data or cell-pointer location are assumed to be in the current worksheet file unless the range names are preceded with a specific filename or the wildcard filename <<?>>.

For example, suppose you have a Release 3 macro which refers to a range name like LHERE that changes the contents of LHERE or moves the cell pointer to LHERE with a {goto} command. You will see the wildcard filename <<?>> in the following types of commands:

```
{let <<?>>LHERE,+53}
{goto}<<?>>LHERE~
{blank <<?>>LHERE}
{if <<?>>LHERE=999}{quit}
```

Note, however, the wildcard filename <<?>> is *not* required when the macro flow switches to a subroutine named LHERE. Thus, you might see a return to a place-marker that looks like this:

```
{goto}{LHERE}~
```

where the macro flow is interrupted, runs at LHERE, then continues where it left off (at the tilde, in this case). Yet in the same macro, you might see a command that looks like this:

```
{goto}<<?>>LHERE~
```

where the macro is not running a subroutine at LHERE, but simply moving the cell pointer to the cell named LHERE. In that case, the wildcard filename <<?>> is required so the macro knows to look outside the current file if LHERE is not found.

The Titles Toggle Macro

The Titles Toggle Macro provides a very useful utility, as well as another fine example of a toggle macro. This macro solves a typical frustration for 1-2-3 users: the cumbersome cell pointer movement you have to go through to reset your titles if for some reason you have to clear them temporarily.

Before we get into the macro itself, you should know about a couple of handy tricks for moving past locked-in titles without having to clear the titles first. The first trick involves use of the F5 Goto key. If, for example, you have two spreadsheets in a single file where the second spreadsheet is below the first, you may have discovered the /Worksheet Titles Horizontal command as a way to restrict yourself to the second spreadsheet. Unfortunately, you find that when you want to visit the first spreadsheet, the titles keep you out.

Try the F5 Goto key—it will allow you to move the cell pointer right past your titles. So, to visit the first spreadsheet, press F5 Goto, move your cell pointer there, and press Esc when you want to return. If you want to stay at the first spreadsheet to make changes or enter data, press Enter instead of Esc. Then when you want to jump back to the second spreadsheet, press End Home to go to the lower right corner of the worksheet and Home to jump to the cell in the upper left corner under the locked-in titles of the second spreadsheet.

Our second trick involving locked-in titles is a handy way to change a cell of your titles. Suppose, for example, that you notice that the heading TOTAL in cell J14 of your titles should have read SUBTOTAL. You could clear your titles to change it, you could use the F5 Goto technique to move there and make the change, or you could try this technique: Move your cell pointer to a blank cell near your current cell and type SUBTOTAL. Then select /Move, press Enter, and at the message *"Enter range to move to:"* type J14 and press Enter. The title cell is changed instantly and you hardly had to move your cell pointer at all.

This brings us to the Titles Toggle macro in Figure 8.8. Like the Home Alternate Toggle, this macro requires a little advance setup. Move to the first cell beneath your horizontal titles and the first cell to the right of your vertical titles, and range-name that cell T_CORNER. Then move to the upper left cell of the titles themselves and give that cell the range name T_START. Now you can move to any area below the rows you will be locking in as titles and press Alt+T (Ctrl+T in 1-2-3 for Windows). If you've done your range-naming properly, the titles you prepared for should appear, locked in and ready to use. If you want the titles to clear, just press Alt+T (or Ctrl+T) again—the macro has already toggled to the Titles-off position, so it will clear the titles instantly. Invoke the macro again and the titles will lock in again.

{}   The macro begins with a null pass-through command, which allows the macro to have alternate starting names: You can invoke the \T starting name by pressing Alt+T (Ctrl+T in 1-2-3 for Windows), and the _TITLETOG starting name by pressing the

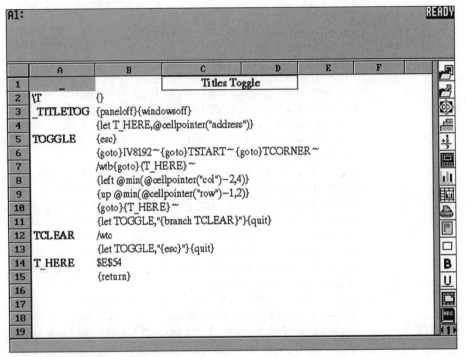

Figure 8.8 Titles Toggle macro.

Alt+F3 Run key in Release 2.2 and higher or with the Macro Launcher shown earlier in Figure 8.5.

{windowsoff}{paneloff}   Suppresses screen flicker.

{let T_HERE,@cellpointer("address")}   This is a place-marker command that stores the current cell address in the cell named T_HERE.

{esc}   This cell has been range-named TOGGLE because it provides the pivotal direction of the flow of the macro. With the {esc} command in this cell (we could have used the {} null command), the macro simply passes through to the next cell down. However, in the tenth line of the macro, the macro self-modifies. The cell named TOGGLE will be changed to the command {branch TCLEAR}, which will cause the macro to operate quite differently the next time you run the macro.

{goto}IV8192~{goto}TSTART~{goto}TCORNER~   Sends the cell pointer to the lower right corner of your worksheet, then to the range name TSTART, which brings the title rows into full view. The cell pointer then jumps to TCORNER, where you would ordinarily place your cell pointer to lock in these particular titles.

/wtb{goto}{T_HERE}~ Selects /Worksheet Titles Both, which accomplishes the title lock. The {goto} command continues at the part of the macro named T_HERE, which contains the absolute address of the original cell. The {return} command below that cell tells the macro to continue at the tilde after the {T_HERE} subroutine branch.

{left @min(@cellpointer("col")-2,4)} Moves the cell pointer left either two cells less than the current column or four cells, whichever is less. This is done to reorient the original cell location more towards the center of the screen.

{up @min(@cellpointer("row")-1,2)} For the same reason, this line of the macro moves the cell pointer up either one cell less than the current row or two cells, whichever is less.

{goto}{T_HERE}~ Jumps the cell pointer back to the original location.

{let TOGGLE,"{branch TCLEAR}"}{quit} Changes the instruction in TOGGLE so the macro will branch to TCLEAR the next time you run it. The macro quits at this point.

/wtc The next time you invoke the macro, it branches to this command to do a /Worksheet Titles Clear.

{let TOGGLE,"{esc}"}{quit} The macro changes the instruction in TOGGLE back to {esc} so the macro will continue its normal flow without branching the next time you run it.

Using the Titles Toggle Macro in Release 3 and Higher

As noted earlier, you can run most .WK1 versions of macros without changes in Release 3 and higher, so long as you are running the macro from within the current worksheet file. However, to run the macro from a background Macro Library in Release 3 and higher, you must insert the wildcard filename <<?>> before certain of the range names in the macro.

Refer now to Figure 8.9. You will see that lines 3, 10, and 12 have been modified to include the wildcard filename <<?>>. This is because all three of these range-name references are contained in {let} commands which make some change to the data in the referenced cells.

All other references to range names, however, are contained in branches or subroutine calls, so the wildcard filename <<?>> is not required. Understanding this difference will save you a great deal of typing as you become more proficient with the macro language.

Switching Spreadsheet Areas with Titles

The use of titles in your worksheets can make your view of a given spreadsheet area clearer and more understandable, but it is not at all easy to

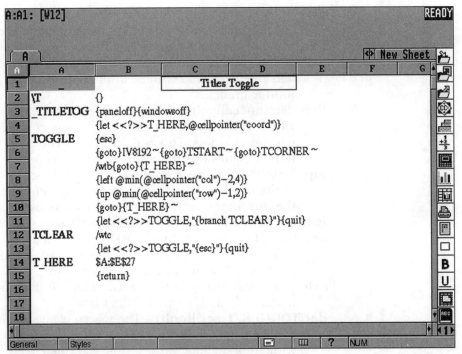

FIGURE 8.9 Using the Titles Toggle macro in Release 3.

switch between spreadsheet areas, each with its own set of titles. Manually, doing this would mean clearing your current titles, moving to a location to bring an alternate set of titles into view, and then setting those titles before you move to the location in this spreadsheet area where you want to work.

Fortunately, you can accomplish this with a simple menu macro, as shown in Figure 8.10.

Before you start the macro, you should find three areas with titles in your worksheet that you think you might be visiting often, and using /Range Name Create, name the upper left corner of the first set of titles using the range name **#1**, the second set of titles using the range name **#2**, and the third set of titles using the range name **#3**. Name the cell below and to the right of your vertical titles **VLOCK1**, **VLOCK2**, and **VLOCK3**.

Here's how the macro works:

{windowsoff}{menubranch VMENU}{quit}   Begins by turning off the windows to suppress screen flicker, and calls up the menu choices First Area, Second Area, and Third Area.

{paneloff}/wtc{goto}IV8192~   The upper panel could not be turned off until this point or the custom menu would not have been visi-

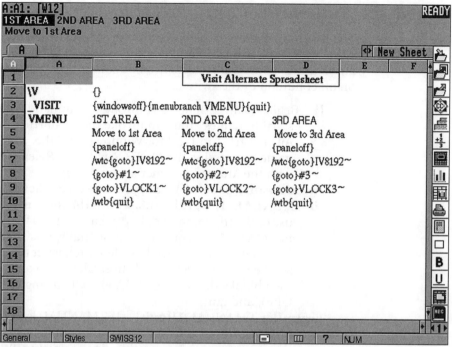

FIGURE 8.10 Macro to visit alternate spreadsheet areas.

ble. The macro turns off the upper panel to suppress screen flicker, selects /Worksheet Titles Clear, and moves the cell pointer clear of the cell (to IV8192) to ensure your titles end up in the upper right corner of the screen.

{goto}#1~{goto}VLOCK~ Jumps the cell pointer to the upper left corner of the first set of titles you have previously given the range name **#1**, then moves to the cell below and to the right of your vertical titles, to the cell you have named **VLOCK1**.

/wtb{quit} With the new spreadsheet area in place, the macro selects /Worksheet Titles Both and quits.

Note, this macro can be used without modification as a background macro in a Release 3 Macro Library, even though it references six location range names and one macro range name. The reason has to do with the range names themselves. The six location range names represent locations in the current file, and so do not need to be preceded with a wildcard filename <<?>>. As for the macro range name, it is found in a {branch} command, which never requires a wildcard filename.

Toggle for Automatic/Manual Recalc

The macro in Figure 8.11 shows a different way to create a toggle. In this case, the macro is a simple five-line macro that instantly toggles between automatic and manual recalculation by setting a switch, then testing for the on/off condition of the switch.

{}   Begins with a null pass-through command, allowing alternate starting names: You can invoke the \T starting name by pressing Alt+T (Ctrl+T in 1-2-3 for Windows) and the _TOGLCALC starting name by pressing the Alt+F3 Run key in Release 2.2 and higher or with the Macro Launcher shown in Figure 8.5.

{windowsoff}{paneloff}   Suppresses screen flicker.

{if TMANUAL=1}/wgra{blank TMANUAL}~{quit}   This is another use of the {if} command. In this case, it tests for whether the value in TMANUAL is equal to 1. Essentially, this is equivalent to testing whether your special toggle switch is set to the ON position. If so, the macro selects /Worksheet Global Recalculation Automatic, then blanks the value in TMANUAL (turning the toggle switch to OFF), and quits.

/wgrm{let TMANUAL,1}{quit}   If TMANUAL is *not* equal to 1, or in other words, if your toggle switch is not set to the ON position, the macro continues at this line, selecting /Worksheet Global Recalculation Manual, then changes the value in TMANUAL to 1 (turning the toggle switch to ON), and quits.

The Release 3 Macro Library version of this macro is almost identical, except that every reference to TMANUAL should be changed to <<?>> TMANUAL as shown in Figure 8.12 so the macro can run in the background in a separate active file.

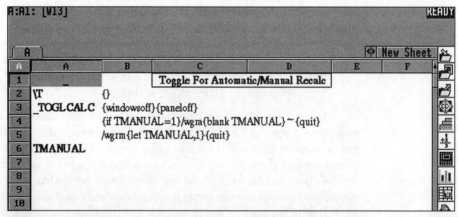

FIGURE 8.11 Toggle for automatic/manual recalculation.

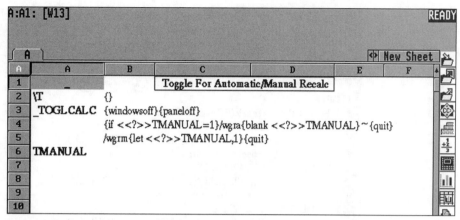

FIGURE 8.12 Release 3 toggle for auto/manual recalculation.

This toggle-switch technique can be used in other macros where you need to toggle between alternating results each time a macro or subroutine is activated. Don't overlook the fact, however, that you can always achieve the same result as a toggle by using a custom menu. In the example of a switch between Automatic and Manual Recalculation, the menu choices would look like this:

```
AUTO                MANUAL
AUTOMATIC RECALC    MANUAL RECALC
/wgra               /wgrm
{quit}              {quit}
```

On the one hand, this is a simpler macro to write. On the other hand, it takes one more keystroke to activate and you have to think about your choices when the menu comes up. You may want to experiment with both methods and decide which method makes more sense for your own specific applications.

The File Directory Toggle

1-2-3 Release 2.x has an unfortunate drawback in the /File Directory menu selection: To make a change to the directory, you must completely retype the drive letter and directory path directory offered instead of simply editing it when you want to make a change. Of course, if you make a typing mistake, your only option is to start over and type the drive letter and directory path again.

Release 3 does give you editing capabilities at this level, but even editing can take quite a few keystrokes. Consider, then, a toggle macro that will automatically toggle between three separate file directories whenever you press Alt+F (Ctrl+F in 1-2-3 for Windows). Such a macro is shown in Figure 8.13.

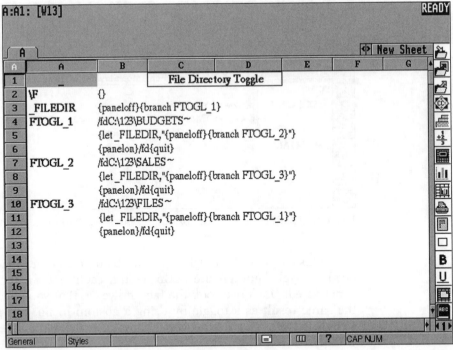

FIGURE 8.13 A file directory toggle using preset directories.

This macro requires a slight modification before it will work on your computer. The particular drives and directory paths shown at the beginning of each routine FTOGL_1, FTOGL_2, and FTOGL_3 are examples only. For your version of the macro, you must enter the drive letters and directory paths that are appropriate for your own 1-2-3 subdirectories.

{paneloff}{branch FTOGL_1} Turns off the upper panel and branches to the first routine, FTOGL_1. (Since FTOGL_1 begins at the next line of the macro, the {branch} command is not strictly required, but it helps to make the macro more easily understood.)

/fdC:\123\FILES~ Selects /File Directory, then enters the drive letter and directory path (changed to correspond to your own most often used directory).

{let _FILEDIR,"{paneloff}{branch FTOGL_2}"} As in the Home Alternate Toggle, this is a self-modifying macro that copies the commands {paneloff} {branch FTOGL_2} to its own beginning cell, so the next time you use the macro it starts by branching to the second subroutine at FTOGL_2 rather than FTOGL_1.

{panelon}/fd{quit}   Turns on the upper panel and selects /File Directory so you can see the directory entered for you. The macro quits, leaving you at the /File Directory menu level. If you like what you see, you can simply press Enter. If you want to enter another selection, you can do so by manually typing a different selection at this point.

Alternatively, press Enter and Alt+F (Ctrl+F in 1-2-3 for Windows) to have the macro automatically enter another pre-established directory for you. The macro has already modified its start, so pressing Alt+F (or Ctrl+F) this time will change the directory to the directory shown at FTOGL_2. In this same way, invoking the macro a third time will change the directory to the directory shown at FTOGL_3.

Switching Directories to Match Retrieved Files

If you select files from different directories often, you may be interested in a macro that selects /File Retrieve, offers you a full-screen view of subdirectories, waits for your selection of subdirectory and specific file, then changes the /File Directory for you automatically to correspond to the subdirectory of the file selected.

For example, suppose you have three subdirectories under your main 1-2-3 directory named C:\123\SALES, C:\123\BUDGET, and C:\123\TRENDS. You have been working in the SALES subdirectory, but now you want to retrieve a file from the BUDGET directory and have your /File Directory changed to C:\123\BUDGET at the same time. Refer to the macro in Figure 8.14.

This macro will not work in Release 2 or 2.01, because it is designed to continue working after it leaves the current file to retrieve another file. In fact, it will only work in a Release 2.2 .MLB Macro Library file or in a separate active file in Release 3.

{let RNAME,@cellpointer("filename")}   This uses the @cellpointer function in a {let} command as a type of place-marker command similar to the command, {let RNAME,@cellpointer("address")}. However, instead of storing the current cell address in RNAME, the macro is storing the current drive, directory path, and filename. The "filename" attribute of @cellpointer is unique to Release 2.2 and 3 and will not work in Release 2 or 2.01.

/fr{bs}{name}   Selects /File Retrieve, backs up from the current subdirectory to the main 1-2-3 directory, then presses F3 Name to show a full-screen view of all your subdirectories under the 1-2-3 directory.

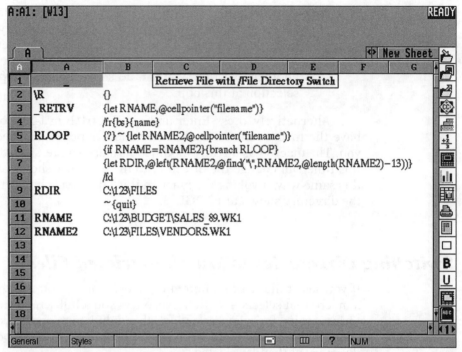

FIGURE 8.14 Macro to retrieve file with /File Directory switch.

{?}~{let RNAME2,@cellpointer("filename")} Pauses for your selection of a subdirectory, then stores the name of the current file in RNAME2. At this point, that name should correspond to the name stored in RNAME.

{if RNAME=RNAME2}{branch RLOOP} Since you have not selected a different file yet, this {if} statement is found to be true, and the macro branches back to RLOOP, where it pauses again—this time for your selection of a file to retrieve. As soon as that file is retrieved, the {let} command at RLOOP changes RNAME2 to the new drive, directory path and filename selected, and the macro continues again at this {if} statement. This time, RNAME will not be equal to RNAME2 and the macro skips the rest of the line to continue at the next line.

{let RDIR,@left(RNAME2,@find("\",RNAME2,@length(RNAME2)-13))} This {let} command introduces use of three @functions not discussed before in this book: @left, @find, and @length. The purpose of this line is to truncate the information in RNAME2, eliminating the filename and placing just the drive letter and directory path in the cell named RDIR.

The @left function has the syntax, @left(*location or string, number of characters*), and is used to return a number of leftmost characters in an entry. Thus, @left(J57,3) will return SAL if the entry in J57 is "SALES", and @left("BUDGET",3) will return BUD.

However, instead of a value (like 3, for example), you can use another set of @functions, (@find and @length) to establish the *number of characters* required for an @left function.

The @find function has the syntax, @find(*item to search for ,string or location to search,start-point*). Thus, the @find function in this case returns a value for the *number of characters* required by @left by searching for the last backslash-character in RNAME2 that comes after the subdirectory and before the filename. It starts its search at a point 13 characters from the right of the entry in RNAME2 (using @length(RNAME2)-13) because the maximum length of a filename in 1-2-3 is 12 including the .WK1 file extension.

We will be seeing more examples of the use of string-manipulating @functions in macros later in the book, including @left, @right, @mid, @find, @length, and @string.

/fd   Selects /File Directory in advance of the self-modified cell shown just below at RDIR.

C:\123\FILES   This is just an example of the type of entry you might see in RDIR after using the macro once. Actually, to type this macro into your own worksheet, you would leave this cell blank initially. It will be completed for you by the {let} command two lines above.

~{quit}   The /File Directory command has been completed, a tilde is typed to enter the directory, and the macro quits. The remaining two cells of the macro are storage cells only.

A variation of this macro is shown in Figure 8.15 to provide its use as a Macro Library macro in a separate active file in Release 3. Notice that the wildcard filename <<?>> has been added to the beginning of every range-name reference in the macro *except* in the {branch} command in the fifth line, where it is not required. Some of the range names have also been shortened, but this is only to allow more of the macro line to fit on a single screen as you type it in.

The Pop-up Notepad and Appointment Calendar

Other interesting uses of the toggle method which also take advantage of the place-marker techniques of this chapter are found in macro-driven pop-up utilities like the Notepad Macro and the Appointment Calendar Macro. The Notepad Macro is shown in Figure 8.16.

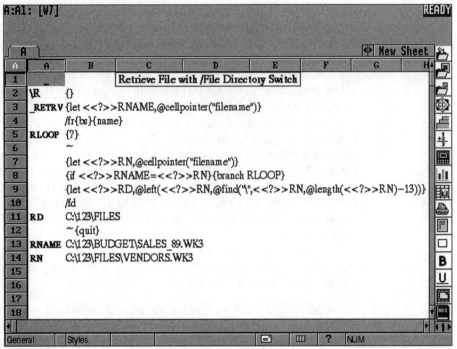

FIGURE 8.15 Retrieve File with directory switch for Release 3.

{windowsoff}{paneloff}{let NHERE,@cellpointer("address")} Turns off windows and panel and creates a place-marker so that it can return to the current cell after using the notepad.

{goto}IV8192~{goto}NOTEPAD~{end}{down} Moves the cell pointer far from the cell which has been range-named NOTEPAD, then jumps to NOTEPAD to bring it into view. The End Down commands move the cell pointer to the first blank area below the last note entered.

{let _NOTEPAD,"{BRANCH NRETURN}"}{quit} Copies a new branching command to the first active line of the macro, so the next time the macro is activated, it toggles to NRETURN. The macro quits at this point, so you are free to explore the items in the notepad, change them or add new items. When you want to return to the area where you started out, press Alt+N (Ctrl+N in 1-2-3 for Windows) again. The macro will run the routine at NRETURN.

{windowsoff}{paneloff}{goto}{NHERE} Turns off windows and panel and jumps the cell pointer back to the original location.

{up @min(@cellpointer("row")-1,3)} Moves the cell pointer up either one cell less than the current row or three cells, whichever

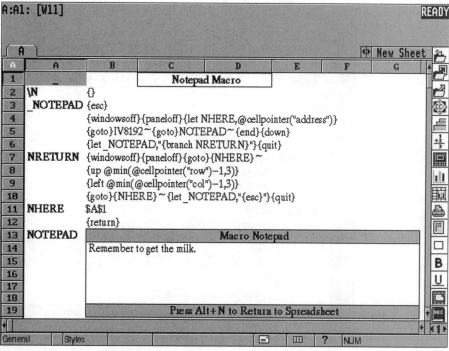

FIGURE 8.16 The Pop-up Notepad macro.

is less, to reorient the original cell location more towards the center of the screen.

{left @min(@cellpointer("col")-2,4)}   For the same reason, this line moves the cell pointer left either one cell less than the current column or three cells, whichever is less.

{goto}{NHERE}~{let _NOTEPAD,"{esc}"}{quit}   Jumps the cell pointer back to the original location, then changes the instruction in the first active line of the macro so the macro will not branch to NRETURN the next time you invoke the macro. The macro quits at this point.

The end result of all this is that you can use this macro to move to a different location; the macro quits so you can move around, enter data, or make changes without the constraints of being in a macro. Then by invoking the macro again, you can return to where you started in your spreadsheet.

If you will compare the Notepad in Figure 8.16 with the Appointment Calendar in Figure 8.17, you will see that the individual lines of both macros are almost identical. The difference is in the area marked off for notes, whether to be entered in a notepad form or entered in a columnar layout. These areas, incidentally, can be placed anywhere in the work-

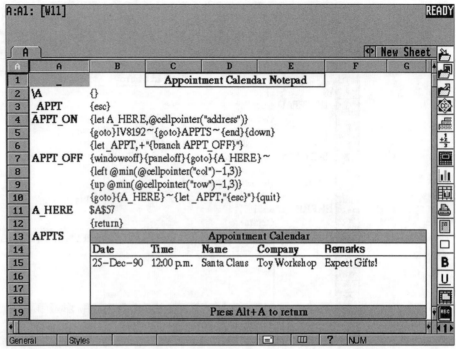

FIGURE 8.17 The pop-up Appointment Calendar.

sheet—they do not have to remain attached to the macros themselves as demonstrated here.

You could also combine the two macros into one with a menu choice of the area you want to visit, still using the same toggle feature to return to your original cell location in the worksheet.

The Automatic Tickler

The macro shown in Figure 8.18 does not have a toggle feature in the same sense as the other toggle macros covered in this chapter, but it will give different results depending on the current date.

The purpose of the macro is to alert you about an important date, meeting, appointment, or occasion without your having to invoke it. As you might guess, this is designed to be an automatic executing macro that starts running as soon as you retrieve the file.

This macro requires some setup before it will operate correctly. To do this, change the input at the DATE_1, DATE_2, and DATE_3 by typing in three appointment dates using the @date format. Then change the notes at

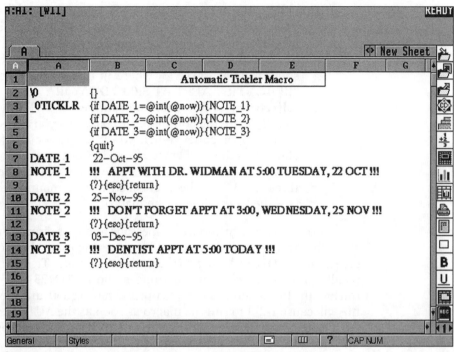

FIGURE 8.18 Automatic Tickler macro using {If}.

NOTE_1, NOTE_2, and NOTE_3. You can use any appropriate reminders or messages you like.

Here's how the macro works:

{if DATE_1=@int(@now)}{NOTE_1}   This is another example using the {if} command as discussed in other macros in this chapter. If the statement is true, the macro continues on the same line. If it is false, the macro skips to the next line down. In this case, if the date entered in DATE_1 is the same as the integer of today's date, the macro skips to the subroutine at NOTE_1. In the example in Figure 8.18, this subroutine causes the macro to type the message, **"!!! APPT WITH DR. WIDMAN AT 5:00 TUESDAY, 22 OCT !!!"** in the upper panel.

{if DATE_2=@int(@now)}{NOTE_2}   Whether the macro runs the subroutine at NOTE_1, it continues at the second line where it tests for whether the date stored in DATE_2 is the same as the integer of today's date. If so, the macro skips to the subroutine at NOTE_2, where in this case it types the message, **"!!! DON'T FORGET APPT AT 3:00, WEDNESDAY, 25 NOV !!!"** in the upper panel.

{if DATE_3=@int(@now)}{NOTE_3} Again, whether the macro runs the subroutines at NOTE_1 or NOTE_2, it continues at the third line, where it tests for whether the date stored in DATE_3 is the same as the integer of today's date. If so, the macro skips to the subroutine at NOTE_3, where in this case it types the message, **"!!! DENTIST APPT AT 5:00 TODAY !!!"**.

{?}{esc}{return} After each subroutine at NOTE_1, NOTE_2, and NOTE_3, are the commands to pause so you can see the message in the upper panel. When you press Enter, the {esc} command eliminates the typed message so it is not entered in a cell, then the flow of the macro returns to the place where it left off. After all three dates have been checked in this manner, the macro quits (see the fourth line of the macro).

If you have a very important message and there is no particular spreadsheet that you are certain you will be retrieving every day, you may want to create an AUTO123 file that contains this Automatic Tickler macro. As you'll recall from earlier chapters, naming a file AUTO123 will cause 1-2-3 to retrieve the file as soon as it boots up; and having a \0 autoexec macro in that file will cause 1-2-3 to run the macro as soon as the AUTO123 file appears.

Note, you can also combine several \0 autoexec macros into one. You may, for example, want to create an AUTO123 file which starts with the Automatic Tickler macro, but instead of a {quit} statement in the fourth line, the macro might branch to another macro that automatically attaches and invokes your MACROMGR.ADN file (in Release 2.2 only), then loads your favorite Macro Library macros.

Summary

In this chapter you were introduced to the following new concepts:

- You can use the F5 Goto key with the F3 Name key to instantly jump to named ranges in your worksheet. Naming your most often-visited ranges #1, #2, #3, and so on will cause those ranges to appear as the first choices when you press Alt+F3 Run F3 Name.
- Both Release 2.2 and Release 3.0 have included a new feature, the Alt+F3 Macro Run key. By giving your macros range names that start with an asterisk, they will appear among the first names you see when you decide to run your macros with the Alt+F3 Run key. Now, instead of a maximum of 26 macros that you invoke by pressing the Alt key and the letters A to Z, you can name the first cells of your macros with an almost unlimited number of asterisk range names that will be accessed through the Alt-F3 Run key.

- You can also press the F3 Name key after the Alt+F3 Run key to get a full-screen view of your macro range names. If any range names follow the first set of backslash-letter names in Release 2.2, these represent range names found in a loaded Macro Library .MLB file.
- In Release 3, pressing Alt+F3 Run and F3 Name causes the screen to show your range names and bracketed filenames for any other active files. If you point to a bracketed filename in this screen and press Enter, you will see another set of range names pertaining to that active file.
- Those with Release 2.0 or 2.01 can simulate the Alt+F3 Run key with the Macro Launcher as shown in Figure 8.5.
- You can use toggles to achieve multiple functions from a single Alt+letter macro.

Macros covered in this chapter which use these techniques are summarized as follows:

- A Macro Launcher to simulate pressing the Alt+F3 Run key and F3 Name key.
- A Home Alternate Toggle for instantly jumping the cell pointer to prime locations on your worksheet.
- A Titles Toggle to automatically turn your titles off and on.
- A Macro to Visit Alternate Spreadsheet Areas, each with its own set of titles.
- A Recalc Toggle to turn manual recalculation off and on.
- A /File Directory Toggle using preset file directory paths.
- A /File Retrieve macro with File Directory Switch.
- Pop-up macros including a pop-up Notepad and Appointment Calendar.
- An Automatic Tickler macro designed to alert you about an important date, meeting, appointment, or occasion.

In the next chapter we will look data entry and data modification macros using the {if} command with @cellpointer ("type"). We will also introduce another type of prompt for the user: the {getlabel} and {getnumber} commands that pause for your entry of a string or a value.

9

Data Entry and Modification

This chapter explores macros that use the {if} command with the @cell-pointer function to facilitate data entry and changes in data. You will also learn about two prompt commands—{getlabel} and {getnumber}—that pause for your entry of a string or value, storing the entry in a designated cell. This feature is especially useful for self-modifying macros that prompt you for information and then use your responses to accomplish different tasks.

Using the {if} Command

So far, we have made a limited use of the {if} command. In one example in Chapter 8, the {if} command tests for whether one entry equals another. If the entries are equal, the macro continues on the same line. Otherwise, the macro skips to the next line and continues there. This chapter takes the concept farther to explore other uses of the {if} command.

You are no doubt familiar with the @if formula as used in a standard 1-2-3 worksheet. As it happens, the *If-Then-Else* concept is common to most programming languages. Basically, the idea is to compare two elements or states. **If** the statement of comparison is true, **Then** one thing happens; otherwise, something **Else** happens.

The @if formula in a standard worksheet has a structure like this:

```
@if(A23=B23,999,@na)
```

which can be read, *"If the contents of cell A23 equal the contents of B23, then display the number 999 in the current cell; else display NA."* In addition to values or the results of @functions, you can have an **@if** statement that returns a label, as in the example:

```
@if(A23=B23,"YES","NO").
```

The {if} command is the macro equivalent to an @if function, except that the following example,

```
{if A23=B23}999~{quit}
@na~
```

would be read, *"If the contents of cell A23 equal the contents of B23, continue at the same line (enter 999 and quit); otherwise skip to the next line down and enter NA in the current cell."*

You should be aware of one more difference between @if functions and {if} commands. In an {if} command, there is always a space between the word **if** and the rest of the statement (in this case, between **if** and A23=B23).

You can use the {if} command to compare the contents of a cell against the contents of another cell, or you can compare cell contents against a string, so long as you put the string in quotes. If you want to test whether cell A23 contains the word **CONFIRMED**, for example, your macro {if} statement would look like this:

```
{if A23="CONFIRMED"}999~{quit}
@na~
```

This demonstrates the most important difference between the @if formula and the {if} macro command. In our example, the @if formula is typed into a cell in the spreadsheet and stays there, displaying either 999 or NA, depending on whether the statement is true or false. If the contents of A23 or B23 change, the results displayed in the @if formula cell will change. The {if} command, on the other hand, is typed into a macro. You can run the macro at any cell, but instead of displaying the answer, it *takes an action* (in this case, to enter an answer). And if you want the A23 = B23 statement tested again—after the content of either cell has changed, for example—you must run the macro again.

Finally, the {if} macro command allows you to design in more than simple typing of a number or a string. Unlike an @if statement, you can use {if} to cause your macro to accomplish a whole series of tasks depending on whether the test is true or false.

The Label-Format Macro

Suppose you have a column of data entries that you need to modify. To make the changes manually, you typically visit each entry in turn, make the change, and continue in this way until you reach the last entry in the series. Imagine instead a macro that moves quickly through the entire range of data entries, automatically modifying every one until it reaches the last entry.

You may have had this problem. You enter a column of part numbers, only to find after an hour of number entries that the numbers should have been entered as labels. You may find, for example, that there are some dash-number suffixes, or some part numbers with the letter A or B at the end. Whatever the reason, you now have to go back to the top of the column and put an apostrophe in front of each number.

This is a perfect job for a looping macro with an {if} statement, like the Label-Format macro in Figure 9.1. This macro changes the numbers or formulas in a column to their label equivalents by typing a label prefix in front of each value and then uses an {if} command to quit when the cell pointer reaches the blank cell at the end of the column.

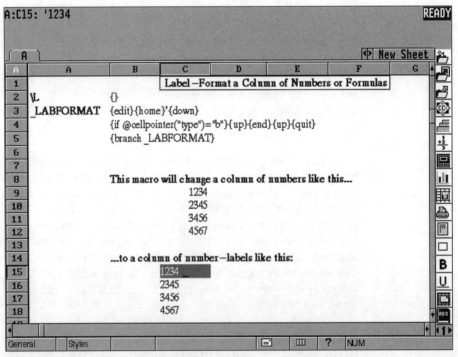

FIGURE 9.1 Label-Format a column of numbers or formulas.

To check whether the current cell contains a label, contains a value, or is completely blank, the macro uses an {if} command with @cellpointer ("type"). The syntax arguments for these types of tests read like this:

```
{if @cellpointer("type")="l"}    This {if} condition is true if
                                 the current cell is a label.
{if @cellpointer("type")="v"}    This {if} condition is true if
                                 the current cell is a value.
{if @cellpointer("type")="b"}    This {if} condition is true if
                                 the current cell is blank.
```

Before you start the macro, place your cell pointer at the first cell of the column you want changed. Here's how the macro works:

{edit}{home}'{down}   The macro switches to the Edit mode, presses Home to move to the beginning of the number or formula, types an apostrophe, then moves down one cell. This changes the entry from a number to a label, and positions the cell pointer to check for an empty cell.

{if @cellpointer("type")="b"}{up}{end}{up}{quit}   This line uses an {if} command with @cellpointer("type")="b" to test whether the current cell is blank. If the statement is true—if the cell is blank—the cell pointer is moved up one cell, then {end}{up} to the top of the column where you started.

{branch _LABFORMAT}   If the cell pointer "type" is *not* equal to "b," the macro loops back to the beginning and changes the next number to a label, moves down to test the next cell and so forth, until it reaches a blank cell or until you press Ctrl-Break to make it quit.

The Number-Format Macro

What if you need to accomplish the opposite task: to change a column of number-labels to their equivalent values? To do this manually, you might typically visit each entry in turn, switching to Edit mode and removing the entry's label prefix. Of course, a macro can do the job for you in a fraction of the time. As you might imagine, a macro to *delete* the apostrophe from the beginning of each entry in a column, as shown in Figure 9.2, is only a slightly modified version of the Label-Format macro.

{edit}{home}'{down}   This is the one line of the Number-Format macro that differs from the Label-Format macro. Instead of inserting an apostrophe each time it loops, this macro deletes the apostrophe, changing your number-labels to straight numbers.

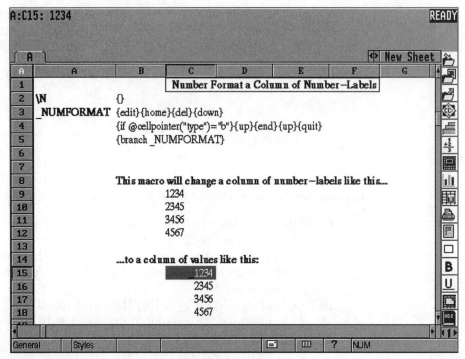

FIGURE 9.2 Number Format a column of number-labels.

As with the earlier example, this macro employs {if @cellpointer ("type")="b"} to test for a blank cell. This particular use of the {if} command can be handy in a variety of situations, as the next few macros will show.

Indent Five Spaces

The macro in Figure 9.3 is used to move down a column and indent every entry five spaces. Of course, since values are already right-justified, this macro is designed to operate only on a column of labels. If you make the mistake of trying to use it on a column that contains values, the macro attempts to insert five spaces between the first digit and the rest of the digits of that value; and since values do not start with an apostrophe, this attempt causes an error that makes the macro quit.

As with the Number-Format and Label-Format macros, this macro uses {if @cellpointer("type")="b"} to test for a blank cell.

{edit}{home}{right} {down} The macro starts by switching to the Edit mode and inserting five spaces in front of the label. The

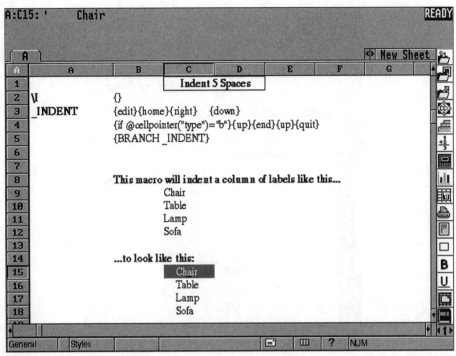

FIGURE 9.3 Indent all entries in a column five spaces.

{down} command enters the change and moves the cell pointer down one cell.

{if @cellpointer("type")="b"}{up}{end}{up}{quit}   If the cell is blank, the cell pointer moves to the top of the column and the macro quits.

{branch \I}   Otherwise, the macro loops back to the beginning and adds five spaces to the front of the next label. The macro continues until it reaches a blank space or until you press Ctrl+Break to quit.

The Leading Zeros Macro

The macro in Figure 9.4 is similar to the Label-Format macro, except that in addition to changing a number to a label, it provides leading zeros in front of the entry. This type of exercise would be handy if, for example, you entered an entire column of zip codes as numbers, only to realize that the only way to get a zip code to show leading zeros is to enter it as a label. This macro will correct the problem after the fact.

{edit}1/1000000{calc}   Switches to the Edit mode, tacks the number 1 to the end of the number, then divides the number by 1,000,000

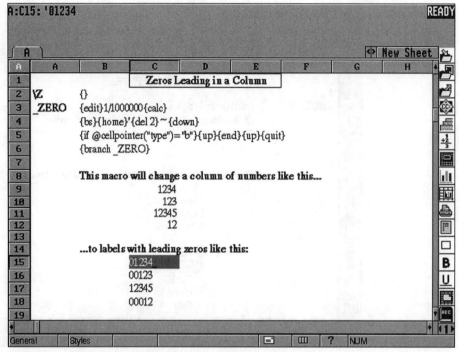

FIGURE 9.4 Macro to leading zeros in a column of numbers.

and calculates the cell—which turns it into a calculated value rather than a division formula. If the number is 777, for example, it becomes 7771/1000000, then 0.007771.

{bs}{home}'{del 2}{down}   Since you are still in the Edit mode, the Backspace command erases the number 1 at the end, pressing Home moves the cursor to the beginning of the entry, apostrophe turns it into a label, and {del 2} eliminates the zero in front of the decimal point, as well as the decimal point itself.

The rest of the macro is a repeat of the looping macros shown above, using **{if @cellpointer("type")="b"}** to test for blank cells so that the macro will know when to stop.

The @Round Macro

From time to time you may find it necessary to add the @round formula to the front of all of the entries in a column. You may find, for example, that the vertical sum in your spreadsheet does not equal the horizontal sum due to differences in rounding.

Since adding @round to each entry manually requires 14 keystrokes per cell, this is the type of chore that should be handled by a looping macro. See the @Round macro in Figure 9.5.

{edit}{home}@ROUND({end},0){down}　The macro switches to the Edit mode, moves to the front of the entry, types @round and an opening parenthesis, moves to the end of the entry and types a comma and a zero, and closes the parenthesis.

The macro then loops back to the beginning and works on the next cell down, continuing in this way until it reaches a blank cell or you press Ctrl-Break to stop it.

Incidentally, another way to get your macro to stop is to place a number like 999 at the end of the column and use the formula **{if @cell-pointer("contents")=999}** as the condition to tell the macro it's time to stop. In fact, you can combine both techniques to have the macro pause when it reaches a blank cell (where you can decide whether to have the macro continue or quit), and end when it reaches the number 999.

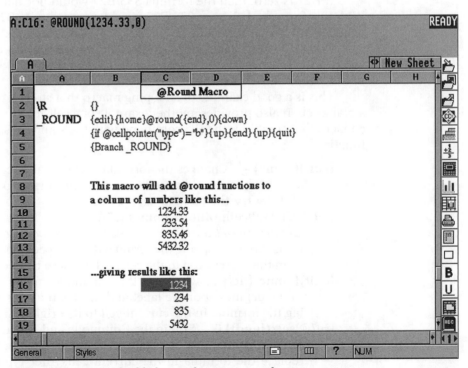

FIGURE 9.5　@Round added to each entry in a column.

A Macro to Eliminate the @ERR Message

The are several types of formulas that can cause an error message (ERR) to appear in one of the cells of your spreadsheet, but perhaps the most common involves formulas that try to divide by zero—a mathematical no-no. For example, if you copy a formula down an entire column that divides the number 333 by the cell to the left and some of the cells to the left of the column are not filled in yet, the formulas in those cases will return ERR. This can make a spreadsheet look unprofessional, error-prone, and highly suspicious if you have to distribute it to others.

One solution, of course, is to erase the offending cells until such time as the cells to the left are filled in. But having to go through the exercise of erasing and then replacing the formulas seems wasted energy and could easily result in a true error if you forget to replace one of the cell formulas later.

The better solution is to surround the formula with an @if statement which essentially states, *"If ERR is displayed by this formula, display a zero instead, otherwise display the true results of the formula."* Such a formula in cell C27 might look like this:

```
@if(@iserr(333/B27),0,333/B27)
```

If B27 is zero, then the formula 333/B27 would normally return ERR. With this formula, however, 333/B27 would return zero if B27 is zero, or it would return the actual value of 333/B27 if B27 is a number.

The macro in Figure 9.6 is designed to move down a column where some of the cells return (or might return) ERR and surround each formula of the column with **@if(@iserr(...)).**

This is a good example of a looping macro that stops when it comes to a blank cell. It also provides another example of a self-modifying macro and a macro that combines the **{if}** command with the standard spreadsheet **@if** function.

{edit}{home}'~ Changes the formula in the current cell to a label by switching to the Edit mode, moving the cursor to the beginning of the entry, then adding an apostrophe.

{let ENTRY,@cellpointer("contents")} This formula could be read, *"Let the cell called ENTRY become like the cellpointer contents."* This is the same as copying the formula that has been turned into a label from the current cell to the cell of the macro named ENTRY.

{edit}{home}{del} Switches to the Edit mode, moves the cell pointer to the beginning of the label and deletes the apostrophe, returning the formula in the current cell to its original state.

@if(@iserr({end}),0, Still in the Edit mode and still at the beginning of the formula, this line starts typing the @if statement that will replace the formula in the current cell. After typing **@if(@iserr** and a parenthesis, the cell pointer moves to the end of the for-

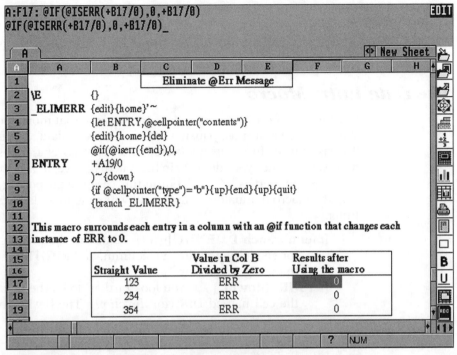

FIGURE 9.6 A macro to eliminate ERR messages in a column.

mula, closes the parenthesis, and types a comma, a zero, and another comma.

The next line of the macro will contain the original formula, inserted there as a label by the third line of the macro. The macro "reads" the line at this point, typing the information into the new @if formula.

)~{down}   Closes the parenthesis and moves the cell pointer down to the next cell in the column.

{if @cellpointer("type")="b"}{up}{end}{up}{quit}   Tests for a blank cell. If the macro finds a blank cell, it moves the cell pointer up to the top of the column and quits.

{branch \E}   If the macro does not find a blank cell, it loops back to the beginning and starts over. It continues in this way until it reaches a blank cell or until you press Ctrl+Break.

If you want to include this macro in Release 3 as a Macro Library item that will operate across active files, you must include a wildcard filename <<?>> in front of the range name ENTRY in the {let} command in the third line of the macro, as follows:

```
{let <<?>>ENTRY,@cellpointer("contents")}
```

This is required so 1-2-3 will know to look beyond the current file for the location of the cell named ENTRY you want to change.

The Data Entry Macro

Chapter 5 introduced a simple data entry macro that moves down the spreadsheet one cell at a time, pausing for your entry of data. The macro in Figure 9.7 has that feature, plus additional choices to cover the possible ways you may want to enter your data. As in the macros above, it uses the {if} command with @cellpointer("type")="b"; but in this case the purpose is to allow you to stop the macro manually at any point by moving to a blank cell and pressing Enter.

> **{menubranch DMENU1}{quit}**   Calls up the menu choices DOWN, for entries going down a column, and RIGHT, for entries moving to the right in a row.
>
> **{let DIR,"{down}"}**   If you look farther down the macro, you will see the cell named DIR (for *direction*). The {let} command tells the

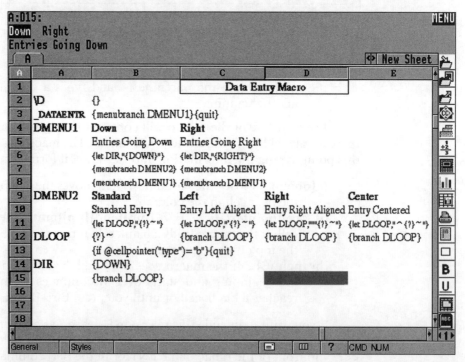

FIGURE 9.7 A Data Entry macro with range label types.

macro to *"Let the cell named DIR become like the word {down}"*. As a result, the macro modifies itself so it will move *down* rather than *across* the spreadsheet during the data entry process.

{menubranch DMENU2}{menubranch DMENU1}   Calls up the second menu, with choices *Standard, Left, Right,* and *Center.*

The *Standard* choice causes the macro to pause for standard entry of a number or a label. This means that values entered with this choice will be right-justified and labels will be left-justified.

The *Left* choice begins every entry with an apostrophe, which means your data will be entered left-justified as a label. This is especially handy when you are entering number-label combinations that must start with an apostrophe. In the same way, the *Right* choice begins every entry with full quotation marks so the entries will be right-justified. The *Center* choice begins every entry with a centering caret (^).

> **{let DLOOP,"{?}~"}**   Selecting the choice *Standard* causes the macro to *Let DLOOP become {?}~, copying {?}~* into the cell named DLOOP. This is the second running modification of the macro based on your menu selection. As you will see, you are able to put any symbols between quotation marks in a {let} command and they will be read as string entries rather than as macro commands.
>
> **{?}~**   This is where the macro pauses for your entry. Had you selected *Left*, this cell would have been modified to '{?}~. Selecting *Right* would have modified it to "{?}~, and *Center* would have changed it to ^{?}~. After each of these changes the macro loops back to this cell, as a result of the {branch DLOOP} command.
>
> **{down}**   This line will always read either {down} or {right}, depending on the choice you made at the first menu level. It causes the cell pointer to move one cell down or to the right after your entry.
>
> **{branch DLOOP}**   Branches back to the cell named DLOOP, where once again the macro pauses for your entry.
>
> **{if @cellpointer("type")="b"}{quit}**   When you are finished entering data and you want the macro to quit, press Ctrl-Break or move to any blank cell and press Enter. This {if} command will cause the macro to quit.

Take a look now at the commands under the menu choice *Right*. You will see that the **{let DLOOP,""""{?}~"}** command seems to have one too many quotation marks. Since the symbols which you want to appear in the cell named DLOOP after selecting *Right* are "{?}~, you might expect that **{let DLOOP,""""{?}~"}** with two quotation marks preceding the bracketed pause would do the trick. As it happens, however, the first quotation mark identifies the string and the second quotation mark would close the string if there were not a third quotation mark.

But if that's the case, you may wonder why there isn't a fourth quotation mark to start the string which consists of the bracketed pause. The answer is that the closing quotation mark for the first string (consisting of ″) can also be used as the opening quotation mark for the second string (consisting of {?}~).

This is all very complicated; fortunately, it doesn't come up often. But if you find in writing your own macros using strings and quotation marks that things just don't seem to work as you expected, try varying the number of quotation marks. This is all covered in more detail in Chapter 10.

This Data Entry Macro is an all-purpose entry macro that moves down your spreadsheet or to the right, entering data in the standard way, with an apostrophe, with full quotes, or with a centering caret depending on your menu selection. It also provides another example of a way to get your macro to modify itself.

For Release 3 users, you may want to use this as a background macro in a separate active Macro Library file. To do so, the only change you need to make is to add a wildcard filename <<?>> in front of the range names DIR and DLOOP in the fifth and tenth lines of the macro. (Don't forget to make this change in all four columns of these rows as required.)

Non-Standard Entries Corrected

This next macro uses the {if} command with @exact as well as with the @cellpointer("type")=″b″ function already covered. Shown in Figure 9.8, this macro is designed to help you identify items in a large database that may be out-of-place, misspelled, plural when they should be singular, singular when they should be plural, or typed using an upper, lower, or proper case inconsistently.

Imagine a sorted database of part numbers, for example, where a given part number appears 21 times. If the twenty-first occurrence of the part number is entered incorrectly, it will not match the item immediately above it. This macro identifies any item that does not match the item above it, then pauses for your correction of an invalid item or acceptance of the item as valid.

To start the macro, place your cell pointer on the first item in the list you want checked for correctness, and press Alt-N.

{let NTEST,@cellpointer("contents")} Copies the displayed contents of the current cell to the cell in the macro named NTEST. This is done to store an item for comparison with the items below it.

{down}{if @cellpointer("type")=″b″}{quit} Moves down to the next cell. This is a looping point to which the macro will return after checking each item in turn. When the cell pointer comes to a blank cell, which presumably represents the end of the list, the macro quits.

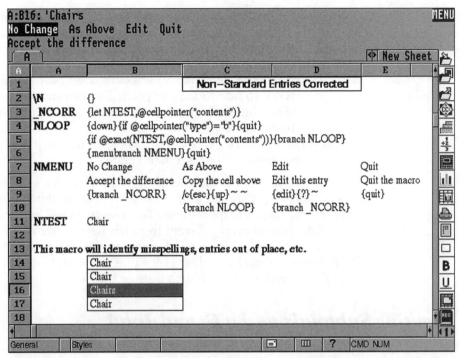

FIGURE 9.8 Macro to correct non-standard entries in a database.

{if @exact(NTEST,@cellpointer("contents"))}{branch NLOOP} This line introduces the @exact function, used to compare strings or cell contents. If the comparison is exact, the {if} statement is evaluated as false and the macro skips to the next line. In this case, the entry in NTEST where the macro has stored a copy of the first cell of the database is compared with the current cell contents. If the comparison is exact, the macro branches back to NLOOP, moves down and checks for a blank cell, then returns to this line to test the next item.

{menubranch NMENU}{quit} If the item stored in NTEST does not exactly match the current cell contents, the difference may be due to misspelling, wrong case, or some other mistake. You will be offered the menu choices *No Change, As Above, Edit,* and *Quit.*

{branch _NCORR} If the item doesn't match the item above it simply because it correctly represents a different item, selecting *No Change* will cause the macro to loop back to the beginning where it stores the new item in NTEST as the item to compare against.

/c{esc}{up}~~{branch NLOOP} If the item should match the item immediately above it, you can select *As Above* to make an instant change. The macro selects /Copy, presses Esc, moves up to the item above for the source cell, and (jumping back) presses Enter at the destination. The macro then continues as before at NLOOP.

{edit}{?}~{branch *NCORR}   If the item is incorrect, but should not match the item above, selecting *Edit* will cause the macro to switch to Edit mode and pause for your manual correction of the item. The macro then branches back to the beginning where it stores the new item in NTEST.

{quit}   Of course, you will always have the option to quit the macro by choosing the *Quit* menu choice.

This macro performs useful housekeeping on a large database. Be aware, however, it should only be used on sorted databases that typically have several entries of most items. This macro would be of no use in a database where each item is different from the item above it.

To use this as a background macro in a separate active Macro Library file in Release 3, add a wildcard filename <<?>> in front of the range name NTEST in the second and fourth lines of the macro.

Creating Subtotals and a Grand Total

If you have had to take a large database and create subtotals for like items, you know what a long and tedious task that can be. Let's suppose, for example, that you have a furniture warehouse and you want a subtotal of the cost of all your chairs, all your tables, and all your lamps. Assuming that like items are grouped together (your database has been sorted), you move to the row just below the last chair entry and select /Worksheet Insert Row, press DownArrow twice, and press Enter. This provides three blank rows in your spreadsheet for the subtotal. Then you move over to the amount column and type the @sum formula to get the total amount for all the chairs. Next you move down to the row just below the last table entry, select /Worksheet Insert Row, press DownArrow twice, and Enter, and move over to the amount column to type the @sum formula for the table amounts. This process is repeated until you have subtotaled all your furniture items. If you have 50 furniture items, this means going through that same process 50 times.

Instead, use the Total macro in Figure 9.9.

Note, there are three conditions that must be met before the macro will work:

1. The column of like items must be just to the left of the column to be subtotaled and totaled. If this is not the case with your database, you should either move the two columns together or change every line in the macro where the words {right} or {left} are used. If, for example, the column of like items is in column A and the col-

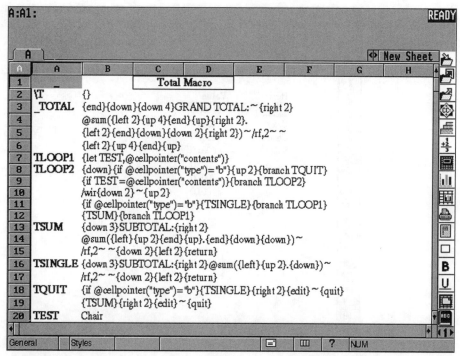

FIGURE 9.9 A macro to subtotal and total all like items.

umn to be subtotaled is in column C, all {right} commands should be changed to {right 2}, and all {left} commands to {left 2}.

2. The column just to the right of the amount column must be empty or used for label entries only (which equate to zero). If this is not the case, the grand total will inappropriately add any values in the column to the sum of all of the subtotals, giving an incorrect answer. Make sure the amount column is followed by a blank or label column or add a /Worksheet Insert Column command to the macro to automatically create a blank column for the subtotals and grand total.

3. There must be no blank spaces between the first entry and the last entry in your column of like items or the first line of the macro will not work correctly.

A glance at Figure 9.10 will show you an example of a simple database to which this macro might apply; Figure 9.11 shows the results you would get by running the macro.

{end}{down}{down 4}GRAND TOTAL:~{right 2} With your cell pointer on the first cell of the item column of the database, invok-

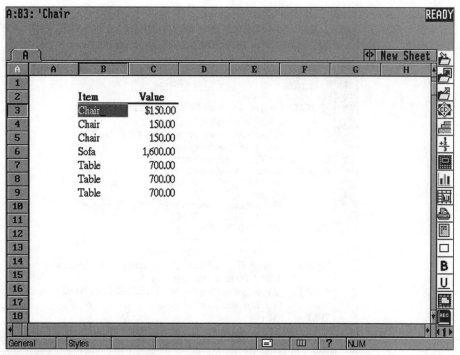

FIGURE 9.10 Sample database for the Total macro.

ing this macro will cause it to move to the last item of your database, then down four more cells where it enters the words *GRAND TOTAL:* and moves to the right two cells.

@sum({left 2}{up 4}{end}{up}{right 2}. This is the beginning of the grand total @sum formula. Since this macro is based on the assumption there are no blank spaces between the first and last entries in the column of like items, the {end} {up} command moves the cell pointer to the top of the amount column. The cell pointer is moved to the left two cells (in our example, that means to column A), then up four cells to the last item of the database, then End UpArrow to the top of the database and two Right-Arrows to the column to the right of the amount column (column C in our example). A press of the Period key (.) locks in the cell pointer.

{left 2}{end}{down}{down 2}{right 2})~/rf,2~~ The macro highlights the area back to the item column, then End DownArrow to the bottom of the column, down two more cells and (unhighlighting the first two columns) to the right two cells. In our example, this means painting in the range from C3 down to two cells

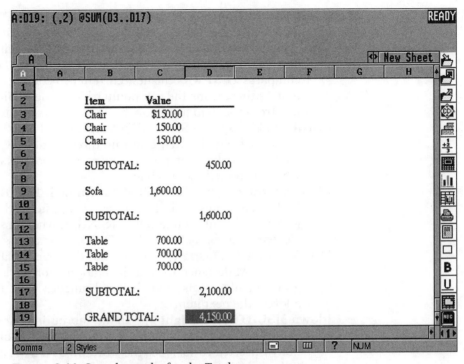

FIGURE 9.11 Sample results for the Total macro.

above the grand total. The tilde enters the formula and the cell pointer jumps automatically back to the grand total cell. This cell is then formatted for commas and two decimal points.

{left 2}{up 4}{end}{up}   Moving back to the last item in the item column, the cell pointer is moved to the top of the column with the {end}{up} command.

{let TEST,@cellpointer("contents")}   Your cell pointer started on the first of the like items. This line, also named TLOOP1, stores a copy of that item in the cell named TEST to test for whether the next item down is a match.

{down}{if @cellpointer("type")="b"}{up 2}{branch TQUIT}   This line of the macro is also the first cell of a loop named TLOOP2. It moves the cell pointer down one cell and tests for whether that cell is blank. Since at this point your cell pointer is only on the second cell of the database, that cell should not be blank and the macro will continue on to the next line. If the cell is blank, the cell pointer is moved up two cells and the macro branches to the routine at TQUIT.

{if TEST=@cellpointer("contents")}{branch TLOOP2}   Compares TEST with the current cell contents. If they match, the macro branches back to TLOOP2 where it moves the cell pointer down one cell to test whether that cell is blank. If not, the macro again compares TEST with the new current cell contents. If they do not match, this means the cell pointer has come to an item that differs from the item just above it. The macro skips to the next line.

/wir{down 2}~{up 2}   Selects /Worksheet Insert Row, presses Down-Arrow twice and Enter, inserting three blank rows in your database. The cell pointer then moves up two rows to check for whether the cell there is blank.

{if @cellpointer("type)="b"}{TSINGLE}{branch TLOOP1}   If the cell is blank, it means the last item was a single item. The macro therefore calls the subroutine called TSINGLE where it subtotals a single item, then branches back to TLOOP1 to address the next item.

{TSUM}{branch TLOOP1}   Otherwise, the macro calls the subroutine TSUM designed to sum the amounts for the latest identified group of like items, and then it branches back to TLOOP1 to address the next item.

{down 3}SUBTOTAL: {right 2}   In the subroutine named TSUM, the macro begins by moving back down to the middle of the three newly inserted rows, types the word SUBTOTAL:, and moves two cells to the right where the subtotal amount is to appear.

@sum({left}{up 2}{end}{up}.{end}{down}{down})~   You may recognize this as a modification of the Add Macro from Chapter 3. In this case it sums a group of numbers one column to the left.

/rf,2~~{down 2}{left 2}{return}   After entering the subtotal, the macro formats the cell for commas and two decimals. The cell pointer moves down two cells and left two cells to the next new item (TABLE in our example) and the macro branches back to the point where it left off at {branch TLOOP1}. Subsequently, that branching command takes the macro back to TLOOP1 to store the name of the next item in the cell TEST in place of the original item.

{down 3}SUBTOTAL:{right 2}@sum({left}{up 2}.{down})~   At the subroutine TSINGLE, the macro moves the cell pointer down to the middle of the newly inserted rows, types the word SUBTO-TAL:, moves the cell pointer two cells to the right where the subtotal amount is to appear, and enters the @sum formula.

/rf,2~~{down 2}{left 2}{return}   As with the TSUM subroutine, the macro formats the cell, moves the cell pointer to the next new item, and branches back to the point where it left off.

{if @cellpointer("type")="b"}{SINGLE}{right 2}{edit}~{quit}   The macro only comes to this line (a separate routine named TQUIT) when the cell pointer reaches a blank cell, indicating that it has come to the end of the database. Before branching to TQUIT (see the seventh line of the macro), the macro moves the cell pointer up two cells. If the cell is blank, it means the last item was a single item. The macro therefore calls the subroutine called TSINGLE where it subtotals a single item, then returns to this line to move two cells to the right, updates the Grand Total cell with {edit}~, and quits.

{TSUM}{right 2}{edit}~{quit}   Otherwise, the macro runs the subroutine TSUM, summing the amounts for the latest identified group of like items, then returns to this line to move two cells to the right, updates the Grand Total cell with {edit}~, and quits.

To use this as a background macro in a separate active Macro Library file in Release 3, add a wildcard filename <<?>> in front of the range name TTEST in the sixth and eighth lines of the macro.

You may be impressed at how quickly this macro runs. In fact, it is so fast that the {windowsoff} {paneloff} commands have been deliberately omitted so you can watch the macro run through its paces. Of course, you can always add these commands at the beginning of the macro. If you do, you may also want to add a command like {indicate **MACRO**} or {indicate **SBTOT**} in the upper right panel as a reminder that a macro is running. Don't forget, though, that another {indicate} command (with no argument so as to return the indicator to **READY**) must appear just before the {quit} command at the end of the second line of the macro.

Adjust Cell Data

Here's another tedious task: You want to change a column of numbers by multiplying every cell by some constant. So you place your cell pointer on the formula of the first cell, make the change, move down one cell, make the change, move down one cell, and so on until you've changed the entire column.

Instead, try using the Modify Cell Data macro in Figure 9.12.

This macro introduces the first of two prompting commands, {getlabel} and {getnumber}.

> **NOTE:** *If you have the latest version of 1-2-3 for Windows, explore the {get-label} and {get-number} commands under User Environment in Appendix A.*

The {getlabel} command is designed to prompt the user for a label— or for a number to be entered as a label. The {getnumber} command

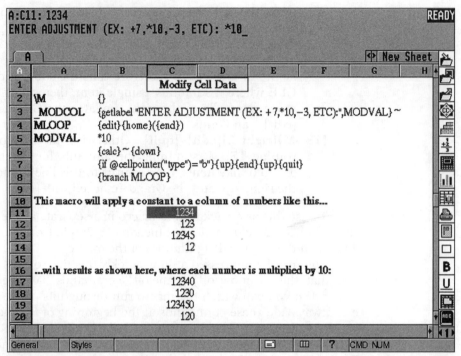

FIGURE 9.12 Macro to modify data in a column.

prompts the user for a value only. The syntax is the same for both commands, as follows:

```
{getlabel "Prompt to the user",Location}
{getnumber "Prompt to the user",Location}
```

The macro puts the user's response in any single-cell location, whether designated by cell coordinates or cell range name.

The Modify Cell Data macro uses {getlabel} to prompt for an arithmetic operator and value to be applied to every cell in a column of values. We have used {getlabel} instead of {getnumber} because of the need for an arithmetic operator and because the response is being entered as a line of the macro—all macro lines must be labels (must begin with an apostrophe).

{getlabel "ENTER ADJUSTMENT (EX: +7,*10,-3 ETC):",MOD-VAL}~ Prompts you to enter a plus (+), minus (−), multiplication (*), or division (/) sign, followed by the constant you want added to, subtracted from, multiplied by, or divided into each cell in the column. Whatever you type at this point will be entered into the self-modifying cell in the macro named MODVAL.

{edit}{home}({end}) The macro requires that you start with your cell pointer at the first value in a column of values. This line of the macro encloses the first value in parentheses by switching to the Edit mode, pressing Home to move the cursor to the beginning of the value, typing an opening parenthesis, pressing End to move to the end of the value, and typing a closing parenthesis.

The next line is the self-modified cell of the macro range-named MOD-VAL. As a result of the {getlabel} command in the beginning of the macro, it contains the factor by which you want to adjust the cell. Although the example in Figure 9.12 shows ***10**, this cell can be left blank when you first enter the macro in your own worksheet.

{calc}~{down} Since you are still in the Edit mode, the macro uses the {calc} command to change the modified cell from a formula to a value. It then moves the cell pointer down to the next cell. If you prefer that the original formula and the new factor remain in the cell rather than the resulting value, you can always eliminate the command {calc} from the macro.

{if @cellpointer("type")="b"}{up}{end}{up}{quit} Tests for a blank cell. If the macro finds a blank cell, it moves the cell pointer up to the top of the column and quits.

{branch MLOOP} Otherwise, the macro branches back to the third line and applies the constant to the next cell. It continues in this way until it hits a blank cell or you press Ctrl-Break.

To use this as a background macro in a separate active Macro Library file in Release 3, add a wildcard filename <<?>> in front of the range name MODVAL in the second line of the macro.

Summary

In this chapter we discussed the *If-Then-Else* concept in both the @if function and the {if} command. The {if} command can be used with @cellpointer("type") to check whether the current cell contains a label or a value or is completely blank. Using the conditional branching {if} command with @cellpointer, you can create a macro that loops until it meets some criteria—such as the determination that the cell pointer has arrived at a blank cell.

You were also introduced to two prompt commands, {getlabel} and {getnumber}, designed to pause for your entry of a string or value, then place that entry in a designated cell. This feature is especially useful for self-modifying macros that prompt you for information, then use that information to accomplish different tasks.

The macros covered in this chapter are:

- A Label-Format macro that will move down a column of numbers, changing each number to a label.
- A Number-Format macro that will move down a column of labels, changing each label to a number.
- A macro to indent each entry in a column by five spaces.
- A macro to add leading zeros to all of the numbers in a column.
- A Rounding macro to add the @round formula to each number or formula in a column.
- A macro to eliminate the ERR messages in a spreadsheet.
- A Data Entry macro to facilitate Standard, Left Justified, Right Justified, or Centered entries in a column or row.
- A macro to identify and allow correction of non-standard entries in a database.
- A Modify Cell Data macro that can apply a constant to every cell in a column of values.

In the next chapter we look at the use in macros of several string and special @functions such as @left, @right, @mid, @length, @replace, @find, @upper, @lower, @proper, @trim, @repeat, and @choose.

String Formulas and String @Functions

In this chapter we look at the underlying concepts and techniques of string manipulation in 1-2-3. As you will see, both string @functions and string formulas can be used to create self-modifying and variable lines in your macros. This can be accomplished by combining string @functions and string formulas with each other as well as with cell addresses, range names, labels, string forms of values, and other @functions.

This chapter explores the purpose and application of string techniques both in cells of the spreadsheet and in macros.

Comparing String @Functions with String Formulas

String @functions allow the 1-2-3 user to manipulate strings, concatenate strings, extract portions of strings, change their case, convert values to strings, and so on. A list of string @ functions is shown in Table 10.1.

In addition to string @functions (and sometimes in combination with them) you can create *string formulas* that use the special string manipulation features of 1-2-3 to combine two or more elements into a single word or phrase. To join the words "IN," "TELL," "I," and "GENT," for example, you can type

Table 10.1 String @Functions

String Function	*Syntax*	*Returns*
@Char	*(number)*	Character for an ASCII Code
@Clean	*(string)*	String without ASCII 0 to 31
@Code	*(character)*	ASCII Code for a character
@Exact	*(1st item ,2nd item)*	1 or 0 Comparing two items
@Find	*(string,from string ,start)*	Offset number of found string
@Length	*(string)*	Length of the string
@Lower	*(string)*	The string in lowercase
@Left	*(string,n characters)*	Leftmost *n* characters
@Mid	*(string,start,n characters)*	Middle *n* characters from start
@N	*(range)*	Value in upper left corner
@Proper	*(string)*	The string in proper case
@Repeat	*(string,n times)*	String repeated *n* times
@Replace	*(string,start,n chars,input)*	String with replacement input
@Right	*(string,n characters)*	Rightmost *n* characters
@S	*(range)*	String in upper left corner
@String	*(value,decimals)*	Value of number-label
@Trim	*(string)*	String without extra spaces
@Upper	*(string)*	The string in uppercase
@Value	*(number-label)*	Value of a number-label

```
"IN"&"TELL"&"I"&"GENT"
```

in any cell. Just as entering an @sum formula into a cell returns the sum in that cell, so entering this string formula into a cell returns the word INTEL-LIGENT.

String formulas must always begin with a plus sign (+) or a string @ function. This example starts with a plus sign and the word SALES in quotes, followed by an ampersand (&). The ampersand is the only operator for string formulas and is used to attach or concatenate the individual strings.

Try this: Combine ALBERT and EINSTEIN by typing

```
+"ALBERT"&" "&"EINSTEIN"
```

in any cell. Again the string begins with a plus sign, followed by the word ALBERT in quotes, followed by an ampersand. In order to separate the first and second words, a single space in quotes is included, like this: " ". The formula ends with another ampersand and the word EINSTEIN in quotes.

By itself, this unique way of entering a word or phrase in a cell seems useless and overly complicated. Combined with @ string functions or references to other cells, however, the string formulas can provide powerful new techniques to create variable titles or headings, to manipulate and change entries in a database automatically, to make some of your macro writing more efficient, and to speed up the execution of certain types of macros.

The example in Figure 10.1 shows how you can use strings to create a variable heading. The entry in cell D13 displays the word OVERRUN, so the formula in cell A1:

```
+"We are running an overhead budget "&D13&" this month.
```

displays as:

```
We are running an overhead budget DEFICIT this month.
```

On the other hand, a display of the word **SURPLUS** in cell D13 would cause the string formula in cell A1 to display:

```
We are running an overhead budget SURPLUS this month.
```

As you might imagine, you can easily create a series of strings that give you status on the individual budgets for rent, utilities, phone, supplies, and so on, all visible at the top of your spreadsheet and all variable depending on the cells to which the strings refer.

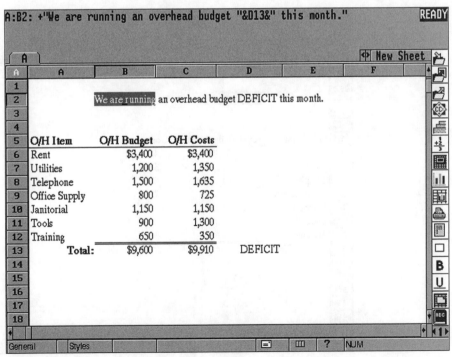

FIGURE 10.1 Using string formulas to create a variable heading.

Using @String in String Formulas

Although you can use string formulas to refer to cells displaying labels, the identical use of string formulas referring to cells with values returns an error. As shown in Figure 10.2, the formula

```
+"The overhead costs came to "&C13&" this month."
```

which one might expect to return a string indicating that the overhead costs are $9,910.00, actually returns ERR.

Fortunately, Lotus has considered this problem and provided a solution. Instead of referring to cell C13, you can refer to the formula @string (C13,0).

The @string function converts numeric values to strings and allows you to specify the number of decimal places to be used for a string. Refer to Figure 10.3. Thus the string formula that returns the desired statement would read:

```
+"The overhead costs came to "&@string(C13,0)&" this month."
```

There are two points regarding this string formula that bear mentioning.

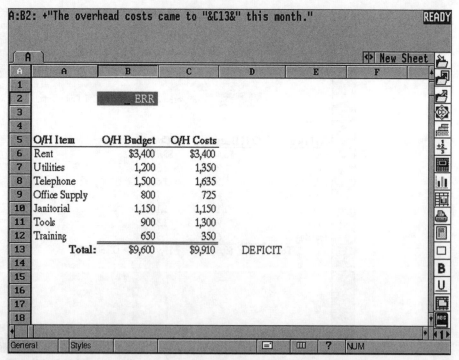

FIGURE 10.2 ERR results from inserting a value cell in a string.

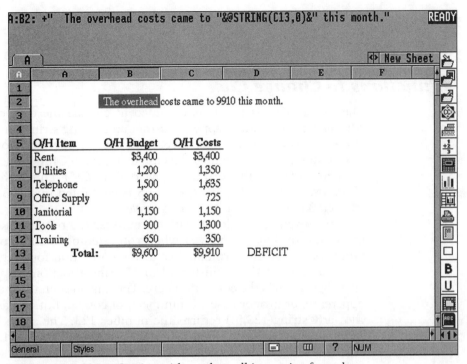

FIGURE 10.3 Using @string with a value cell in a string formula.

 At first glance, it may appear that the characters **&&@string(C13,0)&** are enclosed in quotes. This is not the case. In fact, what may appear to be opening quotes preceding the **&&@string(C13,0)&** are actually closing quotes following the first part of the string. In the same way, what may appear to be closing quotes following the **&&@string (B13,0)&** are actually opening quotes for the last part of the string.

 You may also have noticed that although cell B13 displays a value formatted for currency with two decimal points, the string formula shows only the number 9910 with no formatting. This is because there is no currency format for the @string function, although you can designate two decimal points by typing

```
@string(C13,2)
```

You can also add a dollar sign by typing a dollar sign ($) at the end of the preceding string within its quotation marks, as follows:

```
+"The overhead costs came to $ "&@string(C13,2)&" this month."
```

The @string function always displays a number as a label, but it displays a label as a label-zero in Release 2.01 and up. (In Release 2, using

@string with a label returned ERR—a problem that was corrected with Release 2.01.)

@*Functions to Change Case*

The three string @functions designed to change the case of a string are @lower, @proper, and @upper. Whether an existing string (or a cell containing a string) begins in uppercase, lowercase, proper case, or a mixture of any of these, you can change the case using these @functions.

For example, the formula @lower("*APPLES*") returns the string *apples* all in lowercase. If the string *APPLES* is contained in cell B3, the formula @lower(B3) also returns the string *apples*.

However, using @lower with the number *123* returns ERR. This is similar to the response displayed when you attempt to combine strings with numbers in a string formula. Just as the correction for that kind of string formula error is the inclusion of an @string function, so typing @lower (@string(123,0) is the correction here. There is no such thing as a lowercase, uppercase, or proper case for numbers, of course, but at least the formula @lower(@string(123,0)) returns the number 123. The same is true for the formula @lower(@string(B3,0)) when B3 *contains the value* 123.

Referring to an actual string rather than the cell address containing a string has predictable results. @upper("*sales*") returns the word SALES, and @proper("*12345*")—since "*12345*" in quotes is a string—returns the label-number 12345. Using the formula @lower(NEXTCELL) where the range name NEXTCELL refers to the word *APPLES* returns *apples,* the lowercase version of that cell's label contents.

Manually Changing a Column to Uppercase

Here's a simple way to convert a column of lowercase labels to uppercase. First make sure that the column just to the right of the column of labels is blank. If not, select /Worksheet Insert Column to create a blank column at that spot. Place your cell pointer in the blank column just to the right of the first label in your original column. Type **@upper**, an opening parenthesis, a plus sign, and point to the first label in your original column by pressing LeftArrow. Close the parenthesis to complete the formula and press Enter.

You should now see an uppercase version of the first item. Copy that formula down the exact length of the original column by selecting /Copy and pressing Enter; then at the prompt for a destination range, press the period (.) key, LeftArrow, End, DownArrow, RightArrow, and Enter. Then copy the displayed values of these @upper formulas to the original column by selecting /Range Value, highlighting the new column. An example of this stage of the operation is shown in Figure 10.4.

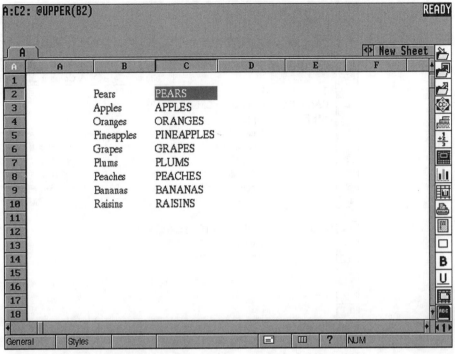

FIGURE 10.4 Manually changing a column of labels to uppercase.

After pressing Enter, you should see another prompt for a destination range. Press LeftArrow to point to the original column and Enter. Instantly the original column is converted all to uppercase. Now erase the new column you created by using /Range Erase or—if you inserted a new column to go through this exercise—by using /Worksheet Delete Column.

Changing a Column to Uppercase with a Macro

This can all be done in a macro, of course. Figure 10.5 shows a macro designed to convert a column of labels entirely to uppercase, lowercase, or proper case, based on your selection.

Before the macro starts, the pointer must be placed on the first cell of the column you want to convert. Since the macro begins by inserting a column to the right of this cell, it is important that the macro not be located in any area to the right of the column to be inserted. If so, the macro is shifted out from under itself and attempts to continue at the next line down, but one cell to the left; and since it cannot continue in that location, it stops or tries to run whatever entry it encounters—with predictably disastrous results.

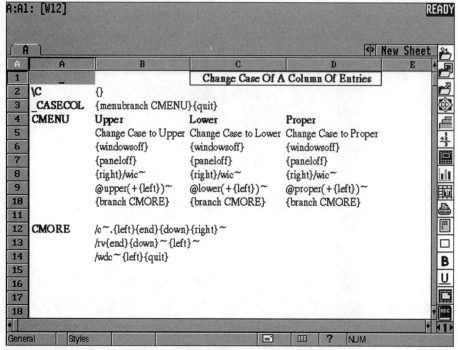

FIGURE 10.5 A macro to change the case of a column of entries.

{menubranch CMENU}{quit}   Offers the menu choices, *Upper,* *Lower,* and *Proper.*

{windowsoff}{paneloff}{right}/wic~   Regardless of which menu choice you select, the windows and panel are turned off, the cell pointer is moved to the right one cell, and the macro selects /Worksheet Insert Column.

@upper(+{left})~ or **@lower(+{left})~** or **@proper(+{left})~**   Types the appropriate case @function and an opening parenthesis, moves left to the first cell of the original column, closes the parenthesis, and enters the function.

{branch CMORE}   Branches to the rest of the commands held in common by all three menu choices.

/c~.{left}{end}{down}{right}~   Selects /Copy and presses Enter; then at the prompt for a destination range, presses the period (.) key, LeftArrow, End, DownArrow, RightArrow, and Enter.

/rv{end}{down}~~   Copies the displayed values of these @ functions to the original column by selecting /Range Value, highlighting the new column, and pressing Enter twice.

/wdc~{left}{quit}   Deletes the temporary column inserted at the beginning of the macro, moves left to the original column, and quits.

Using @Length to Measure a String

The @length function is designed to display the length of a string consisting of a word, a phrase, or a number-label. You can refer to the string directly, as in the following function which returns the value 5:

`@length("Sales")`

or you can indicate the string indirectly by referring to a specific cell containing the string, as in the function

`@length(J23)`

This example returns 5 if J23 has a string with five characters. Be aware, however, this @length function returns ERR if J23 is blank, displays a value, or displays a date based on a value or @date formula in a cell formatted for Date.

There is a way to determine the number of characters in a value when you combine @length with @string, as in the following example providing the length of the string equivalent of the value in B14 with no decimals:

`@length(@string(B14,0))`

You can also use a single-cell range name with @length, as follows:

`@length(CUSTOMER)`

Note that although CUSTOMER has eight letters, this @length function returns 14 if the string contained in the cell named CUSTOMER is GENERAL ELECTRIC.

You can use the @length function with @cellpointer("contents") to return the length of the contents of any cell you highlight with your cell pointer. This is useful for creation of a macro that instantly adjusts the width of the current column as shown in Figure 10.6.

This macro allows you to increase or reduce the width of a column to one space more than the number of characters in the cell you highlight. In the sample column shown, for instance, you can move your pointer to the longest phrase ("Office Supply" in B13) and press Alt+W (Ctrl+W in 1-2-3 for Windows). The column instantly changes to a width of 14 (13+1). If you later decide to change "Office Supply" to just "Supplies," pressing Alt+W (or Ctrl+W) on B13 changes the column width to 9 (8+1).

This macro is short, so it appears deceptively simple. The second line introduces a new command, {recalc}. Its purpose is to recalculate the cell or

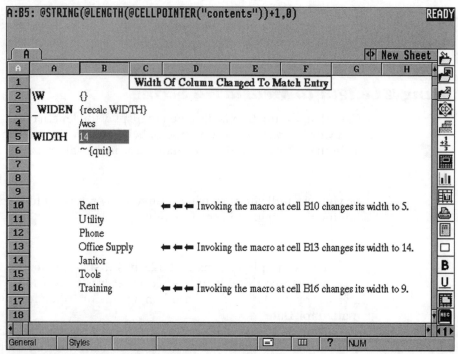

FIGURE 10.6 Adjust column width based on current cell contents.

range referred to in its argument. In this case, it is an instruction to recalculate the cell named WIDTH, cell B6. The third line begins the command to change the column width by selecting /Worksheet Column width Set. The fourth line, though it displays a left-justified number here, is actually the formula

```
@string(@length(@cellpointer("contents")+1),0)
```

as shown in the upper panel. This formula returns ERR when you first enter it as shown. Do not let this worry you, however. If you point to any cell containing a string and press the F9 Calc key, the ERR changes to a number-label (with no decimals) representing one more than the number of characters in that string.

Working from the center of this formula to the outer characters, we can analyze the string starting with the @cellpointer formula.

@cellpointer("contents") Returns the contents of the cell the pointer happens to rest on when the macro is invoked.

@length(@cellpointer("contents"))+1 Returns a value equal to the length of the contents of the current cell, plus 1.

@string(@length(@cellpointer("contents"))+1,0)   The value of the current cell's length is converted to its string equivalent so it can be used in this string formula. The ending zero and closing parenthesis display the label-number with no decimals.

As noted, this macro will not work on cells displaying values.

Using @Find to Search a String

The @find function uses search criteria to search a string for one or more characters starting at a designated position in the string. This function returns ERR if a match with the search criteria is not found. If a match is found, the function displays a number representing the location of its first occurrence in the string. The format of the @find function is as follows:

```
@find(search criteria, entire string or cell, starting point)
```

The starting point and the location number that the @find function returns are both based on the use of position numbers. The first character in a string is the 0 position, the second character is the 1 position, the third character is the 2 position, and so on. (This is similar to the offset principles used in the @dsum, @dcount, @choose, @vlookup, and @hlookup functions.)

Thus a search for position of the first occurrence of the letter "e" in the string Albert Einstein would be typed:

```
@find("e","Albert Einstein",0)
```

and would return the number 3. The formula returns 3 rather than 4 because the letter "e" is the third letter over from the zero position.

Using @find to search for the string "Albert" returns a zero because the name "Albert" starts at the zero position. On the other hand, searching for the uppercase version, "ALBERT," returns ERR because the @find function is case sensitive; it requires that an exact match be found for the search criteria in the searched string or cell, including a match of upper- and lowercase.

Although a search for the letter "e" returns 3 when the starting position of the @find formula is zero, the formula

```
@find("e","Albert Einstein",7)
```

with a starting position of 7 returns the value 12 (the position of the first lowercase "e" after the seventh letter in "Albert Einstein"). Similarly, a search for "e" starting at position 13 returns an ERR message because there is no letter "e" past position 13.

Numbers entered as labels, such as the telephone number 301-555-1212, can be searched with @find, but an attempt to use @find on a number entered as a value returns ERR. The solution in that case, as with the

@length function, is to add the @string function that turns the number into a label. The other possibility, though usually not practical, is to refer to the number directly, typed in quotes.

To locate the second occurrence of a character or string when you do not know the location of the first occurrence, try using a nested @find formula. In other words, instead of using the 0 position as your starting point for the search, substitute another @find function to locate the first occurrence, add the number 1, and provide this information as the new starting point for the second occurrence. For example, a search for the second occurrence of the letter "e" in "Albert Einstein" would be done like this

```
@find("e","Albert Einstein",@find("e","Albert Einstein",0)+1)
```

returning the value 12.

You may wonder about the usefulness of all these explanations about the @find function. After all, knowing that the second letter "e" is the twelfth character over from the beginning of a string does not really provide you with astonishing information. In conjunction with other string formulas, however, this function provides a powerful and much needed element without which many sophisticated manipulations of strings would not be possible.

Using @Left to Extract a String

The @left function uses the syntax

```
@left(string or cell,number of characters)
```

and returns a portion of a string consisting of a designated number of characters from the left side of the string. Thus, @left(*"tangent"*,4) returns the first four letters by displaying the string *tang*. Similarly, the formula @left(*"entertainment"*,5) returns the first five letters by displaying the string *enter*.

Note the @left function does not work on the offset principle. In other words, the @left(*"entertainment"*,5) example does not count up to position 5 (the sixth character), but rather displays the five leftmost characters in the string.

If you enter a number equal to or greater than the number of characters in the string, the @left function simply displays the entire string.

As with the @upper, @lower, and @proper string functions, the @left function works with a string, a cell address, or a range name referring to a single cell containing a string. An ERR message is returned if the referenced cell or range name contains a value rather than a label.

The @left function can also be used in conjunction with the @find function to extract and display a variable length string.

Figure 10.7 shows a list of first and last names in column B, where the names are of various lengths. Using a combination of @left and @find as in the example

```
@left(B6,@find(" ",B4,0))
```

you can create a formula that extracts just the first name by finding the first occasion of a blank space, then using that information to establish how many letters should be extracted from the left side of the string.

The space in the string *William Faulkner* in cell B6, for example, is determined with the function

```
@find(" ",B4,0)
```

where " " refers to the search criteria, B4 refers to the cell being searched, and 0 refers to the search starting point in the cell. This function returns a position number 7, which is used by the @left function to extract 6 characters—the word William.

One of the more sophisticated uses of the @left function is in the creation of variable lines of a macro, especially used in conjunction with the other string-extracting @functions, @right, and @mid.

```
A:D4: @LEFT(B4,@FIND(" ",B4,0))                                    READY
```

	A	B	C	D	E
2		Based on this	Use @left with		
3		list of names:	@find like this:	To return this:	
4		William Faulkner	@left(b4,@find(" ",b4,0))	William	
5		George Gershwin	@left(b5,@find(" ",b5,0))	George	
6		Ludwig Beethoven	@left(b6,@find(" ",b6,0))	Ludwig	
7		George Handel	@left(b7,@find(" ",b7,0))	George	
8		Jean Sartre	@left(b8,@find(" ",b8,0))	Jean	
9		E. Grieg	@left(b9,@find(" ",b9,0))	E.	
10		A. Khachaturian	@left(b10,@find(" ",b10,0))	A.	
11		Franz Kafka	@left(b11,@find(" ",b11,0))	Franz	
12		Fred Chopin	@left(b12,@find(" ",b12,0))	Fred	
13		Scott Fitzgerald	@left(b13,@find(" ",b13,0))	Scott	
14		Aaron Copland	@left(b14,@find(" ",b14,0))	Aaron	
15		Giacomo Puccinni	@left(b15,@find(" ",b15,0))	Giacomo	
16		J. Bach	@left(b16,@find(" ",b16,0))	J.	
17		Marcel Proust	@left(b17,@find(" ",b17,0))	Marcel	

FIGURE 10.7 Extracting a first name with @left and @find.

Using @Right to Extract a String

Similar to the @left function, the @right function uses the syntax

```
@right(string or cell, number of characters)
```

and returns a portion of a string consisting of a designated number of characters from the right side of the string. Thus, @right("*alienation*",5) returns the last five letters by displaying the string *nation*. Similarly, the formula @right("*incidental*",6) returns the last six letters by displaying the string *dental*.

As with the @left function, @right does not work on the offset principle by counting up to position 5 (the sixth character), but rather displays the number of characters entered in the @right function. The @right function works with a string, a cell address, or a range name for a single cell containing a string. And if you enter a number which is equal to or greater than the number of characters in the string, the @right function simply displays the entire string.

Where we were able to extract a variable length string like the first name from a list of first and last names using @left, extracting the last name is a little more difficult using @right. It can be done, however, when the @right function is used in conjunction with the @length and @find functions as in the following example:

```
@right(B4,@length(B4)-@find(" ",B4,0)-1)
```

Figure 10.8 shows a list of first and last names in column B where the names are of various lengths. The formula shown in column C finds the position number of the blank space between first and last name, subtracts that number from the length of the entire name, then reduces that number by 1 to establish the number of characters to be extracted from the right side of the string.

The space in the string *William Faulkner* in cell B4, for example, is determined with the function

```
@find(" ",B6,0)
```

where " " refers to the search criteria, B4 refers to the cell being searched, and 0 refers to the search starting point in the cell. This function returns a position number 8, which is then subtracted from the 16 characters in B4 as determined by the formula @length(B4) to return 8. Subtracting the number 1 from this result provides the number 8—the total number of characters in the last name *Faulkner*.

Since we have presented in Figure 10.7 a method for extracting the first name from a full name string, and in Figure 10.8 a method for extracting the last name, these two formulas can be combined into one formula to change the order of first and last name. The list of names in column A of

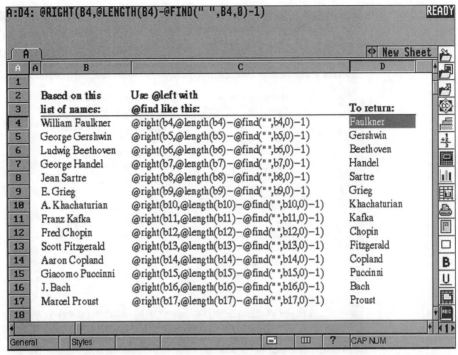

FIGURE 10.8 Extracting last name with @right, @length, and @find.

Figure 10.9 are presented in last name-first name order. The formula in column B is constructed to leave out the comma between names and reverse the order of names from last-first to first-last.

The formula in cell B7 is broken down as follows:

```
@right(A7,@length(A7)-@find(" ",A7,0)-1)
&" "
&@left(A7,@find(" ",A7,0)-1)
```

The first or last name extractions shown in Figures 10.7 and 10.8 are useful for lists where there are no middle initials, but lists of names are rarely so accommodating. The macro in Figure 10.10 takes this into account, however, and extracts the first name, first name and middle initial, or last name from a number of combinations of initials and names.

An example of a database of names is shown in Figure 10.11. Applying the macro in Figure 10.10 to this database, place your pointer in column B to the right of the first full name and invoke the macro. The menu selections *1st Name, First Name & M.I.,* and *Last Name* appear. Selecting *1st Name* causes the macro to type the following @left formula:

A:C4: @RIGHT(B4,@LENGTH(B4)-@FIND(" ",B4,0)-1)&" "&@LEFT(B4,@FIND(" ",B4,0)-1)

	A	B	C	D
1				
2		Based on names	Use string @functions	
3		listed LAST, FIRST	to change to FIRST–LAST	
4		Faulkner, William	William Faulkner	
5		Gershwin, George	George Gershwin	
6		Beethoven, Ludwig	Ludwig Beethoven	
7		Handel, George	George Handel	
8		Lunsford, Hassin	Hassin Lunsford	
9		Grieg, E.	E. Grieg	
10		Khachaturian, A.	A. Khachaturian	
11		Kafka, Franz	Franz Kafka	
12		Chopin, Fred	Fred Chopin	
13		Fitzgerald, Scott	Scott Fitzgerald	
14		Copland, Aaron	Aaron Copland	
15		Puccinni, Giacomo	Giacomo Puccinni	
16				
17	Cell C5:			
18	@right(b4,@length(b4)–@find(" ",b4,0)–1)&" "&@left(b4,@find(" ",b4,0)–1)			

FIGURE 10.9 Reverse the order of names with string @functions.

@left({left},@find(" ",{left},0))~ Types @left and an opening parenthesis and moves the pointer to the left to the first name in the
data base to establish the string to extract from. The macro then
accomplishes an @find function, searching for the first occasion
of a space from that cell starting with the first character (position
0). The result is an extraction of the first name or initial in the
string before the first space.

{branch XQUIT} Branches to a closing routine to copy the @left formula down in a column, change the @left formulas to their corresponding values, and quit.

If you select *First Name & M.I.* from the menu choices, the formula to
extract the first name and middle initial is quite a bit more complicated.
This is due to the necessity for verifying whether a middle initial is included
in the full name being tested.

@if(@iserr(@find(" ",{left},@find(" ",{left},0)+1), Begins typing an
@if statement that checks for an error condition in the search for
two spaces in the string. The nested @find function accomplishes
this search, looking for a second space in the string starting one
space past the position of the first space.

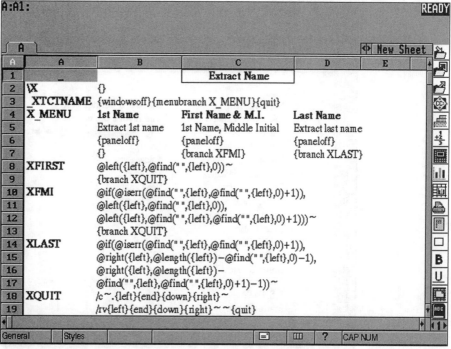

FIGURE 10.10 Extract first name, last name, or middle initial.

@left({left},@find(" ",{left},0)), If the error condition exists, the formula extracts just the first portion of the string up to the first (and only) space in the string.

@left({left},@find(" ",{left},@find(" ",{left},0)+1)))~ If the error condition does not exist, the formula extracts the characters from the leftmost character up to the space found starting at the location after the first space in the string.

If you select *Last Name* from the menu choices, the extraction of the last name follows the same basic principles, including a search for a second space and a determination of whether that search results in an error condition. The only real difference is the formula required to extract the last name. That formula consists of an @right function which pulls out the last name by calculating the position number of the latter space and subtracting that number from the length of the string.

/c~.{left}{end}{down}{right}~ The final routine named XQUIT copies the @left formula from the current cell. The TO cell is established by anchoring the pointer, moving to the contiguous column of full names to the left, moving End DownArrow to the bottom of that column, then moving back to Column B.

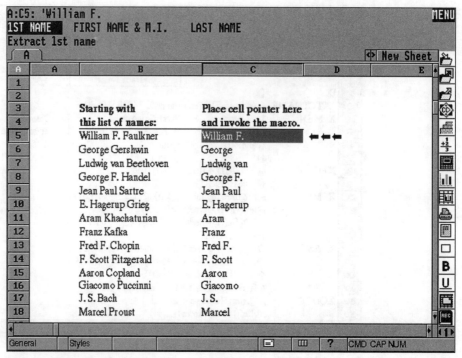

FIGURE 10.11 Database of names to extract.

/rv{left}{end}{down}{right}~~{quit}   Changes the @left formulas to their corresponding values using the /Range Value command, paints in the column with the End DownArrow command, and quits.

Using @Mid to Extract a String

The @mid function uses the syntax

`@mid(string or cell,starting position,number of characters)`

and returns a portion of a string consisting of characters from the middle of the entire string. It does this by extracting, from a starting position in the entire string, a specified number of characters. This definition of a starting position adds an element not required in the @left and @right formulas, as shown in the comparison below:

`@left(string or cell, number of characters)`
`@right(string or cell, number of characters)`
`@mid(string or cell, starting position, number of characters)`

Since the 0 position is the position of the leftmost character in the string, using 0 as the starting position in the @mid function exactly duplicates the effect you can achieve using the @left function. Thus, the formula @mid(*"hopeful"*,0,4) starts counting at the first character (position 0) and counts 4 characters, returning the string *hope*. The formula @mid(*"exclamation"*,2,4), on the other hand, starts counting at the third character (position 2) and counts 4 characters to return the string *clam*.

As with the @left and @right functions, the @mid function works with a string, a cell address, or a range name for a single cell containing a string. If you enter a number which is equal to or greater than the number of characters in the string, the @right function simply displays the entire string.

Some typical uses of the @mid function include extracting the month or day of the month from a date typed as a label. From a typed label date 03/27/90 in cell H37, for example, you can extract the day of the month with the formula

```
@mid(H37,@find("/",H37,0),2)
```

where H37 holds the original string, the formula @find("/",H37,0) establishes the starting point to extract from, and the number 2 establishes the number of characters to extract.

For a more complicated use of @mid with @find, you may be interested in a macro that changes entire label-dates to dates entered in the @date format—and then changes them back again. Refer to the macro called Change Label-Date to @Date Formula shown in Figure 10.12.

To operate this macro, place your cell pointer at the first entry in a column of label-dates or dates entered in the @date format and invoke the macro.

{menubranch CMENU}{quit}   Calls up the menu choices *Label-Date Converted* and *Convert @Date*.

{let CHG,@cellpointer("contents")}   This is the first active line of the *Label-Date Converted* choice. It copies the contents of the first cell in the column to the cell in the macro named CHG. In the example in Figure 10.12, CHG has had the label-date 1/1/88 copied into it. (When you first create this macro, of course, you can leave this cell empty.)

{recalc CALC1}{recalc CALC2}@date(Updates the next two cells in CALC1 and CALC2 to reflect information based on the entry stored in CHG. This is required for self-modifying lines of a macro that consist of string functions or combinations of string functions. The macro then types @date and an opening parenthesis and continues at the next line.

88,1,   Although in Figure 10.12 this line named CALC1 shows as the year and month of the date stored in CHG, it is actually the result of the underlying formula:

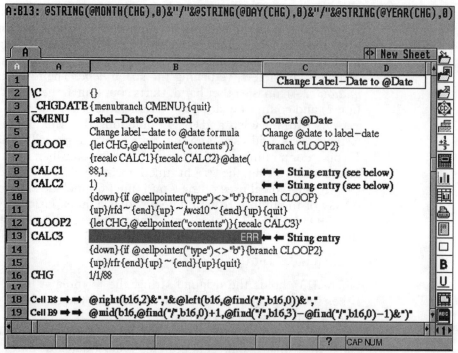

FIGURE 10.12 Macro to change Label-Date to @Date Formula.

```
@right(B16,2)&","&@left(B16,@find("/",B16,0))&","
```

where B16 is the cell address for the cell in the macro named CHG. You can also see this formula redisplayed for clarity at the bottom of the figure in cell A18. (As you type this in yourself, use the cell address that corresponds to CHG in your own worksheet.)

1) In the same way, this line at CALC2 in Figure 10.12 displays the day of the date store in CHG and a closing parenthesis, while it is actually the result of the underlying formula:

```
@mid(B16,@find("/",B16,0)+1,@find("/",B16,3)-@find("/",
B16,0)-1)&")"
```

The purpose of this formula is to extract from the middle of a date like 1/1/88 the day of the month (in this case the number 1). The formula does this by using the @mid(string,start,number) formula, where the start is identified by finding the first forward slash (/), and the number of characters in the day of the month is identified by subtracting the found position of the second slash from the found position of the first slash.

{down}{if @cellpointer("type")<>"b"}{branch CLOOP} Moves the cell pointer down, at the same time entering the @date formula created with the last three lines of the macro. If the cell pointer has not reached the end of the columns of date, the macro loops back to CLOOP to construct the @date formula for the next label-date it encounters.

{up}/rfd~~{end}{up}~/wcs10~{end}{up}{quit}   When the cell pointer does reach a blank cell representing the end of the column, it moves up to the last entry, formats the entire column for date format, changes the column width to 10 to accommodate the date format, moves to the top of the column, and quits.

{let CHG,@cellpointer("contents")}{recalc CALC3}   If you selected *Convert @Date* at the beginning of this macro because the column you want to convert is a column of @date format values, the macro begins by storing a copy of the contents of the first cell to CHG, then recalculates (updates) the next cell at the range name CALC3 and types an label-prefix apostrophe in preparation for entry of the displayed contents of CALC3.

ERR   Although this cell displays ERR at this point, its underlying formula is:

```
@string(@month(B16),0)&"/"&@string(@day(B16),0)&"/"
&@string(@year(B16),0)
```

When placed on an @date format value, this formula concatenates the string value of the month (no decimals), a forward slash (/), the string value of the day (no decimals), a forward slash (/), and the string value of the year (no decimals).

The remainder of this routine named CLOOP2 is the same as the closing line of CLOOP at B11, except that the column width is not changed and the format is reset.

Setting up this macro may seem like a lot to go through to change some dates from one format to another, but if the change is being made to a large database, the trouble of creating the macro is more than offset by the savings in keystrokes and workhours.

@Trim and the [Contents] Command

The purpose of the @trim function is to trim away extraneous spaces in a string. This is especially useful when importing files over from other programs, such as database files that include spaces between the fields.

This function does not trim away all spaces, only leading spaces, trailing spaces, or spaces combined with other spaces. For example, the phrase *General & Administrative* with several spaces between the words would condense to *General & Administrative*. Similarly, the label-number *4 7 3 2* (necessarily entered as a label because it is not possible to place spaces between characters in a value) is displayed with the @trim formula as *4 7 3 2.*

The formula @trim(B13) returns an ERR message when B13 consists of the value 12345. The formula @trim(@string(B14,0)), on the other hand, properly returns the label-number 12345.

The @trim function is especially useful in modifying the results of the {contents} command. The function of the {contents} command is similar to the {let} command in that it causes 1-2-3 to store the contents of one cell at a destination cell. However, there are three major differences between {let} and {contents}, as follows:

 The {contents} command can only store information from a specified cell, while the {let} command can store a specified value or string as well as the contents of a specified cell.

 Whereas the {let} command stores both values and labels, the {contents} command stores only a label version of a value or label.

 When storing a value as a label, the {contents} command also stores the displayed format of that value unless otherwise specified.

The syntax of the {contents} command is as follows:

```
{contents destination,source-cell,[width],[cell-format]}
```

where *[width]* and *[cell-format]* are optional attributes allowing you to specify these attributes that would otherwise default to the width and cell format of the source cell. The *[cell-format]* attribute, if specified, must follow the code numbers as shown in Figure 10.13.

Let's look at an example of the {contents} command that does not include optional attributes. Assuming a spreadsheet where cell F7 has a column width of 11 and contains the value 123 formatted for currency, the command

```
{contents D14,F7}
```

stores a label with three leading spaces and one trailing space in cell D14 as follows:

```
' $123.00
```

This is where the @trim function comes in handy. By trimming the leading and trailing spaces, it allows a change of the result of the {contents} command to a label as follows:

```
'$123.00
```

This can be seen in the sample use of the {contents} command and @trim function in Figure 10.14.

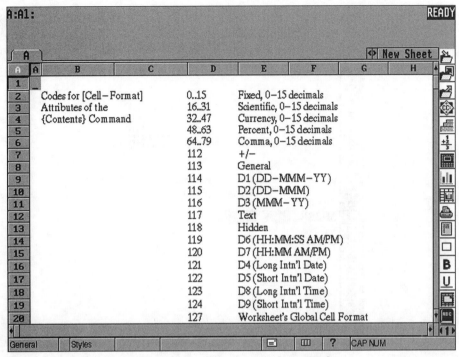

FIGURE 10.13 Codes for [cell-format] attribute in {contents}.

To start, place your cell pointer on cell D7 and invoke the macro.

{contents AHERE,@cellpointer("address")}~ Copies a label version of the current cell location in cell AHERE. In the upper panel you can see the leading and trailing spaces shown in cell B13.

{let BHERE,@trim(AHERE)}~ Copies to BHERE a version of the contents in AHERE with leading and trailing spaces eliminated.

Using @Trim to Change a Column Width

In Figure 10.6, we showed how you can use the @length function in a self-modifying macro to change the width of a column to match the label in the current cell. Unfortunately, that macro will not work on values. In this section we show how you can use the @trim function and the {contents} command to improve the macro so it works on values as well as labels. Refer to Figure 10.15.

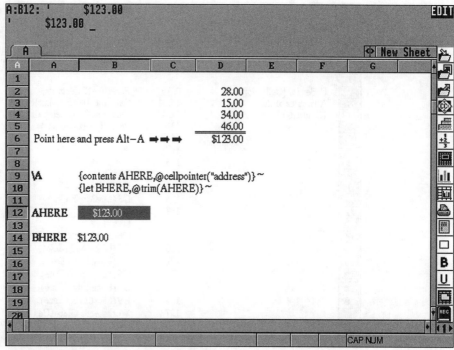

FIGURE 10.14 Sample use of the {contents} command and @trim.

Here's how the macro works:

{windowsoff}{paneloff}   Turns off the windows and panel to suppress screen flicker.

{if @cellpointer("type")="v"}{branch W_VALU}   Checks for whether the current cell contains a label or a value. If it contains a value, the macro branches to W_VALU.

{recalc WIDTH}   Otherwise, the macro recalculates the self-modifying formula in the next cell down, at WIDTH.

/wcs23~{quit}   This is the displayed value of the underlying formula in B6 (also shown at the bottom of Figure 10.15). This formula can be broken down as follows:

```
+"/wcs"
&@string(@length(@cellpointer("contents"))+1,0)
&"~{quit}"
```

The formula calculates a number one greater than the length of the cell pointer contents, turns it into a string showing no deci-

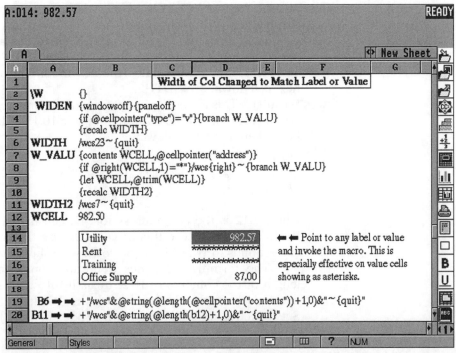

FIGURE 10.15 Width of column changed to match label or value.

mals, precedes the result with the /Worksheet Column width Set sequence, and follows it with a tilde and {quit} command.

> **NOTE:** *When you first enter the formula, it returns ERR. However, don't let that worry you. Simply move to any cell containing a label and press the F9 Calc key to see a display such as shown in cell B6.*

{contents WCELL,@cellpointer("address")} This is the beginning of the routine where the macro branches if the cell pointer starts on a cell containing a value. It copies a label version of the value to WCELL, including the characteristics of the cell's width and format.

{if @right(WCELL,1)="*"}/wcs{right}~{branch W_VALU} If the current cell shows a series of asterisks because it is too narrow to show its value, the macro selects /Worksheet Columnwidth Set, increases the width by one with the {right} command, and branches back to the previous line named W_VALU to once again copy a label version of the current cell's displayed value to WCELL.

{let WCELL,@trim(WCELL)}   Otherwise, the macro uses the {let} command to trim the leading and trailing zeros from the label version of the current cell stored in WCELL. Later, the macro uses this stored label to calculate a revised width.

{recalc WIDTH2}   Recalculates the self-modifying formula in the next cell down, at WIDTH2.

/wcs7~{quit}   This is the displayed value of the underlying formula in B11 (also shown at the bottom of Figure 10.15). This formula can be broken down as follows:

```
+"/wcs"
&@string(@length(B12)+1,0)
&"~{quit}"
```

where B12 is the cell address for the cell in the macro named WCELL. (As you type this in yourself, use the cell address that corresponds to WCELL in your own worksheet.)

The formula calculates a number one greater than the length of the contents of B12, turns it into a string showing no decimals, precedes the result with the /Worksheet Columnwidth Set sequence, and follows it with a tilde and {quit} command.

NOTE: *To use this macro in a Release 3 Macro Library using separate active files, precede every reference to WCELL or cell B12 with the wildcard file-name <<?>>.*

Using {Contents} with Optional Attributes

You may be wondering about the conditions under which you might make use of the optional attributes of the {contents} command. The macro in Figure 10.16 provides one example.

The purpose of the macro is to allow you to edit a formula's range names in Release 2.x without having to retype the entire names. This macro resolves the potential problem in Release 2.x: That pressing the F2 Edit key on a formula causes the formula to display in the Edit Control Panel with cell coordinates in place of any range names the formula may reference.

For example, suppose you have a formula with the range names SALES88 and SALES89 that you would like to edit to reference the range names SALES90 and SALES91. It would be handy to be able to simply press F2 Edit, move the cursor to the numbers 88 and 89 in the range names, and change them to 90 and 91; but when you press F2 Edit in Release 2.x, any range names in the current cell's formula are displayed as cell coordinates. To make this type of change you must manually change these cell coordinates and convert them to their respective range names.

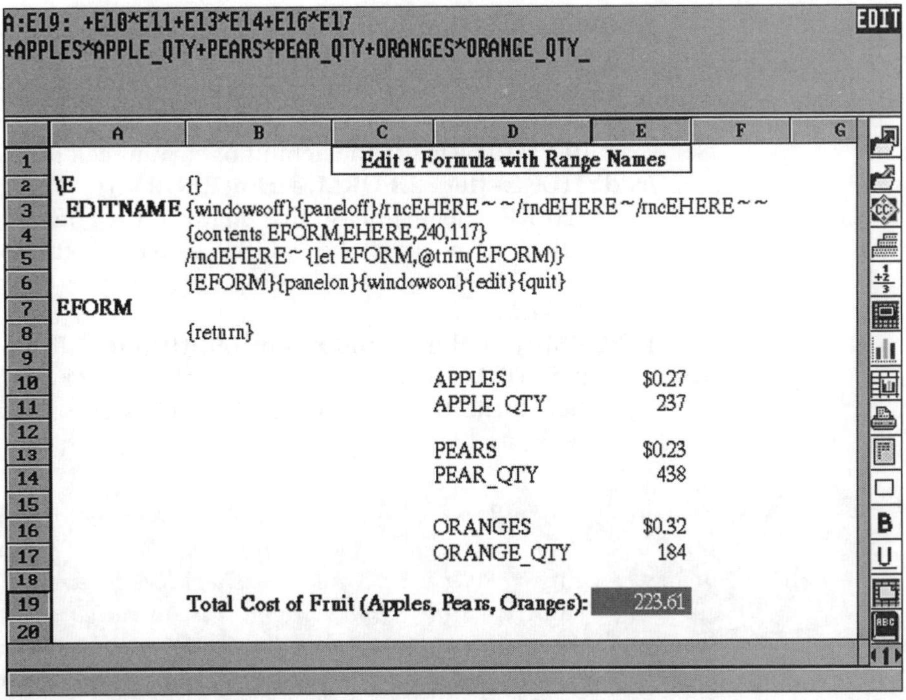

```
A:E19: +E10*E11+E13*E14+E16*E17                                          EDIT
+APPLES*APPLE_QTY+PEARS*PEAR_QTY+ORANGES*ORANGE_QTY_
```

	A	B	C	D	E	F	G
1			Edit a Formula with Range Names				
2	\E	{}					
3	_EDITNAME	{windowsoff}{paneloff}/rncEHERE~~/rndEHERE~/rncEHERE~~					
4		{contents EFORM,EHERE,240,117}					
5		/rndEHERE~{let EFORM,@trim(EFORM)}					
6		{EFORM}{panelon}{windowson}{edit}{quit}					
7	EFORM						
8		{return}					
9							
10				APPLES	$0.27		
11				APPLE_QTY	237		
12							
13				PEARS	$0.23		
14				PEAR_QTY	438		
15							
16				ORANGES	$0.32		
17				ORANGE_QTY	184		
18							
19		Total Cost of Fruit (Apples, Pears, Oranges):			223.61		
20							

FIGURE 10.16 Macro to edit a formula with range names.

In Release 2.0 and 2.01, you can make these changes manually using the F4 Abs key. Press F2 Edit, move to the cell coordinate representing the range name you want to modify, and press F4 Abs. The coordinates will be replaced with an absolute form of the corresponding range name, preceded by the dollar sign ($) absolute indicator. Press the F4 Abs key again to delete the dollar sign and you have a relative form of the range name you can easily change. Unfortunately, if the formula is long and complicated, you may go through quite a number of keystrokes to use this process.

In Release 2.2 through 2.4, you can use the F3 Name key in the same way. If a cell coordinate has one (and only one) corresponding range name, you can place your edit bar on the coordinate and press the F3 Name key once to change it to its range name.

Alternatively, you can use the macro in Figure 10.16 to do all of this for you. Here's how the macro works:

{windowsoff}{paneloff}/rncEHERE~~/rndEHERE~/rncEHERE~~
> Turns off the windows and panel to suppress screen flicker and speed up the macro; then creates, deletes and recreates the range named EHERE at the current cell.

{contents EFORM,EHERE,240,117} Copies the contents of the current cell named EHERE into EFORM. A width of up to 240 characters is specified to override the default: the column width of the current cell. Code 117 specifies Text format (see Figure 10.13) to override the default of current cell format.

/rndEHERE~{let EFORM,@trim(EFORM)) The macro deletes EHERE, then—in case the length of the contents of the current cell is less than the width, causing extraneous spaces in EFORM—it trims any leading or trailing zeros from the copy in EFORM.

{EFORM}{panelon}{windowson}{edit}{quit} Runs the subroutine at EFORM, typing the contents of EFORM in the upper panel, then turns the windows and panel back on, switches to Edit mode, and quits.

NOTE: *This macro will not work in 1-2-3 releases other than 2.x. However, if you have one of the Release 2.x versions, you can see an example of the macro running by setting up your worksheet like Figure 10.16. Don't forget to use /Range Name Labels Right on the range of names in D10 through D17. If you enter the formula shown in the upper panel in E19, and (still at cell E19) press the F2 Edit key, you will see the formula in the Edit Control Panel showing cell coordinates instead of range names. Press Esc, then Alt+E (Ctrl+E in 1-2-3 for Windows). The formula in the Edit Control Panel changes to show range names as in Figure 10.16, which you can then edit.*

Using @Clean to Eliminate ASCII Characters

Just as the @trim function eliminates extraneous spaces from an imported file, so does the @clean function eliminate extraneous characters represented by ASCII codes 0 to 32 that may be imported in the process of pulling in another file. These codes may be special formatting characters, indentations, or print attributes such as those used to print italic type.

The @clean formula works on any string up to 240 characters in Release 2.x and up to 516 characters in all higher releases. As with the other string functions, referencing the string directly requires that you enclose the string in full quotes. A more likely scenario, however, is that the @trim function refers to a cell address or range name representing a single cell. This function will not work on a range of cells, since it can apply to only one string at a time.

Since ASCII characters 0 to 32 are not visible within 1-2-3, the string being "cleaned" and the @clean version of the string look identical. For this reason, it is a good idea to use the @clean function on every string or line being imported where the string is suspected to have one or more of the 0 to 32 ASCII codes.

The @Repeat Function

The @repeat function is used to repeat a character or string a designated number of times by using the syntax:

@repeat(*string*,*n*)

Just as you can fill a cell with multiple instances of a character by typing a backslash and the character (for example, \X fills the cell with a series of X's), you can also repeat a character like the letter X a specific number of times (12, for example) by typing a formula like **@repeat("X",12).** This means that you can use the @repeat function to extend past the width of one cell to any width required, up to 240 characters.

You can also use @repeat in combination with the @char function to repeat symbols not found on the keyboard, as you'll see in the next section.

The @Code and @Char Functions

The @code and @char functions are mirror images of each other and are used to replicate and manipulate the ASCII characters for ASCII codes 33 through 255.

The @code function uses the syntax:

@code(*character*)

and the @char function uses the syntax:

@char(*code*)

For example, **@char(33)** returns the character corresponding to the ASCII code 33: the exclamation point (!). Conversely, typing **@code("!")** returns the number 33.

To explore the ASCII characters that cannot be invoked in 1-2-3 by pressing a single key on your keyboard, follow these steps:

1. Move to an area of your worksheet that has at least two blank columns and select /Data Fill, highlight a vertical range covering 255 cells, and select a Start of 0, a Step of 1, and a stop of 8192.
2. Move to the blank column to the right and type **@char** and an opening parenthesis, type a plus (+) symbol, point to the cell to the left, close the parenthesis, and press Enter.
3. Copy the formula down 255 cells by selecting /Copy; at the prompt for a destination range, highlight to the left one cell, press End Down, unhighlight back to the right, and press Enter twice.

That's all there is to it. Now you can explore the symbols and make a note of the symbols you might like to use to dress up your spreadsheet—perhaps by surrounding the @char function with the @repeat function to create an entire line of a specific symbol.

Figure 10.17 shows a table of codes and their corresponding symbols that you won't find on the keyboard, but which you can create by using **@char(*code*)**.

Of course, you can repeat any of these symbols several times in a cell by using the @repeat function. For example, to repeat the smiling face symbol (☺) 12 times, you simply enter:

```
@repeat(@char(1),12)
```

If you specified the Extended Font set when you installed your version of 1-2-3, you also have access to a complete set of Wingding symbols that go beyond those symbols you can create from the keyboard. Figure 10.18 shows many of the codes and corresponding @char symbols you can access. For example, to repeat a diamond shape (◆) 12 times, use the WYSIWYG command :Format Font to assign the Wingding font to the current cell (typically Font 8), then enter the formula:

```
@repeat(@char(41),12)
```

Code	Char	Code	Char	Code	Char	Code	Char	Code	Char	Code	Char	Code	Char	Code	Char	Code	Char
1	☺	19	‼	135	ç	153	Ö	171	½	189	¢	207	¤	225	ß	243	¾
2	☻	20		136	ê	154	Ü	172	¼	190	¥	208	ð	226	Ô	244	
3	♥	21	§	137	ë	155	ø	173	¡	191	⌐	209	Đ	227	Ò	245	§
4	♦	22	▬	138	è	156	£	174	«	192	└	210	Ê	228	õ	246	÷
5	♣	23	↕	139	ï	157	Ø	175	»	193	┴	211	Ë	229	Õ	247	‚
6	♠	24	↑	140	î	158	×	176	⠿	194	┬	212	È	230	µ	248	°
7	•	25	↓	141	ì	159	ƒ	177	▨	195	├	213	ı	231	þ	249	¨
8	◘	26	→	142	Ä	160	á	178	▦	196	─	214	Í	232	Þ	250	•
9	○	27	←	143	Å	161	í	179	│	197	┼	215	Î	233	Ú	251	¹
10	◙	28	∟	144	É	162	ó	180	┤	198	ã	216	Ï	234	Û	252	³
11	♂	29	↔	145	æ	163	ú	181	Á	199	Ã	217	┘	235	Ù	253	²
12	♀	128	Ç	146	Æ	164	ñ	182	Â	200	╚	218	┌	236	ý	254	■
13	♪	129	ü	147	ô	165	Ñ	183	À	201	╔	219	█	237	Ÿ	255	
14	♫	130	é	148	ö	166	ª	184	©	202	╩	220	▄	238	¯		
15	☼	131	â	149	ò	167	º	185	╣	203	╦	221	¦	239	´		
16	►	132	ä	150	û	168	¿	186	║	204	╠	222	Ì	240	─		
17	◄	133	à	151	ù	169	®	187	╗	205	═	223	▀	241	±		
18	↕	134	å	152	ÿ	170	¬	188	╝	206	╬	224	Ó	242	＿		

FIGURE 10.17 Codes and corresponding @char symbols.

NOTE: *You should be aware that your printer may not print out many of these symbols or may print something different on your paper than you see on the screen. To test which symbols your printer can accommodate, simply print out the range of @char functions you created following the steps above.*

The @Exact Function

The @exact function was covered in the last chapter. To review, this function is used to compare two strings for an exact match, including a match of upper versus lowercase. The syntax of this function is as follows:

```
@exact(first string,second string)
```

If the first string is exactly the same as the second string, this function returns the number 1 indicating the condition is true. If the two strings do not match, a 0 is returned indicating that the condition is false.

Code	Char	Code	Char	Code	Char	Code	Char	Code	Char	Code	Char
33	✂	51	⑧	69	⑥	87	↕	105	⇨	123	↔
34	✁	52	⑨	70	⑦	88	↘	106	⇨	124	➡
35	✂	53	⑩	71	⑧	89	→	107	⇦	125	➡
36	✃	54	❶	72	⑨	90	↗	108	⇨	126	⇨
37	✄	55	❷	73	⑩	91	✈	109	⇩	127	
38	✆	56	❸	74	❶	92	➔	110	⇧	128	
39	☎	57	❹	75	❷	93	→	111	⇨	129	
40	✉	58	❺	76	❸	94	→	112		130	
41	✦	59	❻	77	❹	95	↦	113	⇨	131	
42	✌	60	❼	78	❺	96	➠	114	⊃	132	
43	☞	61	❽	79	❻	97	➡	115	⊨	133	
44	①	62	❾	80	❼	98	≻	116	↘	134	
45	②	63	❿	81	❽	99	≻	117	⊬	135	
46	③	64	①	82	❾	100	➢	118	✗	136	
47	④	65	②	83	❿	101	➡	119	↘	137	
48	⑤	66	③	84	→	102	➡	120	⊬	138	
49	⑥	67	④	85	→	103	▮	121	✈	139	
50	⑦	68	⑤	86	↔	104	➡	122	↔	140	

FIGURE 10.18 Codes and corresponding @char symbols in the Wingding font.

The Non-Standard Entries Corrected macro shown in the last chapter (Figure 9.8) is one example of the use of @exact. That macro is designed to move down a sorted database cleaning up slight variations in the way the data was entered.

The @Replace Function

The @replace function is used to replace a portion of a string with specified characters or to add or delete specified characters in a predefined location of a string. The format is as follows:

```
@replace(string or cell,starting location,# characters,new
string)
```

To apply the @replace function to the word "Application" to return the word "Indication," for example, enter this:

```
@replace("Application",0,4,"Ind")
```

Accordingly, if you have the string ANTELOPE HILL in cell B7, you can use @replace to return the word ANTHILL by typing:

```
@replace(B7,3,6,"")
```

If you have a name like *Edvard H. Grieg* in cell C8 and you want to eliminate the middle initial to display simply *Edvard Grieg,* you can type:

```
@replace(C8,@find(" ",C8,0),3,"")
```

Using @Replace in a Self-Modifying Macro

The View @Sum macro in Figure 10.19 provides an interesting example of a self-modifying macro that uses @replace in combination with @left and @length to create a variable line.

This macro automatically highlights the range in an @sum macro, providing you with a view of the range without your having to manually verify the cell coordinates and visit the range with your cell pointer.

To start, place your cell pointer on any cell with an @sum formula and invoke the macro. The message **SUM RANGE IS:** appears in the left of the top panel and the range coordinates appear in the right. More importantly, the range will be highlighted, so you can verify whether the range is what you want. If not, you can manually adjust the range with your pointer keys. Any adjustment you make automatically updates the @sum formula at the same time.

Here's how the macro works:

{windowsoff}{paneloff}{edit}{home}'~   Turns off the windows and panel to suppress screen flicker and speed up the macro, then converts the @sum formula to a label.

{let VFORM,@cellpointer("contents")}~   Copies the label form of the @sum formula to VFORM.

{edit}{home}{del}~{recalc VRANGE}   Changes the @sum label back to a formula by deleting the apostrophe, then recalculates the self-modifying cell of the macro named VRANGE.

/rncSUM RANGE IS:~~/rndSUM RANGE IS:~/rncSUM RANGE IS:~   Begins the creation of a new range named SUM RANGE IS: in preparation for a later use of this range name as a prompt to the user.

C13..C15   This line establishes the range coordinates for the range name SUM RANGE IS:. Although in our example this cell displays C13..C15, it is actually the result of running the macro on

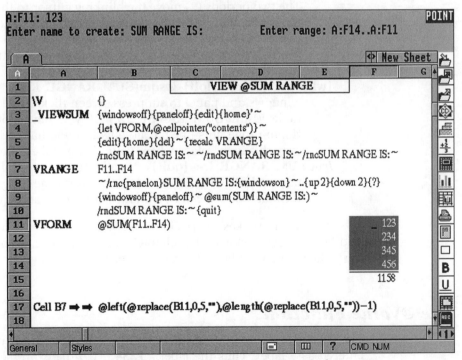

FIGURE 10.19 Macro to view the range of an @Sum Formula.

the @sum formula (that in this case sums the range C13..C15.) Underlying this display is the formula:

```
@left(@replace(B11,0,5,""),@length(@replace(B11,0,5,"")))-1)
```

where B11 is the cell address for the cell of the macro named VFORM. (As you type this in yourself, use the cell address that corresponds to VFORM in your own worksheet.)

The @replace portion of this formula is used to eliminate the five leftmost characters of the @sum formula in B11 by replacing them with the null string "". By itself the formula **@replace (B11,0,5,"")** would display **F11..F14**), with a closing parenthesis. The @left portion of the formula is used To eliminate the parenthesis on the right by extracting the number of characters equal to one less than the length of the results of the @replace formula, leaving us with F11..F14.

~/rnc{panelon}SUM RANGE IS:{windowson}~..{up 2}{down 2}{?} The tilde completes the /Range Name Create sequence. The macro then starts the sequence again, turning on the upper panel this time before SUM RANGE IS: appears. The windows are turned on so you can see the highlighted range in the worksheet. The two periods (..) move the blinking cursor to the upper part of the range, then the cell pointer is moved up two cells, then down two cells to provide a better view of the range. At this point, the macro pauses so you can view the @sum range and accept it or modify it as required.

{windowsoff}{paneloff}~@sum(SUM RANGE IS:)~ Turns off the windows and panel to suppress screen flicker and enters the formula @sum(SUM RANGE IS:). If you have not adjusted the @sum range, this line has no effect. If you have adjusted it, however, this is the place where your change takes effect.

/rndSUM RANGE IS:~{quit} Finally, the macro deletes the range name SUM RANGE IS:, which converts the range of the @sum formula back to cell coordinates, and the macro quits.

This macro makes a very effective and useful companion macro to the Add Macro discussed in earlier chapters, and should be strongly considered for inclusion in any Macro Library collection of macros.

The @Value Function

The @value function is used to return the value of a number that has been entered as a label. Thus the label " **12345**" can be expressed as the value **12345** with the formula **@value(" 12345")**.

The @value formula can convert the label '**123.875** to the value **123.875,** or the scientific notation label '**3.25E3** to **3250**, or the label fraction '**3 3/4** to **3.75**. As you might expect, these @value formulas can be added together. They cannot be used, however, to calculate a sum statement entered as a label. Thus an @value formula such as **@value(''3 3/4 + 7 7/8'')** returns an ERR message.

For this reason, a telephone number such as the '**301-555-1212** is not calculated by the @value function to return the difference of 301 minus 555 minus 1212. Instead the function returns ERR.

However, the @value function returns the value of numbers typed as labels in the currency or percent format. Thus the function **@value (''$123,000.00'')** returns **123000** in F16, and the function **@value(''12.3%'')** returns **0.123**. Of course, you can always format the cell containing the @value function to display Currency or Percent if you want the formats to show in the value version of these numbers.

One format for numbers which cannot be read by the @value function is the +/– format. The @value function **@value(''++++++'')**, for example, returns ERR. Similarly, the formula **@value(''Sales'')** in Cell D20 returns an ERR because the @value function cannot read nonnumeric labels.

The @N Function

The @n function is used to return the value of the upper-left entry in a range. Typing **@n(A5..C9)** where cell A5 contains the value 1234, for example, returns the value 1234.

The @n function also works on a single-cell range such as **@n(A5..A5)** where cell A5 contains the value 1234, still returning the value 1234.

The @n function will not convert a numeric label to a value as the @value function does. And whereas the formula **@value(A1..A1)** returns ERR if A1 contains the word *''Budget,''* the formula **@n(A1..A1)** returns a zero. Using the @n is therefore especially useful when you are not sure whether the cell or upper left corner of the range being referred to begins with a label or a number; but in either case, you do not want ERR displayed.

Even if the range in the @n function is typed in reverse order—if you type **@n(C3..C1)**, for example, instead of **@n(A1..C3)**—the result is still the value of the cell in the upper left corner of the range: A1 in this case. If the range being referred to is entirely blank, the @n function returns a zero.

The @S Function

The @s function is similar to the @n function in that it has as its argument a range address rather than the address of a single cell. But whereas the @n function returns a value when referring to a range of numbers and a zero when referring to a range of labels, the @s function returns a string when referring to a range of labels and a blank cell when referring to a range of numbers.

The formula **@s(A5..C13)**, for example, returns the string *Sales* when A5 contains the string *Sales*. On the other hand, the formula **@s(A5..C13)** referring to a blank range returns a blank cell. The formulas **@s(A5..C13)** referring to a range that begins with the number 1234 also returns a blank cell.

If the @s formula refers to a string as in the example **@s("Sales"),** the result is ERR. This is because the @s and @n functions, unlike most of the other string functions, require a range address or range name and will not accept a string as their argument.

Summary

In this chapter we have reviewed the science of string formulas and the use of the special string manipulation features of 1-2-3 to combine two or more elements into a single word or phrase. We defined the concept of string formulas and the individual string @functions and explored their purpose and application in cells of the spreadsheet to create variable entries and in macros that require variable or self-modifying lines. We also looked at the use of string formulas and string @ functions in combination with other @ functions of 1-2-3.

Uses and techniques of the individual string @functions were reviewed, as follows:

- Using the @string function to change numeric values to strings, allowing you to specify the number of decimal places to be used for a string.
- Using the @upper, @lower, and @proper functions to change a string to uppercase, lowercase, or proper case. These functions will not work on numbers or formulas displayed as values unless such entries are converted to labels with the @string function. A macro to automate the conversion of case in a column was also presented.
- Using the @length function to determine the number of characters in a string. The @length function will not provide the length of a number entered as a value. A Width of Column Changed macro was presented to automatically increase or decrease the width of a column to accommodate the length of a label at the current cell. An enhanced version of this macro was included to accommodate the length of a number at the current cell.
- Using the @find function to search a string for the first occurrence of one or more characters starting at a designated position in the

string. The use of nested @find statements was also presented to locate the second occurrence of the characters established as the search criteria.

- Using the @left function to return a specified number of characters from a string, starting from the leftmost character. Use of @left with @find was reviewed to show a technique for extracting a variable length string, such as the last name from a list of first name-last name entries.

- Using the @right function to return a specified number of characters from a string, starting from the rightmost character. The @right function can also be used in conjunction with the @length and @find functions to extract and display a variable length string or to reverse a last name-first name order of customer names to first name-last name order and vice-versa. A macro was also presented to extract the first name, last name, or middle initial from a database of names.

- Using the @mid function to extract a portion of a string based on a starting position and including a specified number of characters. A macro using @mid was presented, designed to change Label-Dates to @Date Formulas and vice-versa.

- Using the @trim function to trim away extraneous spaces in a string. This is especially useful in conjunction with the {contents} command or when importing files over from other programs such as database files that appear with spaces between the fields. The {contents} command was compared with the {let} command and codes for optional attributes of {contents} were shown. Two macros using {contents} and @trim were presented: one to change the column width to match a label or a value and the other to allow you to edit a formula's range names.

- Using the @clean function to eliminate extraneous ASCII codes from 0 to 32 which may be imported in the process of pulling in another file. These codes may be special formatting characters or indentations or print attributes, such as those used to print italic face type.

- Using the @repeat function to create a string of repeating characters that can extend past the width of one cell. You can have different combinations of repeating characters, including those not found on the keyboard.

- Using the @Code and @Char functions to replicate and manipulate the ASCII characters for ASCII codes 33 through 255. Instructions were given on creation of a table of characters using @Char, including Wingding characters.

- Using the @exact function to compare two strings for an exact match, including a match of upper versus lowercase.

- Using the @replace function to replace a portion of a string with specified characters or to add or delete specified characters in a predefined location of a string. A macro was automatically highlighted to give you a view of the range of any @sum formula.
- Using the @value function to return the value of a number entered as a label. The most useful feature of the @value function is its ability to return the value of numbers typed as labels in the fraction, scientific notation, currency, or percent format.
- Using the @n function to return the value of the upper-left entry in a range. The @n function will not convert a numeric label to a value as the @value function does.
- Using the @s function to return the upper left string in a range. A blank cell is returned when the @s function refers to a range where the upper left cell contains a value or a blank cell.

In the next chapter we review looping macros that include counters using the {let} command. We will also look at counters using the {for} command, especially in conjunction with @index and the {put} command.

11

Counters and the {for} Loop

In Chapter 9, you saw how to use the {if} command in a macro that loops until the cell pointer encounters a blank cell. This chapter explores ways to make your macro loop a designated number of times in two other ways: by using {if} with the {let} command and by using the more advanced {for} command.

Width of Columns Changed

In Release 2.2 and higher, you can change the width of several columns at once using /Worksheet Column Column-Range Set. Up to that point, column widths could only be changed one at a time—unless, of course, you used a macro.

The macro in Figure 11.1 is used in earlier releases of 1-2-3 to change the column widths of any number of columns you designate. Even if you have Release 2.2 or higher, you may find this an interesting use of the {if} and {let} commands to cause the macro to loop a number of times based on an internal counter.

{getlabel "ENTER THE REVISED COLUMNWIDTH: ", WIDTH}
The macro starts with a prompt for the width you want. Notice

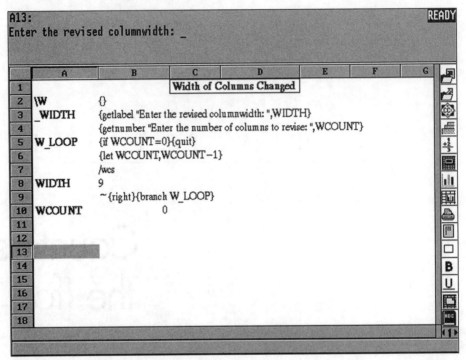

FIGURE 11.1 Using a counter to change a range of column widths.

the use of {getlabel}, which inserts your response in the cell named WIDTH as a label, not as a value. This is done because the response is needed as a self-modifying line of the macro itself, which means it must be entered as a string.

{getnumber "ENTER THE NUMBER OF COLUMNS TO REVISE: ",WCOUNT} This is the beginning of a method for creating a counter. In this case, a counter is set up at the cell named WCOUNT. The {getnumber} prompt allows the user to store a new count value from which the macro will count down to zero. For example, if you wanted to revise the columns F through P, you would enter the number 11 at this point and the macro would count down from 11 to zero.

> **NOTE:** *Here we are using {getnumber} rather than {getlabel}, since the macro will be doing an arithmetic operation on the responded value.*

{if WCOUNT=0}{end}{left}{quit} This line uses the {if} command to test whether the value in WCOUNT has reached zero. If so, the macro moved the cell pointer End LeftArrow and quit.

{let WCOUNT,WCOUNT-1}   Otherwise, the macro changes the cell named WCOUNT to WCOUNT-1, the value which is one number less than the current value of WCOUNT. This is how the macro counts down from 11 to zero.

/wcs   The macro presses /Worksheet Columnwidth Set to change the width of the current column. The next line of the macro is your response to the {getlabel} prompt, reflecting the column width you want.

~{right}{branch W_LOOP}   You might think that a tilde followed by a {right} command is redundant, but both are required. The tilde is the only entry command the /Worksheet Columnwidth Set sequence will recognize to enter your revised column width and the {right} is required to move the cell pointer one cell to the right after the column width is changed.

The macro loops back to the cell W_LOOP and checks and decrements the counter. It will continue in this way until the counter (the value in WCOUNT) reaches zero.

Rather than watching the width of each column change one column at a time, you may want to modify this macro by inserting a row before the W_LOOP line and adding {windowsoff} and {paneloff} commands. This speeds up the macro and delays a display of the resulting changes until the end of the macro.

A Slide Show of Graphs

There are several uses we can make of this ability to create a macro counter that increments or decrements (counts up or down) with each pass through a macro loop. The macro in Figure 11.2 is just such an example, designed to allow a type of slide show of your graphs. This is especially useful during presentations where, instead of having to select /Graph Name Use and point to graphs displayed in alphabetical order, you can simply select *Forward* or *Backwards* to move instantly forward or backwards through graphs named GRAPH1, GRAPH2, GRAPH3, in the order you would like to see them.

Before starting this macro, create or retrieve a worksheet of graphs, then use /Graph Name Create to give the names GRAPH1, GRAPH2, GRAPH3, and so on, to each graph. Be careful not to include a space between the word GRAPH and the number or this macro will not work. For example, do *not* name a graph GRAPH 3.

{blank S_COUNT}   The macro begins by using the {blank} command to zero the counter cell.

{menubranch S_MENU}{quit}   Calls up the menu choices, *Forward* and *Backwards*. To view the first graph, select *Forward*.

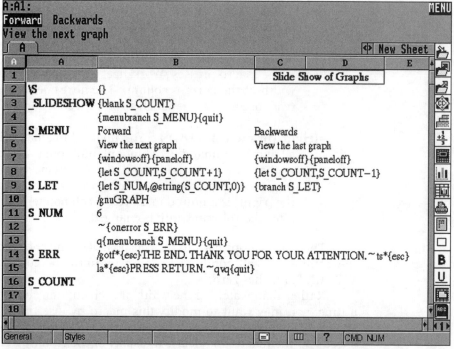

FIGURE 11.2 Using a counter to present a slide show of graphs.

{windowsoff}{paneloff} Strangely, these commands do not affect the display of the graph or the display of the custom menu choices *Forward* and *Backwards*. However, between graphs you will see the *Forward* and *Backwards* menu choices shown on an otherwise blank screen. This isolates the menu commands for your slide show so as not to distract your audience with columns and rows of numbers between graphs.

{let S_COUNT,S_COUNT+1} or **{let S_COUNT,S_COUNT-1}** If you select *Forward,* the counter is incremented by one using the {let} command. If you select *Backwards,* the counter is reduced by one.

{let S_NUM,@string(S_COUNT,0)} Whether you selected *Forward* or *Backwards,* the macro continues at this cell named S_LET. The purpose of this line is to copy a string version (with no decimals) of the new value in S_COUNT to S_NUM, a self-modifying cell of the macro used to designate the next graph name.

/gnuGRAPH Starts the selection /Graph Name Use, then types the word GRAPH. The next line at S_NUM completes the name. Thus, if the next graph to view is GRAPH3, there will be a string version of the number 3 in S_NUM.

~{onerror S_ERR}   The macro completes the /Graph Name Use command with the tilde.

This is our first use of the {onerror} command. This command tells 1-2-3 where to branch in the event the macro comes to an error condition or you decide to stop it by pressing Ctrl+Break. The {onerror} command uses as its argument the cell where the macro should continue. Like the {windowsoff} and {paneloff} commands, it stays in effect until the macro ends or until you disable it. You can disable an {onerror} command with a subsequent {onerror} that includes no argument.

In this case, if there is no GRAPH7, yet 7 is the next number this macro increments to after viewing GRAPH6, operating without an {onerror} command will result in the macro quitting with a beep and an error message. With the command {onerror S_ERR}, however, meeting the error condition will cause the macro to continue to operate at the routine beginning at S_ERR.

q{menubranch S_MENU}{quit}   If the macro does not come to an error, it quits the /Graph menu and branches to the custom menu at S_MENU where it once again offers a screen that is blank except for the two menu choices, *Forward* and *Backwards*.

/gotf*{esc}THE END. THANK YOU FOR YOUR ATTENTION.~ts*{esc}   Otherwise, if there is no graph matching the graph name the macro is attempting to view, the error condition will cause a branch to this cell at S_ERR where it will select /Graph Options Title First, press an asterisk and Esc to clear the first title, enter for your audience the title, "THE END. THANK YOU FOR YOUR ATTENTION," and clear the second title with Title Second and a press of asterisk and Esc.

la*{esc}PRESS ENTER.~qvq{quit}   Finally, the macro changes the Legend for the A-Range to one last instruction, "PRESS ENTER," quits that level of the graph menu and shows a view of the graph. You will see the same graph you last viewed, but with the informative titles as shown in Figure 11.3. After this, the macro quits the /Graph menu and returns to Ready.

> **NOTE:** *In Release 3 and higher, you can clear a prompt with the command {CE} (for "Clear Entry"). The asterisk-Esc sequence is used here to cover all releases, including those before Release 3.*

If you select the *Backwards* menu choice, the slide show of graphs proceeds backwards to GRAPH1, and then to an attempt to view GRAPH0—which does not, of course, exist. In that case, the error causes the macro to branch to S_ERR where the last graph viewed is displayed again with the same ending message.

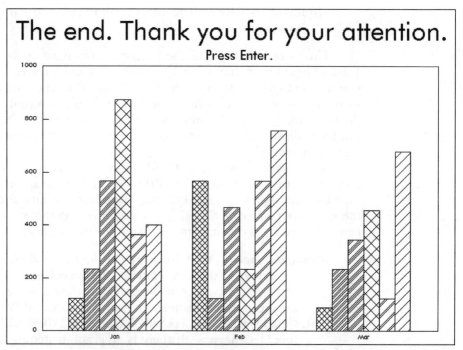

FIGURE 11.3 An example of the last graph in your slide show.

Squeeze a Column to Eliminate Spaces

From time to time you may encounter a situation where blank cells have crept into a column of data. For example, you may have inserted several rows off to the right, not realizing that you were affecting a column to the left that should not include blank cells or rows.

The macro in Figure 11.4 uses a counter to provide a quick fix for this type of problem. Its purpose is to squeeze the filled cells in a column together into one contiguous range of viable data, but without affecting the columns to the right or left of the column being squeezed.

{windowsoff}{paneloff}/rncCOL TO SQUEEZE?~~/rndCOL TO SQUEEZE?~ Turns off the windows and panel to suppress screen flicker, then creates and deletes the range name COL TO SQUEEZE? intended as a user prompt.

/rnc{panelon}COL TO SQUEEZE?~{windowson}{?}~ Again creates the range name COL TO SQUEEZE, turning the panel on just before this prompting range name appears. The windows are turned on just before the macro pause {?} to allow you to paint in the range you want to squeeze.

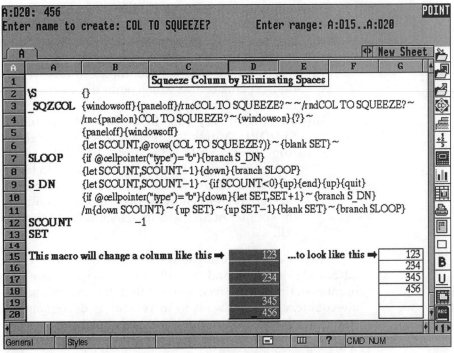

FIGURE 11.4 A macro to squeeze a column by eliminating spaces.

{let SCOUNT,@rows(COL TO SQUEEZE)}~{blank SET} Changes the count in the counter SCOUNT to a value matching the number of rows in the range you have just highlighted. The counter at SET is set at zero by blanking the cell.

{if @cellpointer("type")="b"}{branch S_DN} This is the beginning of the routine named SLOOP. This routine begins by determining if the cell pointer has come to a blank cell. If so, the macro branches to the routine at S_DN.

{let S_COUNT,S_COUNT-1}{down}{branch SLOOP} Otherwise, the counter at S_SCOUNT is decremented by one, the cell pointer is moved down to the next cell, and the macro loops back to SLOOP to check whether the next cell is blank.

{let SCOUNT,SCOUNT-1}~{if SCOUNT <0}{up}{end}{up}{quit} If the next cell is blank, the macro branches to this line at S_DN where it decrements the counter by one and checks for whether the counter is now less than zero. If so, the macro must have run its course and the cell pointer is moved UpArrow End UpArrow to the top of the column of data and the macro quits.

{if @cellpointer("type")="b"}{down}{let SET,SET+1}~{branch S_DN}
Once again the macro checks the cell to determine if it is blank. If so, the cell pointer is moved down one cell, the counter at SET is increased by one, and the macro branches back to the previous macro line at S_DN. It continues in this way until it no longer finds a blank cell, at which point the macro starts the /Move command on the next line.

/m{down SCOUNT}~{up SET}~{up SET-1}{blank SET~{branch SLOOP} Moves the remainder of the original column of data from its current location up to the cell below the last filled cell. The macro knows how many rows down to highlight because the counter at SCOUNT was decremented each time it moved down one cell. It knows how far up to move the column of data because the counter at SET was incremented each time it came to a blank cell.

As you will see throughout the remainder of this chapter, 1-2-3 has an advanced {for} command that allows you to loop your macro a designated number of times. However, you will find that you still have occasions to create counters that you want to increment or decrement and test using {if} statements based on certain established criteria.

Changing Zeros to Blank Spaces

One little-used feature of 1-2-3 is the ability to suppress zero displays in your worksheet by selecting /Worksheet Global Zero Yes. This can be handy when your worksheet is filled with formulas that return scores of unsightly zeros if the cells on which they depend are empty.

Unfortunately, there are two drawbacks to this feature. First, when you save your file, the /File Save command does not remember that you wanted the zeros suppressed, so when you retrieve the file later the zeros are all visible again. Second, the zero suppression is a global command, but you may want to have zeros suppressed in a range of your worksheet only.

Fortunately, there is a simple macro solution to the first of these drawbacks. If you want the zeros permanently suppressed on a given worksheet, you only have to add an autoexecute (\0) macro to type /Worksheet Global Zero Yes, as follows:

```
\0        /wgzy{quit}
```

With this macro, each time this file is retrieved you will see the file for an instant with the zeros visible. Then the autoexec macro runs and all of the zeros in your worksheet are suppressed.

As for the occasional need to suppress zeros in a range of your spreadsheet only, the macro in Figure 11.5, called Omit Zeros, Replace with Blank Spaces, uses a {for} command to accomplish that task.

This macro uses a counter just as in the macros above, but it applies its magic to an entire matrix of cells rather than simply to a column. To do that, it uses an example of a loop-within-a-loop.

{getnumber "ENTER # OF COLUMNS TO TEST: ",OCOL}   Prompts you for the number of columns to the right you want to test for zeros. Your response is stored in the cell named OCOL.

{getnumber "ENTER # OF ROWS TO TEST: ",OROW}   Prompts you for the number of rows down you want to test for zeros. Your response is stored in the cell named OROW. Figure 11.6 is an example of a matrix of values with zero cells, showing the macro prompt for the number of rows to test.

{indicate   MACRO}{windowsoff}{paneloff}   The {indicate} command changes the indicator in the upper right panel from the word READY to a message to the macro user.

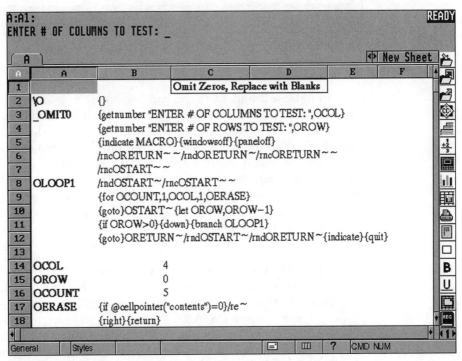

FIGURE 11.5 A macro to omit zeros, replace with blank spaces.

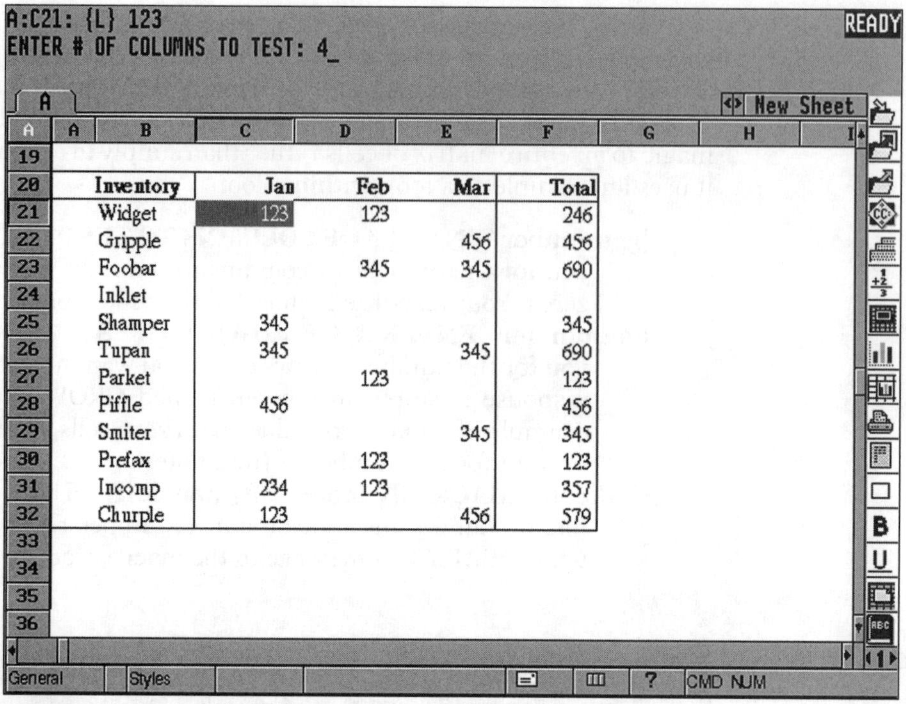

A:C21: {L} 123
ENTER # OF COLUMNS TO TEST: 4_   READY

Inventory	Jan	Feb	Mar	Total
Widget	123	123		246
Gripple			456	456
Foobar		345	345	690
Inklet				
Shamper	345			345
Tupan	345		345	690
Parket		123		123
Piffle	456			456
Smiter			345	345
Prefax		123		123
Incomp	234	123		357
Churple	123		456	579

FIGURE 11.6 An example using the Omit Zeros macro.

In Release 2 and 2.01, you can use any five-letter word with the {indicate} command. In this case, because the windows and panels are being turned off during execution of most of the macro, the indicator changes from READY to the word MACRO to remind you that a macro is running. Of course, you can change the word to something else like ZEROS or BLANK, but keep in mind that only the first five letters of the word you choose will appear in the indicator panel in the early 1-2-3 releases.

In Release 2.2 and higher, you can use any message in the {indicate} command up to 256 letters, but you will want to limit your message to one that fits in the upper panel: typically, 72 characters.

/rncORETURN~~/rndORETURN~~/rncORETURN~~ Creates a place-marker at the original cell of the matrix called ORETURN.

/rncOSTART~~ Begins the create-delete-create sequence for the range name OSTART.

/rndOSTART~/rncOSTART~~ Creates a place-marker called OSTART that moves down row-by-row in this column as each row is processed. Notice that this line of the macro is in a cell called OLOOP1, marking the beginning of a counting loop using {let}, {if}, and a counter. Within this loop (in the next line of the macro) is another counting loop using the {for} command.

{for OCOUNT,1,OCOL,1,OERASE} The {for} command is a short-hand method of creating a way to loop in a macro a designated number of times. Instead of using the {let} and {if} commands at the beginning and end of the counted loop you want to run, you can use a {for} command that goes ahead of the loop and tells it how many times to increment.

The format of the {for} command is *{for* followed by the *counter location*, the *start* value, the *stop* value or *cell location containing the stop* value, the *step* value, and the *loop name}*. This means that you can have a {for} command that looks like this: *{for WCOUNT,1,100,1,WLOOP}* if you know you want it to loop 100 times; or like this: *{for WCOUNT,1,WSTOP,1,WLOOP}* if you have included the stop value in the cell named WSTOP.

The {for} line of this macro, then, might be read like this: *At the cell named OCOUNT, start counting at the number 1, and count until the number in OCOL is reached, counting by ones, and for each increment loop to the subroutine called OERASE.* As you'll see in the last lines in the Figure 11.5 macro, the OERASE subroutine reads

```
{if @cellpointer("contents")=0}/re~
```

which erases every cell displaying a zero. Actually, in Release 2.2 and higher, you can use the commands

```
{if @cellpointer("contents")=0}{blank @cellpointer("contents")}
```

which will operate faster, since no tilde affecting a recalculation is required.

The next cell down reads {right} {return}, moving the cell pointer one cell to the right and returning control of the macro to the line immediately following the {for} command.

{goto}OSTART~{let OROW,OROW-1} The cell pointer moves back to the beginning of the row. You will remember we created a place-marker in the first cell of the row called OSTART. The next command decrements the counter at OROW (where the macro has stored the number of rows you want tested) to record the fact that the first row of the matrix has been processed.

{if OROW>0}{down}{branch OLOOP1} If the row counter is still greater than zero, the cell pointer is moved down to the next row and the whole process starts again on this row via a macro loop back to OLOOP1.

{goto}ORETURN~/rndOSTART~/rndORETURN~{indicate}{quit} Otherwise, the cell pointer is returned to the original upper left cell of the matrix which the macro named ORETURN, the two place-marker range names are deleted, the {indicate} command changes the word MACRO in the upper right indicator to READY, and the macro quits.

> **NOTE:** *Whereas the {windowsoff} and {paneloff} commands do not require corresponding {windowson} and {panelon} commands before a {quit}, the {indicate MACRO} command in the third line does require a corresponding {indicate} command to restore the indicator to READY.*

The next three cells, OCOL, OROW, and OCOUNT, are not a part of the main macro, but rather cells that are referred to in the macro. OCOL stores the number of columns that you want processed and OCOUNT is the cell where the column counting occurs with each loop. When the value in OCOUNT equals the value in OCOL, the column looping stops. The row looping is counted in the cell named OROW, which simply counts backwards to zero before it stops.

Test-and-Replace Macro

This technique of using loops and counters to test an entire matrix for zeros can also be used to test for any specified value, to be replaced with another specified value. Although a search-and-replace feature in Release 2.2 and higher can be used on strings, this feature is not available in any current release to apply to values.

Refer to the macro called Test-and-Replace Values across Columns in Figure 11.7.

This macro is similar to the Omit Zeros macro in Figure 11.5, with its {for} loop within a {let}/{if} loop; but this macro uses a {for} loop within another {for} loop.

{getnumber "ENTER # OF COLUMNS TO TEST: ",TCOL} Prompts you for the number of columns to the right you want to test for zeros. Your response is stored in the cell named TCOL.

{getnumber "ENTER # OF ROWS TO TEST: ",TROW} Prompts you for the number of rows down you want to test for zeros. Your response is stored in the cell named TROW.

{getnumber "ENTER VALUE TO TEST FOR: ",TEST} Prompts you for the value you want the macro to replace with another value. Your response is stored in the cell named TEST. A sample matrix of data with the value 999 sprinkled throughout is shown in Figure 11.8. In this example, the macro is prompting the user to "Enter value to test for."

{getnumber "ENTER REPLACEMENT VALUE: ",T_REPL} Prompts you for the replacement value you want inserted in place

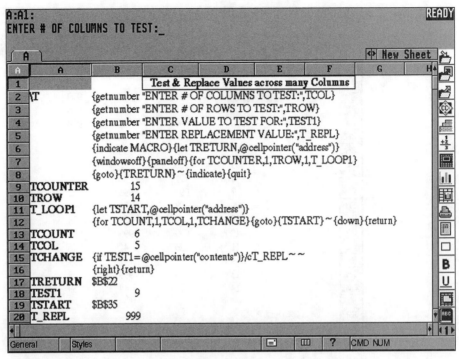

FIGURE 11.7 A macro to test-and-replace values across columns.

of the test value. Your response is stored in the cell named T_REPL.

{indicate MACRO}{let TRETURN,@cellpointer("address")} This line changes the indicator in the upper right panel from the word READY to the word MACRO to remind you that a macro is running. Of course, you can change the word to something else like TEST or REPLC (or, if you have Release 2.2 or higher, to a long message like: "Please wait . . . Macro is running . . ."), but keep in mind that there must also be an {indicate} command without an argument to return the indicator to Ready at the end of the macro.

The {let} command creates a place-marker for the original cell of the matrix by inserting the current address in the cell named TRETURN.

{windowsoff}{paneloff}{for TCOUNTER,1,TROW,1,TLOOP1} Turns off the windows and panels to speed up the macro. The {for} loop can be read: *At the cell named TCOUNTER, start counting at the number 1 and count until the number in TROW is reached, counting by ones, and for each increment loop to the subroutine called TLOOP1.*

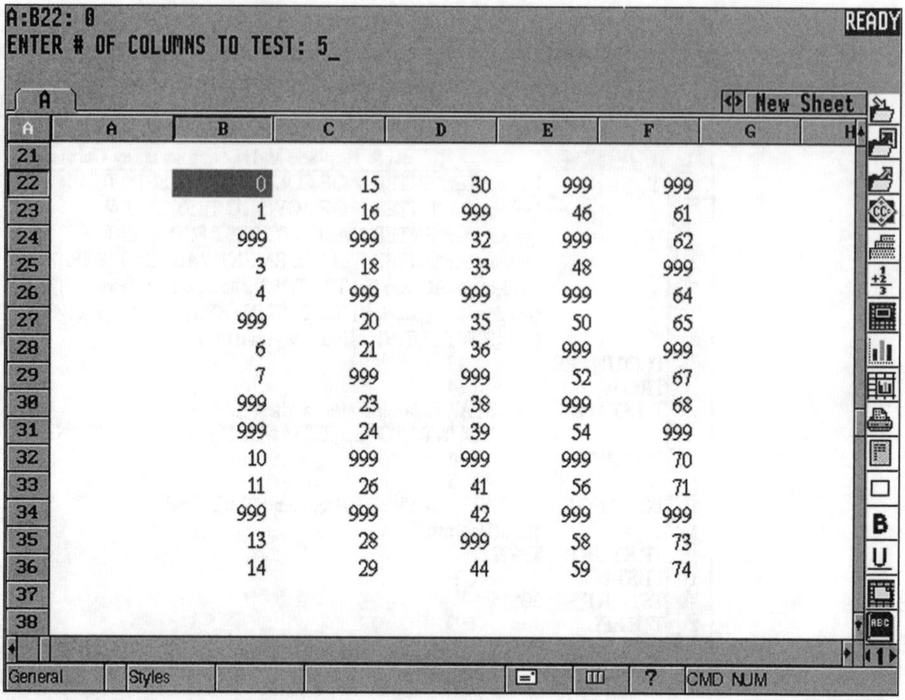

A:B22: 0
ENTER # OF COLUMNS TO TEST: 5_   READY

A	B	C	D	E	F	G
21						
22	0	15	30	999	999	
23	1	16	999	46	61	
24	999	999	32	999	62	
25	3	18	33	48	999	
26	4	999	999	999	64	
27	999	20	35	50	65	
28	6	21	36	999	999	
29	7	999	999	52	67	
30	999	23	38	999	68	
31	999	24	39	54	999	
32	10	999	999	999	70	
33	11	26	41	56	71	
34	999	999	42	999	999	
35	13	28	999	58	73	
36	14	29	44	59	74	
37						
38						

General   Styles   ? CMD NUM

FIGURE 11.8 An example using the Test & Replace Macro.

{goto}{TRETURN}~{indicate}{quit} The bulk of the macro is completed after the required number of passes through the first loop, which also contains the second loop. Although it may not appear so, this line is actually the last line of the macro. To finish up the macro, the cell pointer is returned to the original upper left cell of the matrix which the macro place-marked using the cell named TRETURN. Then the {indicate} command changes the word MACRO in the upper right indicator to READY, and the macro quits.

{let TSTART,@cellpointer("address")} This is the first cell of the subroutine called TLOOP1. It creates a place-marker stored in TSTART which will increment its row number by 1 as each row is processed.

{for TCOUNT,1,TCOL,1,TCHANGE}{goto}{TSTART}~{down}{return} The second {for} loop starts at this line, which can be read: *At the cell named TCOUNT, start counting at the number 1 and count until the number in TCOL is reached, counting by ones, and for each increment loop to the subroutine called TCHANGE.* As you'll see in the cell named TCHANGE, this subroutine reads:

```
{if TEST=@cellpointer("contents")}/cT_REPL~~
```

which replaces every cell displaying the same value as TEST with the value in **T_REPL**. Incidentally, though it will not work in Release 2 or 2.01, if you have Release 2.2 or 3 you can replace the /Copy command in this line with the following {let} command:

```
{let @cellpointer("address"),T_REPL}
```

The next cell down reads **{right}{return}**, which moves the cell pointer one cell to the right and returns control of the macro to the line beneath the {for} command.

The cell pointer moves back to the beginning of the row (you will remember we created a place-marker in the first cell of the row by storing the cell address at TSTART), then down one cell to the next row. The {return} command ends the subroutine called TLOOP1, which returns control of the macro to the macro's final line just above TCOUNTER.

> **NOTE:** *Placement of the subroutines at TLOOP1, TRETURN, TSTART, and TCHANGE is fairly arbitrary. These subroutines could have been shown in any order or in any location on your worksheet. However, you may want to keep your subroutines close to the main macros to which they apply as shown here.*

One additional technique has been used here that you may want to adopt. Neither of the subroutines at TRETURN or TSTART is followed by a cell with the {return} command; yet after running these subroutines, the program flow returns to the place where it left off in the main body of the macro. This is because a blank cell or a value cell is also interpreted by 1-2-3 as the end of the routine. We do not recommend using a blank cell for this purpose, since it can be so easily filled later without your realizing the importance of keeping the cell empty. However, using a value cell is a viable way to end a subroutine, thus saving an extra cell, shortening the length of your macro, and eliminating the need to type in a {return} command.

Adding Another Choice to /Range Search

In addition to using the {for} command with counters to search for and replace values, you can create a macro that will enhance the existing /Range Search capability found in Release 2.2 and higher by adding a new feature called Previous to the current choice for the Next found item.

Currently, selecting /Range Search results in 1-2-3 prompting you for the range, for the string to search for, for whether you want to search Formulas, Labels, or Both, and for whether you want to Find or Replace the searched item. After the first item is found, you are offered the prompts Next or Quit. There is no choice, unfortunately, called Previous. This means you can search for the fifth occurrence of a string, go past it to the sixth occurrence by mistake, and 1-2-3 offers no way to back up to the previous record.

Instead, use the macro in Figure 11.9 called "Find Next or Previous /Range Search Item."

NOTE: *This macro will not work with Release 2 or 2.01.*

/rs{?}~{?}~bf   The macro begins by selecting /Range Search, which causes 1-2-3 to prompt you for the range and string to search. The macro then selects the Both choice from the menu of Formulas, Labels, or Both, and the Find choice from the choices Find or Replace.

{panelon}{windowson}   This line has no effect the first time through, but you will notice this cell of the macro is named FLOOP. When the macro loops back to this point, this line

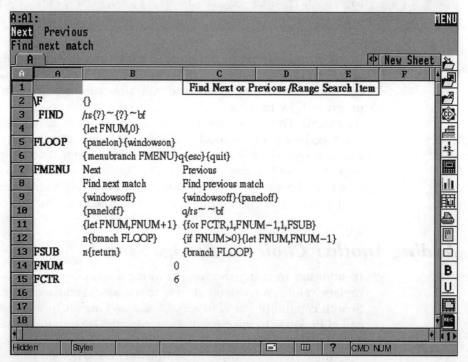

FIGURE 11.9 Macro to find the next or previous /Range Search item.

reverses the effect of the {windowsoff} and {paneloff} commands that occur later in the macro.

{menubranch FMENU}q{esc}{quit}   Calls up the menu choices Next and Previous. An example of this phase of the macro at work on a typical database is shown in Figure 11.10.

    If you press Esc at this point, the macro processes the remainder of the line, selecting Quit, pressing Esc, and quitting the macro to return to Ready.

{windowsoff}{paneloff}{let FNUM,FNUM+1}   If you select Next, the macro turns off the windows and panel and increments the counter at FNUM, storing the number of times you have selected Next. This information is required so the macro will be able to return to the record found just before the current record.

n{branch FLOOP}   The macro presses N for Next, which causes the cell pointer to jump to the line with the next found record. The macro then branches back to FLOOP to turn off the windows and panel and call up the menu choices Next and Previous again.

{windowsoff}{paneloff}q/rs~~bf   If you select Previous, the windows and panel are turned off and the macro presses Q for Quit

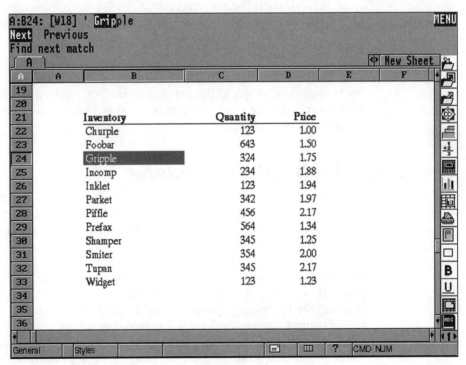

FIGURE 11.10 An example of the Find Next or Previous macro.

to leave the /Range Search menu. It then selects /Range Search and presses Enter twice to accept the already established range and string to search for, as well as repeating the previous menu selections Both and Find. In other words, the macro starts the /Range Search sequence all over again using the same criteria.

{for FCTR,1,FNUM-1,1,FSUB}   This {for} command can be read: *At the cell named FCTR, start counting at the number 1 and count until the number one less than the number in FNUM is reached, counting by ones, and for each increment loop to the subroutine called FSUB.* Since FSUB consists only of a press of N for Next, the effect is to select the next record one less time than the total number of times Next was selected before the Previous choice was made. So if you selected Next up to the sixth record, then selected Previous, this {for} command would start at the beginning and select Next five times, leaving you at the previous record viewed.

{if FNUM>0}{let FNUM,FNUM-1}   Provided FNUM is greater than 0 (which will always be the case unless you select Previous before selecting Next even once), the value in FNUM is reduced by one. This is necessary to reflect in FNUM the number of records found to reach the current record.

{branch FLOOP}   Finally, the macro branches back to FLOOP to turn off the windows and panel and call up the menu choices Next and Previous again.

That's all there is to it. By keeping track of how many times N for Next must be pressed to get to the current record, this macro is able to use a {for} loop to run through the same process that number of times, less one, to reach the previous record.

Changing Label-Numbers to Values

In Chapter 9 we explored a macro that changes numbers entered as labels into straight values. The macro did this by switching to edit mode, moving to the beginning of the entry, deleting the apostrophe in front of the number-label, and pressing Enter.

Unfortunately, this method will not work on number-labels that include commas inserted to delineate the thousandths place or millionths place. If, for example, you have a number entered as **'1,234,567.00**, simply deleting the beginning apostrophe will only result in an error and a beep.

Fortunately, you can create a macro that will take into account number-labels that include commas. The macro in Figure 11.11 uses a prompting range name, self-modifying techniques, string @ functions, recalculation of lines of the macro, and a {for} loop to accomplish this task.

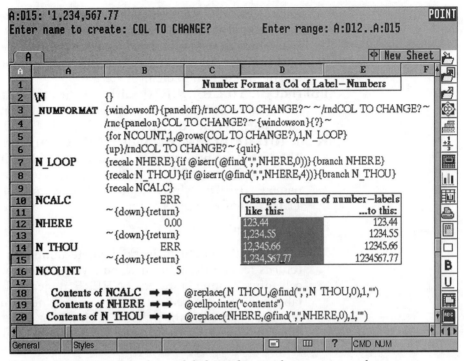

FIGURE 11.11 Macro to change label-numbers with commas to values.

To operate this macro, move to the first entry in a column of number-labels and press Alt+N (Ctrl+N in 1-2-3 for Windows). At the prompt, highlight the column of numbers you want to convert and press Enter. After a short pause, the number-labels disappear and reappear as straight values.

Here's how the macro works:

{windowsoff}{paneloff}/rncCOL TO CHANGE?~~/rndCOL TO CHANGE?~ Turns off the windows and panel to suppress screen flicker, then creates and deletes the range name COL TO CHANGE? intended as a user prompt.

/rnc{panelon}COL TO CHANGE?~{windowson}{?}~ Again creates the range name COL TO CHANGE?, turning the panel on immediately before this prompting range name appears. The windows are turned on just before the macro pause {?} to allow you to paint in the range you want to change.

{for NCOUNT,1,@rows(COL TO CHANGE?),1,N_LOOP} This {for} command can be read: *At the cell named NCOUNT, start counting at the number 1 and count until the number equal to the number of* *rows in COL TO CHANGE? is reached, counting by ones, and for each increment loop to the subroutine called N_LOOP.* Its purpose is to convert a number-label, move down one cell, convert the next number-label, and so on until the cell pointer reaches the end of the column to change.

{up}/rndCOL TO CHANGE?~{quit} At the end of the process, the cell pointer is moved up one cell, the range name COL TO CHANGE? is deleted, and the macro quits.

{recalc NHERE}{if @iserr(@find(",",NHERE,0))}{branch NHERE} This line is the beginning of the loop named N_LOOP, referred to in the {for} command above. Its purpose is to recalculate the cell named NHERE, which (though it appears as ERR in Figure 11.11) actually consists of the formula:

```
@cellpointer("contents")
```

The {if} statement works by determining that if the macro returns an error condition when trying to find a comma in the cell pointer contents stored at NHERE, it means that the number-label has been entered without a comma (the number 123 would be such a case) and the macro can simply branch to NHERE and enter the stored number-label as a value, move down one cell, and return to N_LOOP.

{recalc N_THOU}{if @iserr(@find(",",NHERE,4))}{branch N_THOU} Otherwise, if the macro, upon finding one comma, returns an error condition when trying to find a second comma starting at the fourth position of the cell pointer contents stored at NHERE, it means that the number-label has only one comma (the number 1,234 would be such a case). The macro branches to N_THOU and enters the value returned there, moves down one cell, and returns to N_LOOP.

Although N_THOU shows ERR in Figure 11.11, it returns the proper results when the cell pointer is on a cell with a number-label showing one comma. The formula underlying this cell is as follows:

```
@replace(NHERE(@find(",",NHERE,0),1,"")
```

This formula works by replacing with a null string ("") the first comma it finds in the number-label stored in NHERE, thereby eliminating the comma and showing only numbers.

{recalc NCALC} If the program flow arrives at this line of the macro, proceeding through the two {if} commands in the sixth and seventh lines, that means the macro was not diverted by the check for a number-label with no commas or only one comma. This line prepares for an extract of numbers from a number-label with two commas. It does this by recalculating the formula at NCALC.

Although the formula at NCALC shows ERR in Figure 11.11, it returns the proper results when the cell pointer is on a cell with a number-label showing two commas. The formula uses the same principle as the formula at N_THOU, except that it extracts its results from the results of N_THOU as follows:

```
@replace(N_THOU(@find(",",N_THOU,0),1,"")
```

Thus, if N_THOU displays a result such as 123456,789 from a number-label like 123,456,789, then the formula in NCALC will display a result like 123456789, without commas, by eliminating the one comma in N_THOU.

Although it seems that this macro goes through a long and complicated process to accomplish its task, you will find that it converts a column of number-labels to straight values in a surprisingly short time.

Dates Displayed One Month Apart

Counters and loops are not always required to create a repeating but variable result. Figure 11.12 provides an interesting example of a macro that prompts you for a number, then uses that information to determine how many copies to make of a complicated formula.

The purpose of this macro is to create a series of dates exactly one month apart. This has been added as a new feature of the /Data Fill command in Release 3, but a macro is required to accomplish the same task as quickly in Release 2.x.

Here's how the macro works:

{getnumber "Enter the number of months to display: ",VMONTHS}
Prompts you to enter the number of dates you want shown vertically in a column, each date exactly one month greater than the previous date. In using this macro, be sure that you are not about to write over important data below the current cell.

{getlabel "Enter the date of the 1st month: @date(",V_ENTER}
This prompt is slightly different from previous uses of the {getlabel} command. Prompts usually end with a colon. In this case, however, the prompt ends with **@date(**to indicate that the entry required should be in the @date format; since **@date(**has already been typed all that is needed is the year, the month, and the day. The macro itself will provide the closing parenthesis.

@date(Actually, the beginning of the @date formula has not been typed yet, so the macro does that now. The next line is a self-modifying cell named V_ENTER and is filled in by your response to the {getlabel} prompt.

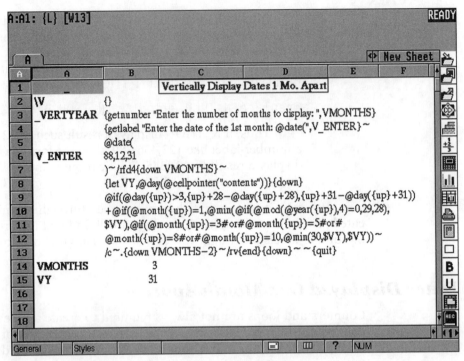

FIGURE 11.12 Vertically display dates one month apart.

)~/rfd4{down VMONTHS}~ Enters the closing parenthesis and formats the cell for date format 4 in the range that includes the current cell plus the number of cells you provided in your response to the opening {getnumber} prompt.

{let VY,@day(@cellpointer("contents"))}{down} Stores in VY the day of the month you just entered and moves down one cell.

@if(@day({up})>3,{up}+28-@day({up}+28),{up}+31-@day({up}+31)) This is the beginning of a long formula being typed into the cell below the first date you entered. Its purpose is to determine whether the day of the month entered is greater than 3 and, if so, it adds 28 to the original date, then subtracts the day of the month for a date 28 days past the original date, thus calculating the end of the month of the original date.

Here is an example using 10 April:

```
Date = 4/10/87
Date + 28 = 5/7/87
Date + 28 - @day(Date+28) = 5/7/87 - 7 = 4/31/87
```

If the day of the month entered is not greater than 3, the macro adds 31 to the original date and subtracts the day of the month for a date 31 days past the original date, which also calculates the end of the month of the original date.

Here is an example using 2 February:

```
Date = 2/2/87
Date + 31 = 3/5/87
Date + 31 - @day(Date+31) = 3/5/87 - 5 = 2/28/87
```

To this calculated end-of-month date is added a value that depends on the particular month of the original date.

+@if(@month({up})=1,@min(@if(@mod(@year({up}),4)=0,29,28),$ VY), If the month of the original date is January, the macro adds to the last day of the original month the value 29 or 28 (depending on whether it is a leap year), or the day of the original month, whichever is less. Thus, using an original date of 2 January 1987, you would get the following:

```
Date = 1/2/87
Date + 31 = 2/2/87
Date + 31 - @day(Date+31) = 2/2/87 - 2 = 1/31/87
Date + 31 - @day(Date+31) + @day(Date) = 1/31/87 +
2 = 2/2/87
```

The remainder of the formula being typed by the macro works in the same way, with slight variations depending on whether the original date is the third, fifth, eighth, or tenth month, or one of the remaining months.

No matter what month the original date is, the macro computes the *end* of the month of the original date, then adds the *day* of the month of the original date, giving you a date exactly one month later than the original date.

/c~.{down VMONTHS-2}~/rv{end}{down}~~{quit} The last line of the macro copies the formula down the number of cells you responded with at the first {getnumber} command, less two, then changes these formulas to their values using /Range Value End DownArrow.

The result is a column of dates, each date exactly one month later than the date above it, and the total number of dates equal to your response at the opening prompt.

Inserting a Prefix in a Column of Entries

This section explores two features of 1-2-3 that can be used in conjunction with the {for} command to affect a column of data: the {put} command and the @index function.

The macro in Figure 11.13 is an excellent example of a macro designed to move quickly down a column of labels making changes with the {put} command. Its purpose is to add a specific prefix to each entry in a column of labels.

{getlabel "Type prefix to insert (add space if required): ",INSERT}
The macro begins by prompting you to type the prefix you want to add to each entry in a column. If, for example, you wanted to add the word NOV, you would type NOV and a space, then press Enter. Your response will be stored in the cell named INSERT.

{windowsoff}{paneloff} Turns the windows and panel off to suppress screen flicker.

/rncICOL~~/rndICOL~/rncICOL~~{end}{down}~ Creates the range name ICOL. The range is everything from the current cell down through the column to the last cell before a blank space.

{for IROW,0,@rows(ICOL)-1,1,ILOOP} This {for} loop can be read: *At the cell named IROW, start counting at zero and count up to the number equal to one less than the number of rows in ICOL, counting by ones, and for each increment loop to the subroutine called ILOOP.*

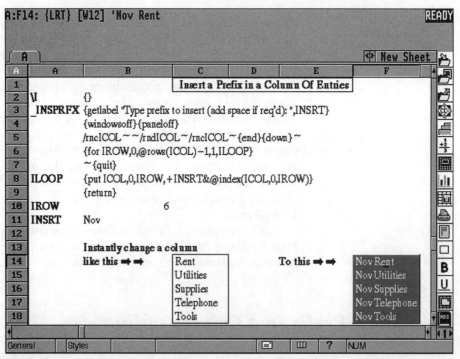

FIGURE 11.13 A macro to insert a prefix in a column of entries.

~{quit}   When the macro has added a prefix to every label in the column, the tilde updates the results and the macro quits.

{put   ICOL,0,IROW,+INSRT&&@index(ICOL,0,IROW)}   This {put} command at ILOOP provides the operation required in the {for} command above. The {put} command has the syntax:

{put *range,column-offset,row-offset,entry*}

and its purpose is to enter a number or label in a cell within a range based on a designated column and row position in that range. In this case, the range is the single column IROW. The offset is the zero column—which would usually be the leftmost column, but here it also represents the only column. The row offset is a variable. As the macro makes each pass through the {for} command, it increments the counter at IROW. That same counter is then used by the {put} command to move down to the next row in turn and "put" its entry there. For an entry, the {put} command uses:

+INSRT&&@index(ICOL,0,IROW)

or in other words, the prefix you have entered in response to the {getlabel} command at the beginning, plus the contents of each entry of the column in turn. Rather than move the cell pointer to each entry and use @cellpointer("contents"), the {put} command is able to determine the contents with the @index function, which has the syntax:

@index(*range,column-offset,row-offset*)

In this case, the range is the single column ICOL; the column offset for that single column is, of course, zero; and the row-offset is the variable counter being incremented by the {for} command at IROW.

This unique combination of the {put} command and the @index function, both of which have the same *range,column-offset,row-offset* locators, provides an almost instantaneous technique for altering the entries in a range.

Deleting a Prefix from a Column of Entries

The {put} and @index combination can be used to delete a prefix from a column of labels almost as easily as it inserts one. It does this by calling on the additional features of the @replace function as shown in Figure 11.14.

To operate the macro, place your cell pointer on the first cell in a column of labels with a common prefix (or prefixes with a common number of letters) you want to delete, and press Alt+D.

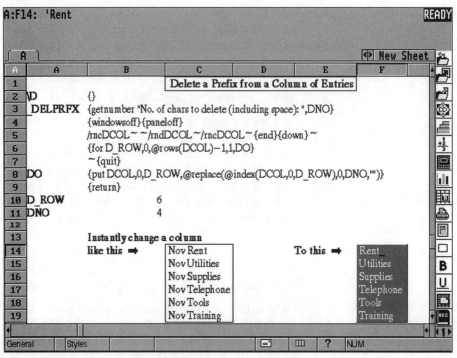

FIGURE 11.14 A macro to delete a prefix from a column of entries.

{getnumber "No. of characters to delete (including space): ",DNO}
The macro begins by prompting you for the number of characters you want to delete, including any spaces, and places your response in the cell named DNO.

The next four lines of the macro follow exactly the same principles as the \I Insert a Prefix macro described above. Only the range names are different.

{put DCOL,0,D_ROW,@replace(@index(DCOL,0,D_ROW),0,DNO,"")}
This {put} command is similar to the {put} command in the \I Insert a Prefix macro, except that instead of adding a prefix to the entry at @index(ICOL,0,IROW) like this:

```
+INSRT&@index(ICOL,0,IROW)
```

the *entry* used by the {put} command in this case removes a prefix with the @replace function like this:

```
@replace(@index(DCOL,0,D_ROW),0,DNO,"")
```

The replacement starts at the zero offset, continues to the offset stored at DNO, and consists of a null string, effectively eliminating the prefix entirely.

You can use these combinations of {for}, {put}, @index, and @replace to great effect in all types of macros where you want to make changes to entire ranges of data. However, these techniques are usually not appropriate in ranges consisting of formulas, unless you are willing to see the formulas converted to straight values at the completion of the macro.

Summary

In this chapter we reviewed ways to make your macro loop a designated number of times in one of two ways: by using {if} with the {let} command or by using the more advanced {for} command with a counter. The format of the {for} command is *{for* followed by the *counter location,* the *start* value, the *stop* value or *cell location containing the stop* value, the *step* value, and the *loop name}.*
We also explored the following concepts:

- Use of the {onerror} command to trap an error and branch the macro in response to an error condition or Ctrl+Break. This command takes as its argument the cell where the macro should continue. Like the {windowsoff} and {paneloff} commands, it stays in effect until the macro ends, or until you disable it. Disabling of an {onerror} command is done with a subsequent {onerror} that includes no argument.
- Suppression of the display of zeros in your worksheet by selecting /Worksheet Global Zero Yes. Unfortunately, when you save your file, the /File Save command in all but Release 3 does not remember that you wanted the zeros suppressed, so when you retrieve the file later the zeros are all visible again. The short autoexecuting macro **/wgzy{quit}** is one solution to this problem.
- Use of the {indicate} command to change the indicator in the upper right panel from the word **READY** to a prompting message. In Release 2 and 2.01, you can use any five-letter word. In Release 2.2 and higher, you can use any message up to 256 letters, but you will want to limit your message to one that will fit in the upper panel: typically, 72 characters.
- Use of a value cell to establish the end of a subroutine, thus saving an extra cell, shortening the length of your macro, and eliminating the need to type in a {return} command.
- Use of a {getnumber} prompt to store information on how many copies to make of a complicated formula. This technique demonstrates how counters and loops are not always required to create a repeating but variable result.
- Use of a prompt that ends with **@date(** to indicate that the entry required should be in the @date format. The idea here is that since

@date(has already been typed by the macro, all that is needed from the user is the year, the month, and the day.

- Use of the {put} command to enter a number or label in a cell within a range based on a designated column and row position in that range, using the syntax:

{put *range,column-offset,row-offset,entry*}

- Use of the @index function to return the contents of a specific column and row location in a range, using the syntax:

@index(*range,column-offset,row-offset*)

The macros covered in this chapter are summarized as follows:

- A macro to automatically change the width of any number of columns in Release 2 and 2.01.
- A macro designed to allow a type of slide show of your graphs.
- A macro to squeeze the filled cells in a column together into one contiguous range of viable data, but without affecting the columns to the right or left of the column being squeezed.
- A macro to change zeros in your worksheet to blank spaces. This macro uses a {for} loop within a {let}/{if} loop to change an entire matrix of cells rather than just one column.
- A Test-and-Replace macro to test a matrix of numbers for a particular value and insert another value in its place.
- A macro to enhance the existing /Range Search capability of Release 2.2 and 3 by adding a new feature called Previous to the current choice for the Next found item.
- A macro to change number-labels to values, taking into account number-labels that include commas.
- A macro to vertically display a series of dates exactly one month apart in 1-2-3 issues before Release 3.
- A macro designed to add a specific prefix to each entry in a column of labels. This macro uses the {put} command and the @index function, both of which have the same *range,column-offset,row-offset* locators.
- A macro designed to delete a common prefix (or prefixes with a common number of letters) from a column of entries. This macro calls on the @replace function to eliminate a specific number of characters.

The next chapter explores the syntax, purpose, and specific uses of the {get} command, especially in conjunction with the {indicate} command and string @functions.

12

Using the {get} Command

This chapter defines and explores the {get} command in combination with macro techniques and commands already covered. You will see how {get} can be used to create a Yes/No prompt; to quit a macro when you press the Esc key; to create a special "action key" for yourself; to differentiate between a press of letter/number keys and directional or function keys; and to have your macro evaluate and act on your response to special {indicate} prompts.

Search and Replace in a Single Column

As mentioned in the last chapter, the /Range Search feature in Release 2.2 and higher is designed to work only on strings. In addressing the limitations of /Range Search, that chapter presented a macro that uses counters and the {for} command to test and replace values across several columns.

The macro in Figure 12.1 is similar in that it accomplishes a test-and-replace function, though only on a single column. It adds an additional feature not included in the Test-and-Replace macro, however, prompting for whether you want to test for labels or values, then for whether to replace with labels or values. This is also an excellent starting point for a review of the {get} command.

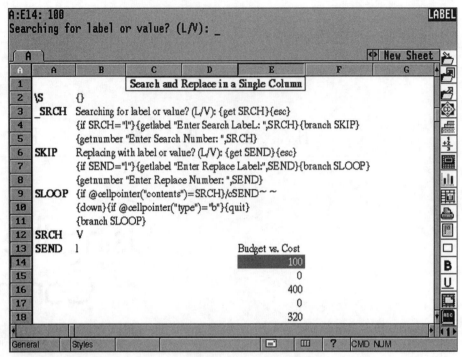

FIGURE 12.1 Macro to search and replace in a single column.

Here's how the macro works:

Searching for label or value? (L/V):{get SRCH}{esc} The macro begins by typing a message into the upper control panel that appears as a prompt. This is somewhat similar to the {getlabel} method of creating a user prompt, except that the message is actually typed, character by character, rather than appearing all at once. On slower computers, you may be able to see the prompt appear character by character.

The macro pauses at the {get} command, waiting for you to press any key. The {get} command uses the syntax, **{get *location*}**, and it operates in a way that will remind you of the bracketed question mark pause {?}. The main difference is that it pauses only until you press a single key. As soon as you have pressed any key, the macro stores the name of that key in the designated cell address or named cell and continues its normal flow. If you press the capital letter P, for example, a capital letter P is stored in the location. If you press the DownArrow key, the macro command **{DOWN}**—shown all in uppercase—is stored in the location.

In this case, the {get} command is designed to store the captured keystroke in cell B12, which has been range-named SRCH. The {esc} command following the {get SRCH} command is intended to eliminate the typed prompt from the upper control panel.

{if SRCH="1"}{getlabel "Enter Search Label:",SRCH}{branch SKIP}
If you press the letter L (using either uppercase or lowercase), a {getlabel} message appears, prompting you for the label to find. Your response to the {getlabel} prompt is stored in the cell named SRCH (which, as you can see, is doing double duty for both the {get} and {getlabel} commands). The macro branches to the routine at the cell named SKIP.

{getnumber "Enter Search Number:",SRCH} Otherwise, if you have not pressed the letter L, it is assumed you pressed an uppercase or lowercase V, and the macro uses {getnumber} to prompt you for a search value that it stores in SRCH.

Replacing with label or value? (L/V):{get SEND}{esc} In the same way that the macro typed a message in the upper control panel to prompt for whether the search item is a label or value, it now types a message that appears as a prompt for whether to replace the searched item with a label or a value. The macro pauses at the {get} command, waiting for you to press any key. Whether you respond with L for Label or V for Value, your response is stored in SEND and the Esc command eliminates the prompt.

{if SEND="1"}{getlabel "Enter Search Label: ",SEND}{branch SLOOP} If you press the letter L (using either uppercase or lowercase), a {getlabel} prompt appears, prompting you for the label you want in place of the searched item. Your response to the {getlabel} prompt is stored in the cell named SEND and the macro branches to the cell named SLOOP.

{getnumber "Enter Replace Number: ",SEND} Otherwise, if you have not pressed the letter L, the macro assumes you pressed an uppercase or lowercase V, and uses {getnumber} to prompt you for a replacement value to store in the cell named SEND.

{if @cellpointer("contents")=SRCH}/cSEND~~ The macro moves through the column, testing for whether the contents of the current cell are the same as the contents of the label or value stored in SRCH. If so, the label or value in SEND is copied to the current cell.

Note, in Release 2.2 and higher, a slightly faster method of replacing the value in the current cell is to replace the command **/cSEND~~** with a {let} command, as follows:

```
{let @cellpointer("address"),SEND}
```

> **NOTE:** *Those of you with Release 2 or 2.01 cannot use @cell-pointer as the first argument in a {let} command. This capability was not made available until Lotus shipped Release 2.2.*

{down}{if @cellpointer("type")="b"}{quit}   The cell pointer is moved down one cell and the macro checks for whether the cell is blank. If so, the macro assumes the cell pointer has reached the end of the column and quits.

{branch SLOOP}   Otherwise, the macro branches back to SLOOP to check the next cell for a match with the contents of SRCH.

In Figure 12.1 you can see a simple example where you might use this macro. If you have a column that subtracts cost from budget, any zero value must mean you are exactly on budget. If you want to replace all zeros with the label "Break-even" in just this column (a task not possible using /Range Search), this macro will handle that chore for you.

Using {get} in a Year-to-Date Macro

You have seen how the {get} command can be used in conjunction with a typed message to provide functionality similar to the {getlabel} command. There are more ways to use the {get} command, as you can see from the Year-to-Date macro in Figure 12.2

Here is a common situation. You have a spreadsheet with a column for the current month and a column for the year-to-date values and you prefer not to show data relating to other months already past, even though the information for those months is included in the year-to-date column.

There are two ways of dealing with this problem manually: You can place the information dealing with past months in some out-of-the-way, off-screen location (usually somewhere to the right) or you can leave the data for those months in the on-screen area, but hide the columns using /Worksheet Column Hide. The advantage of these methods is that you will always have a record supporting the final year-to-date figures shown. The disadvantage is that these columns can be accidentally erased, deleted, or changed in the unseen areas, thereby affecting the year-to-date totals without your necessarily being aware of the change.

One solution is to use a special year-to-date macro. The macro works by prompting you to enter the current month's data. When you finish, the press of a specially designated key can be used to tell the macro to update the year-to-date column automatically.

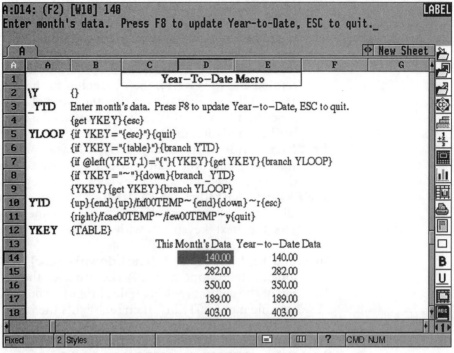

FIGURE 12.2 A macro to update a year-to-date matrix.

Here's how the macro works:

Enter month's data. Press F8 to update Year-to-Date, ESC to quit.
The macro begins by typing a message in the upper panel. It instructs you to enter the month's data, to press F8 when finished and ready for an update, or to press Esc to return to Ready.

{get YKEY}{esc}   The {get} command causes the macro to pause for your press of a single key, which will be stored in YKEY. The Esc command in included to eliminate the typed message.

{if YKEY="{esc}"}{quit}   If you press Esc, the command {esc} is stored in YKEY, and this {if} statement causes the macro to quit.

{if YKEY="{table}"}{branch YTD}   If you press the F8 Table key, this {if} statement operates on the assumption you are finished inputting the month's data and want the year-to-date column updated. It does this by branching to YTD. Incidentally, the F8 Table key was not chosen in this case because the process has anything to do with the Table key, but because it is so rarely pressed by 1-2-3 users and can be considered the most available of function keys.

{if @left(YKEY,1)="{"}{YKEY}{get YKEY}{branch YLOOP} This {if} statement checks for whether the type of key you have pressed starts with opening braces, which would be the case if it were a function key or directional key such as {up}, {down}, {pgdn}, {end}, or {home}. If so, the macro processes that key with the subroutine call to {YKEY}, then branches to the routine at YLOOP. This is a handy way of isolating the types of keys the macro will process, differentiating as it does between a press of letter/number keys and directional or function keys.

{if YKEY="~"}{down}{branch _YTD} If you press Enter, this {if} statement interprets that, moves down one cell without affecting the current cell, and branches back to the beginning at _YTD.

{YKEY}{get YKEY}{branch YLOOP} Otherwise, if the macro passes all four {if} statements above, it processes the keystroke at YKEY, gets the next keystroke with the {get YKEY} command, and branches back to YLOOP.

{up}{end}{up}/fxf00TEMP~{end}{down}~r{esc} This is the beginning of the routine named YTD. It moves the cell pointer to the top of the column, selects /File Xtract Formulas, enters a temporary file name 00TEMP, then highlights the range just entered by pressing End DownArrow to the bottom of the column, then R for Replace, and Esc in case the file does not exist.

{right}/fcae00TEMP~/few00TEMP~y{quit} Once the temporary file with this month's data has been created, the cell pointer is moved one cell to the right, and the macro increases the current year-to-date figures by the amount of the current month by selecting /File Combine Add Entire and entering the file name 00TEMP. The temporary file is then erased and the macro quits. The last line of the macro is simply the storage cell for the {get} command, named YKEY.

In Release 2.2 and higher, you can speed up the message prompt by having it appear in the upper panel as an Indicate message in place of the Ready indicator. This is possible in Release 2.2 and higher because these releases allow a longer Indicator message than the five-character limit of Release 2 and 2.01. Refer to Figure 12.3.

{indicate "Enter mo. data, F8 to update Year-to-Date, ESC to quit"} This message appears instantly and stays in the upper panel until the macro reaches an {indicate} command, returning it to its normal state.

{get YKEY}{if YKEY="{esc}"}{indicate}{quit} If you press Esc upon seeing the prompt, the macro uses {indicate} to return the Indicator to "Ready" and quits.

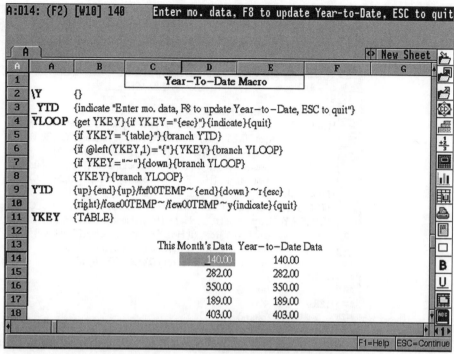

FIGURE 12.3 The Year-to-Date macro using an {Indicate} prompt.

The remainder of the macro is similar to the first version, except that the final {quit} command is also preceded by an {indicate} command.

Using {get} to Toggle Your Hidden Columns

You have already seen how to create toggle macros in 1-2-3. Here we use the same techniques, but add a few new uses of the {get} command to provide even more flexibility for the person who will be using the macro.

Refer to Figure 12.4. The purpose of the Hide Columns Toggle is to alternately prompt you through the hiding of one or more columns at once or offer you the ability to instantly redisplay, or unhide, all hidden columns in your worksheet.

Here's how the macro works:

> **{onerror HTOGGLE}** If you press Ctrl+Break at any time during the operation of the macro or if the macro reaches an error condition that would normally halt its operation, this instruction tells it to

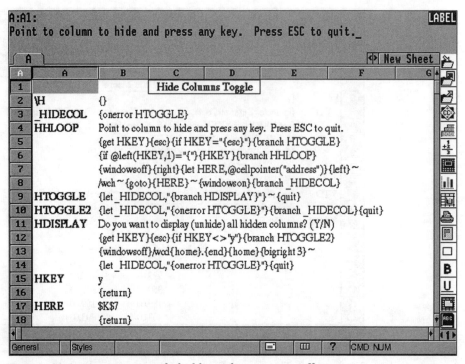

FIGURE 12.4 A macro to toggle hidden columns on or off.

branch to the routine at HTOGGLE, a special toggling line of the macro. The toggle switches the opening command so the next time you press Alt+H (Ctrl+H in 1-2-3 for Windows), the macro will run the {branch HDISPLAY} command and prompt for whether you want to display (unhide) all hidden columns.

Point to Column to hide and press any key. Press ESC to quit. This message is typed in the upper panel, instructing you to point to the column you want to hide. In Release 2.2 and higher, you may want to substitute an {indicate} version of this message. If you do so, however, remember to precede each {quit} command in the macro with a resetting {indicate} command.

{get HKEY}{esc}{if HKEY="{esc}"}{branch HTOGGLE} Pauses for your press of any key, which the macro stores in the cell named HKEY. The {esc} command eliminates the prompt above. If you press the Esc key manually at this point, the macro branches to HTOGGLE, switching the opening command so the next time the macro will branch to HDISPLAY and prompt for whether you want to display (unhide) all hidden columns.

{if @left(HKEY,1)="{"}{HKEY}{branch HHLOOP}   If you pressed a directional key such as {Up} or {Down}, the leftmost character stored in HKEY must be opening braces. In that case, the macro processes the key in HKEY as a subroutine, then branches to HHLOOP where it again prompts you to point to the column you want to hide. You can continue to press any directional key and the macro will continue to process that key, then again prompt you to point to a column to hide. This combination of prompt, {get} command, and {if} command provides a handy way to instruct your user while allowing the freedom to move around in response to the instruction.

{windowsoff}{right}{let HERE,@cellpointer("address")}{left}~   If you press a key whose macro equivalent does not start with braces (such as the Enter key), the macro continues at this line, turning off the windows, moving to the right one cell, recording the address of that cell at the place-marker cell named HERE, then moving back to the left one cell.

/wch~{goto}{HERE}~{windowson}{branch _HIDECOL}   At this point the macro selects /Worksheet Column Hide, moves back to the cell address stored at HERE, turns on the windows, and branches back to the beginning of the macro where you are again prompted for a column to hide. If you press Ctrl+Break or Esc, the {onerror} command or the command that reads {if HKEY= "{esc}"} will branch the macro to HTOGGLE.

{let _HIDECOL,"{branch HDISPLAY}"}~{quit}   This is the routine named HTOGGLE, designed to change the first line of the macro to {branch HDISPLAY} so the next time you press Alt+H (or Ctrl+H), the macro prompts for whether you want to display (unhide) all hidden columns. Once the toggle switch is set, the macro quits.

{let _HIDECOL,"{onerror HTOGGLE}"}{branch _HIDECOL}{quit}   This is the second toggling line, named HTOGGLE2. Its purpose, which becomes clear at the end of the routine called HDISPLAY, is to return the original {onerror} command to the first line of the macro so it runs its primary function.

Do you want to display (unhide) all hidden columns? (Y/N)   This message is the beginning of the routine HDISPLAY, and it prompts you to type Y for Yes or N for No to indicate whether you want to display all hidden columns in the worksheet.

{get HKEY}{esc}{if HKEY<>"y"}{branch HTOGGLE2}   If your next keystroke (which the macro stores in HKEY) is not Y for Yes, the macro branches back to HTOGGLE2, the subroutine that returns the macro to its primary operating function before quitting.

{windowsoff}/wcd{home}.{end}{home}{bigright 3}   Otherwise (assuming you have pressed Y for Yes), the macro turns off the windows, selects /Worksheet Column Display, and highlights the entire worksheet from the Home (A1) position to three screens to the right of the End Home position.

{let _HIDECOL,"{onerror HTOGGLE}"{quit}   This is actually a repeat of the HTOGGLE2 line, except that the macro quits rather than looping back to the beginning to start over.

This macro does not accomplish anything you cannot do for yourself; but it goes through the necessary keystrokes much faster than you could manually and it eliminates the need to remember how to hide columns using /Worksheet Column Hide. If you would like to start making more use of hidden columns in your work, this macro provides a nice beginning to that process.

Creating a Macro to Temporarily View Hidden Columns

You may have noticed that you can temporarily view your hidden columns in a worksheet by pressing /Copy or /Move. Any hidden columns will appear temporarily, designated as hidden by an asterisk that appears to the right of the column letter in the upper border. After the /Copy or /Move command is completed or interrupted, the hidden columns disappear again. This is a handy manual way to bring your hidden columns into view without having to display them with /Worksheet Column Display, then rehide them using /Worksheet Column Hide. Unfortunately, you cannot make changes to hidden columns that are temporarily displayed in this way.

Fortunately, there is a clever macro technique for both displaying and allowing changes to hidden columns in Release 2.x without losing the characteristic that these columns are designated as hidden. Refer to the View Hidden Columns macro in Figure 12.5.

{menubranch VMENU}{quit}   Brings up the menu choices, *View* and *Rehide*. Select *View* to bring all hidden columns temporarily into view and *Rehide* to rehide all columns that you have previously designated as hidden using /Worksheet Column Hide.

{paneloff}/c{CTRL_BREAK}   Turns off the upper panel to suppress screen flicker, selects /Copy, then attempts to process a nonexistent command. Actually, you could use any nonexistent command at this point, such as {VIEW}, or {TEMP}, or {APPLESAUCE}, so long as there is no cell or range in the worksheet that has been given that name. We used {CTRL_BREAK} here because, being nonexistent, it provides an effect similar to the effect you would get if you pressed Ctrl+Break: It interrupts the /Copy command.

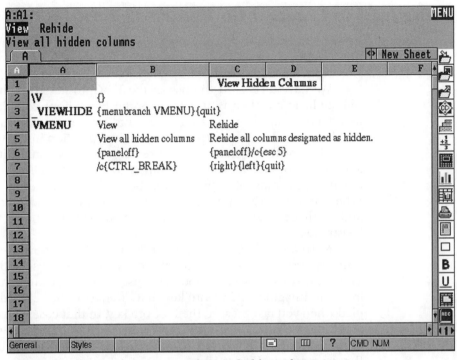

FIGURE 12.5 A macro to temporarily view hidden columns.

In doing so, it does one other strange thing: It freezes any temporarily viewed hidden columns in their temporarily visible state. At this point, if you have Release 2.x, you can erase a cell, edit a cell, or type new information into a cell that is hidden.

> **NOTE:** *If you have Release 4, invoking this macro and choosing View allows you to view any hidden columns that are displayed on the screen, but you cannot make changes to them. Pressing Esc automatically rehides them. If you have Release 3.x, this macro will not work.*

{paneloff}/c{esc 5}{right}{left}{quit}   If you have Release 2.x and, after selecting VIEW once, you decide you want to cause your temporarily viewed columns to disappear again, invoking this macro and selecting REHIDE will cause the macro to turn off the upper panel, select /Copy, press Esc five times to gracefully back out of the /Copy command, then move RightArrow and Left-Arrow to cause the screen to redisplay correctly. At this point the hidden columns will all disappear and the macro quits.

Using {get} to Create a Go-Return Macro

In this section we will explore how you can use the {get} command to continue or interrupt an F5 Goto sequence and thereby allow a modified version of the F5 Goto function.

We have discussed the use of the F5 Goto key to temporarily visit a remote location, then return by pressing Esc before completing the command. For example, you can press F5 and Home, view the area around cell A1, then press Esc to return to your original position in the worksheet.

The Go-Return macro in Figure 12.6 provides that utility and more. It allows you to relocate your cell pointer to a remote cell in your worksheet, but it keeps track of your last location so you can jump back instantly. What's more, it remembers the remote location, so you can toggle back and forth between that location and your starting point with only two keystrokes.

Normally, when you press the F5 Goto key 1-2-3 types the message, *Enter address to go to:* and prompts you with the address of the current cell. This is fairly useless, since you never use the Goto key to go to your current location. Imagine an F5 Goto key that offers you the cell address you occupied when you last pressed the F5 Goto key. In that case, you could press F5 and Enter to instantly jump to a previous location, then F5 and Enter again to return to the cell where you started. This is exactly the effect of the Go-Return macro in Figure 12.6.

{goto}{GLAST}{get GKEY1}{if GKEY1="~"{branch GLOOP} The macro begins by activating the F5 Goto function, then types in the address stored in GLAST. (Note, when you first type this macro into your own worksheet, you must include an address in GLAST or the macro will halt at this point.) The Enter key to complete the Goto sequence is not pressed yet. Instead, the {get} command pauses for your press of a single key.

If you press Enter, the assumption is that you accept the offered address shown at the Goto prompt in the upper panel. This will be the place your cell pointer occupied the last time you used this macro. The macro branches to GLOOP to process your Goto response.

{if GKEY1="{esc}"}{esc 3}{quit} If you press Esc instead, the macro backs out of the F5 Goto sequence and quits.

{let GLAST,@cellpointer("address")}{esc 2} Otherwise, it stores the current cell pointer address in GLAST so the next time you invoke the macro, it will offer this address as the address to go to. The macro presses Esc twice, leaving just the *Enter address to go to:* prompt, repeats the single key you pressed at the {get} pause, and quits.

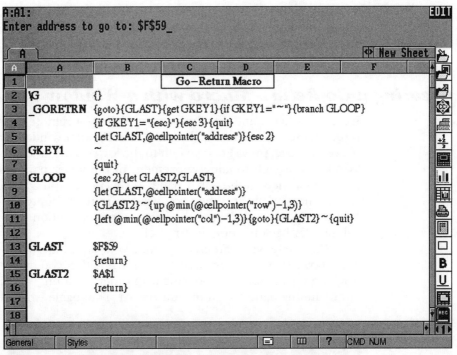

FIGURE 12.6 Using the {Get} command in a Go-Return macro.

Thus, pressing the LeftArrow key after invoking this macro will leave you with the same *Enter address to go to:* prompt you would get by simply pressing F5 and the LeftArrow key.

{esc 2}{let GLAST2,GLAST}   This is the beginning of the routine named GLOOP where the macro processes your acceptance of the last cell location where you used this macro. The macro backs partially out of the F5 Goto sequence, then stores the address in GLAST at GLAST2.

{let GLAST,@cellpointer("address")}   Now that a copy of the address in GLAST has been stored in GLAST2, the macro stores the current address in GLAST.

{GLAST2}~{up @min(@cellpointer("row")-1,3)}   Completes the F5 Goto sequence by typing in the address of the last location where you used this macro, then moves up either three cells or the number of cells equal to one less than the current row, whichever is less. The result is to move the current row more towards the center of the screen.

{left @min(@cellpointer("col")-1,3)}{goto}{GLAST2}~{quit}   Moves left either three cells or the number of cells one less than the current column, whichever is less, relocating the current columns more towards the center of the screen. Then the cell pointer is moved back to the address in GLAST2 and the macro quits.

Creating a Go-Return Macro with a Window Pane

Here's another manual technique for visiting a remote location and easily returning to the original cell. Create a horizontal window pane in the middle of the page, press F6 to switch to the lower pane, and choose /Worksheet Window Unsynch to allow movement in the lower pane without affecting the original view in the upper pane. At this point, you can move to any location in the worksheet. When you want to return, simply choose /Worksheet Window Clear to eliminate the lower pane—an action that also jumps the cell pointer back to your starting cell.

Of course, you can create a macro to automate these actions. Figure 12.7 shows such a macro, written as a toggle that you invoke once to create a window pane for free movement to other locations, and invoke again to eliminate the pane for an instant return. The toggle works by checking for

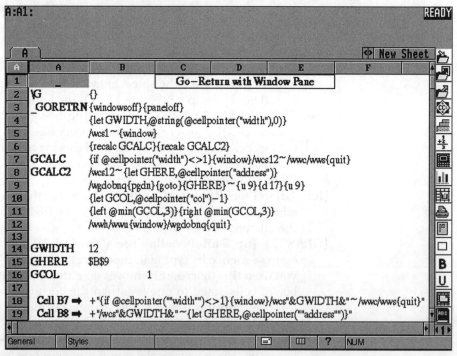

FIGURE 12.7 A Go-Return macro that uses a horizontal window pane.

whether a pane exists. If no pane exists, the macro creates one and unsynchronizes the two panes. Otherwise, the macro removes the pane and the cell pointer returns to the location it held when the pane was first created.

This macro uses an interesting technique for determining whether a window pane exists. As it happens, changing a column's width in one pane has no effect on that same column displayed in the other pane; so the macro stores the current column width, changes the column to a new width of 1, and tries to switch to an alternate pane by using the {window} command. If there is another pane, the macro detects a difference between the upper pane's new column width of 1 and the original width of that same column in the lower pane. In that case, it assumes that you want to return to your original starting point, so it restores the original column width and eliminates the window pane. On the other hand, if the macro does not determine that another pane exists, it restores the column width, creates a horizontal window, switches to the new pane, unsynchronizes the windows, and quits.

{windowsoff}{paneloff}   Turns off the windows and panel to suppress screen flicker.

{let GWIDTH,@string(@cellpointer("width"),0)}   Stores the string version of the current cell width in the cell named GWIDTH.

/wcs1~{window}   Changes the current cell width to 1, a deliberately atypical size. The macro then uses the {window} command to switch to the opposite pane, if one exists.

{recalc GCALC}{recalc GCALC2}   The macro recalculates the next two lines, named GCALC and GCLAC2. Those two lines are actually variable strings that change depending on the column width of the current cell.

{if @cellpointer("width")<>1}{window}/wcs10~/wwc/wws/ wgdobyq{quit}   If another pane exists, the cell pointer probably is now in a column not equal to 1, so the macro uses the {window} command to jump back to the original pane, changes the column back to the width stored in GWIDTH, clears the windows, chooses /Worksheet Window Synchronize, and quits. As shown at the bottom of Figure 12.7, the underlying string for this macro line reads:

```
+"{if @cellpointer(""width"")<>1}{window}/
wcs"&GWIDTH&"~/wwc/wws/wgdobyq{quit}"
```

/wcs10~{let GHERE,@cellpointer("address")}   If no other pane exists, the macro changes the column back to the width stored in GWIDTH and stores the current cell address in GHERE. The underlying string for this macro line reads:

```
+"/wcs"&GWIDTH&"~{let GHERE,@cellpointer(""address"")}"
```

{pgdn}{goto}{GHERE}~{u 9}{d 17}{u 9}   Relocates the current cell to the upper left corner of the screen by moving down one page (which moves the original cell out of sight), then returning to the original cell address stored in GHERE. To relocate the current cell to a more vertically centered position, the cell pointer is moved up nine cells, down 17 cells, then up nine cells again.

{let GCOL,@cellpointer("col")-1}   Stores in GCOL a value equal to the number of columns you would have to move through to get to column A.

{left @min(GCOL,3)}{right @min(GCOL,3)}   Relocates the current cell to a more horizontally centered position by moving left to column A or left three cells, whichever is less, then right the same number of cells.

/wwh/wwu/wgdobyq{window}{quit}   Finally, the macro creates a horizontal window pane, unsynchronizes the windows, and turns the computer's bell on again.

Try this macro for yourself. When you first invoke it, the macro should create a horizontal pane for easy movement to another location. When you invoke it again, the macro eliminates the pane and returns you to your original cell.

Goto Command with a History List

Excel for Windows offers a Goto command that includes a history list of the last few cell locations visited with the F5 Goto key. With this feature you can not only visit a cell and easily return, but you can quickly jump back and forth between the two locations or jump to any of several locations you visited recently with a few keystrokes. In case you'd like to have this feature in 1-2-3, you may be interested in a macro that replicates it by combining the {goto} command and a self-modifying menu, as shown in Figure 12.8.

To create this macro, type it as shown in Figure 12.8. However, in addition to the usual range-naming from column A, you'll need to give the name MENUS2_7 to the cells occupied by the second through the seventh menu items (cells C4..H4 in our example), give the name MENUS3_7 to the cells occupied by the third through the seventh menu items (cells D4..H4 in our example), give the name MENUSTORE to six cells in the next-to-last lines of the macro (cells C8..H8 in our example), and give the name MENUPART to five cells in the next-to-last lines of the macro (cells C8..G8 in our example).

{menubranch GMENU}{quit}   The macro starts by calling up the menu at GMENU, which permits the user to choose from a standard Goto command (that also remembers the current location before going there), up to six rotating history list locations, and a quit command.

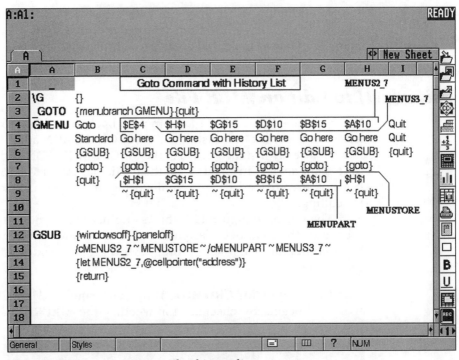

FIGURE 12.8 A Goto macro with a history list.

{GSUB}   No matter which choice the user makes, the macro runs the subroutine at GSUB, which shifts the menu of history list locations one cell to the right.

{goto}   The macro executes the F5 Goto feature. If the user selected the standard Goto choice, the macro quits at this point. If the user selected any of the history list locations, the macro continues at the next cell down, where the GSUB subroutine has copied the appropriate cell addresses.

~{quit}   The macro executes an Enter and quits.

{windowsoff}{paneloff}   This is the first line of the subroutine at GSUB, included to suppress screen flicker and speed the macro.

/cMENUS2_7~MENUSTORE~/cMENUPART~MENUS3_7~   The macro copies the history list locations (the second through the seventh GMENU choices) to MENUSTORE, then copies the first part of MENUSTORE (the six cells in MENUPART) to the third through the seventh GMENU cells.

{let MENUS2_7,@cellpointer("address")}   So as to record the location before leaving it, the macro copies the current cell address to the first cell in MENUS2_7.

{return}   The macro control returns to the main macro.

In addition to providing you with a handy tool for returning to cells previously visited with a Goto feature, this macro provides an excellent example of macro code that creates a self-modifying menu.

Using {get} to Edit an .MLB File

Normally, to edit an .MLB file from your background Macro Library in Release 2.x, you must first Install the MACROMGR.ADN add-in application (if it is not already installed), invoke the MACROMGR.ADN add-in application (if it is not already invoked), load the particular .MLB Macro Library file (if it is not already loaded), and finally bring up the .MLB Macro Library file for editing.

The macro in Figure 12.9 shows another use of the {get} command. In this case, the macro is designed to facilitate and speed up the process involved in pulling a Macro Library .MLB file into your current worksheet for editing.

{if @isapp("MACROMGR")}{app1}{branch EMORE}   The macro begins by checking for whether the MACROMGR.ADN add-in

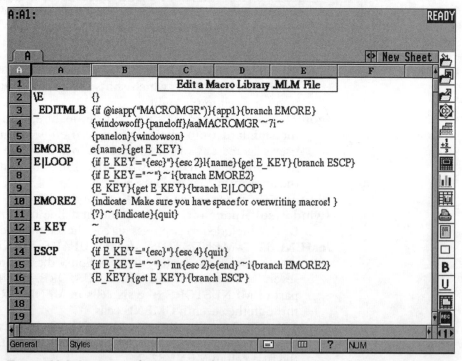

FIGURE 12.9 Macro to edit a Macro Library .MLB file.

application has been attached. If so, the @isapp function is evaluated as true. The {app1} command is the macro equivalent to pressing Alt+F7 to invoke the add-in application attached to Alt+F7. The macro assumes that you have attached the MACRO-MGR.ADN add-in to Alt+F7 either manually or through the /Worksheet Global Default command. At this point the macro branches to the fifth line of the macro at EMORE.

{windowsoff}{paneloff}/aaMACROMGR~7i~   If the MACROMGR.ADN has not been attached, this line selects /Add-in Attach, enters MACROMGR, attaches the add-in to Alt-F7, and invokes the MACROMGR add-in, offering the menu choices Load, Save, Edit, Remove, Name-List, and Quit, and selects Load.

{panelon}{windowson}   Turns off the windows and panel to suppress screen flicker and speed up the macro.

e{name}{get E_KEY}   Selects Edit, presses the F3 Name key to show a full-screen view of the choice of loaded .MLB files to edit, then pauses for your press of a key.

{if E_KEY="{esc}"}{esc 2}1{name}{get E_KEY}{branch ESCP}   If you press Esc, it is assumed that the file you want to edit is not already loaded. The macro backs out of the Edit menu level, selects Load, presses Name to show a full-screen view of the choice of .MLB files you can load, pauses for your press of a key, then branches to ESCP.

{if E_KEY="~"}~i{branch EMORE2}   If you do not press Esc, but press Enter, the macro assumes you are selecting the highlighted .MLB file to edit. That file is selected, and between the menu choices Ignore and Overwrite, I for Ignore is typed. The macro branches to EMORE2.

{E_KEY}{get E_KEY}{branch E|LOOP}   Otherwise, if you have pressed neither Esc nor Enter, the key you pressed (which was stored at E_KEY) is processed. Then the macro pauses for your press of another key and branches back to E|LOOP.

{indicate "Make sure you have space for overwriting macros!"}   Before the .MLB macro library file is brought into the current worksheet, a message is shown in the upper panel warning you to make sure you have enough space for the .MLB file. This is important, since bringing the file into the current worksheet will overwrite anything in its way.

{?}~{indicate}{quit}   The macro pauses for your relocation of the cell pointer, if required, to the place where you want the macros to appear in your worksheet. As soon as you decide and press Enter, the macro also presses Enter, bringing in the .MLB file. The {indicate} command eliminates the warning message in the upper panel, and the macro quits.

The next two lines of the macro consist of the location for the stored keystroke (named E_KEY) and a {return} command to end the subroutine consisting of the single keystroke stored at E_KEY.

{if E_KEY="{esc}"}{esc 4}{quit}   The remaining three lines are the continuation of the condition that you pressed Esc because the file you wanted to edit is not already loaded. At this point, the macro has backed out of the Edit menu level, selected Load, shown a full-screen view of the choice of .MLB files you can load, and paused for your press of a key. If you press Esc again at this point, the macro escapes entirely out of the menu levels and the macro quits.

{if E_KEY="~"}nn{esc 2}e{end}~i{branch EMORE2}   If, on the other hand, you press Enter to select a file to load, it is possible that the file has already been loaded. In that case, you will be given a No/Yes prompt and an explanation that the "*.MLB file already exists in memory. Overwrite it?*" The first N is for No, the second N selects Name-List (a bogus selection). If the file has not already been loaded, pressing NN will simply make a bogus selection of Name-List and a typing of the letter N.

Whichever happens, two presses of Esc return you to the menu choices Load, Save, Edit, and so on. The macro selects Edit, the last .MLB file, and I for Invoke, and the macro branches back to EMORE2.

{E_KEY}{get E_KEY}{branch ESCP}   Otherwise, if you have pressed neither Esc nor Enter, the key you pressed (which was stored at E_KEY) is processed. Then the macro pauses for your press of another key, and it branches back to ESCP.

In Chapter 16 we will look at a macro to facilitate the saving of a .MLB Macro Library file.

Simulating the F10 Quick Graph Key

Release 3 uses the F10 function key as a Quick Graph key for instantly creating a graph based on the data matrix in which the cell pointer currently resides.

While this feature has not been added to Release 2.2, another feature has: the /Graph Group option. This feature allows you to assign all of the graph data ranges (X and A through F) at once when the data is in consecutive columns or rows of a range.

To do this, follow these steps:

1. Select /Graph Group.
2. Specify the group range you want to divide into graph data ranges.

3. Select Columnwise or Rowwise. Columnwise sets the first column of a range as the X data range and each succeeding column as the ranges A through F, while the Rowwise choice sets the first row of the range as the X data range and each succeeding row as the ranges A through F.

Not only is this an important improvement to the /Graph command sequence, but these features can also be used in a macro to simulate in Release 2.2 through 2.4 the F10 Quick Graph feature available in Release 3. Refer to the macro in Figure 12.10.

To operate this macro, place your cell pointer in any cell of a range where the data you want to graph is in consecutive columns or rows and press Alt-Q.

{windowsoff}{paneloff}   Turns off the windows and panel to suppress screen flicker and speed up the macro.

{right}{if @cellpointer("type")="b"}{left}   Moves the cell pointer to the right. If the cell is blank, it is assumed that the starting column was the rightmost edge of the range to graph, so the cell pointer is moved back again.

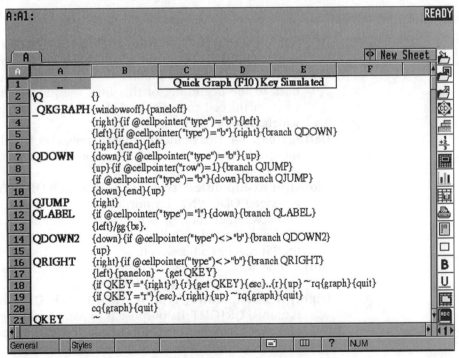

FIGURE 12.10 Macro to simulate the Quick Graph (F10) key.

{left}{if @cellpointer("type")="b"}{right}{branch QDOWN}   In this same way, the cell pointer is moved to the left to determine whether the starting column was the leftmost edge of the range to graph. If so, the cell pointer is moved back to the range and the macro branches to QDOWN.

{right}{end}{left}   Otherwise, the macro moves the cell pointer to the right, then End LeftArrow, to take it to the leftmost edge of the range.

{down}{if @cellpointer("type")="b"}{up}   The cell pointer is moved down and, if the cell is blank, it is moved up again.

{up}{if @cellpointer("row")=1}{branch QJUMP}   The cell pointer is moved up and the macro checks for whether the current row is Row 1. If so, the macro branches to QJUMP.

{if @cellpointer("type")="b"}{down}{branch QJUMP}   If, by moving up one cell, the macro moved above the range to graph (assumed if the cell is blank), the cell pointer is moved back down and the macro branches to QJUMP.

{down}{end}{up}   Otherwise, the macro moves the cell pointer down, then End UpArrow, to take it to the top of the range to graph.

{right}   This is the beginning of the routine named QJUMP. The macro moves the cell pointer one column to the right on the assumption that the current column (leftmost column of the range to graph) consists of labels.

{if @cellpointer("type")="1"}{down}{branch QLABEL}   This line is named QLABEL. Its purpose is to check whether the cell contains a label. If so, the cell pointer is moved down, the macro loops back to the beginning of this line, the macro checks again for whether the cell contains a label, and so on until it reaches a cell which is not a label.

{left}/gg{bs}.   At this point, the macro moves back to the leftmost column, selects /Graph Group, then presses Backspace to free the cell pointer.

{down}{if @cellpointer("type")<>"b"}{branch QDOWN2}   This line is named QDOWN2. Its purpose is to paint down one row and check whether the cell is blank. If not, the macro loops back to the beginning of this line, paints down another row, and so on until it reaches a blank cell.

{up}   Otherwise, if the cell is blank, the cell pointer reduces the highlighted area by moving back up one cell.

{right}{if @cellpointer("type")<>"b"}{branch QRIGHT}   This line is named QRIGHT. Its purpose is to paint to the right one column and check whether the cell is blank. If not, the macro loops back to the beginning of this line, paints down another column, and so on until it reaches a blank cell.

{left}{panelon}~{get QKEY} When a blank cell is reached, the cell pointer moves left, reducing the highlighted area by one column, the panel is turned back on, and the highlighted group of columns and rows to graph is entered by the tilde.

At this point, 1-2-3 automatically offers the menu choices Columnwise and Rowwise described above. The macro pauses for your press of R for Rowwise or RightArrow to point to the Rowwise choice. If you do not press R or RightArrow, it is assumed you pressed C for Columnwise or Enter to select the Columnwise choice.

{if   QKEY="{right}"}{r}{get   QKEY}{esc}..{r}{up}~rq{graph}{quit} If you press the RightArrow key, the cursor moves to the right to point to Rowwise.

Since you have pressed RightArrow to point to the choice Rowwise, the macro pauses again for your press of the Enter key, then escapes from this menu level, presses the Period key twice to reverse the free cursor point in the highlighted range you want to graph, unhighlights the range to the right one column, highlights it up one row, and enters the revised /Graph Group range. It again selects Rowwise and Quit, and displays the graph. After you have viewed the graph and pressed Enter, the macro quits.

{if QKEY="r"}{esc}..{right}{up}~rq{graph}{quit} This line accomplishes the same thing as the last, except that it relies on your pressing R for Rowwise rather than pointing to the Rowwise choice by pressing the RightArrow key.

cq{graph}{quit} Otherwise, the macro assumes you want Columnwise graphing, so it simply selects the menu choices Columnwise and Quit, displays the graph, then returns to Ready mode.

Summary

This chapter showed how the {get} command uses the syntax, **{get *location*}**, to pause until you press a single key, storing a copy of that keystroke in the cell address or named cell you have designated.

The following techniques and concepts were covered:

- The {get} command can be used to allow a typed message in the upper control panel that will appear as a prompt. This is somewhat similar to the {getlabel} method of creating a user prompt, except that the message is actually typed, character by character, rather than appearing all at once, then eliminated by an {esc} command.
- In Release 2.2 and higher, you can speed up the message prompt by having it appear in the upper panel as an Indicate message in place

of the Ready indicator. This is possible because Release 2.2 and higher allow a longer Indicator message than the 5-character limit of Release 2 and 2.01.

- In Release 2.2 and higher, you can improve on use of the /Copy command to copy a label or value to the current cell. This is done by using the {let} command in the configuration

```
{let @cellpointer("address"),location}
```

- This ability to use @cellpointer as the first argument in a {let} command is not available in Release 2 or 2.01.
- The {get} command can be used to create a special "action key" that will accomplish a pre-established action when you press it. We recommend the F8 Table key for this purpose because it is so rarely pressed by 1-2-3 users and can be considered the most available of function keys.
- The {get} command can be used with an {if} command as in the command **{if @left(YKEY,1)="{"}{YKEY}** to check for whether the type of key you have pressed is a letter/number key or a function or directional key such as {edit}, {up}, {down}, {pgdn}, {end}, or {home}. If so, the macro processes that key with the subroutine call. This is a handy way of isolating the types of keys the macro will process.
- The {get} command can be used in conjunction with a typed or {indicate} instruction to point to a location or highlight a range.
- You can temporarily view any hidden columns by pressing /Copy or /Move. The columns will appear temporarily, with an asterisk that appears to the right of the column letter in the upper border. After the /Copy or /Move command is completed or interrupted, the hidden columns disappear again.
- You can use any nonexistent command such as {VIEW}, {TEMP}, or {APPLESAUCE}, to cause an error-message break in a macro, so long as no cells or ranges in the worksheet have been given that name. We suggest using {CTRL_BREAK} because, being nonexistent, it provides an effect similar to the effect you would get if you pressed Ctrl+Break during the macro's execution.
- Since the {get} command can be used to capture a keystroke, you can pass every keystroke through a looping macro with a {get} command and several {if} commands to test and react to the type and nature of every key pressed.
- The /Graph Group option in Release 2.2 through 2.4 allows you to assign all of the graph data ranges (X and A through F) at once when the data to be graphed is in consecutive columns or rows of a range, provided you select Columnwise or Rowwise graphing.

The following macros use the {get} command:

- A macro to search and replace in a single column, prompting for whether you want to test for labels or values, then for whether to replace with labels or values.
- A macro to update a year-to-date matrix, to be used in a worksheet where you have a spreadsheet with a column for the current month and a column for the year-to-date values, and you prefer not to show data relating to other months already past.
- A Hide Columns Toggle for Release 2.x to alternately prompt you through the hiding of one or more columns at once or offer you the ability to instantly redisplay, or unhide, all hidden columns in your worksheet.
- A macro to temporarily view hidden columns, both displaying and allowing changes to hidden columns without losing the characteristic that these columns are designated as hidden.
- A Go-Return macro that allows you to relocate your cell pointer to a remote cell in your worksheet, keeping track of your last location so you can jump back instantly. This macro also remembers the remote location, so you can toggle back and forth between that location and your starting point with just two keystrokes.
- A Go-Return toggle macro that uses a horizontal window pane to permit viewing of the original cell while you visit a remote location and return.
- A Goto macro with a self-modifying menu that provides a history list of locations visited while using this macro.
- A macro to facilitate and speed up the process involved in pulling a Macro Library .MLB file into your current worksheet for editing.
- A macro to simulate the Quick Graph (F10) key in Release 2.2 through 2.4 using the /Graph Group command sequence.

The next chapter explores advanced methods for manipulating strings in your macros.

13

Manipulating Strings in Your Macros

In this chapter we explore ways of using and manipulating strings in your macros to accomplish tasks based on variable input or conditions. You will learn how a macro can use string technology to display a variable message in the upper panel; display changing choice explanations in custom menus; use @cellpointer("address") with {let}, {contents}, and {blank}; combine commands like /Range Unprotect with variable cell addresses; display an absolute cell address as a relative address; create range names that change based on the counter in a {for} loop; and calculate and display a relative cell location based on your current cell address.

You will also learn how to write a macro that offers a vertical custom menu with more than eight choices. Using this approach, you can provide your users with a way to select from the menu by pointing and pressing Enter or by typing an underlined letter—which need not be the first letter in the menu item.

Displaying the ASCII Code for a Keystroke

The macro in Figure 13.1 uses a string to create a temporary and variable message in the upper panel, offering a technique you can use in other

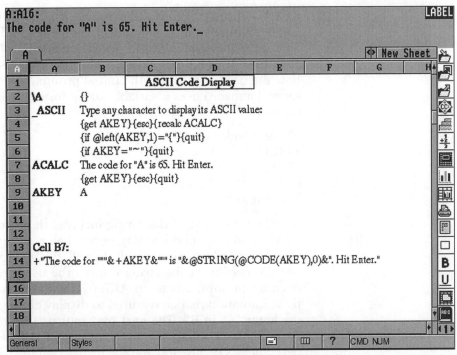

FIGURE 13.1 Using string programming to display an ASCII code.

macros to create a message that can actually change depending on an action by the user. In this case, the message tells the user what ASCII code corresponds to any keystroke typed in response to the macro's prompt.

Type any character to display its ASCII value: The macro begins by prompting the user to type a single keystroke. Note that this message shows in the upper panel because the macro types its individual characters, not because the macro instantly displays it with a {getlabel} or {getnumber} command. This method has an advantage in that it precludes the user having to press Enter after typing the required keystroke.

{get AKEY}{esc}{recalc ACALC} Pauses for the user's press of a single key, then eliminates the typed message in the upper panel with the {esc} command and recalculates the cell of the macro named ACALC.

{if @left(AKEY,1)="{"}{quit} If the user presses a function key or directional key such as {edit}, {home}, {left}, or {pgdn}, the macro quits.

{if AKEY="~"}{quit}   Directs the macro to quit if the user presses Enter. (Without this command, the macro would enter the first half of the message in ACALC into the current cell.)

The code for "A" is 65. Hit Enter.   This line changes depending on how the user responds to the initial prompt. To create this message, the macro uses a variable string formula, broken down as follows:

```
+"The code for """&
+AKEY&
""" is "&
@string(@code(AKEY),0)&
".Hit Enter."
```

The first part of this string includes three quotation marks as required to display opening quotes before the typed character (the letter "A" in the example in cell B7 in Figure 13.1). The +AKEY portion of the string returns the user's response to the opening prompt, stored in AKEY. The third part begins with three quotation marks, required to display closing quotes before the letter "A" in B7. The next part returns the string version of the code that corresponds to the character in AKEY and the last part consists of a period and the instruction to "Hit Enter."

{get AKEY}{esc}{quit}   The last {get} command is included solely to pause the macro so the user can read the message typed into the upper panel. When the user presses any key, the {esc} command eliminates the message and the macro quits.

Creating Changeable Menu Descriptions

Not only can you use string formulas as functioning parts of the program flow of a macro, but you can also include string formulas as variable lines used for the descriptions that appear under custom menus as shown in Figure 13.2. This macro's purpose is to provide a way to store a word or phrase and allow its instant entry into any cell; but it also offers an excellent example of a way to create a custom menu with a variable description line.

{recalc E_CALC}{menubranch EMENU}{quit}   The macro begins by recalculating the cell at E_CALC, which is also the description line for the custom menu at EMENU. The macro then calls up the custom menu choices, *ENTER* and *CHANGE_PHRASE*. If you select the *ENTER* menu choice, the macro instantly enters into the current cell whatever phrase has been stored in the cell named E_ENTER (cell B8 in Figure 13.2). If you select *CHANGE_*

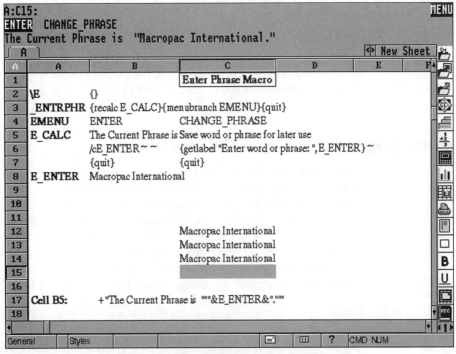

FIGURE 13.2 A macro for instantly entering a word or phrase.

PHRASE, the macro prompts you for the new word or phrase to store for later use by the macro.

The Current Phrase is "Macropac International." This line of the macro is the variable description line that appears under the first custom menu choice, *ENTER.* Its purpose is to show you the word or phrase the macro will enter in the current cell if you make this menu choice. In this case, the phrase is "Macropac International." The string formula underlying this line is best understood broken down as:

```
+"The Current Phrase is """&
E_ENTER&
"."""
```

Notice how the first part ends in three quotation marks. This is required to display one set of opening quotes in front of the displayed phrase, "Macropac International." The second part, of course, returns the phrase you have stored at the cell named E_ENTER. The last part displays as a period (.) and closing quotes.

/cE_ENTER~~   If you select the *ENTER* menu choice, the contents of the cell named E_ENTER are copied to the current cell.

{quit}   At this point, the macro quits. If you decide you want a different phrase stored in the macro, press Alt+E again (Ctrl+E in 1-2-3 for Windows), select CHANGE_PHRASE, and respond as required to the {getlabel} prompt.

Changing the Case of a Cell Entry

In the last chapter, you read about how the @cellpointer function cannot be used in {let} commands in Release 2 and 2.01 as it can in later releases. The macro in Figure 13.3 shows how you can use strings to work around problems like these. In this case, the macro uses string technology to substitute for use of @cellpointer("address") as the first argument in the {let} commands and @cellpointer("contents") as the second argument.

This macro gives you a handy tool for changing the label in a cell to uppercase, lowercase, or proper case. To operate the macro, place your cell

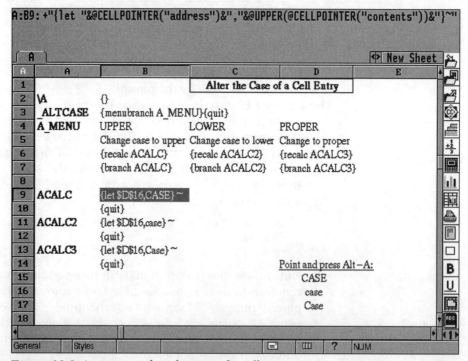

FIGURE 13.3 A macro to alter the case of a cell entry.

pointer on any cell whose case you want to change and press Alt+A (Ctrl+A in 1-2-3 for Windows).

{menubranch A_MENU}{quit}　　The macro begins by calling the menu choices *UPPER, LOWER,* and *PROPER.*

{recalc ACALC}　　The three menu choices begin in the same way, by recalculating ACALC, ACALC2, or ACALC3.

{branch ACALC}　　Strictly speaking, this command under the UPPER choice could have been a null string {} pass-through command. It is written in the same way as the branching commands under the LOWER and PROPER choices for clarity only.

{let $D$16,CASE)~{quit}　　This is the result of a string formula that is best understood broken down as:

```
+"{let "&
@cellpointer("address")&
","&
@upper(@cellpointer("contents"))&
")~{quit}"
```

By now you have no trouble deciphering the components of this string formula. The string formulas in ACALC2 and ACALC3 are almost identical, except that the @function applied to the @cellpointer("contents") component is changed to @lower and @proper, respectively.

If you refer now to Figure 13.4, you will see how this same macro would be written for Release 2.2 or higher. Instead of having string formulas that must be recalculated before they are used by the macro, this example shows how you can use @cellpointer("address") and @cellpointer ("contents") directly in the {let} commands for each menu choice.

Displaying the Difference between Two Dates

The macro in Figure 13.5 provides an example of string formulas that display a variable message in the upper panel. As you will see, the second of the two string formulas in this macro performs calculations based on your input before displaying the results.

Here's how the macro works:

{getlabel "Type 1st date (m/dd/yy) or Press Enter for Today: ",SUB1}　　Prompts for the first date in the configuration m/dd/yy. For example, you might type 3/5/88. Alternatively, you can press Enter for today's date. Your response is stored in SUB1.

{if SUB1=""}{recalc S_NOW}{let SUB1,S_NOW}　　If you press Enter instead of entering a date at the prompt, SUB1 becomes blank. In

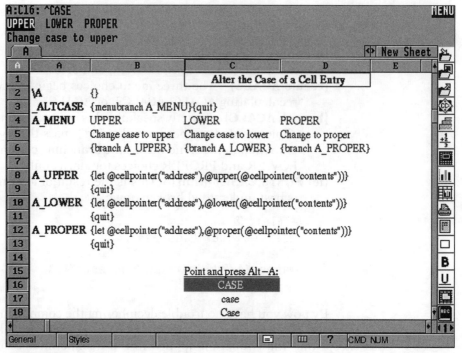

FIGURE 13.4 A macro to change case in Release 2.2 and higher.

that event, the macro is designed to recalculate S_NOW to reflect today's date in the same m/dd/yy format, then copy today's date to SUB1.

{getlabel "Type 2nd date (m/dd/yy) or Press Enter for Today: ",SUB2} Prompts for the second date in the configuration m/dd/yy or you can press Enter for today's date. Your response is stored in SUB2.

{if SUB2=""}{recalc S_NOW}{let SUB2,S_NOW} As before, if you press Enter, S_NOW is recalculated to reflect today's date in the same m/dd/yy format, then copied to SUB2.

{recalc S_MSG}{recalc S_CALC} Recalculates the string formulas in S_MSG and S_CALC.

The number of days between 3/5/88 and 3/8/88 is This line is the displayed result of the string formula in S_MSG and consists of the following:

```
+"The number of days between "&
SUB1&
" and "&
SUB2&
" is"
```

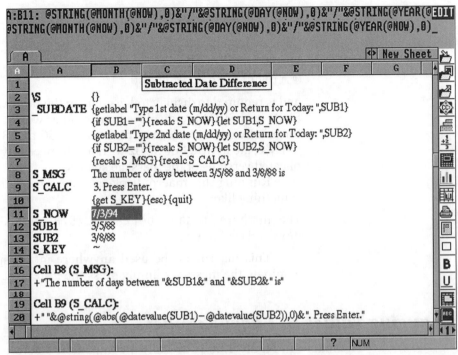

FIGURE 13.5 A macro to show the number of days between two dates.

The macro types this—the beginning of the entire message—in the upper panel.

3. Hit Enter. This is the rest of the message that the macro types. Although the display is short, it consists of:

```
+" "&
@string(@abs(@datevalue(SUB1)-
@datevalue(SUB2)),0)&
".Hit Enter."
```

By calculating the absolute of the difference between the date value of SUB1 and SUB2, the macro comes up with a positive number representing the number of days between the two dates.

{get S_KEY}{esc}{quit} The macro pauses for your press of any key. Whatever key you press, the {esc} command eliminates the message typed in the upper panel and the macro quits.

7/3/94 The date in cell B11 named S_NOW changes based on the date you use this macro. Note, however, the underlying formula shown for this date. You can see it in the upper panel in Figure 13.5. This formula consists of the following parts:

```
@string(@month(@now),0)&
"/"&
@string(@day(@now),0)&
"/"7
@string(*@year(@now),0)
```

and is required to display today's date in the same way the dates in SUB1 and SUB2 are displayed; or in other words, in the m/dd/yy format. Done this way, the strings in S_MSG and S_CALC can use today's date in SUB1 or SUB2 without the necessity for other complicated versions of the message strings.

Running this macro displays a message in the upper panel something like:

```
The number of days between 3/5/88 and 3/8/88 is 3
days. Hit Enter.
```

This macro can be used anywhere in the spreadsheet. To eliminate the message, simply press the Enter key.

Changing Values to Label-Numbers

The macro in Figure 13.6 is actually a companion macro to the macro in Figure 11.11. While the macro in Figure 11.11 was designed to change label-numbers to values, this macro does the reverse, changing values to label-numbers while retaining the displayed format.

This macro is also an interesting example of the use of a string formula to get around the problem that you cannot use @cellpointer("address") as an argument in the {contents} command.

Here's how the macro works:

{windowsoff}{paneloff} Turns off the windows and panel to suppress screen flicker and speed up the macro.

/rncCOL TO CHANGE?~~/rndCOL TO CHANGE?~ Creates, then deletes, the range name COL TO CHANGE? designed as a prompt to the user.

/rnc{panelon}COL TO CHANGE?~{windowson}{?}~ Again creates the prompting range name COL TO CHANGE?, turns on the windows, and pauses for the user's highlighting of the column to convert from values to number-labels.

{for L_COUNT,1,@rows(COL TO CHANGE?),1,LLOOP} This {for} command counts at L_COUNT, starting at the number 1, counting up to the number of rows in COL TO CHANGE?, counting by ones, and for each increment runs the routine at LLOOP.

{up}/rndCOL TO CHANGE?~{quit} At the end of the {for} command, the macro moves the cell pointer (which by this time is one

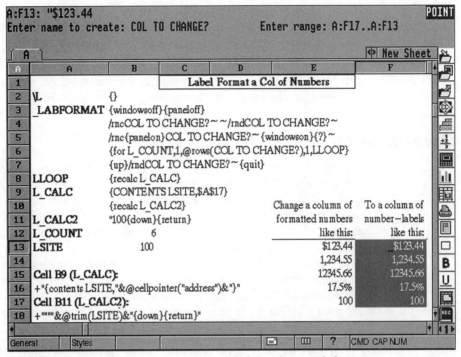

FIGURE 13.6 Macro to change values to label-numbers with formats.

cell below the last entry in the column) up one cell, deletes the range name COL TO CHANGE?, and quits.

{recalc L_CALC} This is the beginning of the routine at LLOOP that the macro runs in its {for} loop as many times as there are rows in the column to change.

{contents LSITE,$A$17} This line is the displayed result of a string formula, consisting of:

```
+"{contents LSITE,"&
@cellpointer("address")&
"}"
```

This line places in LSITE a label copy of the contents of the current cell, including any format identifiers such as dollar signs, commas, percentage signs, and so on.

{recalc L_CALC2} Recalculates the string formula in L_CALC2.

"100{down}{return} This is the displayed result of a string formula, consisting of the following:

```
+""""&
@trim(LSITE)&
"{down}{return}"
```

A string formula is required for this line because LSITE is variable, depending on the current cell pointer contents.

Like the macro in Figure 11.11, this macro works surprisingly quickly to convert values to labels. Note, each resulting label in the column is entered beginning with quotation marks instead of an apostrophe. This ensures that the label is right-justified, as are the values.

Creating a Custom Help Screen

When 1-2-3 Release 2.2 shipped, it provided users the ability to capture a press of the F1 Help key using the {get} command for the first time. This new feature is especially useful for creating custom help screens for your users, but you can also accomplish the equivalent feat by simply capturing another of the function keys. For example, you can capture the little-used F8 Table key in any 1-2-3 release.

The macro in Figure 13.7 allows your users to switch to a custom help screen when they press the F8 key. It also calculates the address of the upper left corner of the help screen and uses that information in strings to limit the user's ability to move around (and potentially damage) the contents of the help screen.

{if 0} Rem: Macro requires an area range-named HELPSCREEN.
This is an interesting use of the {if} command to permit a nonoperational line to be inserted in the beginning of your macro. Since any false statement in an {if} command causes the macro to skip the rest of the line and continue in the line below, starting a line with {if 0}—the equivalent of {if @false}—allows you to create an introductory note like this, giving instructions that the macro requires a range-named HELPSCREEN before it will work. As macro code, this line has no effect whatever on the operation of your macro, but it shows you an easy way to add comments to your macro code.

> **NOTE**: *If you have the latest release of 1-2-3 for Windows, you can use {-- comment} instead of {if 0} followed by a comment.*

{indicate MACRO}{onerror HQUIT} In Release 2.2 and higher, the {indicate} prompt can be quite a bit longer, such as:

```
{indicate "Press the F8 key for more information"}
```

which would also obviate the need for the next line shown here. In any case, the {onerror} command is important in case the user presses Ctrl+Break. Without this {onerror} command, the In-

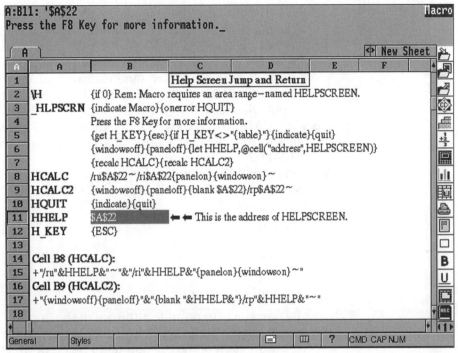

FIGURE 13.7 Macro to jump to help screen and return.

dicator prompt is left on the screen when the macro ends; but with it, the {indicate} command at HQUIT returns the prompt to normal.

Press the F8 Key for more information. The macro types this message in the upper panel. In Release 2.2 and higher, of course, this message can rely on the more intuitive instruction to press the F1 Help key. In that case, the {if} statement in the next line would read:

```
{if H_KEY<>"{HELP}"}
```

{get H_KEY}{esc}{if H_KEY<>"{table}"}{indicate}{quit} The macro pauses so you can press the F8 Table key. After you press any key, the {esc} command that follows eliminates the typed prompt. If you press any key other than F8, the {indicate} command returns the Ready indicator to normal and the macro quits.

{windowsoff}{paneloff}{let HHELP,@cell("address",HELPSCREEN)} Turns off the windows and panel to suppress screen flicker and speed up the macro, and then causes the contents of HHELP to reflect the cell address of the upper left corner of the range you have named HELPSCREEN.

Incidentally, the formula **@cell("address",HELPSCREEN)** was not inserted in HHELP in advance because such a formula cannot be accepted by Release 2.x until the range name HELP-SCREEN exists. Using a {let} command in the macro itself allows you to type in the macro (and transfer it from worksheet file to worksheet file) without having to concern yourself ahead of time about whether HELPSCREEN exists in the worksheet.

{recalc HCALC}{recalc HCALC2}   Recalculates the string formulas in the following two lines of the macro named HCALC and HCALC2.

/ru$A$22~/ri$A$22{panelon}{windowson}~   This display of the string formula in cell B8 named HCALC can be broken down as:

```
+"/ru"&
HHELP&
"~"&
"/ri"&
HHELP&
"{panelon}{windowson}~"
```

Its purpose is to unprotect the cell in the upper left corner of the range named HELPSCREEN, then select /Range Input to limit the movement of the cell pointer to this cell, which should be the sole unprotected cell in HELPSCREEN.

{windowsoff}{paneloff}{blank $A$22}/rp$A$22~   This display of the string formula in B9 named HCALC2 consists of:

```
+"{windowsoff}{paneloff}"&
"{blank "&
HHELP&
"}/rp"&
HHELP&
"~"
```

Once you press Enter, the windows and panel are turned off again, the upper left corner of HELPSCREEN is blanked in case your user made an entry there in error, and the cell is protected again with /Range Protect.

{indicate}{quit}   Finally, the macro returns the Ready indicator to normal and quits.

Creating a Sum-and-Stay Macro

Here's a common annoyance you may have encountered. You want to sum several individual cells, so you press the Plus sign (+), point to a cell, then press Plus (+) again; but the cell pointer jumps back to your starting point. If the second cell you want to sum is beyond the first, you find yourself repeating movement keystrokes unnecessarily as your cell pointer is jumped back to your starting point each time you press the Plus (+) sign.

The macro in Figure 13.8 eliminates this problem. To operate the macro, place the cell pointer at the place where you want the sum to reside, press Alt+S (Ctrl+S in 1-2-3 for Windows), and respond to the menu choices +, −, *EDIT,* and *FINISH* by selecting the Plus (+). Respond to the prompt, "Enter address to go to" by pointing to the first cell to include in the sum. When you press Enter, the cell pointer temporarily jumps to the original location, but when you select the Plus (+) again from the custom menu, it jumps back to the first cell to sum and prompts you from there to "Enter address to go to."

> **/re~{let S_HERE,@cellpointer("address")}~**   The macro begins by erasing the current cell, then stores the current cell address in S_HERE.
>
> **{let STAY,S_HERE}{menubranch S_MENU}{quit}**   Copies the current cell address in S_HERE to the cell named STAY, then offers

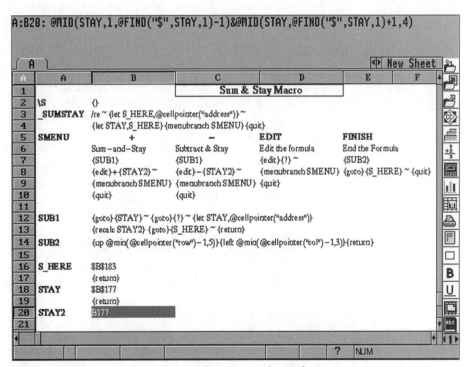

FIGURE 13.8 A summing macro with a sum-and-stay feature.

the menu choices +, −, *EDIT,* and *FINISH.* If you type the Plus (+) or Minus (−) sign, the macro continues by first making a subroutine branch to the code at SUB1.

{goto}{STAY}~{goto}{?}~{let STAY,@cellpointer("address")}   This first line at SUB1 has different effects depending on whether you typed Plus (+) or Minus (−) for the first time since invoking the macro. Since the cell pointer is already at the address in STAY during the first pass through this line of the macro, the command {goto} {STAY}~ has no effect this time through. Subsequently, however, this command plays an important function in keeping the cell pointer from staying at the starting point where the sum formula is being created.

The next part of this macro line, {goto}{?}~, prompts you for the location of the first cell you want in your sum formula. Then the macro uses a {let} command to store the current cell address in the cell named STAY.

{recalc STAY2}{goto}{S_HERE}~{return}   Recalculates the formula in STAY2, moves the cell pointer to the original cell address stored in S_HERE, and returns flow to the main macro code in row 8.

The formula in STAY2, which returns the relative form of the absolute address in STAY, can be broken down as:

```
@mid(STAY,1,@find("$",STAY,1)-1)&
@mid(STAY,@find("$",STAY,1)+1,4)
```

The first part of this formula uses @mid to isolate the column letters from the absolute address in STAY by extracting the number of characters between the first offset (second character) and the number of the offset position of the second dollar sign ($) in the absolute address less one.

The second part of the formula uses @mid to isolate the row number from the absolute address in STAY by extracting the number from the number of the offset position of the second dollar sign ($) in the absolute address plus one, to a position up to a maximum of four characters beyond that point.

> **NOTE:** *You may want to keep this formula handy for use in other cases where you need to display absolute cell addresses (like $B$27) in their relative forms (like B27).*

{edit}+{STAY2}~   This macro code in row 8 switches to Edit mode, types the Plus (+) sign, then types the address in STAY2. Since the cell pointer is back at the starting cell at this point, the effect is to create a summing formula that adds the value in the last cell visited.

{menubranch SMENU}{quit}   Once again calls up the menu choices **+, −, EDIT,** and **FINISH**. When you select the Plus (+) choice this time, however, the first thing the macro does is to jump back to the last cell you indicated you wanted to add, thus saving the keystrokes you would normally have to press to return to that point.

If you select the Minus (−) choice, the macro operates in exactly the same way, except that it subtracts the cell you point to instead of adding it.

If you select *EDIT*, the macro processes the command **{edit}{?}**, then branches back to the menu choices +, −, *EDIT*, and *FINISH* again.

If you select *FINISH*, the macro branches to the subroutine at SUB2 where it uses @min with @cellpointer("row") and @cellpointer("col") to adjust the original cell more towards the center of the screen. Then it moves the cell pointer back to the original cell and quits.

Figure 13.9 shows an example of the type of spreadsheet where this macro might come in handy. If you want a total of all the furniture items sold to be displayed at cell E17, place your cell pointer at E17, press Alt+S (Ctrl+S in 1-2-3 for Windows), select the Plus (+) sign, point to E15, select the Plus (+) sign again and point to E10, select the Plus (+) sign again and point to E5,

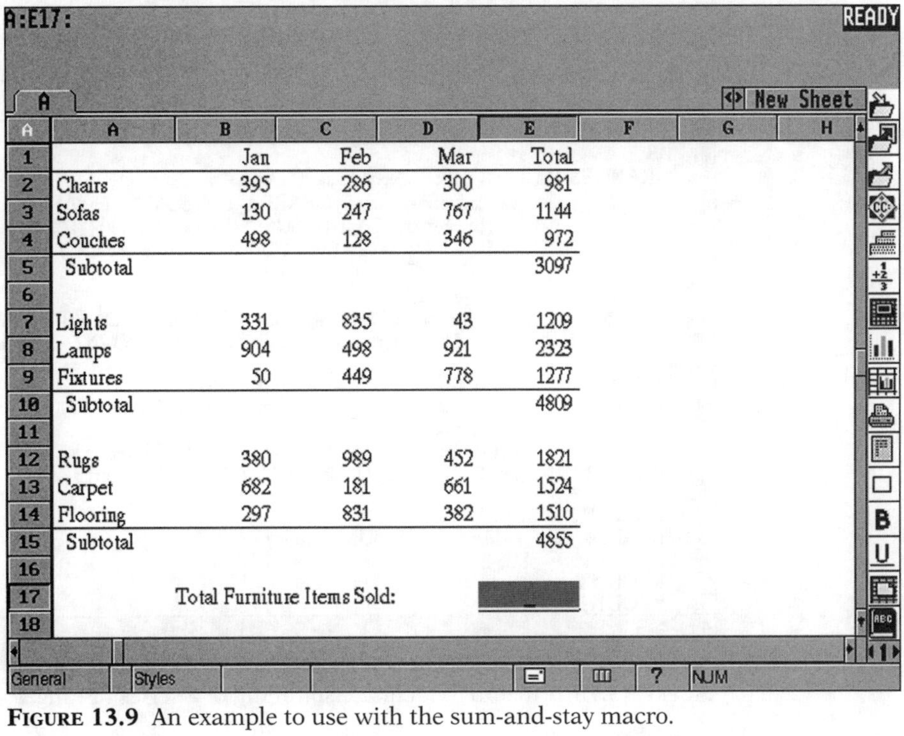

	A	B	C	D	E	F	G	H
1		Jan	Feb	Mar	Total			
2	Chairs	395	286	300	981			
3	Sofas	130	247	767	1144			
4	Couches	498	128	346	972			
5	Subtotal				3097			
6								
7	Lights	331	835	43	1209			
8	Lamps	904	498	921	2323			
9	Fixtures	50	449	778	1277			
10	Subtotal				4809			
11								
12	Rugs	380	989	452	1821			
13	Carpet	682	181	661	1524			
14	Flooring	297	831	382	1510			
15	Subtotal				4855			
16								
17		Total Furniture Items Sold:						
18								

A:E17: READY

New Sheet

General | Styles | NUM

FIGURE 13.9 An example to use with the sum-and-stay macro.

and then select **FINISH.** You will see the formula +E15+E10+E5 appear in cell E20, all done with a minimum of pointer keystrokes.

Summing a Series of Ranges

The macro in Figure 13.10 is like the sum-and-stay macro, except that it sums a series of ranges instead of a series of individual cells. As you can see in Figure 13.11, this macro uses several string formulas, all designed to permit reference to variable range locations as you designate which range locations you want to include in your @sum formula.

After you invoke this macro and indicate the separate ranges to sum, you get a resulting formula like @sum(C43..C46,C39..C41,C33..C37) as shown in Figure 13.12.

Here's how the macro works:

> **{let R_HERE,@cellpointer("address")}** The macro begins by using the {let} command to create a place-marker at R_HERE.

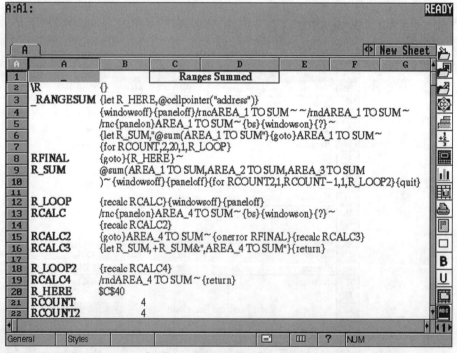

FIGURE 13.10 A macro to facilitate summing of a series of ranges.

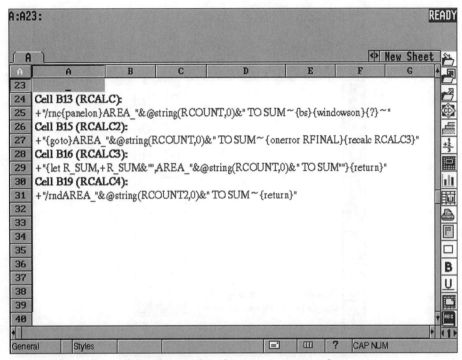

FIGURE 13.11 String formulas used in the Ranges Summed macro.

{windowsoff}{paneloff}/rncAREA_1 TO SUM~~/rndAREA_1 TO SUM~ Turns off the windows and panel, then creates and deletes the range-named AREA_1 TO SUM.

/rnc{panelon}AREA_1 TO SUM~{bs}{windowson}{?}~ Again creates the prompting range name AREA_1 TO SUM, then pauses so you can highlight the first range to be included in your @sum formula.

{let R_SUM,"@sum(AREA_1 TO SUM"}{goto}AREA_1 TO SUM~ Uses the {let} command to store the label, "@sum(AREA_1 TO SUM)" in R_SUM, then moves the cell pointer to the upper left corner of that range.

{for RCOUNT,2,20,1,R_LOOP} This is a {for} loop that counts at RCOUNT, starting with the number 2, counting up to a maximum of 20, counting by ones, and running the routine at R_LOOP with each counter increment. Its purpose is to prompt you for up to 20 areas to include in your ranges to sum.

{goto}{R_HERE}~ This is the cell named RFINAL. The macro flow only reaches this cell after you have highlighted the last range you want to sum. That is, only if you press Ctrl+Break to interrupt the

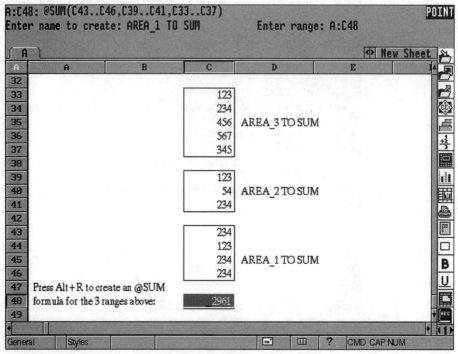

FIGURE 13.12 An example using the ranges summed macro.

{for} loop because you do not want to designate another range or if you actually designate the full limit of 20 ranges to sum. Whatever the circumstance, the macro now moves the cell pointer back to its original location stored in R_HERE.

@sum(AREA_1 TO SUM,AREA_2 TO SUM,AREA_3 TO SUM This cell is named R_SUM; it consists of the beginning of a variable @sum formula as created by the {let} commands in cell B6 or B16. This formula changes based on the number of ranges you decide to include as you run the macro.

)~{windowsoff}{paneloff}{for RCOUNT2,1,RCOUNT-1,1,R_LOOP2} {quit} This line completes the @sum formula, turns off the windows and panel, then starts a {for} loop at RLOOP2 designed to delete the range names such as AREA_1 TO SUM, AREA_2 TO SUM, and so on.

{recalc RCALC}{windowsoff}{paneloff} This is the beginning of the routine of the first {for} loop, starting at the cell named R_LOOP, designed to prompt you for up to 20 areas to include in your ranges to sum.

/rnc{panelon}AREA_4 TO SUM~{bs}{windowson}{?}~ Although this appears as the familiar creation of a prompting range name (in this case, the range name AREA_4 TO SUM?), it is actually the resulting display of the following string formula:

```
+"/rnc{panelon}AREA_"&
@string(RCOUNT,0)&
" TO SUM~{bs}{windowson}{?}~"
```

This formula begins by creating the range name AREA_1 TO SUM, followed by AREA_2 TO SUM in the second pass through the {for} loop, AREA_3 TO SUM in the third pass, and so on.

{recalc RCALC2} Recalculates the next cell, named RCALC2.

{goto}AREA_4 TO SUM~{onerror RFINAL}{recalc RCALC3} Moves the cell pointer to the top of the most recent range designated as an area to sum, through use of the following string formula:

```
+"{goto}AREA_"&
@string(RCOUNT,0)&
" TO SUM~{onerror RFINAL}{recalc RCALC3}"
```

The {onerror} command is included so the macro branches to RFINAL when you press Ctrl+Break after highlighting the last range to sum.

{let R_SUM,+R_SUM&",AREA_4 TO SUM"}{return} Increases the contents of R_SUM to include the most recent range designed as an area to sum. This line is the displayed result of the following string formula:

```
+"{let R_SUM,+R_SUM&
"",AREA_"&
@string(RCOUNT,0)&
" TO SUM""}{return}"
```

{recalc RCALC4} This is the beginning of the routine referred to in the closing {for} loop just before the macro quits at B10. It begins by recalculating the next line of the macro at the cell named RCALC4.

/rndAREA_4 TO SUM~{return} By the time the macro gets to this point, your @sum range has been established. If you are summing three separate ranges, the @sum formula will be something like:

```
@sum(AREA_1 TO SUM,AREA_2 TO SUM,AREA_3 TO SUM)
```

With each pass of the {for} loop at B10, this line deletes each range name in turn. It does this by using the variable string formula:

```
+"/rndAREA_"&@string(RCOUNT2,0)&" TO SUM~{return}"
```

The result is an @sum formula with cell coordinates instead of range names, something like this:

@sum(C43..C46,C39..C41,C33..C37)

Creating a Column Jump Macro

1-2-3 has a drawback in that it does not allow you to easily jump to another off-screen column while staying in the same row without losing your relative position on the screen. For example, if you are positioned at cell A17 and you want to visit Z17, pressing the F5 Goto key, typing Z17, and pressing Enter deposits your cell pointer at the correct location, but in the upper left corner of the screen. Fortunately, you can use string formulas to create a handy Column Jump macro, as shown in Figure 13.13.

NOTE: *If you have the latest release of 1-2-3 for Windows, you may want to explore the Navigation commands in Appendix A.*

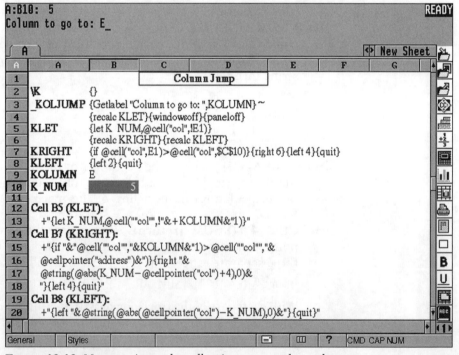

FIGURE 13.13 Macro to jump the cell pointer to another column.

To use this macro, simply press Alt+K (Ctrl+K in 1-2-3 for Windows). At the prompt for a column to go to, enter a single- or double-letter column identifier, and press Enter. The macro instantly jumps your cell pointer to the column you want to go to while leaving your cell pointer properly positioned on the screen.

{Getlabel "Column to go to: ",KOLUMN}~ The macro begins by prompting you for the column letter or letters, placing your response in the cell named KOLUMN.

{recalc KLET}{windowsoff}{paneloff} Recalculates the next cell named KLET, then turns off the windows and panel to suppress screen flicker and speed up the macro.

{let K_NUM,@cell("col",!E1)} This is the displayed result of a string formula, as follows:

```
+"{let K_NUM,@cell(""col"",!"&
+KOLUMN&
"1)}"
```

The purpose of this line is to combine the column letter you entered with an arbitrary row number (we used row number 1), to calculate and store in K_NUM the number of the column that corresponds to your entry. For example, if you entered the column letter K, the macro line would read:

```
{let K_NUM,@cell("col",!K1)}
```

which would cause the number 11 to be entered in K_NUM.

{recalc KRIGHT}{recalc KLEFT} Recalculates the string formulas in KRIGHT and KLEFT.

{if @cell("col",E1)>@cell("col",$E$1)}{right 3}{left 4}{quit} This {if} statement moves the cell pointer to the right if you entered a column letter that resides to the right of your current position. A string formula is required to calculate and display how far to the right the cell pointer should be moved:

```
+"{if"&"@cell(""col"","&KOLUMN&"1)>@cell(""col"","&
@cellpointer("address")&")}{right "&
@string(@abs(KNUM-@cellpointer("col")+4),0)&
"}{left 4}{quit}"
```

{left 1}{quit} Otherwise, the cell pointer is moved to the left, based on the following string formula:

```
+"{left "&
@string(@abs(@cellpointer("col")-K_NUM),0)&
"}{quit}"
```

Since your windows and upper panel have been turned off for the jump to the right or left, all you will see after you enter a column number is a short screen flicker, after which the screen changes to show your cell pointer in the new column, but still in the same row. More importantly, you will still be in the same relative vertical position on the screen instead of being left in the upper left corner.

Jump Left, Right, Top, or Bottom

In Chapter 5 we showed a simple macro designed to jump your cell pointer to the leftmost or topmost cell of the spreadsheet without losing your relative position on the screen. (See Figure 5.8.) Unfortunately, this macro requires use of the /Worksheet Titles command. This means that if you already have your titles locked in, the macro inappropriately eliminates those titles as it attempts to create new titles.

In this section we look at a more advanced macro using string formulas to jump your cell pointer to the leftmost cell (column A) in the current row, the rightmost filled cell in the current row, the top cell (row 1) in the current column, or the lowest filled cell in the current column. Refer to Figure 13.14.

{menubranch L_MENU}{quit}   The macro begins by offering the menu choices RIGHT, LEFT, TOP, and BOTTOM. Select RIGHT to jump your cell pointer to the rightmost filled cell in the current row.

{windowsoff}{paneloff}   Turns off the windows and panel to suppress screen flicker and speed up the macro.

{goto}{end}{home}   Moves the cell pointer to the End Home location in the spreadsheet. (Notice that there is no tilde at this point to complete the {goto} command.)

{let LCOL,@cellpointer("address")}   Creates a place-marker at LCOL to store the address of the cell at the End Home location.

{esc}{recalc LCALC}   Having recorded the End Home location, the macro backs out of the F5 Goto sequence with the Escape key, then recalculates the next cell named LCALC.

{right @cell("col",$A$192)-@cellpointer("col")+2}   Moves the cell pointer to the right a number of cells equal to two cells more than the difference between the current column and the rightmost column. This is actually the displayed result of the following string formula:

```
+"{right @cell(""col"","&+LCOL&")-@cellpointer(""col"")+2}"
```

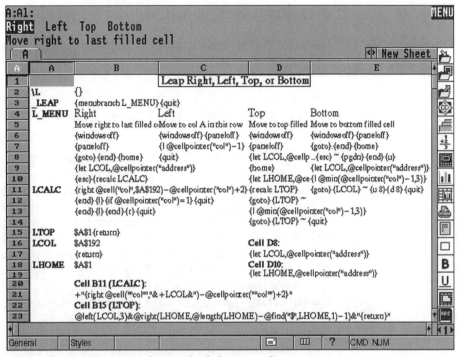

FIGURE 13.14 A macro to leap right, left, top, or bottom.

{end}{left}{if @cellpointer("col")=1}{quit}   Having moved two cells past the rightmost column, the cell pointer is now moved End LeftArrow to the rightmost filled cell in the current row. If that happens to be column A because there is no other entry in the current row, the macro quits.

{end}{left}{end}{right}{quit}   Otherwise, the cell pointer is moved End LeftArrow and End RightArrow to reposition the cell pointer to the right edge of the screen, and the macro quits.

{left @cellpointer("col")-1}{quit}   If you select LEFT, the cell pointer is simply moved left the number of columns necessary to move it to column A, and the macro quits.

{let LCOL,@cellpointer("address")}   If you select TOP, the macro creates a place-marker for the current cell, storing the cell address in the cell named LCOL.

{home}   The cell pointer is moved to the Home position. If there are no titles locked in, this will be cell A1. Otherwise, it will be the cell just below and/or to the right of the titles.

{let LHOME,@cellpointer("address")} The cell coordinates for this Home location are stored at LHOME.

{recalc LTOP}{goto}{LTOP}~ The address at LTOP is recalculated and the macro moves to that address. LTOP is based on the following string formula:

```
@left(LCOL,3)&
@mid(LHOME,@find("$",LHOME,1)+1,4)&
"{return}"
```

This formula isolates the column letter from the starting cell address stored in LCOL, appends the row number from the Home address stored in LHOME, and adds a {return} command to end the subroutine. The effect is to jump the cell pointer to the top cell (below the titles, if any) of the current column.

{left @min(@cellpointer("col")-1,3)} Moves the cell pointer either three cells to the left or one less than the current column, whichever is the lesser. This is done to reposition the top cell more towards the center of the screen.

{goto}{LTOP}~{quit} Finally, the cell pointer is jumped back to the top cell and the macro quits.

{goto}.{end}{home} If you select BOTTOM, you activate an interesting use of the F5 Goto key. The macro presses the F5 Goto key, then does something you would not normally think to do manually: It presses the period to lock in the cell coordinates so that any movement of the cell pointer highlights everything between the original cell and the cell you move to.

...{esc}~ The macro presses the Period (.) key three times to change the cell coordinates around. (Try this manually for yourself to see it clearly.) When the macro processes the {esc} command, the F5 Goto prompt is left with a cell address that combines the current column with the End Home row. The tilde completes the F5 Goto sequence and the cell pointer moves there.

{pgdn}{end}{up} The cell pointer moves down one page, then End UpArrow to ensure that it ends up in the lowest filled cell in the column.

{left @min(@cellpointer("col")-1,3)} Moves the cell pointer either three cells to the left or one less than the current column, whichever is less, to reposition the current cell more towards the center of the screen.

{goto}{LCOL}~{up 8}{down 8}{quit} The cell pointer moves back to the lowest filled cell in the column, then UpArrow eight cells and DownArrow eight cells to reposition the cell vertically, and the macro quits.

Calculating the Median of a Column

If you've ever tried to calculate the median of a range of values, you already know that currently 1-2-3 has no @median function that does the job for you. To compensate for this lack, the macro in Figure 13.15 makes use of the @mod, @index, @int, and @count functions as well as the @string and @cellpointer functions to calculate and display the median of any column of numbers.

To operate the macro, move to a vertical range of numbers for which you want to calculate the median. The numbers need not be sorted and the range can include blank cells. For an example, refer to Figure 13.16.

Here's how the macro works:

{windowsoff}{paneloff}/rncMEDIAN RANGE?~~/rndMEDIAN RANGE?~~ Turns off the windows and panel and begins the sequence to create a prompting range name.

/rnc{panelon}MEDIAN RANGE?~{windowson}{?}~ Creates the prompting range name MEDIAN RANGE?, turning on the upper

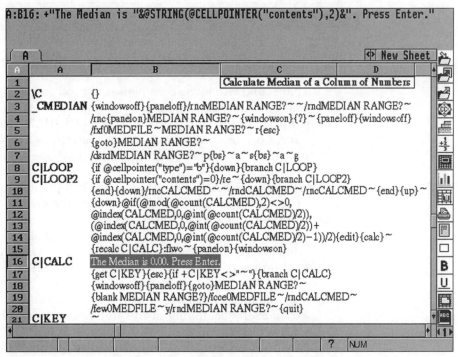

FIGURE 13.15 Calculate the median of a column of numbers.

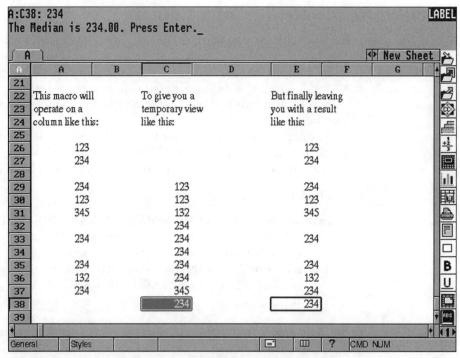

FIGURE 13.16 An example using the Median Calculator macro.

panel and windows, then pauses for you to highlight the vertical range of numbers for which you want the median calculated.

{paneloff}{windowsoff}/fxf0MEDFILE~MEDIAN RANGE?~r{esc} Turns off the windows and panel, then stores a copy of the cells in the range named MEDIAN RANGE? by doing a /File Xtract, naming the file 0MEDFILE.

{goto}MEDIAN RANGE?~ Moves the cell pointer to the top of the range of numbers for which you want the median calculated.

/dsrdMEDIAN RANGE?~p{bs}~a~s{bs}~a~g Sorts the range of numbers in ascending order. This places all blank cells, zero cells, and label cells above the cells with values in them.

{if @cellpointer("type")="b"}{down}{branch C|LOOP} This is the beginning of the loop named C|LOOP. If the current cell is blank, the cell pointer is moved down one cell, and then the macro loops back to the beginning of this line to check for whether the next cell is blank.

{if @cellpointer("contents")=0}/re~{down}{branch C|LOOP2} This is the beginning of the second loop, named C|LOOP2. If the current cell pointer contents are a label or otherwise equal to zero, the cell is erased, the cell pointer is moved down one cell, and the macro loops back to the beginning of this line to check for whether the next cell equals zero.

{end}{down}/rncCALCMED~~/rndCALCMED~/rncCALCMED~
{end}{up}~ By the time this line of the macro is reached, the cell pointer has bypassed all blank or zero cells, coming to the first cell with a value greater than zero. The cell pointer is moved End DownArrow to the bottom of this range of numbers, then the range named CALMED is created by highlighting End UpArrow to the top of the column.

{down 2}@if(@mod(@count(CALCMED),2)<>0, Moves the cell pointer two cells below the last filled cell in the range of numbers to calculate, and begins to type an @if function. The @if function checks for whether the number of units in CALCMED is an odd number or even by using @mod to divide the count in CALCMED by two.

@index(CALCMED,0,@int(@count(CALCMED)/2)), If the count is an odd number, the @if function uses @index to isolate from CALCMED (in this, the zero offset column) the item which is down from the first item the integer of the number exactly one-half the total number of items.

(@index(CALCMED,0,@int(@count(CALCMED)/2))+ Otherwise, if the count is even, the @if function works in two parts. First it uses @index to isolate from CALCMED the item which is in that same location.

@index(CALCMED,0,@int(@count(CALCMED)/2)-1))/2){edit}
{calc}~ Then it adds the item just below that item and divides the sum by two. Finally, the macro presses Edit and Calc to turn the formula to a straight value.

{recalc C|CALC}{panelon}{windowson} The macro recalculates C|CALC and turns the panel and windows off.

The median of this range of numbers is 0.00 . Press Enter. The macro types this message in the upper panel by displaying the result of a string formula:

```
+"The Median is "&
@string(@cellpointer("contents"),2)&
".Press Enter."
```

{get C|KEY}{if +C|KEY<>"~"}{esc}{branch C|CALC} The macro pauses until you press a key. If you do not press Enter, the macro presses Esc to eliminate the typed message, and then branches back to C|CALC to display the message once again.

{esc}{windowsoff}{paneloff}{goto}MEDIAN RANGE?~ Otherwise, the macro presses Esc to eliminate the typed message, the windows and upper panel are turned off, and the cell pointer is moved to the top of the range previously named MEDIAN RANGE?

{blank MEDIAN RANGE?}/fcce0MEDFILE~/rndCALCMED~ To restore the original range to its original location, the macro blanks MEDIAN RANGE? and the macro selects /File Combine Copy Entire of the extracted file named 0MEDFILE. The macro then deletes the range named CALCMED.

/few0MEDFILE~y/rndMEDIAN RANGE?~{quit} Finally, the macro erases the extracted file named 0MEDFILE, deletes the range named MEDIAN RANGE?, and quits.

> **NOTE:** *One last word about this macro: Be sure that you have allowed for at least one blank cell below the range of numbers for which you want the median calculated. This is required for the answer that the macro calculates and inserts at the bottom of the range.*

Creating a Vertical Custom Menu

Earlier in this chapter you saw how to use the {get} command to pause a macro for message viewing or to capture the press of the F1 or F8 keys as an indicator for viewing a separate help screen. In this section you'll see another use of the {get} command—to facilitate the creation of a vertical custom menu.

Chapter 5 demonstrated how to create horizontal custom menus for up to eight menu choices. While this is sufficient in most cases, there may be times when you'd like to have more choices, each with its own activating key—even when several choices start with the same letter. Figure 13.17 provides an example of such a macro.

Before you write the macro, you'll want to set up your menu choices on a separate page. Figure 13.18 shows an example of menu choices that refer to different parts of an overhead expense spreadsheet. When the user chooses one of the menu items, the macro branches the specific routine that sends the cell pointer to where that particular expense is located. Of course, you can use the techniques in this example to create vertical menu choices that branch to any number of macro programs that solve your own spreadsheet needs.

Be sure to assign the range names VERTCORNER, VRTMENU, and VEND as shown in Figure 13.18. Also notice how an individual letter is underlined in each menu item in Figure 13.18. To add an underline attribute at the character level like this, press Ctrl+A, which types an upward solid triangle character (▲) and tells 1-2-3 that the next typing you do represents attribute codes. Then type the attribute codes 1 and an underline. This tells 1-2-3 to underline the next letter(s) you type. Type the letter

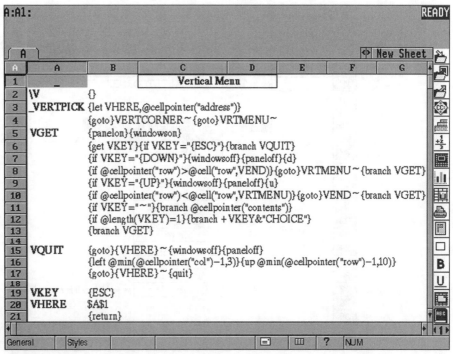

FIGURE 13.17 Creating a vertical custom menu.

you want to underline and press Ctrl+N. This enters a downward solid tri-angle (▼) and informs 1-2-3 to end the attribute. As you can see in Figure 13.18, the entry ▲1_R▼ent shown in the upper panel displays **Rent** in cell C26, with the letter R underlined. Use this same method for underlining specific letters in all of the individual menu items. (Notice that although the letter does not need to be the first character in the menu item, there are no duplications of underlined letters. For example, there is only one under-lined letter M.)

Figure 13.19 shows examples of short macro routines that the macro executes when the user chooses any of the items by the point-and-shoot method or by pressing the underlined letter. Each macro routine has two possible starting points: one with a range name that matches its corre-sponding menu item (attributes, underlines, and all) and the other with a range name that combines a starting letter with the word CHOICE.

> **NOTE:** *To make sure that you create range names that exactly match the corre-sponding menu items, use the /Copy command to simply copy the attributed menu items to this area of your spreadsheet.*

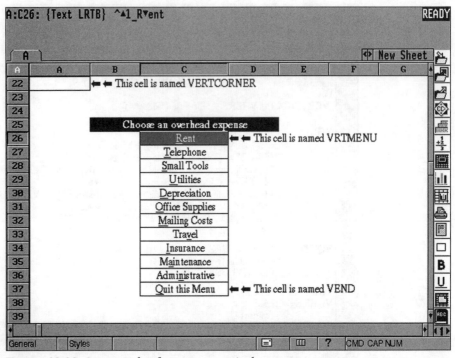

FIGURE 13.18 An example of a custom vertical menu.

In Figure 13.19, the macro routines are designed to use the {goto} command to simply jump the cell pointer to pre-established cells. Of course, in your own macro writing, you'll want to use different menu items that accomplish tasks specific to your own spreadsheet work.

Here's how the macro in Figure 13.17 works:

{let VHERE,@cellpointer("address")}   Begins by storing the current cell pointer address in the cell named VHERE.

{goto}VERTCORNER~{goto}VRTMENU~   Calls up the page where the vertical menu is stored by sending the cell pointer to the cell named VERTCORNER. Then the macro places the cell pointer at the first menu item, located in the cell prenamed VRTMENU.

{panelon}{windowson}   Later in the macro, the windows and panel are turned off to suppress unwanted cell pointer activity. This line of the macro, named VGET, is actually a looping point in the macro that has no effect in the beginning, but later restores the window and panel activity so the user can see the results of scrolling through the menu.

{get VKEY}{if VKEY="{ESC}"}{branch VQUIT}   This use of the {get} command waits for the user to press a single key. If the user

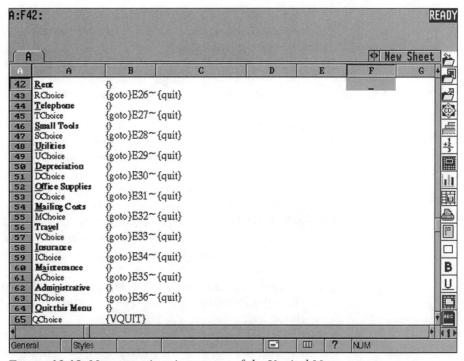

FIGURE 13.19 Macro routines in support of the Vertical Menu macro.

presses Esc, the macro branches to VQUIT, causing the cell pointer to return to its original position, and quits.

{if VKEY="{DOWN}"}{windowsoff}{paneloff}{d} If the user presses the DownArrow instead, the macro turns off the windows and panel and moves down one cell.

{if @cellpointer("row")>@cell("row",VEND)}{goto}VRTMENU~ {branch VGET} If the cell pointer is now past the cell VEND containing the last menu item, this line tells it to wrap around to the first menu item by sending it to VRTMENU, then branches back to VGET where the window and panel activity are restored.

{if VKEY="{UP}"}{windowsoff}{paneloff}{u} If instead of the DownArrow the user has pressed the UpArrow key, the macro turns off the windows and panel and moves up one cell.

{if @cellpointer("row")<@cell("row",VRTMENU)}{goto}VEND~ {branch VGET} If the cell pointer is now above the cell VRT-MENU containing the first menu item, this line tells it to wrap around to the last menu item by sending it to VEND, then branches back to VGET where the window and panel activity are restored.

{if VKEY="~"}{branch @cellpointer("contents")} Once the user has moved the cell pointer to the desired menu item and pressed

Enter, this line detects the press of the Enter key and branches to the cell (shown in Figure 13.19) whose name matches the current cell pointer contents.

{if @length(VKEY)=1}{branch+VKEY&"CHOICE"}   This line detects the user pressing a single letter and branches to the range name that matches a concatenation of the letter pressed and the word CHOICE.

{branch VGET}   If the user has not pressed a key that matches any of the {if} commands designed to trap specific keystrokes, this line simply branches back to the looping point in the macro named VGET.

That's all there is to the main macro. If you explore the subroutine at VQUIT, you'll see that it consists of only three lines:

{goto}{VHERE}~{windowsoff}{paneloff}   Sends the cell pointer back to the original cell where the macro was invoked, then suppresses unnecessary screen activity with the {windowsoff} and {paneloff} commands.

{left @min(@cellpointer("col")-1,3)}{up @min(@cellpointer("row") -1,10)}   Relocates the current cell more towards the center of the screen.

{goto}{VHERE}~{quit}   Finally, the macro returns the cell pointer to the original cell one last time and quits.

Incidentally, if you'd like to experiment with other attributes you can add at the character level, try using the :Text Edit command followed by the F3 Name key or manually enter examples from the following table:

Table 13.1 Formatting Attributes at the Character Level

To Use This Code	Type This	For This Effect
▲b	Ctrl+A,b,Rent	Rent in bold
▲d	Ctrl+A,d,Rent	Rent in subscript (shifted down)
▲f	Ctrl+A,f,Rent	Rent in a flashing mode
▲i	Ctrl+A,i,Rent	Rent in italics
▲u	Ctrl+A,u,Rent	Rent underlined
▲x	Ctrl+A,x,Rent	Rent with letters reversed
▲y	Ctrl+A,y,Rent	Rent with upside down letters
▲1_	Ctrl+A,1_,Rent	Rent with a single underline
▲2_	Ctrl+A,2_,Rent	Rent with a double underline
▲3_	Ctrl+A,3_,Rent	Rent with a wide underline
▲4_	Ctrl+A,4_,Rent	Rent with a box around it
▲5_	Ctrl+A,5_,Rent	Rent with a strike-through
▲1c	Ctrl+A,1c,Rent	Rent with the default color
▲2c	Ctrl+A,2c,Rent	Rent with the color red

Table 13.1 (*Continued*)

To Use This Code	*Type This*	*For This Effect*
▲3c	Ctrl+A,3c,Rent	Rent with the color green
▲4c	Ctrl+A,4c,Rent	Rent with the color dark-blue
▲5c	Ctrl+A,5c,Rent	Rent with the color cyan
▲6c	Ctrl+A,6c,Rent	Rent with the color yellow
▲7c	Ctrl+A,7c,Rent	Rent with the color magenta
▲8c	Ctrl+A,8c,Rent	Rent with colors reversed
▲1F or ▲A	Ctrl+A,A,Rent	Rent set for Font 1
▲2F or ▲B	Ctrl+A,B,Rent	Rent set for Font 2
▲3F or ▲C	Ctrl+A,C,Rent	Rent set for Font 3
▲4F or ▲D	Ctrl+A,D,Rent	Rent set for Font 4
▲5F or ▲E	Ctrl+A,E,Rent	Rent set for Font 5
▲6F or ▲F	Ctrl+A,F,Rent	Rent set for Font 6
▲7F or ▲G	Ctrl+A,G,Rent	Rent set for Font 7
▲8F or ▲H	Ctrl+A,H,Rent	Rent set for Font 8
▲–127k to ▲127k	Ctrl+A,–127k,Rent	Rent with a different kerning
▲1o to ▲255o	Ctrl+A,1o,Rent	Rent with an outline font

Don't forget that you can end an attribute at any character in a string by pressing Ctrl+N, which enters the downward-pointing triangle (▼).

Summary

In this chapter we explored the use of strings to create variable code in your macros. This chapter covered the following concepts:

- Strings can be used to create a temporary and variable message in your upper panel.
- The {if} command **{if @left(AKEY,1)="{"}** can be used to identify whether you pressed a function key or directional key such as {edit}, {home}, {left}, or {pgdn}.
- If you have Release 2 or 2.01, the {let} command will not accept an @function as its first argument. Thus, the command, **{let @cell-pointer("address"),999},** designed to place 999 in the current cell, gives the error message, "Invalid range in LET." This deficiency was corrected in Release 2.2. Alternatively, you can work around this problem by using @cellpointer("address") in an underlying string formula.
- Double quotes are required within a string function to return single quotes in the results.

- You can use string formulas not only as functioning parts of the program flow of a macro, but also as variable lines used for the descriptions that appear under custom menus.
- You can use a string formula to substitute for the use of @cell-pointer("address") as an argument in the {contents} command.
- Release 2.2 and higher have the ability to capture a press of the F1 Help key using the {get} command. This new feature is especially useful for creating custom help screens for your users, but you can also accomplish the equivalent feat by capturing another of the function keys—like the little-used F8 Table key.
- You can use {if 0} to create a remarks line. Since any false statement in an {if} command causes the macro to skip the rest of the line, starting a line with {if 0} or {if @false} allows you to end the line with a remark. As macro code, this line has no effect whatever on the operation of your macro.
- You can use @mid to isolate the column letter(s) and row number from an absolute address by extracting characters based on the offset position of the dollar signs ($) in the absolute address.
- Using strings, you can create a variable line in a macro that changes with each pass of a {for} loop.
- You can create a macro that makes an interesting use of the F5 Goto key, pressing the F5 Goto key, pressing the period to lock in the cell coordinates so that any movement of the cell pointer highlights everything between the original cell and the cell you move to, then pressing the period key again to reverse the offered cell coordinates before pressing Escape or Enter.

The following macros were shown in this chapter:

- A macro using string programming to display an ASCII code. This macro includes a temporary message typed in the upper panel, telling you the ASCII code that corresponds to the keystroke provided in response to a prompt.
- A macro for storing and instantly entering a word or phrase. This macro includes the use of string formulas to create a variable description line under a custom menu.
- A macro that allows you to change the label in any cell to uppercase, lowercase, or proper case.
- A macro to show the number of days between two dates.
- A macro to change values to label-numbers with formats. This macro is also an interesting example of the use of a string formula to get around the problem that you cannot use @cellpointer ("address") as an argument in the {contents} command.
- A macro to jump to a custom help screen and return by pressing the F8 key. This macro also calculates the address of the upper left cor-

ner of the help screen and uses that information in strings to limit the user's ability to move around (and potentially damage) the contents of the help screen.

- A summing macro with a sum-and-stay feature that offers the custom menu choices +, −, *EDIT,* and *FINISH.*
- A macro to facilitate the summing of a series of ranges. The result of this macro will be an @sum formula such as @sum(C43..C46, C39..C41,C33..C37).
- A macro to jump the cell pointer to another column, but still in the same row. Using this macro, you will be left in the same relative vertical position on the screen as you started instead of being sent—as you are if you use the F5 Goto key—to the upper left corner.
- A macro to jump your cell pointer to the leftmost cell (column A) in the current row, the rightmost filled cell in the current row, the top cell (row 1) in the current column, or the lowest filled cell in the current column.
- A macro to calculate the median of a column of numbers. This macro makes use of the @mod, @index, @int, and @count functions as well as the @string and @cellpointer functions to calculate and display the median of the range you highlight.
- A macro that shows you how to create a vertical custom menu with all the features of a standard horizontal scrolling macro, but with the possibility of more than eight choices. This macro lets your users select from the menu by pointing and pressing Enter, or by typing an underlined letter which can be other than the first letter in the menu item.

In the next chapter we explore macros that use 1-2-3's Wysiwyg (What-you-see-is-what-you-get) features. The examples we explore include shortcut macros to toggle between Wysiwyg attributes, frame types, display sizes, and printer orientations. We'll also take a look at macros that automate the loading of Wysiwyg add-ins and provide instant manipulation of Wysiwyg features.

14

Wysiwyg Macros

When you press the Colon (:) key in 1-2-3, you gain access to its most important features for controlling the display in Wysiwyg (What-you-see-is-what-you-get) format. In this chapter you'll learn how to speed up your spreadsheet publishing tasks using macros that access 1-2-3's Wysiwyg commands. Among these macros you'll find shortcuts for toggling between Wysiwyg attributes, frame types, display sizes, and printer orientations; automating the loading of Wysiwyg add-ins; changing Wysiwyg attributes the instant you retrieve a file; automating standard 1-2-3 /Copy and Wysiwyg :Copy commands; increasing the size of an outline box created with single, double, or wide lines; and instantly deleting a line that exists in both of two adjacent cells.

Toggle Macros

As you learned in earlier chapters, a toggle macro performs one action the first time you activate it and another action the next time. In this section, you'll read about toggle macros that make your Wysiwyg and spreadsheet publishing tasks easier.

Bold Attribute Toggle

Figure 14.1 shows a toggle macro that applies bold formatting the first time you press Alt+B (Ctrl+B in 1-2-3 for Windows), then clears the bold formatting when you run the macro again.

Here's how the Bold Attribute Toggle macro works:

{} The macro begins with a null pass-through command that permits the macro to start at either B2 or B3. Invoke the macro by pressing Alt+B (Ctrl+B in 1-2-3 for Windows) or by pressing Alt+F3 and selecting_BOLD.

{if BTOGGLE=0}{branch BOLDOFF} The first command is an {if} command that tests whether the value in BTOGGLE is equal to zero. If so, the macro skips down to cell B6, named BOLDOFF. If not, the macro simply continues with the next line down, at cell B5.

:fbs~{let BTOGGLE,0}{quit} The macro selects :Format Bold Set and presses Enter, then uses a {let} command to cause the value in BTOGGLE to become zero and quits. This sets the macro up

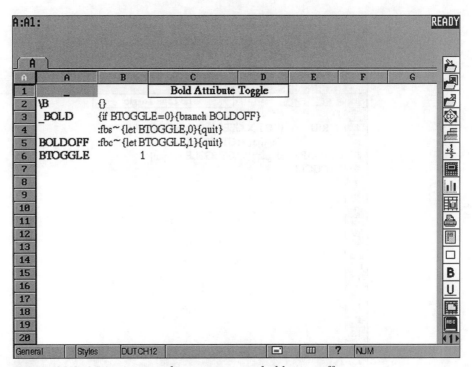

FIGURE 14.1 A Wywisyg toggle macro to turn bold on or off.

for its next use when the {if} statement in cell B4 will be found to be true and the macro will skip ahead to BOLDOFF.

:fbc~{let BTOGGLE,1}{quit}   This is the line named BOLDOFF. It selects :Format Bold Clear, presses Enter, then uses the {let} command to change the value in BTOGGLE to 1 so the next time you use the macro it will not skip ahead to BOLDOFF, but instead runs the commands at B5 setting the bold format.

The last line in the macro is named BTOGGLE and starts with a value of 1. This is not a part of the flow of the macro, but rather a named cell that the macro tests, acts on, then changes each time you press Alt+B (or Ctrl+B).

Grid Line Toggle

The Grid Line Toggle in Figure 14.2 alternately turns the worksheet grid lines on or off using Wysiwyg each time you press Alt+G (or Ctrl+G in 1-2-3 for Windows). Unlike the previous macro, this one works on the entire session, not on a specific cell or range.

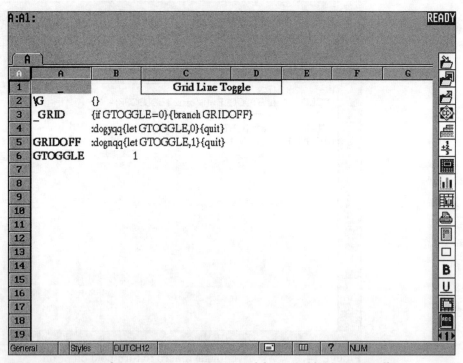

FIGURE 14.2 A Grid Line macro to turn spreadsheet grid lines on or off.

{} As with the last macro, the first line is a null, pass-through command.

{if GTOGGLE=0}{branch GRIDOFF} If the value in GTOGGLE is set at zero, the macro skips ahead to GRIDOFF.

:dogyqq{let GTOGGLE,0}{quit} The macro selects :Display Options Grid Yes Quit Quit, then uses a {let} command to change the value in GTOGGLE to zero, so the next time you press Alt+G (or Ctrl+B) the macro will skip ahead to GRIDOFF. At this point the macro quits.

:dognqq{let GTOGGLE,1}{quit} This is the cell named GRIDOFF where the macro branches if the toggle is set to zero. The macro selects :Display Options Grid No Quit Quit, then uses a {let} command to change the value in GTOGGLE to 1, so the next time you press Alt+G (or Ctrl+B) the macro will *not* skip ahead to GRID-OFF.

As with the previous macro, the cell named GTOGGLE starts with a value of 1, which changes to zero after you press Alt+G (or Ctrl+G) and the macro turns on the grid. The next time you press Alt+G (or Ctrl+G), the macro turns the grid off and changes the toggle back to 1.

Lines Attribute Toggle

The Lines Attribute Toggle in Figure 14.3 works like the toggles in Figure 14.1 and 14.2, except that it allows for a cycle through three choices instead of two. When you press Alt+L (or Ctrl+L in 1-2-3 for Windows) using this macro, the current cell or preselected range is alternately formatted using :Format Lines Outline, :Format Lines All, or :Format Lines Clear All.

{} The first line is a null, pass-through command.

{if LTOGGLE=0}{branch LINEOFF} If the value in LTOGGLE is set at zero, the macro skips ahead to LINEOFF.

{if LTOGGLE=1}{branch LINEALL} If the value in LTOGGLE is set at 1, the macro skips ahead to LINEALL.

{windowsoff}:flca~:flo~{let LTOGGLE,0}{quit} Alternatively, the screen is frozen with the {windowsoff} command to speed up the macro and the macro invokes the commands :Format Lines Clear All and :Format Lines Outline. The {let} command changes the value at LTOGGLE to zero and the macro quits.

:flca~{let LTOGGLE,1}{quit} This is the cell named LINEOFF where the macro branches if the value at LTOGGLE is set at zero. The macro selects :Format Lines Clear All, then changes LTOGGLE to 1 and quits.

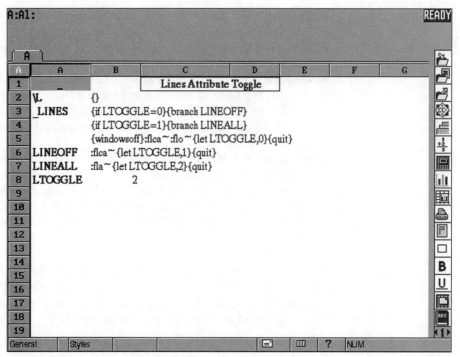

FIGURE 14.3 A Lines Attribute Toggle to cycle through three line choices.

> **:fla~{let LTOGGLE,2}{quit}** This is the cell named LINEALL where the macro branches if the value at LTOGGLE is set at one. The macro selects :Format Lines All, then changes LTOGGLE to 2 and quits.

The cell named LTOGGLE starts with a value of 2 which will change to zero after you press Alt+L (Ctrl+L in 1-2-3 for Windows) and the macro changes the formatting to Outline. The next time you press Alt+L (or Ctrl+L), the macro clears all the lines and changes LTOGGLE to 1. When you press Alt+L (or Ctrl+L) again, the macro changes the lines to ALL and changes LTOGGLE to 2.

Shade Attribute Toggle

The Shade Attribute Toggle in Figure 14.4 cycles through four types of shading: Clear, Light, Dark, and Solid.

If you compare this macro with the previous one, you can see that the principle is the same; only the toggle tasks and the number of toggles has changed. Depending on whether STOGGLE is set at 0, 1, 2, or 3, the macro selects :Format Shade Clear, Light, Dark, or Solid.

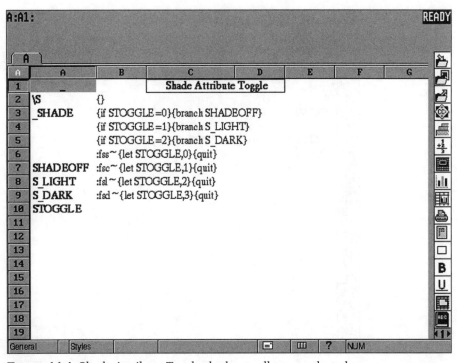

FIGURE 14.4 Shade Attribute Toggle shades a cell or preselected range.

Frame Toggle

The Frame Toggle in Figure 14.5 alternately changes the worksheet frame to the standard 1-2-3 type or to the special frame showing inches.

The macro begins in the usual way with a null, pass-through command and a command that checks for the value in the toggle cell named FTOGGLE. If the value is zero, the macro skips to the cell named FRAME and selects :Display Options Frame Special Inches Quit Quit, changes the value in FTOGGLE to 1, and quits. If the value is 1, the macro selects :Display Options Frame 1-2-3 Quit Quit, changes the value in FTOGGLE to zero, and quits.

Display Zoom Toggle

The macro in Figure 14.6 cycles through Small, Tiny, and Normal views of the spreadsheet, so that you can get different zoomed displays of your data.

The macro starts with a null, pass-through command, then checks for whether DTOGGLE equals zero. If so, it skips to DSMALL, which selects :Display Zoom Small, then selects Rows 25 to change the number of rows (assuming default size) that will show on the screen. Selecting a small view and a row count of 25 is perfect for displaying in two screens, one over the

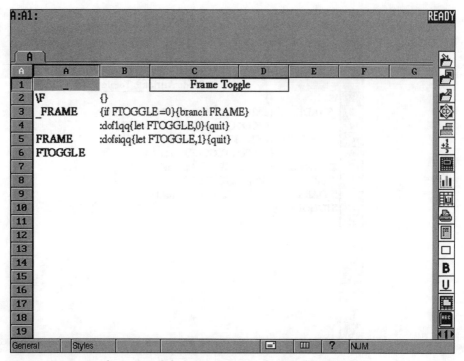

FIGURE 14.5 Toggle to switch between 1-2-3 and special inches frame.

other, a single print range that covers an 8½″ by 11″ sheet of paper when printed. In other words, you will not have to scroll past the last column to the right to see the rightmost boundary of your print range in Portrait mode and you need only press PgDn once to see the bottom boundary.

If DTOGGLE is equal to 1, the macro selects :Display Zoom Tiny, then selects Rows 25 before changing DTOGGLE to 2 and quitting. This size is perfect for being able to view a standard 8½″ × 11″ range when Wysiwyg's page orientation is set to Landscape.

If DTOGGLE is equal to 2, the macro selects :Display Zoom Normal, then selects Rows 20 before changing the value of DTOGGLE and quitting.

Orientation Toggle

Figure 14.7 shows the last toggle in this section—a macro that toggles between the Landscape and Portrait views using Wysiwyg. This toggle can be very useful for those spreadsheets that have multiple ranges where some need to be printed in Landscape layout and others in Portrait.

The macro works as the other toggles we have looked at in this section. It starts with a null, pass-through command, then tests for whether OTOGGLE equals zero. If so, the macro branches to OLANDSCAPE.

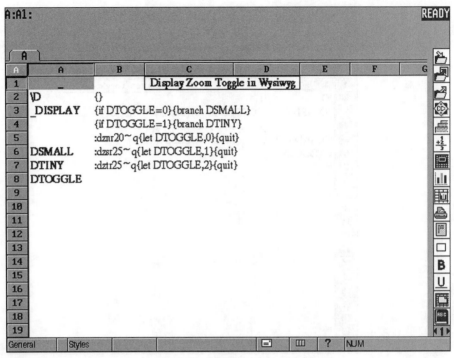

FIGURE 14.6 Macro to cycle through display zoom settings.

Otherwise, the macro selects :Print Configuration Orientation Landscape Quit Quit, changes the value of OTOGGLE to zero, and quits.

If the macro finds a zero in OTOGGLE (or if it's blank), it selects :Print Configuration Orientation Portrait Quit Quit, changes the value of OTOGGLE to 1, and quits.

Autoexec Macros with Wysiwyg

An autoexec macro that runs automatically as soon as the file containing it is retrieved can be especially useful for changing global features in ways that are appropriate for specific files. For example, if you want all the zeros suppressed in a particular file, you can save the global commands/ Worksheet Global Zero Yes in a short autoexec macro in that file so the zeros are automatically suppressed as the file is retrieved.

Automatically Loading Wysiwyg

The examples in Figure 14.8 show macros that load Wysiwyg automatically.

The first macro is designed to load Wysiwyg in Release 2.3. Note this macro makes the assumption that no Alt+Function key combination should

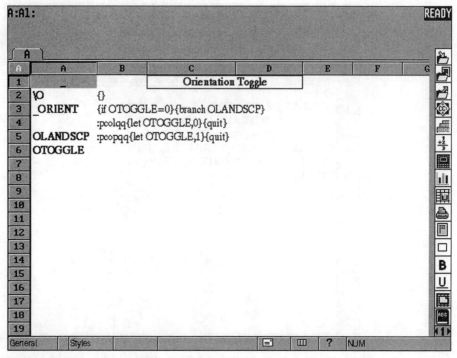

FIGURE 14.7 Toggle to switch between Landscape and Portrait mode.

be assigned to the add-in, since attaching Wysiwyg automatically invokes it as well.

The macro starts with a null, pass-through command, then continues at the cell named _WYSIWYG where it uses the {if} command to test for whether WYSIWYG.ADN is currently attached—this is the function of @isapp. If it is not currently attached, the {if} statement is true, and the macro processes the rest of that line. It uses /a to call up the Add-in menu choices Attach, Detach, Invoke, Clear, and Quit, presses "a" for Attach, types WYSIWYG, presses Enter, selects No-Key, then processes the {quit} command on the next line.

If Wysiwyg is already attached, the macro does not process the rest of line B4 after the {if} command, but simply proceeds to the {quit} command on the next line.

The second macro in Figure 14.8 is designed to attach Wysiwyg in Release 3.x, again choosing No-Key at the prompt for a key combination to assign to the add-in. Though the macros look quite different, they actually function the same way. The @isapp function does not work in Release 3.x, so we use a trick instead. The macro issues the colon (:) keystroke and stores the result of @info("mode") in WYS_TEST. It then clears the colon with

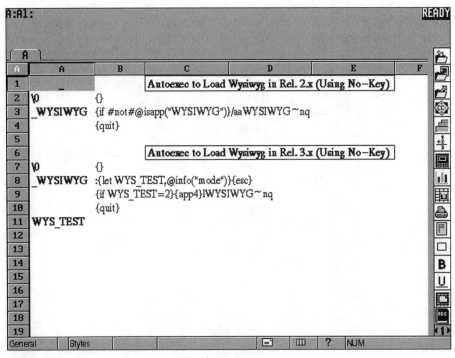

FIGURE 14.8 Autoexec macros to load Wysiwyg.

{esc} and tests WYS_TEST to see what mode 1-2-3 is in. If it's 2, which is label mode, then Wysiwyg must not be attached. Therefore, the macro uses {app4} to perform the equivalent of Alt+F10, types "1" for Load; then, exactly like the previous macro, it types WYSIWYG, presses Enter, selects No-Key, and processes the {quit} command on the next line.

You may want to consider modifying this macro to create a menu choice of whether to attach Wysiwyg. Such a macro could then be stored in an AUTO123 file which 1-2-3 will automatically retrieve as you start the 1-2-3 session each day. That way, you will have the option each time you load 1-2-3 of whether you want to start out with spreadsheet publishing. If you go this route, however, be sure that your default is not set for automatic attachment of the add-in.

Autoexec Macros to Change Display to Small

The :Display setting is a global feature that is not saved with the specific worksheet file. Figure 14.9 provides autoexec macros for storage in individual files that will take care of this task for you.

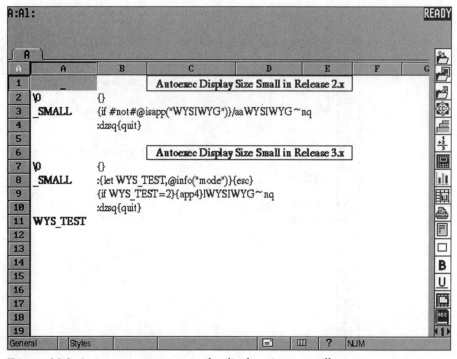

FIGURE 14.9 Autoexec macros to set the display size to small.

Instead of selecting :Display Zoom Small Quit to change your view so you can see more of the spreadsheet, use one of the two macros in Figure 14.9. The first is intended for Release 2.x, while the second is intended for 3.x.

Both macros assign Wysiwyg to No-Key if it is not already attached. The commands **:dzsq** apply the Small view to your worksheet.

Using :Special Copy in Macros

Two macros in this section make use of the :Special Copy command. The first macro combines :Special Copy with the 1-2-3 /Copy command so you can copy data and lines in one stroke; the second uses :Special Copy in a macro designed to increase the size of an outline box with very few keystrokes.

A Macro to Both /Copy and :Special Copy

When you use the standard 1-2-3 /Move command to move a cell in Wysiwyg, the data, SSP formatting, lines, and shading all move at once. However, when you use the /Copy command, the only elements that copy are the data, SSP formatting, and shading. The lines do not copy until you go through the process again using the :Special Copy command.

The macro in Figure 14.10 is designed to accomplish both the /Copy and :Special Copy commands at once.

{}   The macro begins with a null, pass-through routine.

{paneloff}/rncCOPY FROM?~~/rndCOPY FROM?~   This line of the macro, named_COPYBOTH, begins by freezing the upper panel with the {paneloff} command to suppress unnecessary screen flicker. Then it selects /Range Name Create, types the range name COPY FROM?, and presses Enter twice to select the currently offered location. The macro then selects /Range Name Delete, types the range name COPY FROM? again, and presses Enter to delete the range name.

This process ensures that the range name COPY FROM? has been deleted from the worksheet before establishing the range name again in the next line of the macro. Another option for accomplishing the same thing in Release 3.x is the line:

```
{paneloff}{if @isrange("COPY FROM?")}/rndCOPY FROM?~
```

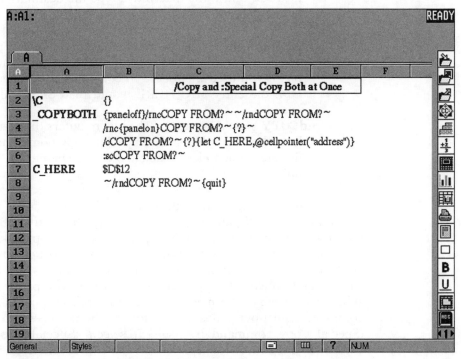

FIGURE 14.10 A macro to both /Copy and :Special Copy a range.

but the line chosen for Figure 14.10 works with any version of 1-2-3.

/rnc{panelon}COPY FROM?~{?}~ This line begins by selecting /Range Name Create, unfreezes the upper panel with the {panelon} command, enters the range name COPY FROM?, then uses the {?} question mark in braces to pause for your painting of a range. When you press Enter after highlighting the range you want to copy, the macro uses the ending tilde to enter the range.

/cCOPY FROM?~{?}{let C_HERE,@cellpointer("address")}~ This line selects /Copy, enters the range name COPY FROM? (which you just assigned to a range in your worksheet), then pauses with the {?} command so you can establish a destination to copy your range to. Before entering that destination, the macro uses a {let} command to store in the cell named C_HERE the address of the cell your pointer is occupying at that instant. Then the macro enters that cell as the destination cell for the /Copy command.

:scCOPY FROM?~ At this point the macro selects :Special Copy, and uses the range name COPY FROM? as the source range. In the next cell down, the macro will type the destination cell as stored by the {let} command in the last line.

$D$12 In this case, the macro reads $D$12 in the cell named C_HERE, but this is a variable that will change depending on the last location where you copied data using this macro. For example, if you used the macro to copy data to a range that starts at E14, the entry at C_HERE would read $E$14 after the macro ended.

~/rndCOPY FROM?~{quit} The macro enters the address in the last line, thus completing the :Special Copy command, then selects /Range Name Delete to delete the range name COPY FROM?, and quits.

This macro creates, then deletes, then begins to create a range name, COPY FROM?, and pauses so you can highlight a range. But to you, the user, the range name will simply appear to be a prompt, asking you where you want to copy data from. When you respond with a range, the macro starts a real /Copy command, using the range name COPY FROM? as the source, and pausing for your response to the prompt for a destination. When you respond, the macro records that cell and completes the /Copy command. But now it has all the information it needs to accomplish a :Special Copy command by itself. It selects :Special Copy, uses COPY FROM? as the source range, and uses the address it stored in C_HERE as the destination. Finally, it deletes COPY FROM?, and the macro quits.

Adding Size to a Box

The macro in Figure 14.11 lets you quickly expand an outline box horizontally from its current size to a larger size. This is a complicated macro, as you will see, but it can be a real timesaver when compared to the alternatives.

Without a macro, the fastest way to increase the width of an outline box in Wysiwyg is to use :Special Move to move one end of the box to the right or left, then use :Special Copy to copy lines from one part of the box into the area that has been left without lines by the :Special Move command. This macro goes through those rather laborious tasks automatically with very little input required from you.

{} The macro begins with a null, pass-through command to the next line of the macro named _AUGMENT.

{paneloff}/rndHILITE BOX END~~/rndHILITE BOX END~ This combination of commands should be familiar from the last macro. The upper panel is frozen and the range name HILITE BOX END is created, then deleted, in preparation for its recreation in the next line.

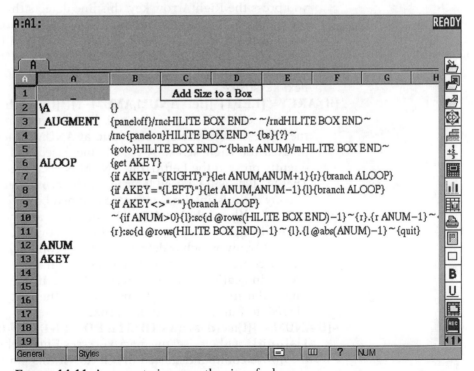

FIGURE 14.11 A macro to increase the size of a box.

/rnc{panelon}HILITE BOX END~{bs}{?}~ The macro selects
/Range Name Create, turns the upper panel on, enters the range
name HILITE BOX END, presses Backspace to free the cell
pointer, then pauses for your highlighting of the last cells at the
right or left end of the box you want to expand. You might
respond, for example, by highlighting the range D13..D17 if those
cells represent the right or left end of your outline box.

{goto}HILITE BOX END~{blank ANUM}/mHILITE BOX END~
The macro then moves the cell pointer to the first cell of the
range given the range name HILITE BOX END, blanks the value-
storage cell named ANUM (cell B13 in Figure 14.11), and begins
the /Move command by entering HILITE BOX END as the source
range.

{get AKEY} The next cell, named ALOOP, is a command that tells
1-2-3 to pause and "get" your next press of a key. No matter what
key you press at this point, it will be stored in the cell named
AKEY (cell C14 in Figure 14.11). As you will see, the macro then
uses the next three lines to act on the information about which
key you pressed.

{if AKEY="{RIGHT}"}{let ANUM,ANUM+1}{r}{branch ALOOP} If
you press the RightArrow key, this line detects that. It then adds
the value 1 to the current value at ANUM (which, you will remember, was blanked; and a blank cell plus the value 1 equals 1). The
macro then moves the cell pointer one cell to the right and
branches back to the {get} command at ALOOP to wait for your
next keystroke.

{if AKEY="{LEFT}"}{let ANUM,ANUM−1}{l}{branch ALOOP} If
you pressed the LeftArrow key, this line detects that and subtracts
the value 1 from the current value at ANUM. Thus, if you first
pressed the RightArrow, ANUM is increased to 1; if you subsequently pressed the LeftArrow, ANUM is decreased back to zero.
These values will be used later by the macro to determine where
to copy the missing lines in your expanded box.

{if AKEY<>"~"}{branch ALOOP} If you press anything other than
the RightArrow, which is detected by the first {if} statement, or
the LeftArrow, which is detected by the second {if} statement, the
macro comes to this {if} statement which looks for a tilde in
AKEY, indicating that you pressed Enter. If you did not press
Enter, the macro simply loops back to the {get} command at
ALOOP to wait for another keystroke.

**~{if ANUM>0}{l}:sc{d @rows(HILITE BOX END)−1}~{r}.{r ANUM−
1}~{quit}** Otherwise, the macro presses Enter, which completes
the /Move command started in cell A6. At this point, if ANUM is
greater than zero, it means you have used the RightArrow to

move the end of your outline box to the right, so the macro moves the cell pointer one cell to the left, begins the :Special Copy command, and uses the **{d @rows(HILITE BOX END)–1}** command to highlight down one less than the number of rows you highlighted when responding to the HILITE BOX END prompt. For a destination cell, the macro moves back to the right (to the original cell), locks in the cursor, and paints to the right one less than the number of cells you moved originally to establish the destination cell for the /Move command. This process seems complicated, but it actually does nothing more than copy box lines from the left into the gap in the box created by the /Move command, at which point the macro quits.

{r}:sc{d @rows(HILITE BOX END)–1}~{l}.{l @abs(ANUM)–1}~ {quit}   If the macro did not process the last line, the value in ANUM must have been less than zero, which means you moved the left end of the outline box. The macro therefore moves the cell pointer to the right, selects :Special Copy, highlights a height equal to one cell less than the height of the range named HILITE BOX END, and presses Enter. For a destination cell, it moves to the left, locks in the cursor, paints in a range one column less than the number of cells you moved to get to your /Move destination cell, and presses Enter. At this point the macro quits. The result is a :Special Copy of outline box lines into the gap to the left.

Eliminating Shared Lines

Because Wysiwyg can put lines on all sides of a cell, you have to go through a lengthy process to eliminate a line when the adjacent cell is also formatted for the same line. For example, if cell B3 is formatted for a right line and cell B4 is formatted for a left line, you cannot eliminate the line by selecting :Format Lines Clear in only one cell. You must either select :Format Lines Clear All and highlight both cells—which may clear more lines than you want—or select :Format Lines Clear Right in the left cell, then select :Format Lines Clear Left in the right cell.

Eliminating Shared Lines from Adjacent Cells

Fortunately, you can use the menu macro in Figure 14.12 to eliminate lines in both cells with fewer keystrokes than it would take to manually eliminate the left, right, top, or bottom line in just a single cell.

{}   The macro begins with a null, pass-through routine to the next cell, named _ELIM.

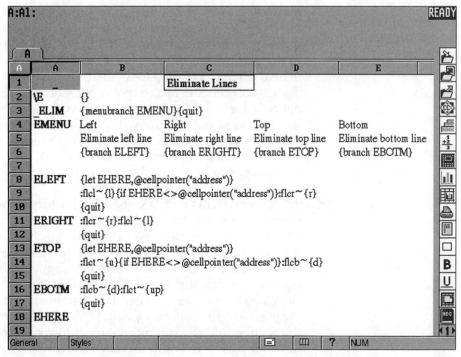

FIGURE 14.12 A macro to eliminate shared lines in adjacent cells.

{menubranch EMENU}{quit} This line informs 1-2-3 that a set of menu choices exists in the row starting at the range name EMENU and instructs 1-2-3 to call up those choices. The {quit} command after the {menubranch} command is only processed if you press Escape after the menu shows in the upper panel. The menu choices are Left, Right, Top, and Bottom. The menu descriptions in Row 6 that will appear in the top panel as you scroll through the choices are Eliminate left line, Eliminate right line, Eliminate top line, and Eliminate bottom line.

{branch ELEFT} If you choose Left, the macro will continue at the cell named ELEFT. In the same way, the branch commands under the Right, Top, and Bottom choices (depending on which you select) will cause the macro to continue at ERIGHT, ETOP, and EBOTTOM.

{let EHERE,@cellpointer("address")} The first line at ELEFT uses the {let} command to store the current cell address in the cell named EHERE. It then uses that address in the {if} statement in the next line.

:flcl~{l}{if EHERE<>@cellpointer("address")}:flcr~{r} The macro selects :Format Lines Clear Left and presses Enter, then uses the {l} command to move one cell to the left. The {if} command checks for whether the cell stored in EHERE (where you started out) is equal to the current cell after the command to move left. If the two cell addresses are not the same, it means that nothing prevented the cell pointer from moving left (like locked-in titles or the left edge of the worksheet), so the macro proceeds to select :Format Lines Clear Right, presses Enter, then moves back to the original cell to the right.

{quit}   Otherwise, if the cell pointer could not be moved to the left, the macro simply quits.

:flcr~{r}:flcl~{l}   This is the first line of the subroutine at ERIGHT. It selects :Format Lines Clear Right, presses enter, moves to the right and (since it is highly unlikely that anything would prohibit that move), selects :Format Lines Clear Left, presses Enter, and moves back to the original cell to the left.

{quit}   At this point the macro quits.

The rest of the macro is fairly obvious. If you select Top, the routine at ETOP includes an {if} statement along the same lines as the {if} statement at ELEFT. It checks for whether the cell pointer could be moved up one cell and, if the cell pointer moves, it proceeds to clear the bottom line in that cell.

Eliminating Shared Lines from Adjacent Ranges

The macro we just described is fairly straightforward and easy to understand, but it can only be used to eliminate shared lines from adjacent cells, not adjacent ranges. If you want a more powerful macro that will eliminate shared lines from two adjacent columns or two adjacent rows of cells, refer to Figure 14.13.

{}   The macro begins with a null, pass-through command to the cell named _X_LINES.

{paneloff}/rncDELETE LINES?~~/rndDELETE LINES?~   You should recognize this from the macros in Figures 14.10 and 14.11. Its purpose is to freeze the upper panel, then create and delete the range name DELETE LINES? that will be used in the rest of the macro.

/rnc{panelon}DELETE LINES?~{?}   The macro recreates the range name DELETE LINES?, then pauses for your highlighting of the range of cells in which you want to delete single, double, or wide lines.

{let XROW,@cellpointer("row")}{let XCOL,@cellpointer("col")}
This line stores the cell pointer's current row number in the cell named XROW (cell C17 in Figure 14.13), and the cell pointer's current column number in the cell named XCOL (cell C16 in Figure 14.13).

	A	B	C	D	E
1			**Xtra Lines Shared by 2 Ranges Deleted**		
2	\X	{}			
3	_X_LINES	{paneloff}/rncDELETE LINES?~~/rndDELETE LINES?~			
4		/rnc{panelon}DELETE LINES?~{?}			
5		{let XROW,@cellpointer("row")}{let XCOL,@cellpointer("col")}			
6		{if @cell("row",DELETE LINES?)<>XROW}{menubranch XMENU}{quit}			
7		{menubranch XMENU1}{quit}			
8	XMENU	Left	Right	Quit	
9		Delete left lines	Delete right lines	Return to Ready	
10		{windowsoff}	{branch XRIGHT}	{quit}	
11		{paneloff}			
12		:flclDELETE LINES?~/rncDELETE LINES?~..{l}			
13		{if @cellpointer("col")<>XCOL}..{l}~:flcrDELETE LINES?~			
14		/rndDELETE LINES?~{quit}			
15	XCOL				
16	XROW				
17	XRIGHT	{windowsoff}{paneloff}:flcrDELETE LINES?~			
18		/rncDELETE LINES?~{r}..{r}~:flclDELETE LINES?~			
19		~/rndDELETE LINES?~{quit}			
20	XMENU1	Top	Bottom	Quit	
21		Delete top lines	Delete bottom lines	Return to Ready	
22		{windowsoff}	{branch XDOWN}	{quit}	
23		{paneloff}			
24		:flctDELETE LINES?~/rncDELETE LINES?~..{u}			
25		{if @cellpointer("row")<>XROW}..{u}~:flcbDELETE LINES?~			
26		~/rndDELETE LINES?~{quit}			
27	XDOWN	{windowsoff}{paneloff}:flcbDELETE LINES?~			
28		/rncDELETE LINES?~{d}..{d}~:flctDELETE LINES?~			
29		~/rndDELETE LINES?~{quit}			
30					

FIGURE 14.13 A macro to eliminate lines shared by two ranges.

**{if @cell("row",DELETE LINES?)<>XROW}{menubranch XMENU}
{quit}** This line tests for whether you have moved your cell
pointer out of the current row. If so, the macro assumes that you
have just highlighted a column, so it skips ahead to the menu
choices at XMENU. These menu choices call for the elimination
of either left or right lines.

{menubranch XMENU1}{quit} Otherwise, the macro assumes that
you have just highlighted a row, so it skips ahead to the menu
choices at XMENU1. These menu choices call for the elimination
of either top or bottom lines.

{windowsoff} If you highlight a column and select the menu choice
Left, the macro freezes the current view with the {windowsoff}
command.

{paneloff} It then freezes the upper panel with the {paneloff} command.

:flclDELETE LINES?~/rncDELETE LINES?~..{l} At this point the
macro selects :Format Lines Clear Left, types the range name
DELETE LINES? you highlighted earlier, and presses Enter to
clear all the left lines of that range. The macro then selects /Range

Name Create, types the range name DELETE LINES? again, and at the prompt for a range types the Period key twice to rotate the coordinates to the opposite corner, and uses the {l} command to increase the range one column to the left.

{if @cellpointer("col")<>XCOL}..{l}~:flcrDELETE LINES?~ If the move to the left was successful as tested by this {if} statement (in other words, neither locked-in titles nor the left edge of the work-sheet prohibited the move), the macro presses the Period key twice more to move back to the original corner, moves left to shrink the right edge of the range of DELETE LINES? by one column, and uses a tilde to enter the new range. It then selects :Format Lines Clear Right to clear all right lines from this new range.

~/rndDELETE LINES?~{quit} The tilde in this line is only neces-sary to complete the /Range Name Create command in case the {if} command in the last line is not passed successfully. The macro then deletes the range named DELETE LINES? and quits.

{windowsoff}{paneloff}:flcrDELETE LINES?~ This is the line at XRIGHT, cell C18 in Figure 14.13. If you selected the choice Right at the menu shown in cell C9, the macro would have branched to this cell. The screen and upper panel are frozen with the {windowsoff} and {paneloff} commands and the macro selects :Format Lines Clear Right for the range named DELETE LINES?.

/rncDELETE LINES?~{r}..{r}~:flclDELETE LINES?~ The macro then uses the /Range Name Create command to shift the range one column to the right (try this manually for yourself to watch how it works), then selects :Format Lines Clear Left for the new range assigned to DELETE LINES?.

/rndDELETE LINES?~{quit} Finally, the macro deletes the range named DELETE LINES? and quits.

The remainder of the macro works along the same lines as the portion we have described above, except that it deletes top or bottom lines.

Summary

This chapter explored how macros work and presented examples that toggle between Wysiwyg attributes, frame types, display sizes, and printer orienta-tions, macros that automate the loading of Wysiwyg; autoexec macros that run when the files containing them are retrieved; a macro that does a stan-dard 1-2-3 /Copy and a Wysiwyg :Copy both at the same time; a macro to increase the size of an outline box; and macros to quickly eliminate lines established two adjacent cells or ranges.

- You can create a set of Wysiwyg macros that toggle your bold for-matting and grid lines on and off by pressing Alt+B or Alt+G (Ctrl+B or Ctrl+G in 1-2-3 for Windows), as well as macros that let you toggle through the various lines and shade types by pressing Alt+L or Alt+S (Ctrl+L or Ctrl+S in 1-2-3 for Windows).

- The Frame Toggle alternates the frame between the standard 1-2-3 type and the special frame showing inches.
- The Display Zoom macro cycles between Small, Tiny, and Normal views of the spreadsheet. The Small size is best for viewing a standard 8½″ by 11″ range when Wysiwyg is set for Portrait and the Tiny size is perfect for viewing a standard 8½″ × 11″ range set for Landscape.
- The Orientation Toggle switches between the Landscape and Portrait views. This toggle is useful for worksheets that have multiple ranges that need to be printed, some Landscape and others Portrait.
- Autoexec macros are especially useful for changing global features in ways that are appropriate for specific files. To create macros ensuring that Wysiwyg is loaded, use the {if} command with @isapp to test for whether the add-in has been attached yet in Release 2.3, or @info("mode") in Release 3.1.
- To change Print Orientation for spreadsheets with multiple print ranges and different orientations, use a macro designed to toggle between portrait and landscape mode.
- Some features are not saved with the worksheet file, such as the size of the display view, so it makes sense to create an autoexec macro to automatically change the size to small when the file is retrieved.
- When you use the /Copy command in Graphic mode, the only elements that copy are the data, SSP formatting, and shading. The lines do not copy until you go through the process again using the :Special Copy command. Instead of going through the process twice, use a macro that will accomplish both types of copying at once.
- To add size to a box, use a macro to expand an outline box horizontally from its current size to a larger size.
- It can be a complicated process to eliminate a line when the adjacent cell is also formatted for the same line. You must either select :Format Lines Clear All and highlight both cells—which may clear more lines than you want—or select :Format Lines Clear Right in the left cell, then select :Format Lines Clear Left in the right cell. A better method is to use a macro that accomplishes these tasks for you.

In the next chapter we explore the use of string formulas in macros designed to manipulate the elements of a database. The examples we investigate include macros to create date headings, view duplicate entries, find a string within a string, delete blank or zero-value rows, and subtotal like items in a database.

C H A P T E R | **15**

Macros to Manipulate
a Database

In this chapter we look at macros that use variable strings and the combination of several features including operators, such as #not#, and @functions, such as @exact, @iserr, @value, and @choose to facilitate the use and manipulation of databases in 1-2-3.

Automating the Creating of Date Headings

The macro in Figure 15.1 addresses one of the most common tasks 1-2-3 users encounter: the creation of date headings across the top or along the side of a spreadsheet.

This repetitive task usually takes anywhere from 48 to over 80 keystrokes for a 12-month period, depending on whether you spell out the names of the months or use the shorter forms like JAN, FEB, and so on. However, with the Headings of Dates macro, this can be reduced to six keystrokes.

{menubranch HMENU}{quit}   The macro begins by offering the menu choices ACROSS and DOWN. Select ACROSS to have your headings typed across in a row, with each heading underlined,

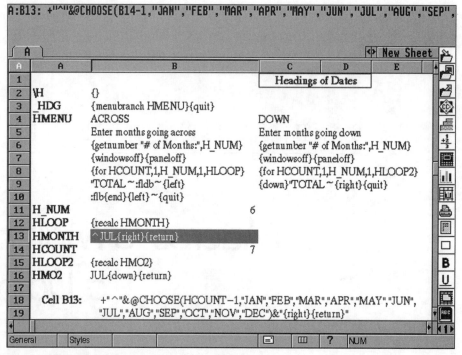

FIGURE 15.1 A macro to create date headings.

and the word TOTAL entered and double-underlined at the end of the row.

{getnumber "# of Months:",H_NUM} Prompts you for the number of months you want in your headings, storing your response in the cell named H_NUM.

{windowsoff}{paneloff} Turns off the windows and panel to suppress screen flicker and speed up the macro.

{for HCOUNT,1,H_NUM,1,HLOOP} or **{for HCOUNT,1,H_NUM,1, HLOOP2}** This {for} loop counts at HCOUNT starting with one, counting up to the number of months you stored in H_NUM—in increments of one—and for each increment runs the routine at HLOOP or HLOOP2.

If you select ACROSS, the routine at HLOOP begins by recalculating HMONTH, enters a centering caret and the name of a month, then executes a {right} command and starts over, repeating this loop until the last month has been entered.

After all months have been entered, the macro enters the word TOTAL, moves down one cell, enters a double underline, moves left, enters a repeating underline symbol, copies it to the left, moves back to the right, and quits.

If you select DOWN, the routine at HLOOP2 recalculates HMO2, enters a month (without a caret), moves down one cell, then starts over, repeating the loop until the last month has been entered. Finally, the cell pointer is moved down one more cell, the word TOTAL is entered right-justified, and the macro quits.

The real magic of this macro is contained in the string formulas behind cells B13 and B16. The two formulas are almost identical, so we will look only at the formula behind cell B13. As you can see at the bottom of Figure 15.1, this formula consists of three parts: a caret, an @choose function that returns a month, and the ending {right}{return} commands.

The @choose function selects JAN (the zero offset) at the first pass of the {for} loop when HCOUNT equals 1 (and HCOUNT –1 = 0). At the second pass of the {for} loop, HCOUNT equals 2 (and HCOUNT minus 1 = 1), so the @choose selects offset 1 or FEB. The macro continues in this way, changing the name of the month to select, until the last month is entered.

Creating a Worksheet Matrix

This same technique, using variable data entry based on passes through a {for} loop, can be used to create an entire worksheet matrix of variable size. Such a macro is shown in Figure 15.2.

To operate this macro, press Alt+W (or Ctrl+W in 1-2-3 for Windows). At the range-name prompt, WKSHT AREA?, highlight the size of the matrix you want to create, starting in column A. When you press Enter, the macro will type date headings and a Total label across the top of your highlighted range, enter the word "Siding" and a Total label down the left side of the range, enter @sum formulas under the Total label down the right side, enter underline cells and @sum formulas across the bottom row of the range, and finally enter a Grand Total summing formula in the lower right cell of the range. In addition to all this, the macro formats the matrix with colors and grid lines for a polished look.

Figure 15.3 shows the results you will get by invoking this macro and highlighting, for example, the range A33...G45 as the size of the worksheet matrix you would like to create.

Of course, the "Siding" labels down the left side are only there to represent the siding labels you will actually be using. Once the worksheet matrix is completed, you should replace these labels with the appropriate titles for your own spreadsheet. If necessary, you can also change the date headings to any other headings that may be appropriate.

Here's how the macro works:

{windowsoff}{paneloff}/rncWKSHT AREA?~~/rndWKSHT AREA?~
Turns off the windows and panel to suppress screen flicker and

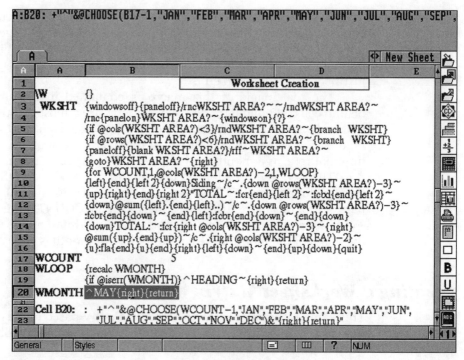

FIGURE 15.2 A macro to automatically create a worksheet matrix.

speed up the macro, then creates and deletes the prompting range name, "WKSHT AREA?".

/rnc{panelon}WKSHT AREA?~{windowson}{?}~   Again creates the range name WKSHT AREA?, then pauses for your highlighting of the size of worksheet matrix to create.

{if @cols(WKSHT AREA?)<3}/rndWKSHT AREA?~{branch_WKSHT}   If the number of columns you highlight are less than three, the macro deletes the prompting range name WKSHT AREA? and starts over again. This is necessary because the sidings, at least one column of data, and @sum formulas to the right require three columns by themselves.

{if @rows(WKSHT AREA?)<6}/rndWKSHT AREA?~{branch_ WKSHT}   If the number of rows you highlight is less than six, the macro deletes the prompting range name WKSHT AREA? and starts over again. This is necessary because of the number of rows required for headings, minimum lines of data, and @sum formulas at the bottom.

{paneloff}{blank WORKSHEET AREA?}/rff~WKSHT AREA?~   The range you highlighted is blanked and formatted for Fixed Format

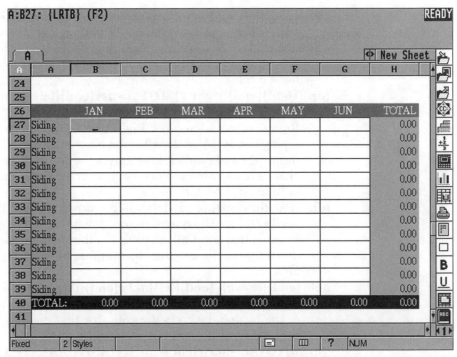

FIGURE 15.3 Results after using the Worksheet Creation macro.

with two decimals. Of course, you should feel free to change the range formatting to any other type.

{goto}WKSHT AREA?~{right} In case the cell pointer is not already there, this command sends it to the upper left corner of the range you highlighted, then moves one cell to the right.

{for WCOUNT,1,@cols(WKSHT AREA?)–2,1,WLOOP} This {for} command counts at WCOUNT starting with the number one, counting up to two less than the number of columns in the highlighted range, incrementing by ones; for increment it runs the routine at WLOOP designed to insert the names of months across the top of the highlighted range. If your range is greater than 12 months, the word HEADING is used (see line B21).

The string formula used to calculate the appropriate month and enter it is shown at the bottom of Figure 15.2 and displayed in cell B20. As with the Headings of Dates macro, this formula consists of three parts: a caret, an @choose function that returns the appropriate month based on the number of passes through the {for} loop recorded at WCOUNT, and the ending {right}{return} commands.

{left}{end}{left 2}{down}Siding~/c~.{down @rows(WKSHT AREA?)
–3}~   This line moves the cell pointer back to column A and
down two cells, where the Siding label is entered and copied
down three less cells than the total number of rows in the highlighted range.

{up}{right}{end}{right 2}"TOTAL~:fcr{end}{left 2}~:fcbd{end}{left
2}~   The cell pointer is moved back up to the top row, then End
RightArrow, and another RightArrow to the correct location for
typing the TOTAL title. After the macro types the word TOTAL, it
moves the cell pointer down, gives the row a reverse color (white
characters against a black background), and changes the background color to dark blue.

{down}@sum({left}.{end}{left}..)~/c~.{down @rows(WORKSHEET
AREA?)–3}   The macro moves down one cell to enter an @sum
formula that sums all the values in the current row, then copies it
down three cells less than the number of rows in the highlighted
area.

:fcbr{end}{down}~{end}{left}:fcbr{end}{down}~{end}{down}
Reverses the color for the current column, moves the cell pointer
to the far left, reverses the color for that column, and moves to
the bottom of the column.

{down}TOTAL:~:fcr{right @rows(WKSHT AREA?)–3}~{right}
Moves down, enters the word TOTAL, reverses the color for the
current row, and moves to the right one cell.

@sum({up}.{end}{up})~/c~.{right @cols(WKSHT AREA?)–2}~
Sums the current column and copies that formula across the bottom row of your matrix.

{u}:fla{end}{u}{end}{right}{left}{down}~{end}{up}{down}{quit}
Moves up one cell, uses :Format Line All to add a grid to the
matrix of data, moves to the upper left corner of that data area,
and quits.

Automatically Creating /Data Query Ranges

Creating /Data Query Input and Criterion ranges in your database so you
can execute a /Data Query Find operation can take quite a number of keystrokes and requires meticulous attention to detail. The macro in Figure
15.4 is designed to automate the process, first by creating your /Data Query
Input and Criterion ranges, then by initiating your first /Data Query Find
operation based on those ranges.

To operate this macro, create or move to a pre-established database
and press Alt+Q (or Ctrl+Q in 1-2-3 for Windows).

Point to the first title of your input range. ESC to quit.   The macro
begins by typing a prompt in the upper panel. If you have Release

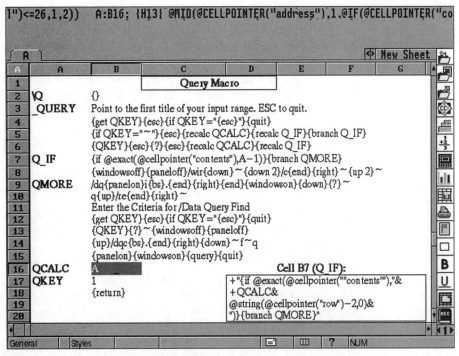

FIGURE 15.4 Macro to automatically create /Data Query Ranges.

2.2 or higher, you may want to replace this with a long {indicate} prompt. In that case, don't forget to include an {indicate} command at the end of the macro to return your indicator prompt to Ready.

{get QKEY}{esc}{if QKEY="{esc}"}{quit}   If you press the Escape key, the macro quits.

{if QKEY="~"}{esc}{recalc QCALC}{recalc Q_IF}{branch Q_IF}   If you press Enter, the {esc} command deletes the typed message and the macro recalculates the string formulas at QCALC and Q_IF before branching to Q_IF.

The string formula at QCALC is designed to extract and display the letter or letters representing the current column. The macro uses that information in the string formula in Q_IF. Since using @cellpointer("col") provides only the *number* of the column, not the letter(s), you'll need to use a combination of @cellpointer functions to extract the column letter from the current address, as follows:

```
@mid(@cellpointer("address"),1,@if(@cellpointer
("col")<26,1,2))
```

If the current column is any column from A to Z (less than or equal to the 26th column), this formula extracts one column letter. Otherwise, it extracts two, such as AA, AB, and so forth.

{QKEY}{esc}{?}{esc}{recalc QCALC}{recalc Q_IF} If you do not press Enter at the initial prompt, the {esc} command still deletes the typed message and the macro pauses to allow you to move to the first title of your database. The second {esc} will eliminate any keystrokes you inadvertently press while moving around. When you press Enter, the string formulas at QCALC and Q_IF are recalculated.

{if @exact(@cellpointer("contents"),D15)}{branch QMORE} This is the result of a string formula that checks the contents of the cell two rows above the current cell.

The reason for this line has to do with the creation of the /Data Query Input and Criterion ranges. The macro is designed to place duplicates of the Input range headings in an area two rows above the database, then use /Data Query Criterion to establish those two rows as your Criterion range. That way, your Criterion headings will exactly match your Input headings and will be immediately accessible just above the Input range. However, in case you have already established Criterion headings in that location, the macro checks for an exact match; upon finding a match, it branches two lines down to QMORE. Refer to the example in Figure 15.5.

In order to calculate and display the cell two rows above the current cell, the macro uses the string formula:

```
+"{if @exact(@cellpointer("contents"),"&
+QCALC&
@string(@cellpointer("row")-2,0)&
")}{branch QMORE}"
```

You can see now why we had to extract the current column letter as shown in QCALC. By referring to QCALC, the string formula in Q_IF can include a reference to that current column letter.

{windowsoff}{paneloff}/wir{down}~{down 2}/c{end}{right}~{up 2}~ The windows and panel are turned off, two new rows are inserted, and a copy of the Input headings is made two cells above the Input range—to be used for Criterion headings.

> **NOTE:** *Since this line inserts two rows, there should be no data off to the right of your database when you use this macro.*

/dq{panelon}i{bs}.{end}{right}{end}{windowson}{down}{?}~ Selects /Data Query Input, uses Backspace to eliminate any previously established Input range, locks in the cursor, moves End

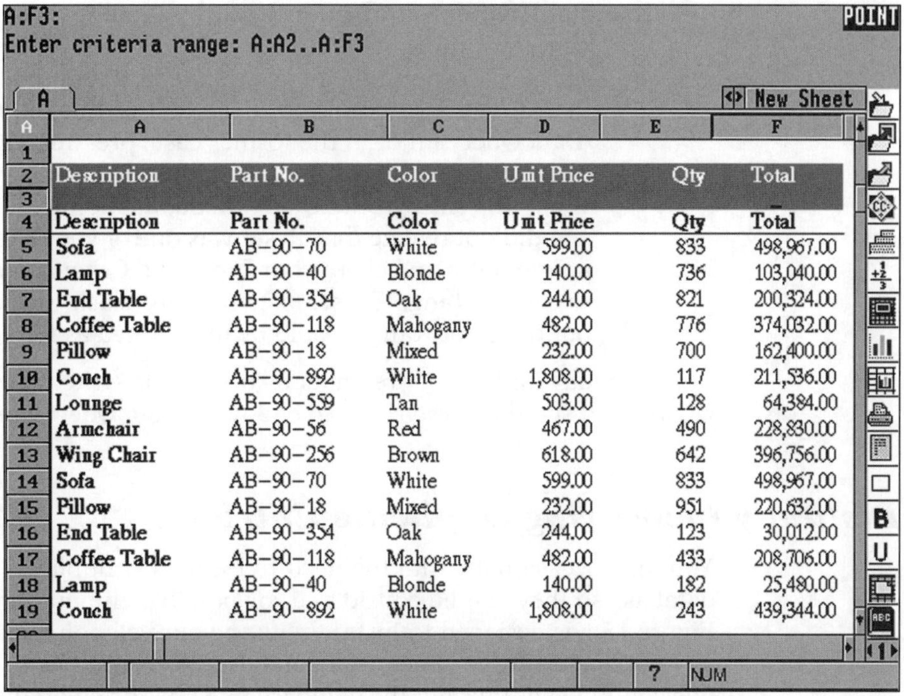

A:F3:
Enter criteria range: A:A2..A:F3

POINT

A | New Sheet

A	A	B	C	D	E	F
1						
2	Description	Part No.	Color	Unit Price	Qty	Total
3						
4	**Description**	**Part No.**	**Color**	**Unit Price**	**Qty**	**Total**
5	**Sofa**	AB–90–70	White	599.00	833	498,967.00
6	**Lamp**	AB–90–40	Blonde	140.00	736	103,040.00
7	**End Table**	AB–90–354	Oak	244.00	821	200,324.00
8	**Coffee Table**	AB–90–118	Mahogany	482.00	776	374,032.00
9	**Pillow**	AB–90–18	Mixed	232.00	700	162,400.00
10	**Couch**	AB–90–892	White	1,808.00	117	211,536.00
11	**Lounge**	AB–90–559	Tan	503.00	128	64,384.00
12	**Armchair**	AB–90–56	Red	467.00	490	228,830.00
13	**Wing Chair**	AB–90–256	Brown	618.00	642	396,756.00
14	**Sofa**	AB–90–70	White	599.00	833	498,967.00
15	**Pillow**	AB–90–18	Mixed	232.00	951	220,632.00
16	**End Table**	AB–90–354	Oak	244.00	123	30,012.00
17	**Coffee Table**	AB–90–118	Mahogany	482.00	433	208,706.00
18	**Lamp**	AB–90–40	Blonde	140.00	182	25,480.00
19	**Couch**	AB–90–892	White	1,808.00	243	439,344.00

? NUM

FIGURE 15.5 Database with Input and Criterion Ranges established.

RightArrow and End DownArrow to highlight the Input range, then pauses for your acceptance or revision of the Input range.

q{up}/re{end}{right}~ Quits the /Data Query command sequence, moves up one cell (to the second row of the Criterion range), and erases any single entry in that row that may be left over from a previous /Data Query Find operation.

Enter the Criteria for /Data Query Find Prompts you to enter criteria in this row before the macro executes a /Data Query Find operation.

{get QKEY}{esc}{if QKEY="{esc}"}{quit} If you press Escape at this point, the macro simply quits, leaving your /Data Query Input range intact.

{QKEY}{?}~{windowsoff}{paneloff} Otherwise, the macro executes the keystroke you pressed, pauses for you to point to any cell and enter your criteria, then turns off the windows and panel.

{up}/dqc{bs}.{end}{right}{down}~f~q The macro moves your cell pointer up one cell to the Criterion headings, selects /Data Query Criterion, eliminates any previously established Criterion range with Backspace, locks in the cursor, highlights the Criterion range using End RightArrow DownArrow, selects Find, then selects Quit.

{panelon}{windowson}{query}{quit} Finally, the macro turns the windows and panels back on, presses the F7 Query key, and quits. This leaves you in the first found record, but in a better situation than if you had been left at the end of the command sequence /Data Query Find. In the former case, pressing Enter returns you to the Ready prompt. In the latter case, pressing Enter returns you to the entire /Data Query menu, including the Reset choice. If you did not realize that Reset was one of your choices, you could accidentally cancel out your Input and Criterion ranges simply by selecting /Range Erase. (The forward slash would cause a beep, but the R for Range would be interpreted as Reset.)

You may find, therefore, that any macro you write that ends with /Data Query Find should be rewritten to end with /Data Query Find Quit {query}.

Instantly Identifying Duplicate Entries

You may occasionally find the need to locate any duplicate entries in your database so they can be considered for possible elimination. The macro in Figure 15.6 is designed to instantly jump your cell pointer to the second of any duplicate entries in a sorted database. Note, the macro will only check one column at a time and the database must be sorted on that same column before it will work correctly.

{recalc VCALC} The macro begins by recalculating the string formula in the next cell down, named VCALC.

{if @left(@cell("contents",$A$9),5=":"}{down 2}{up}{quit} This is the displayed result of the string formula as follows:

```
+"{if @left(@cell("contents","&
@LEFT(@CELLPOINTER("address"),3)&
@STRING(@CELLPOINTER("row")+1,0)&
"),5)=""&
@LEFT(@CELLPOINTER("contents"),5)&
"""}{down 2}{up}{quit}"
```

Its purpose is to compare the first five characters of the current cell with the first five characters of the cell below (notice how the third part of this string formula uses @cellpointer("row")+1). If they are the same, the macro moves down two cells to bring the second cell more into view, then up one cell, leaving the cell pointer at the second entry.

Checking only the first five characters is an arbitrary convention that allows you to identify entries that are almost, but not necessarily entirely, identical. You may want to modify this string

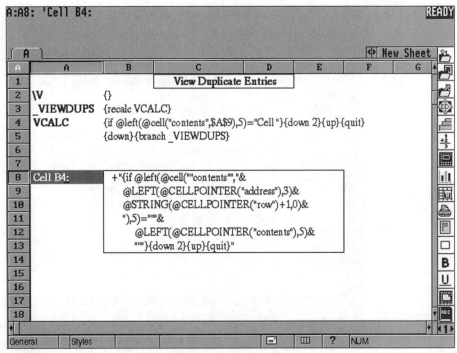

FIGURE 15.6 A macro to jump to the second of any duplicate entries.

> formula to check the entire entry or to check less than the first five characters of the entry.
>
> **{down}{branch_VIEWDUPS}**   If the macro does not find a match at the first cell in the current column, the cell pointer is moved down one cell and the macro repeats. It continues in this way until it finds the first duplicate, then quits.

To use the macro, press Alt+V (or Ctrl+V in 1-2-3 for Windows). If a duplicate is found, make your decision to retain or eliminate it, then press Alt+V (or Ctrl+V) to view the next duplicate.

Finding Strings-within-Strings in Release 2/2.01

We have looked at a couple of macros designed to enhance or substitute for the /Range Search feature found in Release 2.2 and higher, but none of the examples explored so far have the ability to search for a string-within-a-string. If you have Release 2 or 2.01, you may be interested in a way to duplicate this feature. Refer to the macro shown in Figure 15.7.

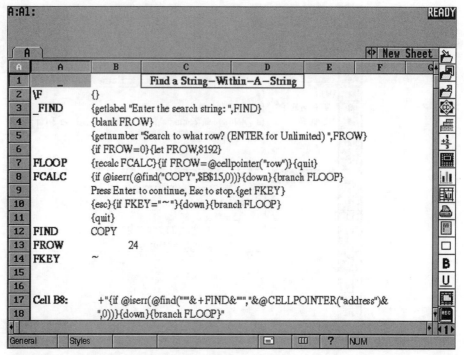

FIGURE 15.7 A macro to find a string-within-a-string.

{getlabel "Enter the search string: ",FIND} The macro begins by prompting you for the string you want to search for and places your answer in the cell named FIND. You can enter a portion of a string or an entire string at this point.

{blank FROW} Blanks the cell in the macro named FROW.

{getnumber "Search to what row? (ENTER for Unlimited) ",FROW} Prompts you for the row you want to search down to. If you press Enter, the macro will search in the current column to end of the worksheet at row 8192.

{if FROW=0}{let FROW,8192} If you press Enter at the prompt, FROW will remain blank, which means its contents equal zero. In that case, the macro converts the contents of FROW to 8192.

{recalc FCALC}{if FROW=@cellpointer("row")}{quit} Recalculates the string formula at FCALC. If the row number at FROW equals the cell pointer row, the macro quits.

{if @iserr(@find("COPY",$B$15,0))}{down}{branch FLOOP} This is the result of the string formula in FCALC, which consists of the following:

```
+"{if @iserr(@find(""&
+FIND&
""","&
@CELLPOINTER("address")&
",0))}{down}{branch FLOOP}"
```

This line determines whether the string you stored in FIND at the starting prompt is found in the current cell. If not, the @find formula returns an error, which causes the remainder of this line to be executed. The cell pointer is moved down to the next cell, and the macro loops back to FLOOP.

Press Enter to continue, Esc to stop.{get FKEY} Otherwise, a prompting line is typed into the upper panel and the macro pauses until you press any key. If you have Release 2.2 or higher, you may want to replace the typed message with a long {indicate} prompt.

{esc}{if FKEY="~"}{down}{branch FLOOP} The message is eliminated with the {esc} command. If you press Enter, the cell pointer is moved down to the next cell and the macro loops back to FLOOP.

{quit} If you press any other key (including Escape), the macro quits.

When you use this macro, the cell pointer will move rapidly down the current column until it reaches a found string. If you press Enter, the search will continue until another matching string is found or until the cell pointer reaches the designated row to quit or the end of the worksheet. If you press any other key at a found record, the macro will quit.

Locating a String with /Data Query Find

The above macro works in any column in the worksheet to locate a string or a portion of a string. But, although it moves down the column fairly quickly, it does have to visit each cell in turn to check for the record you want. If you are developing an application that requires a more instant jump to a found string in a large database, you may want to set up /Data Query Input and Criterion ranges and use the macro in Figure 15.8.

The last macro we looked at is not case sensitive, which means you can enter your search string using uppercase, lowercase, or proper case. However, because the /Data Query Find sequence in 1-2-3 is case sensitive, the macro in Figure 15.8 includes some complicated string formulas to check for a match in your database using all uppercase, lowercase, or proper case versions of your search string. While this does not ensure absolute identification of all matches to the string you are trying to locate (it will not properly identify a match with the string dBASE, for example), it will catch most occurrences.

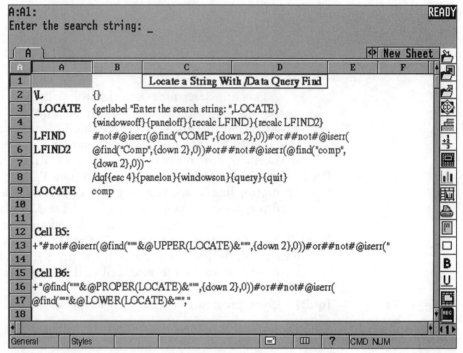

FIGURE 15.8 A macro to locate a string with /Data Query Find.

Here's how the macro works:

{getlabel "Enter the search string: ",LOCATE} Prompts for the search string, placing your response in LOCATE.

{windowsoff}{paneloff}{recalc LFIND}{recalc LFIND2} Turns off the windows and panel, and recalculates the string formulas in LFIND and LFIND2.

#not#@iserr(@find("COMP",{down 2},0))#or##not#@iserr(This is the displayed result in LFIND of the string formula as follows:

```
+"#not#@iserr(@find(""&
@UPPER(LOCATE)&
"",{down 2},0))#or##not#@iserr("
```

The purpose of this line is to begin typing a formula in the current criterion cell. Once fully entered, the formula determines that there is no error when the macro tries to find at least one of the following: the uppercase version of the search string, the lowercase version, or the proper case version.

@find("Comp",{down 2},0))#or##not#@iserr(@find("comp", This is the displayed result in LFIND2 of the string formula as follows:

```
+"@find("""&
@PROPER(LOCATE)&
""",{down 2},0))#or##not#@iserr(
@find(""&
@LOWER(LOCATE)&
""","
```

Its purpose is to continue typing the formula described above.

{down 2},0))~ This is the completion of the formula.

/dqf{esc 4}{panelon}{windowson}{query}{quit} Once the formula is entered in the current criterion cell, the macro executes a /Data Query Find, escapes from the /Data Query menu, then presses the F7 Query key to instantly jump the cell pointer to the search string. At this point you can edit the found record by pressing F2, stay at the found record by pressing F7 Query, find the next record by pressing DownArrow, find the previous record with PgUp, or return to the original cell by pressing Enter.

Deleting Zero and Blank Rows

If you have a very large database filled with blank rows that you want to eliminate, you may find the task tedious and unnecessarily timeconsuming. If your database is in alphabetical order except for the blank rows, the easiest way to isolate and delete the rows may be to select /Data Sort, which combines all blank rows into one block, then deletes that entire block.

If your database is not in alphabetical order, you can insert a new column, select /Data Fill to fill the column with consecutive numbers, then sort on some other cell (which again will combine all the blank rows into one block), delete the block of blank rows, then re-sort the database by the new /Data Fill column, and finally delete the /Data Fill column. Alternatively, you may be interested in the macro in Figure 15.9.

{let DHERE,@cellpointer("address")}{blank DCOUNT} The macro begins by creating a place-marker for the current cell at DHERE, then blanks DCOUNT.

{getnumber "Test how many cols across for row deletion? ",DELT} Prompts for the number of columns across you want the macro to test for zero or blank cells before doing a /Worksheet Delete Row. Your response is stored in DELT.

{menubranch DMENU}{quit} Calls up the menu choices, End of Worksheet and Specified-Row. If you select End of Worksheet,

	A	B	C	D	E	F	G
1				Delete 0 and Blank Rows across Range			
2	\D	{}					
3	_DELROW	{let DHERE,@cellpointer("address")}{blank DCOUNT}					
4		{getnumber "Test how many cols across for row deletion? ",DELT}					
5		{menubranch DMENU}{quit}					
6	DMENU	End of Worksheet		Specified-Row			
7		Delete to worksheet end		Delete empty rows to a specified row.			
8		{indicate WAIT}		{indicate WAIT}{branch DSPEC}			
9		{goto}{end}{home}					
10		{let DENDHM,@cellpointer("address")}{esc}					
11	DLOOP1	{recalc DENDROW}{recalc DCALC}					
12	DCALC	{if @cellpointer("row")>@cell("row",A71)}{branch DQUIT}					
13		{if @length(@cellpointer("contents"))>0}{down}{branch DLOOP1}					
14		{if @cellpointer("contents")>0}{down}{branch DLOOP1}					
15		{for DCTR,1,DELT,1,DLOOP2}					
16		{if @length(@cellpointer("contents"))>0}{recalc DCALC2}{branch DCALC2}					
17		{if @cellpointer("contents")=0}/wdr~{up}{let DCOUNT,DCOUNT+1}					
18		{recalc DCALC2}					
19	DCALC2	{goto}A$1~{down}{branch DLOOP1}					
20	DLOOP2	{right}{if @length(@cellpointer("contents"))>0}{forbreak}					
21		{if @cellpointer("contents")>0}{forbreak}					
22		{return}					
23	DSPEC	{getlabel "Delete empty rows down to what row number? ",DNUM}					
24		{recalc DCALC3}					
25	DCALC3	{let DENDHM,"$A$80"}{branch DLOOP1}					
26	DENDHM	$E$73					
27	DENDROW			73			
28	DCOUNT			2			
29	DHERE	$A$63					
30		{return}					
31	DNUM	80					
32	DQUIT	{goto}{DHERE}~{indicate}{quit}					
33	DCTR			1			
34	DELT			5			
35							
36	Cell B12:						
37	+"{if @cellpointer(""row"")>						
38	@cell(""row"",A"&@STRING(DENDROW-DCOUNT,0)&")}{branch DQUIT}"						
39							
40	Cell B19:						
41	+"{goto}"&@MID(DHERE,1,2)&@STRING(@CELLPOINTER("row"),0)&						
42	"~{down}{branch DLOOP1}"						
43							
44	Cell B25:						
45	+"{let DENDHM,""A"&+DNUM&"""}{branch DLOOP1}"						
46							
47	Cell B27:						
48	@VALUE(@RIGHT(DENDHM,@LENGTH(DENDHM)-(@FIND("$",DENDHM,1)+1)))						
49							

FIGURE 15.9 A macro to delete zero and blank rows across a range.

the macro operates until it reaches the row in which resides the End Home cell. If you select Specified-Row, you will be prompted for the row down in which you want the macro to operate.

{indicate WAIT} or **{indicate WAIT}{branch DSPEC}**   Whether you select End of Worksheet or Specified-Row, the macro changes the Ready indicator to the word WAIT. If you have Release 2.2 or higher, of course, you can use a longer Indicator message, such as "Macro is eliminating rows, please wait."

{goto}{end}{home}   If you selected End of Worksheet, the macro presses the F5 Goto key, then End Home to send the cell pointer temporarily to the End Home location. Notice there is no tilde at this point.

{let DENDHM,@cellpointer("address")}{esc}   The macro stores the address of the End Home location in DENDHM, then presses Esc to back out of the F5 Goto sequence and return the cell pointer to its previous location.

{recalc DENDROW}{recalc DCALC}   Recalculates DENDROW, which consists of the string formula:

```
@value(@right(DENDHM,@length(DENDHM)-
(@find("$",DENDHM,1)+1)))
```

The purpose of this string formula is to return, as a value, the row in which resides the End Home location of the spreadsheet. It does this by finding the second dollar sign ($) in the absolute address stored in DENDHM and extracting the rightmost characters from that point on.

{if @cellpointer("row")>@cell("row",A71)}{branch DQUIT}   This is the cell named DCALC, which displays its results based on the following string formula:

```
@if(@cellpointer("row")>
@cell("row",A"&
@STRING(DENDROW-DCOUNT,0)&
")}{branch DQUIT}"
```

This line determines whether the current row is greater than the End Home row (less the number of rows already deleted). If so, the macro branches to DQUIT, where the cell pointer is returned to its original position, the indicator is returned to normal, and the macro quits.

{if @length(@cellpointer("contents"))>0}{down}{branch DLOOP1}   This is where the macro establishes whether the cell consists of a label. If not, the cell pointer is moved down one cell and the macro loops back to DLOOP1.

Note, we could have used {if @cellpointer("type")="L"} here, but that would not have eliminated rows that included those troublesome cases of cells that look like blank cells, but actually consist of a single apostrophe.

{if @cellpointer("contents")>0}{down}{branch DLOOP1}   If the current cell contents are greater than zero, the cell pointer is moved down to the next cell, and the macro loops back to DLOOP1.

{for DCTR,1,DELT,1,DLOOP2}   This {for} loop counts at DCTR starting with the number one, counting up to the number of columns you stored in DELT, incrementing by ones, and for increment runs the routine at DLOOP2. The routine at DLOOP2 moves to the right and checks for a label or contents greater than zero; if it finds either, it breaks the {for} loop with the {forbreak} command.

{if @length(@cellpointer("contents"))>0}{recalc DCALC2}{branch DCALC2}   Once the macro completes or breaks out of the {for} loop, the current cell is tested again. If it consists of a label, DCALC2 is recalculated and the macro branches to that line.

{if @CELLPOINTER("CONTENTS")=0}/wdr~{up}{let DCOUNT, DCOUNT+1}   Otherwise, if the current contents are equal to zero, the macro selects /Worksheet Delete Row, moves up one cell, then increments DCOUNT by one.

{recalc DCALC2}   DCALC2 is recalculated.

{goto}A$1~{down}{branch DLOOP1}   This is the cell DCALC2, the displayed result of the following string formula:

```
+"{goto"&
@MID(DHERE,1,2)&
@STRING(@CELLPOINTER("row"),0)&
"~{down}{branch DLOOP1}"
```

Its purpose is to send your cell pointer to the leftmost cell in the current row of the range you are searching. It does this by combining the column letter of the starting column with the current cell pointer row. The cell pointer is then moved down to the next row and the macro loops back to DLOOP1.

{right}{if @length(@cellpointer("contents"))>0}{forbreak}   This and the next two lines are the routine at DLOOP2, already described.

{getlabel "Delete empty rows down to what row number? ",DNUM}   If, at the beginning of the macro, you selected SPEC-IFIED-ROW, this {getlabel} command prompts you for the row down to which you want the macro to operate, then stores your response in DNUM.

{recalc DCALC3}   Recalculates the string formula in DCALC3.

{let DENDHM,"$A$80"}{branch DLOOP1}   This is the displayed result in DCALC3 of the string formula as follows:

```
+"{let DENDHM,"$A$"&
+DNUM&
"""}{branch DLOOP1}"
```

Its purpose is to change the contents of DENDHM to an address consisting of column A and the row down to which you want the macro to operate. Then the macro branches back to DLOOP1 and continues in the same program flow as it uses for the END OF WORKSHEET choice. The difference is that the macro will stop at a designated cell rather than stopping at the row containing the End Home cell of the spreadsheet.

Eliminating Completely Empty Rows

The macro in Figure 15.10 is similar to the last macro described, except that it eliminates rows it identifies as completely empty, starting in Column A. Even though this macro checks the entire width of the worksheet, it actually operates faster than the previous macro that only checks a specified number of columns.

The similarities between the two macros are easy to spot, so we will focus here on the lines that constitute the real differences in approach.

{if @cellpointer("type")<>"b"}{down}{branch ELOOP}   This is the line at cell B10 in Figure 15.10, named ELOOP. Its purpose is to check for whether the current cell is blank. If the cell is not blank, there is no reason to test further. The cell pointer is moved down to the next cell and the macro branches back to the beginning of this line to test that next cell.

{end}{right}{recalc ENDROW}{recalc ECALC}   If the current cell is not blank, the cell pointer is moved End RightArrow, and the cells named ENDROW and ECALC are recalculated.

{if @cellpointer("row")>@cell("row",A35)}{branch EQUIT}   This is the cell named ECALC, which displays its results based on the following string formula:

```
@if(@cellpointer(""row"")>
@cell(""row"",A"&
@STRING(ENDROW-ECOUNT,0)&
")}{branch EQUIT}"
```

As with the previous macro, the purpose of this line is to determine whether the current row is greater than the End Home

	A	B	C	D
1				Eliminate Completely Empty Rows
2	\E	{}		
3	_ELIMROW	{let E_HERE,@cellpointer("address")}{blank ECOUNT}		
4		{menubranch E_MENU1}{quit}		
5	E_MENU1	End of Worksheet	Specified-Row	
6		Delete to worksheet end	Delete empty rows to a specified row.	
7		{windowsoff}	{indicate WAIT}{branch ESPEC}	
8		{indicate WAIT}{paneloff}		
9		{goto}{end}{home}{let ENDHOME,@cellpointer("address")}{esc}		
10	ELOOP	{if @cellpointer("type")<>"b"}{down}{branch ELOOP}		
11		{end}{right}{recalc ENDROW}{recalc ECALC}		
12	ECALC	{if @cellpointer("row")>@cell("row",A35)}{branch EQUIT}		
13		{if @cellpointer("col")<>256}{end}{left}{down}{branch ELOOP}		
14		{end}{left}/wdr~{let ECOUNT,ECOUNT+1}{branch ELOOP}		
15	ESPEC	{getlabel "Delete empty rows down to what row number? ",ENUM}		
16		{windowsoff}{paneloff}{recalc ECALC2}		
17	ECALC2	{let ENDHOME,"$A$37"}{branch ELOOP}		
18		{branch ESPEC2}		
19	ENDHOME	$A$37		
20	ENDROW		37	
21	ECOUNT		2	
22	E_HERE	$A$28		
23		{return}		
24	ENUM	37		
25	EQUIT	{goto}{E_HERE}~{indicate}{quit}		
26				
27				
28	Cell B12:			
29	+"{if @cellpointer(""row"")>			
30	@cell(""row"",A"&@STRING(ENDROW-ECOUNT,0)&")}{branch EQUIT}"			
31				
32	Cell B17:			
33	+"{let ENDHOME,""A"&+ENUM&"""}{branch ELOOP}"			
34				
35	Cell B20:			
36	@value(@right(ENDHOME,@length(ENDHOME)-(@find("$",ENDHOME,1)+1)))			
37				

FIGURE 15.10 A macro to eliminate completely empty rows.

row (less the number of rows already deleted). If so, the macro branches to EQUIT, where the cell pointer is returned to its original position, the indicator is returned to normal, and the macro quits.

{if @cellpointer("col")<>256}{end}{left}{down}{branch ELOOP}

You will remember that two lines ago the macro moved the cell pointer End RightArrow, which causes it to travel until it reaches a filled cell or the extreme right cell of the worksheet. If the resulting location is not in the farthest possible cell to the right (column IV, also the 256th column), there must be a cell with contents somewhere in the row. In that case, the cell pointer is moved End LeftArrow back to Column A, then down to the next row, and the macro loops back to continue at ELOOP.

The remainder of the macro is similar enough to the previous macro that it should require no further explanation. Be sure to remember when using this macro, however, that you must start with your cell pointer in Column A.

Deleting Rows Based on a Single Blank Cell

The macro in Figure 15.11 is of the same general type, except that this macro is designed to eliminate rows based on whether the cell in a particular column in each row is blank.

Hit Enter to ZAP every row with a blank cell. Press Ctrl+Brk to Stop This is a warning that appears in the upper panel, prompting you to press Enter to continue with the macro or Ctrl+Break to quit. If you have Release 2.2 or higher, you may want to replace this with a long {indicate} prompt, but be sure to include an {onerror} command that sends the program flow to an {indicate} command to restore the Ready Indicator if you press Ctrl+Break.

{?}{esc} Pauses so you can press Enter or Ctrl+Break. Actually, this is not as effective a way of pausing after having your macro type a message in the upper panel, because the user might press a directional key at this point. If that happens, the typed message will be entered into the current cell, potentially destroying important data that may be in that location. If anything else is typed (such as a letter or number), the {esc} command eliminates your extra keystroke(s) before the macro continues.

{goto}{end}{home}{let ZENDHM,@cellpointer("address")}{esc} As with the two previous macros, the End Home location is recorded through use of an interrupted {goto} command and a {let} command.

{if @cellpointer("type")<>"b"}{down}{branch ZLOOP} If the current cell is not blank, the cell pointer is moved down to the next cell and the macro loops back to the beginning of this cell.

{recalc ZCALC} Otherwise, the macro recalculates the string formula in ZCALC.

{if @cellpointer("row")>@cell("row",$D$186)}{quit} This is the displayed result in ZCALC of the string formula as follows:

```
+"{if @cellpointer(""row"")>@cell(""row"","&
ZENDHM&
")}{quit}
```

The purpose of this line is to determine whether the macro has yet reached the row in which resides the End Home cell. If so, the macro quits.

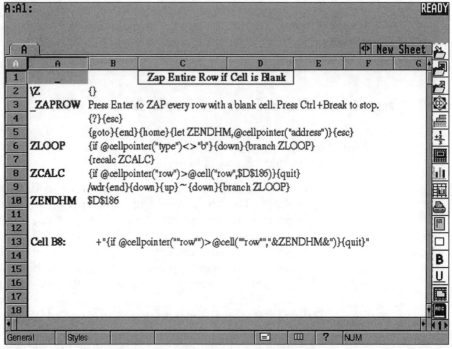

FIGURE 15.11 A macro to delete rows based on a single blank cell.

/wdr{end}{down}{up}~{down}{branch ZLOOP} Deletes all rows down to the next filled cell in the column, then branches back to ZLOOP.

This is the fastest of the three row deletion macros, because this macro deletes entire blocks of rows at once, based on the ability to identify more than one blank cell in sequence.

Subtotaling Like Items in a Database

Chapter 9 presented a macro designed to subtotal and total all like items in a database. In this section we look at an improved version of that macro. Whereas the macro in Figure 9.9 required that the Like Items column and the Subtotal column be side by side, the macro in Figure 15.12 will work with your Like Items column separated from the Subtotal column by any number of cells.

Further, the macro in Figure 15.12 adds a subtotal identifier, something like this:

```
Subtotal for Armchair:
```

	A	B	C	D	E	F
1				Subtotal Like Items in a Database		
2	\S	{ }				
3	_SUBTOT	Point to 1st of the Like Items and hit any key. Press ESC to quit.				
4		{get S_KEY}{esc}{if S_KEY="{esc}"}{quit}				
5		{if @left(S_KEY,1)="{"}{S_KEY}{branch _SUBTOT}				
6		{if S_KEY<>"~"}{branch _SUBTOT}				
7		{let S_COL,@cellpointer("col")}				
8		{let SUBHERE,@cellpointer("address")}				
9	SUBTOT2	Point to Amount Column to Subtotal.				
10		{get S_KEY}{esc}{if S_KEY="{esc}"}{quit}				
11		{if @left(S_KEY,1)="{"}{S_KEY}{branch SUBTOT2}				
12		{if S_KEY<>"~"}{branch SUBTOT2}				
13		{let S_COL2,@cellpointer("col")}{goto}{SUBHERE}~				
14		{recalc SPAN}{recalc SPANEX}				
15	SUBLOOP	{let STEST,@cellpointer("contents")}				
16	SUBLOOP2	{down}{if @cellpointer("type")="b"}{down}{SUBHEAD}{SQUIT}				
17		{if STEST=@cellpointer("contents")}{branch SUBLOOP2}				
18		/wir{down 2}~{down}{SUBHEAD}				
19		{up 3}{if @cellpointer("type")="b"}{SINGLE}{branch SUBLOOP}				
20		{down 3}{SUM}{down 2}{branch SUBLOOP}				
21	SUBHEAD	{recalc SUBCALC}				
22	SUBCALC	SUBTOTAL FOR EASTERN DIVISION:				
23	SPAN	{right 3}{return}				
24	S_COL		2			
25	S_COL2		5			
26	SUM	@sum({up 2}{end}{up}.{end}{down}{down})~/rf,2~~{SPANEX}{return}				
27	SINGLE	{down 3}@sum({up 2}.{down})~/rf,2~~{SPANEX}{down 2}{return}				
28	SQUIT	{up 3}{if @cellpointer("type")="b"}{SINGLE}{quit}				
29		{down 3}{SUM}{down 2}{quit}				
30	STEST	EASTERN DIVISION				
31	S_KEY	~				
32		{return}				
33	SUBHERE	$B$82				
34		{return}				
35	SPANEX	{left 3}{return}				
36						
37	Cell B22:					
38	+"SUBTOTAL FOR "&					
39	@if(@cell("type",STEST)="v",@string(STEST,0),STEST)"&					
40	": "					
41						
42	Cell B23:					
43	+"{"&@if(S_COL>S_COL2,"left","right")&" "&					
44	&@string(@abs(+S_COL-S_COL2),0)&"}"&"{return}"					
45						
46	Cell B35:					
47	+"{"&@if(S_COL>S_COL2,"right","left")&" "&					
48	@string(@abs(+S_COL-S_COL2),0)&"}"&"{return}"					
49						

FIGURE 15.12 A macro to subtotal like items in a database.

Here's how the macro works:

Point to 1st of the Like Items and hit any key. Press ESC to quit.
The macro begins by typing a prompt in the upper panel. If you
have Release 2.2 or higher, you may want to replace this with a
long {indicate} prompt, but be sure to include an {onerror} command that sends the program flow to an {indicate} command to
restore the Ready indicator if you press Ctrl+Break.

{get S_KEY}{esc}{if S_KEY="{esc}"}{quit} Pauses for your press of
a single key, then eliminates the typed message. If you press Esc,
the macro quits.

{if @left(S_KEY,1)="{"}{S_KEY}{branch_SUBTOT} If you press a
function key or directional key, the macro processes that key, then
branches back to the beginning to type the prompt in the upper
panel again. This allows you to move around the worksheet to
point to the first of the like items you want to subtotal.

{if S_KEY<>"~"}{branch_SUBTOT} If the key you press is not the
Enter key, the macro branches back to the beginning to type the
prompt in the upper panel again.

{let S_COL,@cellpointer("col")} Saves the number of the Like
Items column in the cell named S_COL.

{let SUBHERE,@cellpointer("address")} Creates a place-marker
for the current cell, saving the address at SUBHERE.

Point to Amount Column to Subtotal. Types another message in
the upper panel, this time prompting you to point to the Amount
column you want to subtotal.

{get S_KEY}{esc}{if S_KEY="{esc}"}{quit} Pauses for your press of
a single key, then eliminates the typed message. If you press
Escape, the macro quits.

{if @left(S_KEY,1)="{"}{S_KEY}{branch SUBTOT2} If you press a
function key or directional key, the macro processes that key, then
branches back to the beginning to type the prompt in the upper
panel again.

{if S_KEY<>"~"}{branch SUBTOT2} Similarly, if the key you press
is not the Enter key, the macro branches back to SUBTOT2 to
once again type the prompt in the upper panel.

{let S_COL2,@cellpointer("col")}{goto}{SUBHERE}~ Saves the
number of the Subtotal column in the cell range-named S_COL2,
then returns the cell pointer to the first of the like items in the
database.

{recalc SPAN}{recalc SPANEX} Recalculates the string formulas at
SPAN and SPANEX.

{let STEST,@cellpointer("contents")} Stores the contents of the
first of the like items in STEST.

{down}{if @cellpointer("type")="b"}{down}{SUBHEAD}{SQUIT}
Moves down and tests for a blank cell. If the cell is blank, it is assumed the macro has come to the end of the database, a closing subroutine at SUBHEAD is executed, and the macro branches to SQUIT to execute subtotal of the last item before quitting.

{if STEST=@cellpointer("contents")}{branch SUBLOOP2} At this point, the macro tests for whether the current cell matches the contents of STEST. If so, the macro branches to back to the previous line at SUBLOOP2, moving down to the next cell and testing for a blank cell and a match with STEST.

/wir{down 2}~{down}{SUBHEAD} If there is no match with STEST, that means the cell pointer is on a cell with a different item description. In that case, the macro inserts rows between the last group of like items and the current item by selecting /Worksheet Insert Row, painting down two more cells, and pressing Enter. The cell pointer moves down to the middle row of the three newly inserted rows and the macro calls the subroutine at SUBHEAD designed to type the subtotal identifier for the most recently identified like items.

{up 3}{if @cellpointer("type")="b"}{SINGLE}{branch SUBLOOP}
The cell pointer moves back up three cells to check for a blank cell. If the cell is blank, that means the current item is unique (there are no other items that match it), so the @sum formula must be for only one record. In that case, the macro branches to the subroutine at SINGLE before it branches back to the cell at B15 named SUBLOOP.

{down 3}{SUM}{down 2}{branch SUBLOOP} Otherwise, if there is more than one like item in the current batch, the macro runs the subroutine at SUM, then moves down two cells and branches back to SUBLOOP.

{recalc SUBCALC} Recalculates the string formula in the next line named SUBCALC.

SUBTOTAL FOR EASTERN DIVISION: This is the displayed result of a string formula, as follows:

```
+"SUBTOTAL FOR
"&@if(@cell("type",STEST)="v",@string(STEST,0),STEST)&"
":"
```

The string begins typing SUBTOTAL FOR, then checks for whether STEST is a value. If so, the string of the value is used; otherwise, the label in STEST is used. Finally, it types a colon and a space. The result is a subtotal identifier that includes the name of the most recent item subtotaled.

{right 3}{return} This is the displayed result of the string formula at SPAN, as follows:

```
+"{"&
@IF(S_COL>S_COL2,"left","right")&
" "&
&@string(@abs(+S_COL-S_COL2),0)&
"}"&
"{return}"
```

This formula calculates the number columns between the Like Items column and the Subtotal column, then moves right the number of cells required to span that distance.

@sum({up 2}{end}{up}.{end}{down}{down})~/rf,2~~{SPANEX} {return} Having moved to the Subtotal column, an @sum formula is entered to sum the last identified like items. The cell is formatted for Fixed Format with two decimals (though you can easily change this) and the subroutine at SPANEX returns the cell pointer back to the Like Items column using a formula similar to the string formula in SPAN.

{down 3}@sum({up 2}.{down})~/rf,2~~{SPANEX}{down 2}{return} This is the subroutine named SINGLE, designed to create an @sum formula for a single item only. It operates in a way similar to the previous line, but it only sums the two cells immediately above the current cell.

{up 3}{if @cellpointer("type")="b"}{SINGLE}{quit} This is the beginning of the subroutine named SQUIT, designed to check for whether the latest group consists of one or more than one item to subtotal. If there is only one item, the macro runs the subroutine SINGLE, then quits.

{down 3}{SUM}{down 2}{quit} Otherwise, the cell pointer is moved back down, the macro runs the subroutine named SUM, the cell pointer is moved down two more cells, and the macro quits.

An example of the type of results you can get using this macro is shown in Figure 15.13.

Summary

In this chapter we looked at the use of variable string formulas to create macros that will allow you to manipulate elements of your database. Concepts covered in this chapter include:

- The use of @choose in a string formula to enter a data item that varies according to the number of passes through a {for} loop.
- The use of a string formula to extract and display the letter or letters representing the current column. Since using @cellpointer("col")

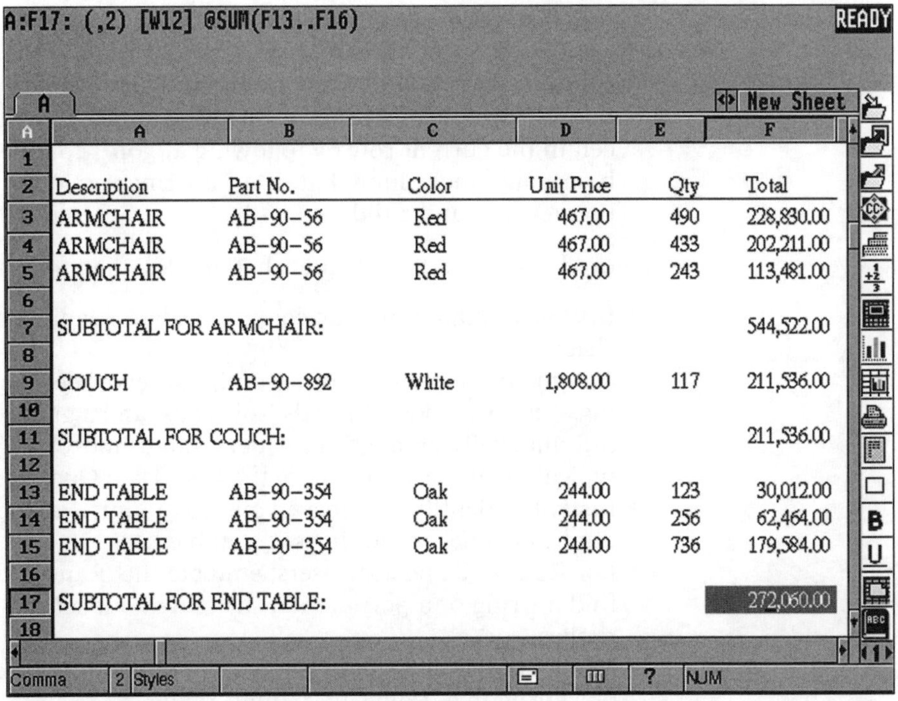

A:F17: (,2) [W12] @SUM(F13..F16)   READY

A	A	B	C	D	E	F
2	Description	Part No.	Color	Unit Price	Qty	Total
3	ARMCHAIR	AB−90−56	Red	467.00	490	228,830.00
4	ARMCHAIR	AB−90−56	Red	467.00	433	202,211.00
5	ARMCHAIR	AB−90−56	Red	467.00	243	113,481.00
6						
7	SUBTOTAL FOR ARMCHAIR:					544,522.00
8						
9	COUCH	AB−90−892	White	1,808.00	117	211,536.00
10						
11	SUBTOTAL FOR COUCH:					211,536.00
12						
13	END TABLE	AB−90−354	Oak	244.00	123	30,012.00
14	END TABLE	AB−90−354	Oak	244.00	256	62,464.00
15	END TABLE	AB−90−354	Oak	244.00	736	179,584.00
16						
17	SUBTOTAL FOR END TABLE:					272,060.00
18						

Comma   2 Styles   ?   NUM

FIGURE 15.13 Example of the results of the Subtotal macro.

provides only the column number, not the letter(s), a combination of @cellpointer functions must be used to extract the column letter from the current address.

- The duplication of Input range headings two rows above your database to establish headings for your Criterion range. This technique will ensure that your Criterion headings exactly match your Input headings and will make your Criterion range immediately accessible just above the Input range.

- Use of the {query} command after the command sequence /Data Query Find at the end of a Query macro. Using this technique, pressing Enter at any found record returns you to Ready mode instead of to the /Data Query menu with its potentially dangerous Reset choice.

- Elimination of blank rows in a database by selecting /Data Sort, which will combine all blank rows into one block, then selecting /Worksheet Delete Row and highlighting the entire block of blank rows. If your database is not in alphabetical order, insert a new column, select /Data Fill to fill it with consecutive numbers, then sort on some other cell (which again will combine all the blank rows into one block), delete the block of blank rows, then resort the database by the new /Data Fill column, and finally delete the /Data Fill column.

- Creation of a string formula to send your cell pointer to the leftmost cell in the current row by following a {goto} command with a combination of the column letter "A," a string version of the current cell pointer row, and a tilde.

We explored macros in this chapter that are designed to:

- Instantly create a row or column of date headings in your spreadsheet.
- Automate the creation of an entire spreadsheet matrix with headings, sidings, underline cells, subtotals, and a grand total.
- Automatically create /Data Query Input and Criterion ranges in a typical database, and initiate the first /Data Query Find operation.
- Instantly identify and leave your cell pointer at the second of any duplicate label entries in your database.
- For Release 2 and 2.01 users, emulate the /Range Search feature to find a string or a portion of a string without setting up /Data Query ranges.
- Modify the /Data Query Find feature to allow a search for a portion of a string in a /Data Query Input range.
- Automatically delete all rows that consist only of zero-value or blank cells in the range that you specify.
- Eliminate all completely empty rows from the current position to the End Home position or to any row that you specify.
- Delete all rows that have a blank cell in the current column, from the current position to the End Home location of the spreadsheet.
- Subtotal all like items in a database, displaying an identifier for each subtotal.

In the next chapter we will look at macros designed to control and manipulate the /File features of 1-2-3, including macros to switch the file directory; to save a file, save a backup and beep when finished; to view the size of a file in bytes; to list a filename table in your worksheet; to create a table of active files in Release 3.x; and to save a Macro Library .MLB file in Release 2.x.

16

Using File Control Macros

In this chapter we explore macros to control and manipulate 1-2-3's file features using variable string formulas, custom menus, @ functions, file-processing macro commands, and the /File Administration of Release 2.2 and higher. You'll learn about macros to automatically save a file, save a backup and beep when finished, present a message in your upper screen indicating the size of a file in bytes, list a filename table in your worksheet, create a table of active files in Release 3 and higher, and save a Macro Library .MLB file in Release 2.x.

Save File and Backup

In Chapter 5, we looked at a simple /File Save macro that calculates the worksheet, saves the file, and prints the data, giving beeps to indicate each operation is complete. (See Figure 5.2.)

The macro in Figure 16.1 is a more advanced /File Save macro that displays the time and date you last saved the file using this macro and prompts for whether you want to save it again. If you type Y for Yes, it saves the file, beeps, then prompts you to save a backup copy or quit. If you elect to save a backup copy, the macro saves a copy on your backup drive, the computer

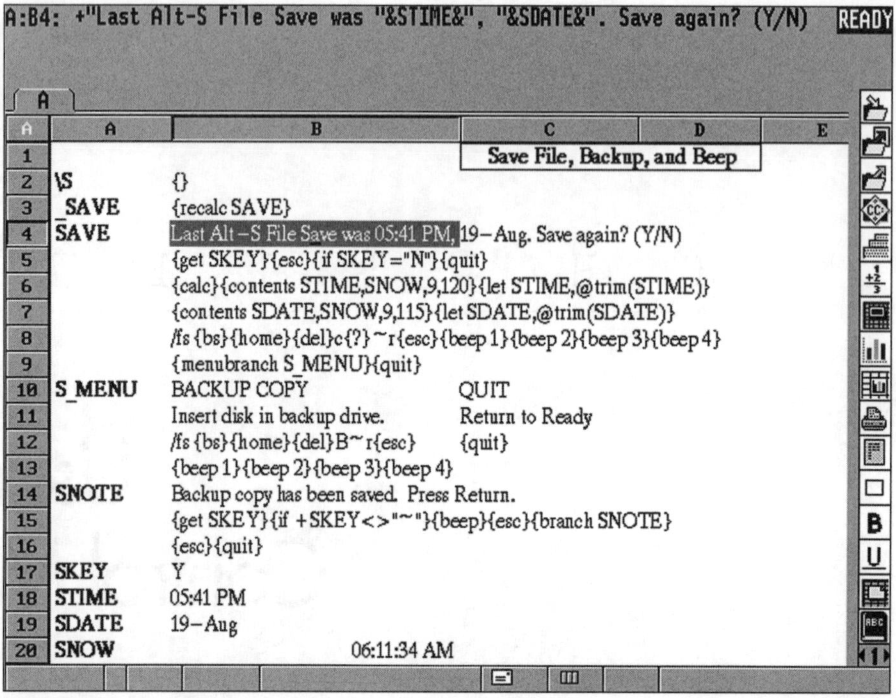

```
A:B4: +"Last Alt-S File Save was "&STIME&", "&SDATE&". Save again? (Y/N)    READY
```

A	A	B	C	D	E
1			Save File, Backup, and Beep		
2	\S	{}			
3	_SAVE	{recalc SAVE}			
4	SAVE	Last Alt −S File Save was 05:41 PM, 19−Aug. Save again? (Y/N)			
5		{get SKEY}{esc}{if SKEY="N"}{quit}			
6		{calc}{contents STIME,SNOW,9,120}{let STIME,@trim(STIME)}			
7		{contents SDATE,SNOW,9,115}{let SDATE,@trim(SDATE)}			
8		/fs {bs}{home}{del}c{?}~r{esc}{beep 1}{beep 2}{beep 3}{beep 4}			
9		{menubranch S_MENU}{quit}			
10	S_MENU	BACKUP COPY	QUIT		
11		Insert disk in backup drive.	Return to Ready		
12		/fs {bs}{home}{del}B~r{esc}	{quit}		
13		{beep 1}{beep 2}{beep 3}{beep 4}			
14	SNOTE	Backup copy has been saved. Press Return.			
15		{get SKEY}{if +SKEY<>"~"}{beep}{esc}{branch SNOTE}			
16		{esc}{quit}			
17	SKEY	Y			
18	STIME	05:41 PM			
19	SDATE	19−Aug			
20	SNOW	06:11:34 AM			

FIGURE 16.1 A macro to save file, save backup, and beep.

beeps, and a message in the upper panel tells you that a backup copy was saved.

{recalc SAVE}   The macro begins by recalculating the string formula in the next line named SAVE.

Last Alt+S File Save was 05:41 PM, 19-Aug. Save again? (Y/N) This is a message typed in the upper panel, the displayed result of a string formula:

```
+"Last Alt+S File Save was "&
STIME&
", "&
SDATE&
".Save again? (Y/N)"
```

The string formula uses the information stored in STIME and SDATE from the last time you used the macro. This means, of course, that the first time you press Alt+S (Ctrl+S in 1-2-3 for Windows) it will not provide the correct information; but after one use, this line displays the last time and date you saved the file with this macro.

Use this macro, especially for larger files, instead of the usual /File Save sequence. That way, you won't have to wonder whether you saved a particular file recently and end by resaving the file just to be sure. The larger the file you avoid resaving, the more time this macro saves you.

{get SKEY}{esc}{if SKEY="N"}{quit}   Pauses for your press of a single key and executes {esc} to eliminate the message in the upper panel. If you press N for No at the message prompt, this means you do not want the file saved again, and the macro quits.

{calc}{contents STIME,SNOW,9,120}{let STIME,@trim(STIME)}
Otherwise, the worksheet is calculated, the current time from the @now formula at SNOW is copied to the cell named STIME using the {contents} command, and the extra spaces in the results are eliminated with a {let} command and the @trim function.

{contents SDATE,SNOW,9,115}{let SDATE,@trim(SDATE)}   The same techniques are used to copy the current date from the @now formula in SNOW to SDATE.

/fs {bs}{home}{del}c{?}~r{esc}{beep 1}{beep 2}{beep 3}{beep 4}
The macro selects /File Save and presses Space, then eliminates the space with Backspace. This allows editing of the offered filename. Then the macro uses {home} to take the cursor to the beginning of the filename, deletes the drive letter, replaces it with the letter C, saves the file (the letter R is for Replace), and beeps to let you know it's done.

{menubranch S_MENU}{quit}   Calls up the menu choices BACKUP COPY and QUIT.

/fs {bs}{home}{del}B~r{esc}   If you select BACKUP COPY, the macro selects /File Save, changes the drive letter to B (you may want to rewrite this to drive A or a separate directory in drive C), enters the filename, and selects Replace.

{beep 1}{beep 2}{beep 3}{beep 4}   Beeps to let you know the backup copy has been saved.

Backup copy has been saved. Press Enter.   This message is typed in the upper panel.

{get SKEY}{if +SKEY<>"~"}{beep}{esc}{branch SNOTE}   Pauses for your press of any key. If you do not press Enter, the macro beeps and loops back to SNOTE to display the same message again.

{esc}{quit}   Otherwise, if you press Enter, the message is eliminated and the macro quits.

Using this macro, if you save and back up a file, then leave your desk, you won't have to wonder when you return whether you saved the file—a message will show in the upper panel reminding you that the file has been saved.

Saving a File with an Alternate Name

You have seen how to save a file that already has a /File Save name by using **/fs{?}~r{esc}.** If you write a macro that prompts you to enter a completely new /File Save name, however, you will need a way to keep from entering an already existing filename, and thus writing over other important files.

The macro in Figure 16.2 provides such a technique. Designed to be used as a part of a larger macro that includes a prompted /File Save of a new file, this macro waits for you to enter the new name of the file to save, and checks for whether the name already exists. If not, the /File Save operation is completed as expected. On the other hand, if the filename already exists, the macro offers the choices CANCEL, REPLACE, and ALT_NAME to deal with that.

Here's how the macro works:

{getlabel "Enter name of file to save: ",NSAVE}   Prompts you to enter the name of the file you want to save and places your response in the cell named NEW_SAVE.

{open +NSAVE&".WK1",r}/fs{NSAVE}.WK1~{quit}   This is our first use of the {open} command, a file-processing command

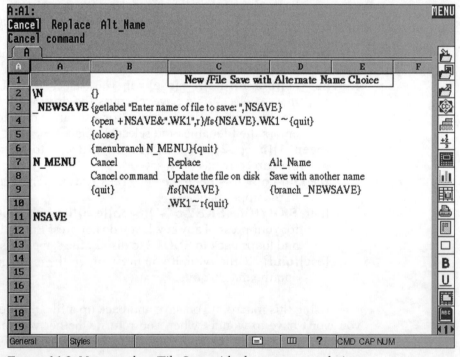

FIGURE 16.2 Macro to do a /File Save with alternate name choice.

designed to open the named file in either Read mode, Write mode, or Modify mode (type **R**, **W**, or **M**). In this case, the file-name you provided in response to the prompt is given a .WK1 suffix, then the macro attempts to open that file in the Read mode.

   If the {open} command is *not* successful, the macro executes the rest of the line. This is the exact opposite of the way an {if} command works, where if a condition is false, the macro skips down to the next line. With the {open} command, if 1-2-3 is *not* able to open the file (in other words, if the file does not exist yet), the rest of the line is processed. In this case, the macro proceeds to select /File Save, types the contents of NSAVE, enters the file-name, and quits. The macro has been written to do this because nonexistence of the file means it is safe to save the current work-sheet using that filename.

{close}   If the {open} command *is* successful, the macro skips the rest of the line and proceeds to this line, where a {close} command closes the pre-existing file.

{menubranch N_MENU}{quit}   Since the filename already exists, the menu choices CANCEL, REPLACE, and ALT_NAME appear. The first two choices, CANCEL and REPLACE, will be familiar to you. If you select CANCEL, the macro quits. If you select REPLACE, the macro selects /File Save of the filename, then selects R for Replace. The new choice, ALT_NAME, simply causes the macro to branch back to the beginning at _NEWSAVE, where it prompts you for another name under which to save the current file.

By itself, this macro is not useful. Included as a part of a larger macro that involves a prompted /File Save of a new file, however, it can save you or your users from inadvertently destroying already existing files.

File-Processing Macro Commands

Some of 1-2-3's file-processing macro commands are used in the macro above, so this is a good place to list and describe the function of these types of commands.

   The standard file commands such as /File Save, /File Retrieve, and /File Combine manipulate 1-2-3 worksheet files. Some of the standard com-mands such as /File Import also work with ASCII files, but only in a limited way. The nine advanced macro commands we will describe here signifi-cantly extend 1-2-3's file-processing capabilities, including the ability to open and close files, access and transfer data from any text or sequential disk file into 1-2-3, and write data from 1-2-3 to a wide variety of file formats outside 1-2-3.

{open *file name,access character***}**   Opens a file in either Read, Write, or Modify mode. In Read mode, information can be transferred only from the disk file to the worksheet. In Write mode, information can be transferred only from the worksheet to the disk file. In Modify mode, information can pass in both directions.

For the access character, type **R**, **W**, or **M**. If you use a letter other than these three, the file is opened in Read mode. Whatever the mode, opening a file places the byte pointer at the beginning of the file (the byte at position 0).

If the {open} command fails, macro execution continues in the same cell. Otherwise, if the command succeeds, any remaining commands on the same line are ignored and execution skips to the cell below. This is the exact opposite of the way an {if} command works, where a false condition causes any remaining commands on the same line to be ignored and a true condition causes the macro to execute the rest of the line.

{close}   Closes any file opened with the {open} command. You must close one file before opening another, although 1-2-3 will do this automatically for you if you omit the {close} command before doing another {open}. If you use the {close} command when there are no open files, 1-2-3 ignores it. On the other hand, any other file-manipulation commands will fail after a {close} command, unless preceded by another {open} command.

{filesize *location***}**   Returns the size (in bytes) of the currently open file. The position of the byte pointer is irrelevant. The result appears in the cell location you specify. If no file is currently open, the {filesize} command fails and macro execution continues in the same cell. Otherwise, the command succeeds and execution skips to the cell below. In other words, any command following a successful {filesize} command in the same macro line will be ignored.

{getpos *location***}**   Returns your current position in the open file where the first character in a file is considered position 0. The result appears in the cell location you specify. Specifying a range is equivalent to specifying the range's top left cell. As with the {filesize} command, if no file is currently open, the {getpos} command fails and macro execution continues in the same cell. Otherwise, the command succeeds, any remaining commands on the same line are ignored, and execution skips to the cell below.

{setpos *file position***}**   Moves the cursor to any file position you specify, where *position* is any number, a range name assigned to a single numeric cell, or a numeric formula. Negative values are not acceptable, however. The move is absolute, not relative, which means the position is counted from the zero position rather than from the current position of the byte pointer.

{read *byte count,location*}   Reads the number of bytes you specify into the location you define, starting at the cursor's current file position. This command transfers into 1-2-3 the specified number of bytes, creating a label in the named cell. This command is intended for use with sequential files; for text files, the {readln} command is preferred.

{readln *location*}   Reads a single line of text from the currently open text file and places it as a label in the cell location you specify. Specifying a range is equivalent to specifying the range's top left cell.

Starting at the current position of the byte pointer (typically the beginning of a text line), this command reads to the end-of-line sequence marked by a carriage return and a line feed, converts each byte to an LICS character, stores the string as a label in the specified cell location (minus the CR-LF sequence), and advances the byte pointer just past the CR-LF sequence to prepare for another {readln} command.

If no file is open, or the current file was opened in Write mode, or the byte pointer is already at the end of the file, the {readln} command fails and the macro continues in the same cell. Otherwise, the command succeeds, any remaining commands on the same line are ignored, and execution skips to the cell below.

{write *string*}   Writes any string of characters you specify to the current byte position in the currently open file. The argument *string* is a character string, an expression evaluating to a character string, or a range name assigned to a single cell that contains a string. This command converts each LICS character in the string to a DOS code, sends the string to a file (extending the length of the file if necessary), and advances the byte pointer just beyond the last character written to prepare for another {write} command.

{writeln *string*}   Writes any string of characters you specify to the current byte position in the currently open file, but adds a 2-character end-of-line sequence. This command converts each LICS character in the string to a DOS code, sends the string to a file (extending the length of the file if necessary), writes a carriage return and a line feed to the file as an end-of-line sequence, and advances the byte pointer just beyond the last character written to prepare for another {writeln} command.

Creating a Message Showing a File Size

We can make use of the {open}, {close}, and {filesize} commands to create a macro that will report on the size of a given file. Such a macro is shown in Figure 16.3.

Here's how the macro works:

{getlabel "Enter file name:",V_NAME} Prompts you to enter the name of the file for which you want a report on the file size (in bytes).

{open +V_NAME&".wk1",R}{branch V_ISNT} The macro attempts to open a version of this file with its .WK1 suffix. If the {open} command fails because the file does not exist, the macro continues on this same line. The remainder of the line causes a branch to V_ISNT where the message, *"No such file exists. Press Enter"* is typed into the upper panel, the macro pauses so you can read it, the message is eliminated, and the macro quits.

{filesize V_SIZE} Otherwise, if the file does exist, the macro skips to this line where the size of the open file is calculated and stored in V_SIZE.

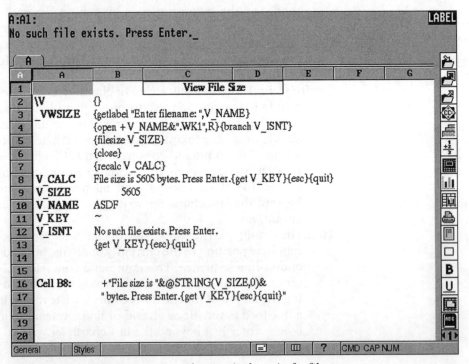

FIGURE 16.3 Macro to report on the size (in bytes) of a file.

{close} The macro closes the open file.

{recalc V_CALC} Recalculates the string formula at V_CALC.

File size is 5605 bytes. Press Enter.{get V_KEY}{esc}{quit} This is a message typed in the upper panel, the displayed result of a string formula, as follows:

```
+"File size is"&
V_SIZE&
" bytes. Press Enter.{get V_KEY}{esc}{quit}"
```

This message displays differently, of course, depending on the actual size of the file you are checking.

Saving a Macro Library File

We have explored macros to save .WK1 files (Figures 5.2, 16.1, and 16.2) and a macro to edit Macro Library .MLB files (Figure 12.9 in Chapter 12). In this section we look at a macro to save a Macro Library .MLB file. Because it addresses the Macro Library capability, this macro, shown in Figure 16.4, works for Release 2.2, 2.3, and 2.4 only.

This macro is based on the assumption that the current worksheet file contains macro code that you want to save to a Macro Library .MLB file. In fact, it assumes that the code you want to save starts at cell A1 and goes to the end of the file. During its process, it highlights the entire file, from the Home to the End Home position, but it also pauses in case you want to limit the save-range to any reduced size.

{indicate "Save file first? (Y/N): (ESC to Cancel)"}{get MKEY} The macro begins by displaying a message in place of the Ready indicator, prompting for whether you want to save the current file before saving a portion of the file as a Macro Library .MLB file. The {get} command pauses for your press of Y for Yes, N for No, or Escape to cancel the macro.

{indicate}{if MKEY="{esc}"}{quit} Returns the indicator to normal. If the key you pressed is Escape, the macro quits.

{if MKEY<>"Y"}{branch M_APP} If the key is not Y for Yes (presumably it was N for No), the file is not saved, and the macro branches to M_APP.

/fs{?}~r{esc}{home} Otherwise, the macro selects /File Save, pauses for your acceptance of the filename or entering of a new filename, selects R for Replace and presses Escape in case Replace is not offered, then moves the cell pointer to the Home position in the Worksheet.

{if @isapp("MACROMGR")}{app1}{branch MORE} Checks for whether the MACROMGR.ADN add-in application has been

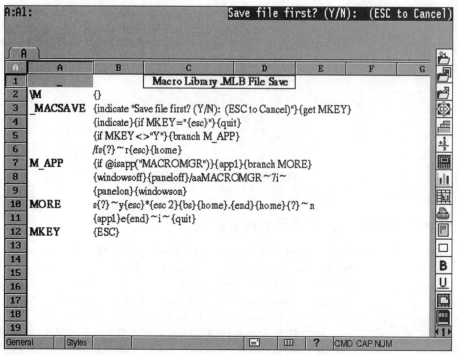

A:A1:   Save file first? (Y/N):   (ESC to Cancel)

	A	B	C	D	E	F	G
1			Macro Library .MLB File Save				
2	\M	{}					
3	_MACSAVE	{indicate "Save file first? (Y/N): (ESC to Cancel)"}{get MKEY}					
4		{indicate}{if MKEY="{esc}"}{quit}					
5		{if MKEY<>"Y"}{branch M_APP}					
6		/fs{?}~r{esc}{home}					
7	M_APP	{if @isapp("MACROMGR")}{app1}{branch MORE}					
8		{windowsoff}{paneloff}/aaMACROMGR~7i~					
9		{panelon}{windowson}					
10	MORE	s{?}~y{esc}*{esc 2}{bs}{home}.{end}{home}{?}~n					
11		{app1}e{end}~i~{quit}					
12	MKEY	{ESC}					
13							
14							
15							
16							
17							
18							
19							

General   Styles   ▱   ▥   ?   CMD CAP NUM

FIGURE 16.4 A macro to save a range to a Macro Library .MLB file.

attached. If so, the macro assumes that you have assigned Alt+F7 as the key to invoke it and it executes the command equivalent for Alt+F7, **{app1}.** At this point the macro branches to MORE to continue with the .MLB file-save.

{windowsoff}{paneloff}/aaMACROMGR~7i~   If the MACROMGR. ADN has not been attached, this line selects /Add-in Attach, enters MACROMGR, attaches the add-in to Alt+F7, and invokes the MACROMGR add-in.

{panelon}{windowson}   Turns off the windows and panel to suppress screen flicker and speed up the macro.

s{?}~y{esc}*{esc 2}{bs}{home}.{end}{home}{?}~n   This is the cell named MORE where the file-saving occurs. From the MACRO-MGR.ADN menu choices Load, Save, Edit, Remove, Name-List, and Quit, the macro selects Save, then pauses for your selection or entry of a Macro Library .MLB file-save name. If the file already exists, a No/Yes menu comes up with the instructions, "Macro Library already exists on disk. Write over it?". The macro types Y for Yes, then Esc in case the file did not already exist. At the prompt for a range to save, the macro types an asterisk and

Esc twice to clear the default range, highlights the range from Home to the End Home position, pauses for your acceptance or modification of the range, then types N for No at the request for password attachment.

{app1}e{end}~i~{quit}   Saving a range to a macro library erases the contents of that range from the current worksheet. This may not be what you want, so the macro again invokes the MACRO-MGR.ADN, bringing up the choices Load, Save, Edit, Remove, Name-List, and Quit. Then it selects the Edit choice and presses End to highlight and select the last .MLB file saved. The macro selects I for Ignore, presses Enter for the current cell-pointer location, and quits.

Creating a Filename Table

If you select /File Admin Table in Release 2.2 or higher, 1-2-3 offers the menu choices Reservation, Table, and Link-Refresh. If you then select Table, 1-2-3 prompts you for the type of files (.WK1 Worksheet files or .PRN Print files, for example), the directory from which you want your table to extract its list of files, and the location in the current worksheet where you want your table to appear.

Unfortunately, the table 1-2-3 enters in the worksheet, though it provides you with filenames, file dates, file times and bytes, might well be unreadable due to the possibility of inappropriate column widths and displayed format. For example, the file dates typically appear as straight numbers like 32073 and the file time usually appears in a form like 0.507186.

The macro in Figure 16.5 is designed to prompt you for a location for your table, then allows you to choose the type of files you want listed and the directory from which the table is to pull its list. The macro enters table headings, changes column widths, formats the columns, inserts the table, and finally prompts you for whether you want the table erased.

{indicate "Point to location for File Table . . ."}   The macro begins by changing the Ready indicator to a prompt to point to the location where you want your file table. If you aren't careful, you may write over existing data, so you may want to press End Home Ctrl+RightArrow to ensure that you move to a clear area for the table.

{onerror LQUIT}   If the macro quits because of an error or your press of Ctrl+Break, this command sends the program flow to LQUIT where it processes an {indicate} command to return the Ready indicator to normal before the macro quits.

{get LKEY}{if LKEY="~"}{branch LMORE}   The macro pauses for your press of a single key. If you press Enter, the macro assumes

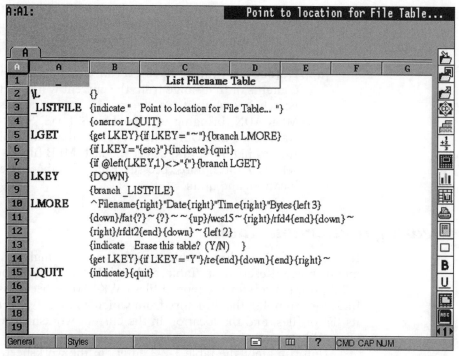

FIGURE 16.5 A Filename Table macro for Release 2.2 and higher.

you are already at the location where you want your table, so it skips to the routine where the table is created.

{if LKEY="{esc}"}{indicate}{quit}   If you press Esc instead, the macro processes an {indicate} command to return the Ready indicator to normal, then quits.

{if @left(LKEY,1)<>"{"}{branch LGET}   If the key you press is not a function key or directional key, this command causes the macro to ignore it, and the macro branches back to LGET to get the next keystroke.

{DOWN}   Otherwise, the macro continues to the next cell, which is LKEY where your keystroke was stored. In this example, the contents of LKEY show **{DOWN}**, but this will vary depending on what keystroke you press.

{branch_LISTFILE}   The macro branches back to the beginning and continues in this way until you press Enter, indicating that your cell pointer is finally at the location where you want your filename table.

^File Name{right}"Date{right}"Time{right}"Bytes{left 3}   Types the headings, Filename, Date, Time, and Bytes.

{down}/fat{?}~{?}~~{up}/wcs15~{right}/rfd4{end}{down}~   Moves down one cell, selects /File Admin Table, and pauses for your selection of the type of file to list. The macro then pauses for your selection of the file directory from which to list the files, enters your current location as the appropriate location for the table, and moves up one cell. The first column is changed to a width of 15, and the next column is given a date format.

{right}/rfdt2{end}{down}~{left 2}   The next column is given a time format and the macro moves back to the first column.

{indicate Erase this table? (Y/N) }   The ready indicator is changed to prompt for whether you want to erase the table.

{get LKEY}{if LKEY="Y"}/re{end}{down}{end}{right}~   The macro prompts for your press of any key. If you press Y for Yes, the table is erased.

{indicate}{quit}   Finally, the indicator is returned to normal and the macro quits.

For an example of the type of results you will get using this macro, refer to Figure 16.6

Active Filename Tables in Release 3 and Higher

1-2-3 provides several additional features accessible from the /File Administration command sequence in Release 3 and higher, including the ability to create a table showing the names of the currently active files.

In Release 3 and higher, you are only limited by memory in the number of files you can have active at any one time, so being able to list those active files is important for record-keeping, for recreating an important multiple-file session later, or simply for resolving any confusion you may have about the files you have active at any one time.

In addition to listing the active files for a current session, the /File Admin Table Active sequence lists the number of worksheets in each file and indicates whether they have been modified since their retrieval, and whether you have the reservation for these files.

The macro in Figure 16.7 is similar to the macro in Figure 16.5 in that it creates a table of files. The difference is that the file list in Figure 16.7 is for currently active files in Release 3 or higher and the headings of the table include the headings, # Wkshts, Modified, and Reservation.

It would be redundant to go through this macro line by line, but it should be pointed out that a wildcard filename <<?>> has been added before every occurrence of the range name A|KEY to provide for use of this macro in a Macro Library file as described in Chapter 7.

An example showing the results of this macro can be seen in Figure 16.8. Note, the number 1 in the column labeled, "# Wkshts" represents a

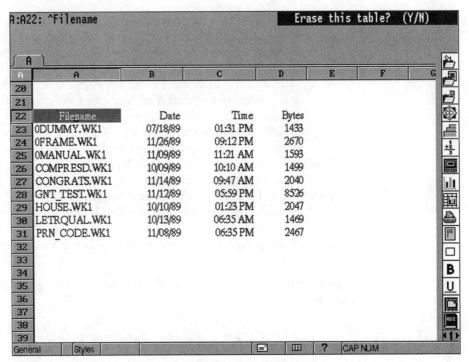

A:A22: ^Filename   Erase this table? (Y/N)

	A	B	C	D	E	F	G
20							
21							
22	Filename	Date	Time	Bytes			
23	0DUMMY.WK1	07/18/89	01:31 PM	1433			
24	0FRAME.WK1	11/26/89	09:12 PM	2670			
25	0MANUAL.WK1	11/09/89	11:21 AM	1593			
26	COMPRESD.WK1	10/09/89	10:10 AM	1499			
27	CONGRATS.WK1	11/14/89	09:47 AM	2040			
28	GNT_TEST.WK1	11/12/89	05:59 PM	8526			
29	HOUSE.WK1	10/10/89	01:23 PM	2047			
30	LETRQUAL.WK1	10/13/89	06:35 AM	1469			
31	PRN_CODE.WK1	11/08/89	06:35 PM	2467			
32							
33							
34							
35							
36							
37							
38							
39							

General   Styles   ▢ ▥ ? CAP NUM

FIGURE 16.6 Sample results of the Filename Table macro.

quantity, while the number 1 in the columns labeled "Modified" and "Reservation" represents a true condition. If a given file has not been modified or you do not have its reservation, the table displays a zero in the appropriate column.

Summary

In this chapter we looked at macros to control and manipulate the file features of 1-2-3 using variable string formulas, custom menus, @ functions, file-processing macro commands, and the /File Administration of Release 2.2 and higher. Concepts and techniques covered in this chapter include:

- The {contents} command and @trim function can be used to copy the current date into one cell and the time into another, both copies being taken from a single cell containing an @now function.
- The {open} command opens a file in either Read, Write, or Modify mode. If the {open} command fails, macro execution continues in the same cell. Otherwise, if the command succeeds, any remaining commands on the same line are ignored and execution skips to the

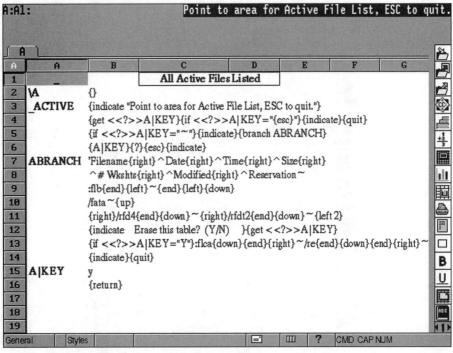

FIGURE 16.7 A macro to list active files in Release 3 or higher.

cell below. This is the exact opposite of the way an {if} command works, where a false condition causes any remaining commands on the same line to be ignored and a true condition causes the macro to execute the rest of the line.

- The {close} command closes any file opened with the {open} command. You must close one file before opening another, although 1-2-3 will do this automatically for you if you omit the {close} command before doing another {open}.
- The {filesize} command returns the size (in bytes) of the currently open file. The result appears in the cell location you specify. If no file is currently open, the {filesize} command fails and macro execution continues in the same cell.
- The {getpos} command returns your current position in the open file. The result appears in the cell location you specify. As with the {filesize} command, if no file is currently open, the {getpos} command fails and macro execution continues in the same cell.
- The {setpos} command moves the cursor to any file position you specify. The position must be counted from the zero position rather than from the current position of the byte pointer.

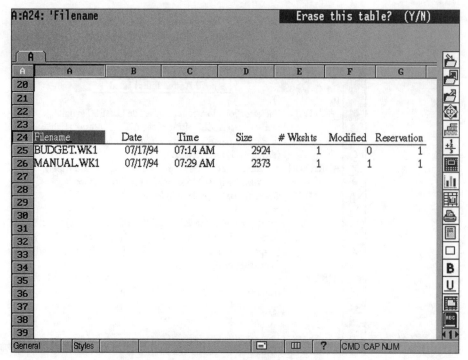

FIGURE 16.8 Sample results of the Active File Table macro.

- The {read} command reads the number of bytes you specify into the location you define, starting at the cursor's current file position. This command is intended for use with sequential files; for text files, the {readln} command is preferred.
- The {readln} command reads a single line of text from the currently open text file and places it as a label in the cell location you specify.
- The {write} command writes any string of characters you specify to the current byte position in the currently open file.
- The {writeln} command writes any string of characters you specify to the current byte position in the currently open file, but adds a 2-character end-of-line sequence.
- If you select /File Admin Table in Release 2.2 or higher, you will see the menu choices Reservation, Table, and Link-Refresh. Unfortunately, if you select Table, the filenames, file dates, file times, and bytes might well be unreadable until you adjust its column widths and range formats.
- Release 3 introduced several additional features accessible from the /File Administration command sequence, including the ability to

create a table of your currently active files. This table also lists the number of worksheets in each file and indicates their modification and reservation status.

This chapter also presented and explored:

- A macro that shows the time and date you last saved the file using this macro, saves the file, saves a backup copy, and beeps when done.
- A macro for use with a larger macro, designed to do a /File Save, to check for whether the /File Save name already exists, and to prompt you with the choices CANCEL, REPLACE, and ALT_NAME if so.
- A macro that uses the {open}, {close}, and {filesize} commands to report on the size of a user-specified file.
- A macro designed to save a range in the current file as a Macro Library .MLB file.
- A Filename Table macro for Release 2.2 and higher that prompts you for a location for your table, the type of files to list, and the appropriate directory. The macro enters table headings, changes column widths, formats the columns, inserts the table, and prompts you for whether you want the table erased.
- A macro to list active files in Release 3 and higher. The headings of the table created are similar to the Filename Table, except that they also include the headings for a number of worksheets and modification and reservation status of your active files.

In the next chapter we look at special applications you can create using the macro techniques covered in this book. These applications include programs to automate and maintain an address database, print form letters and address labels from that database, create a checkbook ledger, and print out your checkbook amounts in words as they might be written on a check.

17

Creating Macro Applications

In this chapter we look at special applications you can create using the macro techniques covered in this book. You'll learn how to create a program that enables prompted data entry into an address database. Then, once you've entered the data, you'll be interested in an application that automatically prints form letters and labels from that database. Using the prompted data entry techniques you learned, you'll find out how to create an easy-to-use checkbook ledger. Finally, you'll learn how to write a macro program that automatically types out your checkbook amounts in words as they might be written on a check.

Creating an Address Database

In Chapter 9 we looked at a data entry macro that includes the typing of a label prefix before each entry (see Figure 9.7). Unfortunately, that macro has no built-in way of shifting from label entry (making entries that require a label prefix) and value entries without your stopping the macro, then starting it again and manually selecting the different entry type.

In this section we present a macro that adds more intelligence to the data entry process. Called the Add to Address Database macro, this macro determines in advance what type of entry is required for a particular column. It differentiates, based on the way you set up the worksheet, between columns dedicated to labels, columns used for values, and columns that contain only dates shown in the date format.

As you can see in Figure 17.1, this macro uses the {get} command to capture every keystroke and the {if} command to test for the type of column into which the data is being entered. Because of the way it is designed, it has the following additional features:

 You can move right, left, up, or down, without being limited by the fact that a macro is running.

 If you switch columns by moving right or left, the data entry prompt instantly switches to match the new column.

 You have full access to the /Copy, /Move, /Range Erase, /Worksheet Delete Row, and /Worksheet Insert Row commands just as if the macro were not active.

To use this macro, you must first set up database titles like the ones shown at the bottom of Figure 17.1. If you want to modify the database, enter the macro with the recommended database structure first, make sure the macro works as it should, and only then make your required modifications. Some suggestions on how to modify both the database and the macro are included in the description of the macro below.

You must also create a range name at the first title, called ADRS. If you want your database to begin in column A, you should know it is not necessary to include the range-name label as shown in Cell A41 of Figure 17.1. However, if you decide to omit the label, you must move your cell pointer to the first title (in our example, that means cell B41), select /Range Name Create, type ADRS, and press Enter.

> **{goto}ADRS~{let ADRSCOL,@cell("col",ADRS)}** The macro begins by sending your cell pointer to the cell range-named ADRS, and records the column of that cell in ADRSCOL.

> **{end}{down}{down}{recalc A|CALC}** The macro moves the cell pointer down to the first blank record and recalculates the string formula at A|CALC.

> **{let A|COL,@cellpointer("col")}** Records the number for the current column in A|COL, to be used by the next nine {if} statements to determine the type of entry required.

> **{if A|COL=ADRSCOL}Enter first name: {branch ALABEL}** If the current column number is the same as ADRSCOL (which it will be in the first pass through this macro), the macro types the prompt, "Enter first name:" into the upper panel and branches to the routine named ALABEL.

	A	B	C	D	E	F	G	H	I
1		Add to Address Database
2	\A	{}
3	_ADRS	{goto}ADRS~{let ADRSCOL,@cell("col",ADRS)}
4		{end}{down}{down}{recalc A\CALC}
5	AGAIN	{let A\COL,@cellpointer("col")}
6		{if A\COL=ADRSCOL}Enter first name: {branch ALABEL}
7		{if A\COL=ADRSCOL+1}Enter last name: {branch ALABEL}
8		{if A\COL=ADRSCOL+2}Enter company: {branch ALABEL}
9		{if A\COL=ADRSCOL+3}Enter address: {branch ALABEL}
10		{if A\COL=ADRSCOL+4}Enter City, State: {branch ALABEL}
11		{if A\COL=ADRSCOL+5}Enter Zip: {branch ALABEL}
12		{if A\COL=ADRSCOL+6}Enter Code: {branch AVALUE}
13		{if A\COL=ADRSCOL+7}Enter month, day: @date(89,{branch ADATE}
14	A\CALC	{if A\COL>ADRSCOL+7}{down}{left 8}{branch AGAIN}
15	ALABEL	{let ACHANGE,"{branch ALABEL2}"}{branch ASUB}
16	ALABEL2	'{AKEY}{?}~{right}{branch AGAIN}
17	AVALUE	{let ACHANGE,"{branch AVALUE2}"}{branch ASUB}
18	AVALUE2	{AKEY}{?}~{right}{branch AGAIN}
19	ADATE	{let ACHANGE,"{branch ADATE2}"}{branch ASUB}
20	ADATE2	@date(95,{AKEY}{?})~/rfd4~{right}{branch AGAIN}
21	ASUB	{get AKEY}{esc}{if AKEY="{esc}"}{quit}
22		{if AKEY="~"}{ABLANK}{right}{branch AGAIN}
23		{if AKEY="{edit}"}{edit}{?}~{right}{branch AGAIN}
24		{if @left(AKEY,1)="{"}{AKEY}{branch AGAIN}
25		{if AKEY="/"}/{branch ASLASH}
26	ACHANGE	{branch ALABEL2}
27	AKEY	{ESC}
28	A\COL	2
29	ABLANK	{if @cellpointer("type")="b"}'{return}
30	ADRSCOL	2
31	ASLASH	{get AKEY}{if AKEY="c"#or#AKEY="m"}{AKEY}{?}~{?}~{branch AGAIN}
32		{if AKEY="r"#or#AKEY="w"}{AKEY}{?}~{branch AGAIN}
33		{esc}{branch AGAIN}
34		
35		
36	CELL B14:	+"{if A\COL>ADRSCOL+"&@string(@rows(b16..b6)-4,0)&
37		"}{down}{left "&@string(@rows(b16..b6)-3,0)&"}{branch AGAIN}"
38		
39		
40		
41	ADRS	First	Last	Company	Address	City, St.	ZIP	Code	Date
42		I.B.	Empicee	Big Blue	9 Munchkin La	Dvorak, NJ	72532	3	01/22/95
43		Mac N.	Tosh	Big Red	123 Apple St	Graphic, CA	95014	2	01/22/95
44		Nick	Smashing	Blackbox	567 Main St	Pine,WY	01864	4	01/22/95
45		
46		

FIGURE 17.1 A macro to add to an address database.

{if A\COL=ADRSCOL+1}Enter last name: {branch ALABEL} If the current column number is one greater than ADRSCOL, the macro prompts you to "Enter last name:" and branches to ALABEL.

{if A\COL=ADRSCOL+2}Enter company: {branch ALABEL} If the current column number is two greater than ADRSCOL, the macro prompts you to "Enter company:" and branches to ALABEL.

{if A|COL=ADRSCOL+3}Enter address: {branch ALABEL}   If the current column number is three greater than ADRSCOL, the macro prompts you to "Enter address:" and branches to ALABEL.

{if A|COL=ADRSCOL+4}Enter City, State: {branch ALABEL}   If the current column number is four greater than ADRSCOL, the macro prompts you to "Enter City, State:" and branches to ALABEL.

{if A|COL=ADRSCOL+5}Enter Zip: {branch ALABEL}   If the current column number is five greater than ADRSCOL, the macro prompts you to "Enter Zip:" and again branches to ALABEL. (Zip codes must be entered as labels, in case they start with a zero.)

{if A|COL=ADRSCOL+6}Enter Code: {branch AVALUE}   If the current column number is six greater than ADRSCOL, the macro prompts you to "Enter code:", but this time it branches to AVALUE.

{if A|COL=ADRSCOL+7}Enter month, day: @date(89,{branch ADATE}   If the current column number is seven greater than ADRSCOL, the macro prompts you to "Enter month, day:" in the @date format (the @date portion is entered for you) and branches to ADATE.

{if A|COL>ADRSCOL+7}{down}{left 8}{branch AGAIN}   If the current column number is seven greater than ADRSCOL, the cell pointer must be beyond the end of a database row, so the macro moves you Down Left 8 to the beginning of the next row, and branches to AGAIN to start over.

The string formula that underlies this displayed result is:

```
+"{if A|COL>ADRSCOL+"&
@string(@rows(b16..b6)-4,0)&
"}{down}{left "&
@string(@rows(b16..b6)-3,0)&
"}{branch AGAIN}"
```

You may be wondering why we bothered to enter this as a string formula. After all, the only string @functions are the second and fourth parts, which return the numbers 7 and 8. Why not simply type the numbers 7 and 8 into the {if} statement as a straight label?

The answer has to do with the generic quality of this macro. It allows you to delete or add rows of the macro in the range between B6 and B16 without having to revisit this line. For example, suppose you do not want a prompt that reads, "Enter Code" in your address database. After the entire macro is typed into your worksheet, simply do a /Worksheet Delete Row to delete row 12, and the string formula at A|CALC on row 14 will adjust automatically to accommodate the fact that there are now fewer prompts, representing fewer headings.

{let ACHANGE,"{branch ALABEL2}"}{branch ASUB}   This is the line of the macro named ALABEL, where the program branches when a label entry is required. It begins by changing the cell named ACHANGE to a new branch command, then branches to ASUB. As you will see, ASUB is the subroutine where the macro checks your keystroke for Esc, Enter, a press of the F2 Edit key, another function key or directional key, or a forward slash (/) key.

{AKEY}{?}~{right}{branch AGAIN}   If the ASUB subroutine does not identify your keystroke as any of those described above, the macro returns to this cell at ALABEL2 (via the branching command at ACHANGE) where it types a label prefix, processes the character key you pressed, does a bracketed question mark pause {?} for the remainder of the entry, then moves right and branches back to the fourth line of the macro at AGAIN.

{let ACHANGE,"{branch AVALUE2}"}{branch ASUB}   This is the line of the macro named AVALUE, where the program branches when a value entry is required. It converts the cell named ACHANGE to a new branch command, then branches to ASUB to check for special keystrokes.

{AKEY}{?}~{right}{branch AGAIN}   If you have not pressed a special keystroke such as Esc, Enter, Edit, and so on, the macro returns to this cell (via the branching command at ACHANGE) where it processes the character key you pressed without a label prefix, does a bracketed question mark pause {?} for the remainder of the entry, then moves right and branches back to the fourth line of the macro at AGAIN.

{let ACHANGE,"{branch ADATE2}"}{branch ASUB}   This is the line of the macro named ADATE, where the program branches when a date entry is required. It converts the cell named ACHANGE to a new branch command, then branches to ASUB to check for special keystrokes.

@date(95,{AKEY}{?})~/rfd4~{right}{branch AGAIN}   If you have not pressed a special keystroke, the macro returns to this cell (via the branching command at ACHANGE) where it types **@date(95,** and processes the character key you pressed, then does a bracketed question mark pause {?} for the remainder of the entry (the month, a comma, and the day). It then closes the parenthesis, formats the cell for date format, moves right, and branches back to the fourth line of the macro at AGAIN.

{get AKEY}{esc}{if AKEY="{esc}"}{quit}   This line and the next four lines of the macro constitute the subroutine where the macro takes special steps if certain keys are pressed. In this line, pressing Esc causes the macro to quit.

{if AKEY="~"}{ABLANK}{right}{branch AGAIN}   If you press Enter, the macro runs the subroutine at ABLANK where it checks for a blank cell and, if it finds one, inserts a label prefix (apostrophe) in the cell. This is an optional part of the macro that assumes you would like to have an entry of some type in every cell, even if it is only an apostrophe that shows as a blank cell in your worksheet display. This will make maneuvering around your database with End LeftArrow and End RightArrow much easier when all the data entry is done.

{if AKEY="{edit}"}{edit}{?}~{right}{branch AGAIN} If you press Edit, the macro executes an {edit} command, then pauses for your modification of a cell and press of Enter when completed. The macro then moves right one cell and branches back to the beginning at AGAIN.

{if @left(AKEY,1)="{"}{AKEY}{branch AGAIN} If the leftmost character of the stored keystroke representing the key you pressed is an opening bracket, it means you have pressed another function key or a directional key. The key is processed and the macro branches back to the beginning at AGAIN.

{if AKEY="/"}/{branch ASLASH} If you pressed a forward slash, the macro assumes you want to access the command menu to do a /Move, /Copy, /Range Erase, /Worksheet Delete Row, or /Worksheet Insert Row, so it branches to ASLASH to process your command. If, on the other hand, you actually want a slash key typed into a cell, pressing it again types it in the upper panel as you intended.

{branch ALABEL2} This is a variable line of the macro that changes depending on the routine that sent the program flow to ASUB. In this case, the flow is sent back to the portion of the macro that deals with entries of labels.

The rest of the macro should be easy to follow. You will find, as you run this macro, that it provides a surprising amount of freedom while providing you with prompts and automatic data entry that greatly speed the process of creating an address database.

If you have Release 2.2 or higher, however, you will find that the macro's typing of prompts is not as efficient or fast as using an Indicator prompt. For those of you with these later releases, try the more advanced version (not useable in Release 2 or 2.01) as shown in Figure 17.2.

Printing Form Letters from a Database

Once you have your address database set up, you might be interested in having a macro that automatically prints custom form letters to the addressees. An advanced method for doing this is shown in Figure 17.3.

This macro makes heavy use of the string @functions covered in previous chapters. You will find them a little complicated and difficult to enter, but the flexibility they offer in printing custom form letters is indispensable.

	A	B	C	D	E	F	G	H	I
1				Add to Address Database					
2	\A	{}							
3	_ADRS	{goto}ADRS~{let AIM,@cell("col",ADRS)}							
4		{end}{down}{down}{recalc A|CALC}{onerror A_QUIT}							
5	AGAIN	{let A|COL,@cellpointer("col")}{if A|COL<AIM}{right}							
6		{if A|COL=AIM}{indicate +" Enter first name: "&AZURE}{branch ALABEL}							
7		{if A|COL=AIM+1}{indicate +" Enter last name: "&AZURE}{branch ALABEL}							
8		{if A|COL=AIM+2}{indicate +" Enter company: "&AZURE}{branch ALABEL}							
9		{if A|COL=AIM+3}{indicate +" Enter address: "&AZURE}{branch ALABEL}							
10		{if A|COL=AIM+4}{indicate +" Enter City, State: "&AZURE}{branch ALABEL}							
11		{if A|COL=AIM+5}{indicate +" Enter Zip: "&AZURE}{branch ALABEL}							
12		{if A|COL=AIM+6}{indicate +" Enter Code: "&AZURE}{branch AVALUE}							
13		{if A|COL=AIM+7}{indicate +" Enter mo,day (MM,DD) "&AZURE}{branch ADATE}							
14	A|CALC	{if A|COL>AIM+7}{down}{left 8}{branch AGAIN}							
15	ALABEL	{let ACHANGE,"{branch ALABEL2}"}{branch ASUB}							
16	ALABEL2	'{AKEY}{?}~{right}{branch AGAIN}							
17	AVALUE	{let ACHANGE,"{branch AVALUE2}"}{branch ASUB}							
18	AVALUE2	{AKEY}{?}~{right}{branch AGAIN}							
19	ADATE	{let ACHANGE,"{branch ADATE2}"}{branch ASUB}							
20	ADATE2	@date(95,{AKEY}{?})~/rfd4~{right}{branch AGAIN}							
21	ASUB	{get AKEY}{esc}{if AKEY="{esc}"}{indicate}{quit}							
22		{if AKEY="~"}{ABLANK}{right}{branch AGAIN}							
23		{if AKEY="{edit}"}{edit}{?}~{right}{branch AGAIN}							
24		{if @left(AKEY,1)="{"}{AKEY}{branch AGAIN}							
25		{if AKEY="/"}/{branch ASLASH}							
26	ACHANGE	{branch ALABEL2}							
27	AKEY	{ESC}							
28	A|COL	2							
29	ABLANK	{if @cellpointer("type")="b"}'{return}							
30	AIM	2							
31	ASLASH	{get AKEY}{if AKEY="c"#or#AKEY="m"}{AKEY}{?}~{?}~{branch AGAIN}							
32		{if AKEY="r"#or#AKEY="w"}{AKEY}{?}~{branch AGAIN}							
33		{esc}{branch AGAIN}							
34	A_QUIT	{indicate}{quit}							
35	AZURE			<---- @repeat(" ",20)					
36									
37	B14:	+"{if A|COL>AIM+"&@STRING(@ROWS(B64..B54)-4,0)&"}							
38		{down}{left "&@STRING(@ROWS(B64..B54)-3,0)&"}{branch AGAIN}"							
39									
40									
41	ADRS	First	Last	Company	Address	City, St.	ZIP	Code	Date
42		I.B.	Empicee	Big Blue	9 Munchkin La	Dvorak, NJ	72532	3	01/22/95
43		Mac N.	Tosh	Big Red	123 Apple St	Graphic, CA	95014	2	01/22/95
44		Nick	Smashing	Blackbox	567 Main St	Pine,WY	01864	4	01/22/95
45									
46									

FIGURE 17.2 Adding to an address database in Release 2.2 or higher.

You will be able to start your printing from any record in the database and continue it automatically down to any other record you like.

{indicate PRINT}{goto}ADRS~{down}{down}{goto}{?}~ The macro begins by changing the Ready indicator to the word PRINT, moves the cell pointer to the top of the address database, moves down two cells to the first record, then gives you a Goto prompt so you can point to the first record you want to include in a form letter.

	A	B	C	D	E	F	G
1				Build Form Letters			
2	\B	{}					
3	_BFORM	{indicate PRINT}{goto}ADRS~{down}{down}{goto}{?}~					
4		{let BSTART,@left(@cell("address",ADRS),3)}{recalc BGOTO}					
5	BGOTO	{goto}$C$3~					
6	B_LOOP	{recalc BCOL1}{recalc BCOL2}{recalc BCOL3}					
7		{recalc BCOL4}{recalc BCOL5}{recalc BCOL6}					
8		{recalc BROW}{recalc LETTER}					
9		/pparLETTER~gpq{down}					
10		{if @cellpointer("type")<>"b"}{branch B_LOOP}					
11		{indicate}{quit}					
12	BROW	3					
13	BCOL1	G					
14	BCOL2	H					
15	BCOL3	I					
16	BCOL4	J					
17	BCOL5	K					
18	BCOL6	L					
19	BSTART	C					
20							
21							
22	B5:	+"{goto}"&BSTART&@string(@cellpointer("row"),0)&"~"					
23							
24	B12:	@string(@cellpointer("row"),0)					
25							
26	B13:	@mid(@cellpointer("address"),1,@if(@cellpointer("col")<=26,1,2))					
27							
28	B14:	@if(@length(BCOL1)=2,@if(@right(BCOL1,1)="z",					
29		@char(@code(@left(BCOL1,1))+1)&"a",@left(BCOL1,1)&					
30		@char(@code(@right(BCOL1,1))+1)),					
31		(@if(BCOL1="z","aa",@char(@code(BCOL1)+1))))					
32							

FIGURE 17.3 A macro to print form letters from a database.

{let BSTART,@left(@cell("address",ADRS),3)}{recalc BGOTO}

Stores in BSTART the column letter of the first column of your address database, then recalculates the string formula in the next cell named BGOTO.

{goto}$C$1~ This is the displayed result of a string formula as follows:

```
+"{goto}"&
BSTART&
@string(@cellpointer("row"),0)
&"~"
```

Its purpose is to send the cell pointer to the first column of your address database (in case you have strayed right or left in choosing the record to print), while still remaining in the same row.

{recalc BCOL1}{recalc BCOL2}{recalc BCOL3} Recalculates BCOL1, BCOL2, and BCOL3. These cells return the first three column letters for your address database. The column letters will not be used in macro code, but rather in string formulas in the form letter itself, as you will see.

The underlying string formula in BCOL1 reads:

```
@mid(@cellpointer("address"),1,@if(@cellpointer
("col")<=26,1,2))
```

It extracts the column letter from the absolute address of the current cell by taking the character from position 1, or (if the column number is not less than or equal to 26) from position 1 and 2.

The string formula in BCOL2 is more complicated, as follows:

```
@if(@length(BCOL1)=2,@if(@right(BCOL1,1)="z",
@char(@code(@left(BCOL1,1))+1)&
"a",@left(BCOL1,1)&
@char(@code(@right(BCOL1,1))+1)),
(@if(BCOL1="z","aa",@char(@code(BCOL1)+1)))))
```

This formula operates based on the column letter in BCOL1 as previously shown.

If BCOL1 consists of two characters where the second is the letter Z, the formula takes one letter greater than the first letter in BCOL1 and tacks an A onto it. Otherwise, it takes the first letter in BCOL1 and tacks on one letter greater than the second letter in BCOL1.

If BCOL1 consists of one character and that character is the letter Z, the formula returns the letters AA. Otherwise, it returns one letter greater than the letter in BCOL1.

The formulas in BCOL3, BCOL4, BCOL5, and BCOL6 are relative copies of the formula in BCOL2, so once you have entered BCOL2, simply use the /Copy command to duplicate that formula in the other cells.

{recalc BCOL4}{recalc BCOL5}{recalc BCOL6} Recalculates BCOL4, BCOL5, and BCOL6.

{recalc BROW}{recalc LETTER} Recalculates the underlying string formula in BROW which reads:

```
@string(@cellpointer("row"),0)
```

This provides the current row of the cell pointer, information required for string formulas in the form letter.

/pparLETTER~gpq{down} Selects /Print Printer Align Range, uses the range name LETTER as the range to print, then selects Go Page Quit and moves down to the next record.

{if @cellpointer("type")<>"b"}{branch B_LOOP} If the next record is not blank, the macro branches back to B_LOOP to recalculate ranges and print the form letter for the next record.

{indicate}{quit}   Otherwise, the indicator is returned to normal and
the macro quits.

None of this will work, of course, until you have constructed your form
letter, using the string formulas as shown in Figure 17.4.

At the top of this letter, you see the headings as follows:

```
First Last
Company
Address
City, St. ZIP

Dear First Last,
```

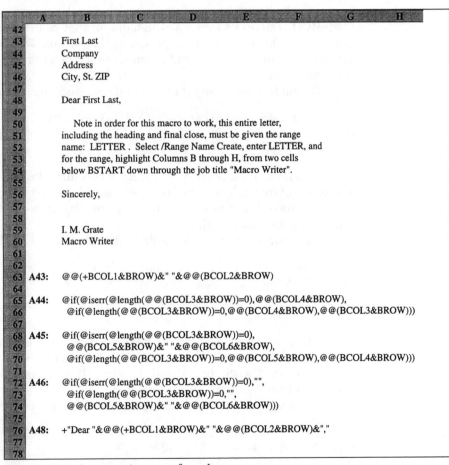

	A	B	C	D	E	F	G	H
42								
43		First Last						
44		Company						
45		Address						
46		City, St. ZIP						
47								
48		Dear First Last,						
49								
50		Note in order for this macro to work, this entire letter,						
51		including the heading and final close, must be given the range						
52		name: LETTER . Select /Range Name Create, enter LETTER, and						
53		for the range, highlight Columns B through H, from two cells						
54		below BSTART down through the job title "Macro Writer".						
55								
56		Sincerely,						
57								
58								
59		I. M. Grate						
60		Macro Writer						
61								
62								

A43:   @@(+BCOL1&BROW)&" "&@@(BCOL2&BROW)

A44:   @if(@iserr(@length(@@(BCOL3&BROW))=0),@@(BCOL4&BROW),
            @if(@length(@@(BCOL3&BROW))=0,@@(BCOL4&BROW),@@(BCOL3&BROW)))

A45:   @if(@iserr(@length(@@(BCOL3&BROW))=0),
            @@(BCOL5&BROW)&" "&@@(BCOL6&BROW),
            @if(@length(@@(BCOL3&BROW))=0,@@(BCOL5&BROW),@@(BCOL4&BROW)))

A46:   @if(@iserr(@length(@@(BCOL3&BROW))=0),"",
            @if(@length(@@(BCOL3&BROW))=0,"",
            @@(BCOL5&BROW)&" "&@@(BCOL6&BROW)))

A48:   +"Dear "&@@(+BCOL1&BROW)&" "&@@(BCOL2&BROW)&","

FIGURE 17.4 Constructing your form letter.

These are actually the displayed results of string formulas, based on placing the cell pointer on the first of the database titles, rather than on the first record you want included in your form letter. (This is done for clarity only; there would be no purpose in printing a form letter with a heading like this.)

As noted in Figure 17.4, in order for this macro to work, the entire letter, including the heading and final close, must be given the range name: LETTER. Select /Range Name Create and enter LETTER; for the range, highlight Columns B through H, from two cells below BSTART down through the job title "Macro Writer."

The underlying string formula in the first line of the heading reads:

```
@@(+BCOL1&BROW)&" "&@@(BCOL2&BROW)
```

It makes use of the @@ function, which returns the contents of the address typed into the referenced cell. Since +BCOL1&BROW is equivalent to a reference to the first column of your database in the current row, the formula **@@(+BCOL1&BROW)** returns the name in that cell (the first name of the addressee). The **&" "** enters a space, and the formula **@@(BCOL2&BROW)** returns the name in the second column of the current row (the last name of the addressee).

The underlying string formula in the second line of the heading reads:

```
@if(@iserr(@length(@@(BCOL3&BROW)))=0),@@(BCOL4&BROW),
@if(@length(@@(BCOL3&BROW))=0,@@(BCOL4&BROW),@@
(BCOL3&BROW)))
```

If there is no Company entry, (if an error is returned when trying to return the length of that cell or if the length of the cell is zero), this formula returns the contents of the Address cell to the right. Otherwise, it returns the contents of the Company cell.

The underlying string formula in the third line of the heading reads:

```
@if(@iserr(@length(@@(BCOL3&BROW)))=0),
@@(BCOL5&BROW)&" "&@@(BCOL6&BROW),
@if(@length(@@(BCOL3&BROW))=0,@@(BCOL5&BROW),
@@(BCOL4&BROW)))
```

In this line, if there is no Company entry, (if an error is returned when trying to return the length of that cell or if the length of the cell is zero), the contents of the City/State cell and the ZIP cell are returned. Otherwise, the contents of the Address cell are returned.

The underlying string formula in the fourth line of the heading reads:

```
@if(@iserr(@length(@@(BCOL3&BROW)))=0),"",
@if(@length(@@(BCOL3&BROW))=0,"",
@@(BCOL5&BROW)&" "&@@(BCOL6&BROW)))
```

In this last line of the heading, if there is no Company entry, a null string (blank cell) is returned. Otherwise, the macro returns the contents of the City, State cell and the ZIP cell.

In case these formulas seem overly complicated, you should be aware that they take into account that not all addressees will have Company entries; and to simply leave a blank would look unprofessional. Therefore, the string formulas use @if statements to check for that condition and display the Address, City/State, and ZIP information one cell higher than they would normally appear.

The salutation is based on the underlying string formula:

`+"Dear"&@@(+BCOL1&BROW)&" "&@@(BCOL2&BROW)&","`

This formula combines the word "Dear" with the first name from the first column, a space, the last name from the second column, and a comma.

The macro works by calculating the position of the cell pointer (column and row). Then it calculates the string formulas in the heading and salutation of the letter—which will be based on the information in the current cell pointer row—prints the recalculated form letter, moves down to the next record, and repeats the whole process.

If you do not want to print form letters for all the records in your address database from your current location to the last record, do this before starting your macro: Move to the row below the last record you want to see included in a form letter, select /Worksheet Insert Row to create a blank row that will stop the macro, then move back to the first record to print and press Alt-B. The macro will print form letters for every record from the current row to the newly inserted blank row. When the printing is completed, simply delete the blank row to restore your database to its original condition.

Printing Labels from a Database

The macro in Figure 17.5 uses similar techniques to print labels, up to five across, from the same address database.

Here's how the macro works:

{getnumber "Enter Number of Labels Across to Print: ",LCOUNT}
Prompts for the number of labels across you want to print. This has to do with the type of labels you are using in your printer, which can be as much as five across. Your response is saved in LCOUNT.

{windowsoff}{paneloff}/ppoouqq Turns off the windows and panel and selects /Print Printer Option Other Unformatted Quit Quit. This ensures there will be no page breaks in your printed labels.

	A	B	C	D	E	F	G
1			**Labels Printed from Address Database**				
2	\L	{}					
3	_LABEL	{getnumber "Enter Number of Labels Across to Print: ",LCOUNT}					
4		{windowsoff}{paneloff}/ppoouqq					
5		{goto}LABEL~/rndLABEL~/rncLABEL~.{down 3}{left}{right LCOUNT}~					
6		{goto}ADRS~{down}{down}{panelon}{windowson}{goto}{?}~					
7		{let LSTART,@left(@cell("address",ADRS),3)}{recalc LGOTO}					
8	LGOTO	{goto}$C$55~					
9	LOOP	{recalc LCOL1}{recalc LCOL2}{recalc LCOL3}					
10		{recalc LCOL4}{recalc LCOL5}{recalc LCOL6}					
11		{recalc LROW1}{recalc LROW2}{recalc LROW3}					
12		{recalc LROW4}{recalc LROW5}{recalc LABEL}					
13		/pparLABEL~gllq{down LCOUNT}					
14		{if @cellpointer("type")<>"b"}{branch LOOP}					
15		{goto}ADRS~/ppoofqq{quit}					
16	LCOUNT	3					
17	LCOL1	A					
18	LCOL2	B					
19	LCOL3	C					
20	LCOL4	D					
21	LCOL5	E					
22	LCOL6	F					
23	LROW1	55					
24	LROW2	56	NOTE: The width of the cells				
25	LROW3	57	containing the labels must be				
26	LROW4	58	as wide as the widest address.				
27	LROW5	59					
28	LSTART	C					
29							
30	LABEL	ERR	ERR	ERR	ERR	ERR	
31		0	0	0	0	0	
32		ERR	ERR	ERR	ERR	ERR	
33							
34	B8:	+"{goto}"&b28&@string(@cellpointer("row"),0)&"~"					
35	B17:	@mid(@cellpointer("address"),1,@if(@cellpointer("col")<=26,1,2))					
36	B18:	@if(@length(b17)=2,@left(b17,1),"")&@char(@code(@right(b17,1))+1)					
37	B19:	@if(@length(b18)=2,@left(b18,1),"")&@char(@code(@right(b18,1))+1)					
38	B20:	@if(@length(b19)=2,@left(b19,1),"")&@char(@code(@right(b19,1))+1)					
39	B21:	@if(@length(b20)=2,@left(b20,1),"")&@char(@code(@right(b20,1))+1)					
40	B22:	@if(@length(b21)=2,@left(b21,1),"")&@char(@code(@right(b21,1))+1)					
41	B23:	@string(@cellpointer("row"),0)					
42	B24:	@string(@cellpointer("row")+1,0)					
43	B25:	@string(@cellpointer("row")+2,0)					
44	B26:	@string(@cellpointer("row")+3,0)					
45	B27:	@string(@cellpointer("row")+4,0)					
46	B30:	@@(+b17&b23)&" "&@@(b18&b23)					
47	B31:	@if(@iserr(@length(@@(b19&b23))=0),@@(b20&b23),					
48		@if(@length(@@(b19&b23))=0,@@(b20&b23),@@(b19&b23)))					
49	B32:	@if(@iserr(@length(@@(b19&b23))=0),@@(b21&b23)&" "&@@(b22&b23),					
50		@if(@length(@@(b19&b23))=0,@@(b21&b23),@@(b20&b23)))					
51	B33:	@if(@iserr(@length(@@(b19&b23))=0),"",					
52		@if(@length(@@(b19&b23))=0,"",@@(b21&b23)&" "&@@(b22&b23)))					

FIGURE 17.5 Printing labels from an address database.

{goto}LABEL~/rndLABEL~/rncLABEL~.{down 3}{left}{right LCOUNT}~ Moves your cell pointer to the cell in the macro named LABEL, deletes the range name LABEL, then recreates it, but this time with a height of four rows and a width that matches the number of labels you indicated you wanted to see printed.

{goto}ADRS~{down}{down}{panelon}{windowson}{goto}{?}~ Moves the cell pointer to the first title in your address database, then down two cells, turns on the windows and panel, then gives you a Goto prompt to allow you to move to the first record you want printed in a label.

The next six lines of the macro are very similar to the equivalent lines in the Form Letter macro, except that rows relative to the current cell pointer are calculated in addition to columns, using the formulas:

```
@string(@cellpointer("row"),0)
@string(@cellpointer("row")+1,0)
@string(@cellpointer("row")+2,0)
@string(@cellpointer("row")+3,0)
@string(@cellpointer("row")+4,0)
```

(Note, lines 37 through 41 in Figure 17.5 are incomplete as shown, but reference to the Form Letter macro will give you the information you need to enter these formulas correctly.)

/pparLABEL~gllq{down LCOUNT} Selects /Print Printer Align Range, enters the range name LABEL as the range to print, then selects Go Line Line Quit, and moves down a number of cells equal to the number of labels across you decided to print.

{if @cellpointer("type")<>"b"}{branch LOOP} If the next record is not blank, the macro branches back to LOOP to recalculate ranges and print the labels for the next records.

{goto}ADRS~/ppoofqq{quit} Otherwise, the cell pointer is moved to the beginning of the address database, the macro selects /Print Printer Options Other Formatted Quit Quit, and the macro quits.

As for the labels themselves, they consist of string formulas that are based on exactly the same principles as the form letter heading. The one difference is that there are up to five labels, so the second label calculates and returns its information based on the current row plus 1 (the number in LROW2); the third label uses LROW3, the fourth uses LROW4, and the fifth uses LROW5.

Of course, the ERR and zero entries you see in Figure 17.5 will automatically display as regular label addresses once you place your cell pointer on one of the records in your address database and press the F9 Calc key.

The result of all this will be a very fast printout of your address labels, starting with the addressee at the first record you point to after starting the macro. If you want to stop short of the last record in the database, insert a blank row temporarily at your desired stopping point before starting the macro.

Creating a Checkbook Ledger Macro

The same principles as used in the Address Database macro can be applied to any data entry system, including order entry, accounts payable, accounts receivable, inventory, customer lists, personnel lists, and so on. In this section we will look at a long macro designed to facilitate your entry of checks into a checkbook ledger. Refer to Figure 17.6.

This macro requires a database structure with titles such as shown in Figure 17.7. In the cell below the title CHK #, press the spacebar a couple of times and press Enter, then assign that cell the range name CHK #. Initially, you may want to use exactly this layout until you verify that the macro is working correctly. Afterwards, you will want to change the categories in columns F through I and to add category columns of your own past column I.

Here's how the macro works:

{goto}CHK #~{let CHK,@cell("col",CHK #)} Moves the cell pointer to the line below the first title of the checkbook ledger (range named CHK #), then stores the column number of that cell in CHK.

{up}{end}{down}{down}{recalc C_CALC} Moves to the first blank cell after the last check entered and recalculates the string formula in C_CALC.

{let C|COL,@cellpointer("col")} Stores the current column letter in C|COL.

{if C|COL=CHK}Enter check number: (F8 for next #) {branch CNUMBER} If the current column is the first column in the checkbook ledger (which it will be, of course, during the first pass through this the macro), the prompt "Enter check number (F8 for next #)" is typed into the upper panel. You can either type a check number at this point or press the F8 key and the next check number in sequence will be entered. The macro then branches to CNUMBER.

{if C|COL=CHK+1}Enter mo,day: (F8 for Today's Date) {branch CDATE} At the second column you will be prompted to enter the date or press F8 to have today's date entered for you. The macro branches to CDATE.

	A	B	C	D	E	F	G
1				Checkbook Ledger Macro			
2	\C	{}					
3	_CHKBK	{goto}CHK #~{let CHK,@cell("col",CHK #)}					
4		{up}{end}{down}{down}{recalc C_CALC}					
5	CAGAIN	{let C|COL,@cellpointer("col")}					
6		{if C|COL=CHK}Enter check number: (F8 for next #) {branch CNUMBER}					
7		{if C|COL=CHK+1}Enter mo,day: (F8 for Today's Date) {branch CDATE}					
8		{if C|COL=CHK+2}Enter Payee: (F8 for Same-as-Above) {branch CLABEL}					
9		{if C|COL=CHK+3}Enter Amount: (F8 for Same-as-Above) {branch CVALUE}					
10		{if C|COL=CHK+4}Enter Code: (F8 for Same-as-Above) {branch CODE}					
11	C_CALC	{if C|COL>CHK+4}{down}{left 5}{branch CAGAIN}					
12	CNUMBER	{let CHANGE,"{branch CNUMBER2}"}{branch CSUB}					
13	CNUMBER2	{if CKEY="{table}"}+{up}+1{calc}~{right}{branch CAGAIN}					
14		{CKEY}{?}~{right}{branch CAGAIN}					
15	CLABEL	{let CHANGE,"{branch CLABEL2}"}{branch CSUB}					
16	CLABEL2	{if CKEY="{table}"}/c{esc}{up}~~{right}{branch CAGAIN}					
17		'{CKEY}{?}~{right}{branch CAGAIN}					
18	CVALUE	{let CHANGE,"{branch CVALUE2}"}{branch CSUB}					
19	CVALUE2	{if CKEY="{table}"}/c{esc}{up}~~{right}{branch CAGAIN}					
20		{CKEY}{?}~/rff~~{right}{branch CAGAIN}					
21	CODE	{let CHANGE,"{branch CODE2}"}{branch CSUB}					
22	CODE2	{let C|ROW,@string(@cellpointer("row"),0)}					
23		{if CKEY="{table}"}/c{esc}{up}~~{recalc CODE3}{recalc CODE4}{branch CODE3}					
24		{CKEY}{?}~{recalc CODE3}{recalc CODE4}					
25	CODE3	/cD178~E178~					
26	CODE4	{if @sum(F178..AA178)<>+D178}/reF178..AA178~~{branch CODE3}					
27		{right}{branch CAGAIN}					
28	CDATE	{let CHANGE,"{branch CDATE2}"}{branch CSUB}					
29	CDATE2	{if CKEY="{table}"}@now~/rfd4~{right}{branch CAGAIN}					
30		@date(90,{CKEY}{?})~/rfd4~{right}{branch CAGAIN}					
31	CSUB	{get CKEY}{esc}{if CKEY="{esc}"}{indicate}{quit}					
32		{if CKEY="~"}{CBLANK}{right}{branch CAGAIN}					
33		{if CKEY="{edit}"}{edit}{?}~{right}{branch CAGAIN}					
34		{if CKEY="{table}"}{branch CHANGE}					
35		{if @left(CKEY,1)="{"}{CKEY}{branch CAGAIN}					
36		{if CKEY="/"}/{branch CSLASH}					
37	CHANGE	{branch CNUMBER2}					
38	CKEY	{ESC}					
39	C|COL			5			
40	C|ROW	178					
41	CBLANK	{if @cellpointer("type")="b"}'{return}					
42	CHK		1				
43	CSLASH	{get CKEY}{if CKEY="c"#or#CKEY="m"}{CKEY}{?}~{?}~{branch CAGAIN}					
44		{if CKEY="r"#or#CKEY="w"}{CKEY}{?}~{branch CAGAIN}					
45		{esc}{branch CAGAIN}					
46							
47	B11:	+"{if C|COL>chk+"&@string(@rows(a5..a12)-4,0)&"}{down}{left "&					
48		@string(@rows(a5..a12)-3,0)&"}{branch CAGAIN}"					
49	B25:	+"/c"&@char(+63+C|COL)&C|ROW&"~"&					
50		@char(+64+C|COL+@cellpointer("contents"))&C|ROW&"~"					
51	B26:	+"{if @sum("&@char(+65+C|COL)&C|ROW&"..aa"&C|ROW&")<>+"&					
52		@char(+63+C|COL)&C|ROW&"}/re"&@char(65+C|COL)&					
53		C|ROW&"..aa"&C|ROW&"~~{branch CODE3}"					

FIGURE 17.6 A macro to facilitate entry in a checkbook ledger.

A:A1: NOTE: The cell below CHK # must contain invisible spaces and must be

	A	B	C	D	E	F	G	H	I
1	NOTE:	The cell below CHK # must contain invisible spaces and must be range named "CHK #".							
2									
3						1	2	3	4
4	CHK #	DATE	PAYEE	AMT	CODE	Rent	Phone	Util	Misc
5									
6	123	12/07/89	Landlord	800.00	1	800.00			
7	124	12/09/89	A T & T	87.50	3			87.50	
8	125	12/11/89	Oak View	123.23	2		123.23		
9	126	12/13/89	Jeans Inc	47.50	4				47.50
10	127	12/15/89	Safeway	90.00	4				90.00
11	128	01/01/90	Landlord	800.00	1	800.00			
12	129	01/03/90	Michael	130.50	2		130.50		
13	130	01/05/90	Macropac	67.3	3			67.3	
14									
15									
16									
17									
18									
19									
20									

General   Styles

FIGURE 17.7 A sample database for the Checkbook Ledger macro.

{if C|COL=CHK+2}Enter Payee: (F8 for Same-as-Above) {branch CLABEL}   At the third column, you will be prompted to enter the payee or press F8 to enter the same payee as shown in the line above. The macro branches to CLABEL.

{if C|COL=CHK+3}Enter Amount: (F8 for Same-as-Above){branch CVALUE}   At the fourth column, you will be prompted to enter the check amount or press F8 for same-as-above. The macro branches to CVALUE.

{if C|COL=CHK+4}Enter Code: (F8 for Same-as-Above) {branch CODE}   At the fifth column, you will be prompted to enter a code representing the type of check written. For example, you may want to use the code 1 for Rent, 2 for Phone, and so on. Press F8 for same-as-above. The macro branches to CODE.

{if C|COL>CHK+4}{down}{left 5}{branch CAGAIN}   This is the cell named C_CALC. If the current column number is four greater than CHK, the cell pointer must be beyond the end of a check entry row, so you are moved down and to the left to the beginning of the next row, and the macro branches to CAGAIN to start over again.

The string formula that underlies this displayed result is as follows:

```
+"{if C|COL>CHK+"&
@string(@rows(a5..a12)-4,0)&
"}{down}{left "
&@string(@rows(a5..a12)-3,0)&
"}{branch CAGAIN}"
```

The principle here is the same as in the equivalent string formula in the Address Database macro.

{let CHANGE,"{branch CNUMBER2}"}{branch CSUB}   This is the first line of the routine named CNUMBER where the macro branches if you are in the check number column. It begins by changing the cell named CHANGE to a new branch command, then branches to CSUB where a {get} command pauses for your press of any key. As with the ASUB subroutine in the Address Database macro, CSUB is the subroutine where the macro checks your keystroke for Esc, Enter, a press of the F2 Edit key, another function key or directional key, or a forward slash (/) key.

{if CKEY="{table}"}+{up}+1{calc}~{right}{branch CAGAIN}   If you pressed F8, the macro in this instance calculates the last invoice number plus one, enters it, moves to the right one cell, and branches back to the beginning at CAGAIN.

{CKEY}{?}~{right}{branch CAGAIN}   Otherwise, the macro types the character you pressed, pauses for the rest of your entry, moves to the right, and branches back to the beginning at CAGAIN.

{let CHANGE,"{branch CLABEL2}"}{branch CSUB}   This is the line of the macro named CLABEL, where the program branches when the payee is to be entered. It converts the cell named CHANGE to a new branch command, then branches to CSUB to check for special keystrokes.

{if CKEY="{table}"}/c{esc}{up}~~{right}{branch CAGAIN}   If you pressed F8 at the payee prompt, the macro copies the payee entry from the cell above, moves to the right one cell, and branches back to the beginning at CAGAIN.

'{CKEY}{?}~{right}{branch CAGAIN}   Otherwise, the macro types a label prefix and the character you pressed, pauses for the rest of your entry, moves to the right, and branches back to the beginning at CAGAIN.

{let CHANGE,"{branch CVALUE2}"}{branch CSUB}   This is the line of the macro named CVALUE, where the program branches when the check amount is to be entered. It converts the cell named CHANGE to a new branch command, then branches to CSUB to check for special keystrokes.

{if CKEY="{table}"}/c{esc}{up}~~{right}{branch CAGAIN} As before, if you pressed F8, the macro copies the entry from the cell above, moves to the right one cell, and branches back to the beginning at CAGAIN.

{CKEY}{?}~/rff~~{right}{branch CAGAIN} Otherwise, the macro types the character you pressed, pauses for the rest of your entry, formats the cell for Fixed with two decimals, moves to the right, and branches back to the beginning at CAGAIN.

{let CHANGE,"{branch CODE2}"}{branch CSUB} This is the line of the macro named CODE, where the program branches when the check code is to be entered. It converts the cell named CHANGE to a new branch command, then branches to CSUB to check for special keystrokes.

{let C|ROW,@string(@cellpointer("row"),0)} The current row is stored in C|ROW as a label.

{if CKEY="{table}"}/c{esc}{up}~~{recalc CODE3}{recalc CODE4} {branch CODE3} If you pressed F8, the macro copies the entry from the cell above, recalculates CODE3 and CODE4, and branches to CODE3.

{CKEY}{?}~{recalc CODE3}{recalc CODE4} Otherwise, the macro processes your keystrokes, pauses for the rest of the entry, and recalculates CODE3 and CODE4.

/cD178~F178~ This is the cell named CODE3, the displayed result of the string formula as follows:

```
+"/c"&
@char(+63+C|COL)&
C|ROW&
"~"&
@char(+64+C|COL+@cellpointer("contents"))&
C|ROW&
"~"
```

Its purpose is to copy the amount from the amount column to the column represented by the code in the current cell.

{if @sum(F178..AA178)<>+D178}/reF178..AA178~~{branch CODE3} This is the displayed result in the cell named CODE4 of a string formula as follows:

```
+"{if @sum("&
@char(+65+C|COL)&C|ROW&
"..aa"&
B|ROW&")<>+"&
@char(+63+C|COL)&
C|ROW&"}/re"&
```

```
@char(65+C|COL)&
C|ROW&"..aa"&
b40&
"~~{branch code3}"
```

If you have previously entered an amount and a different code on the current row (which would cause an extraneous amount to appear in the one of the category columns following the Code column), this line of the macro erases the range from the first category column through column AA.

{right}{branch CAGAIN}   Moves the cell pointer to the right one cell and branches back to the beginning at CAGAIN.

{let CHANGE,"{branch CDATE2}"}{branch CSUB}   This is the line of the macro named CDATE, where the program branches when a date entry is required. It converts the cell named CHANGE to a new branch command, then branches to CSUB to check for special keystrokes.

{if CKEY="{table}"}@now~/rfd4~{right}{branch CAGAIN}   If you pressed F8, the current date is entered automatically, the cell if formatted for date format, the cell pointer moves right, and the macro branches back to the beginning at CAGAIN.

@date(94,{AKEY}{?})~/rfd4~{right}{branch CAGAIN}   If you have not pressed a special keystroke, the macro returns to this line of code (via the branching command at CHANGE) and types **@date(94,** and processes the character key you pressed, then does a bracketed question mark pause {?} for the remainder of the entry (the month, a comma, and the day). It then closes the parenthesis, formats the cell for date format, moves right, and branches back to the fourth line of the macro at CAGAIN.

{get CKEY}{esc}{if CKEY="{esc}"}{quit}   This line and the next five lines of the macro constitute the subroutine where the macro takes special steps if certain keys are pressed. For a better understanding of this and the subroutine at CBLANK, refer to the equivalent lines in the Address Database macro at the beginning of this chapter.

Typing Your Checkbook Amounts

Once you have created a Checkbook Ledger spreadsheet, you will still need a way to print out your checks. This may sound fairly straightforward, but the amounts on a check appear in two forms and 1-2-3 has no easy way of converting an amount written in numbers to an amount written out in words. For a macro to handle this task for you, refer to Figure 17.8.

	A	B	C	D	E	F	G
1			**Check Writing Amount in Words**				
2	\C	{}					
3	_CHKBK	{getnumber "Enter dollar amount (no commas please): $",CDOLLARS}					
4		{recalc CBLOCK}{recalc CBLOCK}{recalc CCALC1}					
5	CCALC1	ONE THOUSAND TWO HUNDRED THIRTY-FOUR AND 22/100 DOLLARS					
6		~{quit}					
7	CDOLLARS	1234.22					
8							
9		ONE					
10		THOUSAND			➡	This range, from CDOLLARS	
11		TWO				through C_ONES, must be	
12		HUNDRED				range-named CBLOCK.	
13		THIRTY					
14		FOUR					
15		AND 22/100 DOLLARS					
16	C_THOUS	ONE					
17	C_ONES	FOUR					
18							
19							
20	B8:	@IF(B9<>""#AND#B10<>"",B9&"-",B9&" ")&@IF(B10<>"",B10&					
21		" ","")&B11&@IF(B12<>"," "&B12&" ","")&@IF(B13<>"",B13&					
22		" ","")&@IF(B14<>""#AND#B15="",B14&" ","")&					
23		@IF(B14<>""#AND#B15<>"",B14&"-","")&@IF(B15<>"",B15&" ","")&B16					
24							
25	B9:	@IF(B7>9999#AND#B7<20000,@CHOOSE(@VALUE(@LEFT(@STRING(B7,2),2))					
26		-10,"TEN","ELEVEN","TWELVE","THIRTEEN","FOURTEEN","FIFTEEN",					
27		"SIXTEEN","SEVENTEEN","EIGHTEEN","NINETEEN","TWENTY"),+B16)					
28							
29	B10:	@IF(B7>999.99,"THOUSAND"," ")					
30							
31	B11:	@CHOOSE(@INT(@MOD(B7,1000)/100),"","ONE","TWO","THREE","FOUR",					
32		"FIVE","SIX","SEVEN","EIGHT","NINE","TEN")					
33							
34	B12:	@IF(B7>99#AND#@INT(@MOD(B7,1000)/100)<>0,"HUNDRED"," ")					
35							
36	B13:	@IF(B7>19,@CHOOSE(@INT(@MOD(B7,100)/10),"","","TWENTY","THIRTY",					
37		"FORTY","FIFTY","SIXTY","SEVENTY","EIGHTY","NINETY"),"")					
38							
39	B14:	@IF(@INT(@MOD(B7,100))<21#AND#@INT(@MOD(B7,100))>10,					
40		@CHOOSE(@INT(@MOD(B7,10)),"","ELEVEN","TWELVE","THIRTEEN",					
41		"FOURTEEN","FIFTEEN","SIXTEEN","SEVENTEEN","EIGHTEEN",					
42		"NINETEEN","TWENTY","TEN"),+B17)					
43							
44	B15:	+"AND "&@RIGHT(@STRING(@MOD(B7,1),2),2)&"/100 DOLLARS"					
45							
46	B16:	@IF(B7>999,@CHOOSE(@INT(@MOD(B7,10000)/1000),"","ONE","TWO",					
47		"THREE","FOUR","FIVE","SIX","SEVEN","EIGHT","NINE"),"")					
48							
49	B17:	@IF(@INT(@MOD(B7,10))<>0,@CHOOSE(@INT(@MOD(B7,10))-1,"ONE",					
50		"TWO","THREE","FOUR","FIVE","SIX","SEVEN","EIGHT","NINE"),					
51		@IF(@INT(@MOD(B7,100)/10)=1,"TEN",""))					
52							

FIGURE 17.8 A macro to write a check amount in words.

Here's how the macro works:

{getnumber "Enter dollar amount (no commas please):$",CDOL-LARS} Prompts for the dollar amount and places your response in CDOLLARS. This portion of the macro can be modified, of course, to take the amount from a database.

{recalc CBLOCK}{recalc CBLOCK}{recalc CCALC1} Recalculates the entire block of string formulas in the area named CBLOCK, then recalculates CCALC1.

ONE THOUSAND TWO HUNDRED THIRTY-FOUR AND 22/100 DOLLARS This is the displayed result of the string formula in CCALC1, as it would appear when you enter 1234.22 in response to the opening prompt. The macro types the letters of this cell into the upper panel, enters the label, and quits.

The more important (and more difficult) part of this macro is contained in the string formulas in CCALC1 and CBLOCK as shown in Figure 17.8. After typing these formulas into your own macro, be sure to range name the acres from CDOLLARS through C_ONES with the range name CBLOCK.

Summary

In this chapter we covered some of the longer applications you can create using macros. Some of the concepts explored here were as follows:

- You can use string formulas to design a macro line that allows you to delete or add rows of the macro without having to revisit the string formula line of the macro.
- You can use the @@ function in macros and variable print areas to return the contents of the address typed into the referenced cell.
- You can combine the current row with a recorded column letter to create a macro that prints different records based on the location of the cell pointer.

The macros covered in this chapter were as follows:

- An Add to Address Database macro that determines in advance what type of entry is required for a particular column. It differentiates—based on the way you set up the worksheet—between columns dedicated to labels, columns used for values, and columns that contain only dates shown in the date format.
- This macro also allows you to move with your directional keys, changing the displayed prompt as you move. Further, you have full access to the /Copy, /Move, /Range Erase, /Worksheet Delete Row, and /Worksheet Insert Row commands just as if the macro were not active.

- A macro to print form letters from a database, allowing you to start your printing from any record in the database and continue automatically to any other record you like.
- A macro used for printing labels from an address database up to five across.
- A macro designed to facilitate your entry of checks into a checkbook ledger.
- A macro designed to convert an amount written in numbers to an amount written out in words.

Macro Commands Specific to 1-2-3 for Windows

Microsoft Windows offers special features not found in the DOS environment, such as a Clipboard for cut, copy and paste operations, resizable worksheet windows, dynamic data exchange (DDE), and the ability to open more than one application at a time. To take advantage of these extra features, and to provide a few extra features of its own, Lotus provides several macro commands in 1-2-3 for Windows not found in its DOS versions, as well as a few commands that you can find only in the more advanced DOS releases such as the 3.0 and higher. This appendix lists and describes the macro commands found in 1-2-3 for Windows Release 4.0 and higher.

Edit Commands

The Edit macro commands correspond to the Edit menu commands. They include the cut-and-paste commands that clear data, cut and copy to the Clipboard, paste from the Clipboard, or create a link between the worksheet file and the file referenced on the Clipboard. Arguments with the square brackets are optional.

{DELETE-COLUMNS [*range*],[*delete-selection*]} deletes all of each column that includes cells in *range*; or deletes only the part of the columns covered by *range*.

{DELETE-ROWS [*range*],[*delete-selection*]} deletes all of each row that includes cells in *range*; or deletes only the part of the rows covered by *range*.

{DELETE-SHEETS [*range*]} deletes all of each worksheet that includes cells in *range*.

{EDIT-CLEAR *[selection],["property"]*} clears all data and formatting without moving it to the Clipboard like the Edit Clear Special command. In case a range is preselected, the optional *selection* argument can specify another range to clear. The optional *property* argument specifies whether to clear contents, formats, styles, or graphs.

{EDIT-COPY *[selection],["format"]*} copies data and formatting from the worksheet to the Clipboard. In case a range is preselected, the optional *selection* argument can specify another range to copy. The optional *format* argument specifies a Clipboard Metfilepict or Bitmap format instead of the default Clipboard Text format.

{EDIT-COPY-FILL *direction,[range]*} copies the contents of one row, column, or worksheet in *range* to all of *range*, based on a specified *direction*.

{EDIT-COPY-GRAPH} copies the contents of the active Graph window to the Clipboard. If the active window is not a Graph window, this command returns an error.

{EDIT-CUT *[selection],["format"]*} cuts data and formatting from the worksheet to the Clipboard. In case a range is preselected, the optional *selection* argument can specify another range to copy. The optional *format* argument specifies a Clipboard Metfilepict or Bitmap format instead of the default Clipboard Text format.

{EDIT-FIND *[search-for],[look-in],[search-through]*]} finds the first instance of specified characters in lables, formula, or both.

{EDIT-FIND?} displays the Edit Find and Replace dialog box. After the user leaves the dialog box, 1-2-3 continues the macro.

{EDIT-PASTE *[selection],["format"]*} copies data and formatting from the Clipboard to the current worksheet file. In case a range is preselected, the optional *selection* argument can specify another range to copy. The optional *format* argument specifies a Clipboard Metfilepict or Bitmap format instead of the default Clipboard Text format.

{EDIT-PASTE-LINK *[range]*} creates a link between the specific *range* of a worksheet file and the file referenced on the Clipboard.

{EDIT-PASTE-SPECIAL [*destination*],[*property*]} inserts data on the Clipboard into the worksheet.

{EDIT-QUICK-COPY *destination*,[*source*]} copies data and related formatting from the *source* range to the *destination* range, without using the Clipboard.

{EDIT-QUICK-MOVE *destination*,[*source*]} moves data and related formatting from the *source* range to the *destination* range, without using the Clipboard.

{EDIT-REPLACE [*search-for*],[*look-in*],[*replacement*],[*search-through*]} finds the first instance of specified characters in labels, formulas, or both, and replaces them.

{EDIT-REPLACE-ALL [*search-for*],[*look-in*],[*replacement*],[*search-through*]} finds all instances of specified characters in labels, formulas, or both, and replaces them.

{FILE-UPDATE-LINKS} recalculates formulas in the current file that contain links to other files.

{INSERT-COLUMNS [*range*],[*number*],[*insert-selection*]} inserts one or more blank columns in the current file, or inserts only the part of the columns covered by *range*.

{INSERT-ROWS [*range*],[*number*],[*insert-selection*]} inserts one or more blank rows in the current file, or inserts only the part of the rows covered by *range*.

{INSERT-SHEETS [*where*],[*number*][*range*]} inserts one or more blank worksheets in the current file.

Window and Screen Control Commands

The Window and Screen Control commands are designed to control different parts of the screen display and activate, move, resize, or arrange windows on the screen.

{APP-ADJUST *x,y,width,height*} positions and resizes the 1-2-3 window on the screen by moving it to x pixels from the left and y pixels from the top of the screen, and changing the *height* and *width* to a designated number of pixels.

{APP-STATE *"state"*} minimizes, maximizes, or restores the 1-2-3 window as if you had pressed the corresponding button. The *state* argument is the word Minimize, Maximize, or Restore.

{BREAK} clears the edit line when data is being entered or edited, or leaves the current dialog box during selection of a 1-2-3 command, and returns 1-2-3 to READY mode. In any other situation, {BREAK} has no effect.

{BORDERSOFF} Same as {FRAMEOFF}

{BORDERSON} Same as {FRAMEON}

{CLEARENTRY} or {CE} clears the current data from the edit line or a text box. For example, {ALT}fo{CE}PHONE.WK3 calls up the File Open dialog box and clears the default path before entering the file name PHONE.WK3.

{FRAMEOFF} suppresses display of the worksheet's column-and-row frame until the macro reaches a {FRAMEON} command or the macro ends.

{FRAMEON} turns display of the worksheet's column-and-row frame back on after a {FRAMEOFF} command.

{GRAPH} duplicates the 1-2-3 Release 3 /Graph View command, creating a graph from a preselected range and bringing it into full-screen view, or bringing an existing graph created in the /Graph menu into full-screen view.

{GRAPHOFF} removes from the screen a graph displayed with the {GRAPHON} command.

{GRAPHON [named graph],[nodisplay]} displays a full-screen view of the current graph (or optionally, a *named graph*) while the macro continues to run. Including both optional arguments makes the *named graph* current without displaying it.

{INDICATE [*text*]} changes the mode indicator to the text you specify or restores the standard mode indicator if you do not specify text. The effects survive past the end of the macro.

{VIEW-ZOOM *how*} decreases or increases the display size of cells, or restores their default display size.

{WINDOW-ACTIVATE [*window-name*],[*reserved*],[*pane*]} makes a window the active window.

{WINDOW-ADJUST *x,y,width,height*} positions and resizes the active window on the screen by moving it to x pixels from the left and y pixels from the top of the 1-2-3 window and changing the *height* and *width* to a designated number of pixels.

{WINDOW-ARRANGE *how*} sizes open windows (Worksheet and Transcript) and either places them side by side or arranges them one on top of the other, with just the title bars showing.

{WINDOW-SELECT *window name*} selects the window in the *window name* argument as the active window.

{WINDOW-STATE *state*} minimizes, maximizes, or restores the active window as if you had pressed the corresponding button. The *state* argument is the word Minimize, Maximize, or Restore.

{WINDOWSOFF} freezes the worksheet window

{WINDOWSON} unfreezes the worksheet window, undoing {WINDOWSOFF}

Program Flow Commands

The Program Flow Commands are designed to direct the flow of the macro using subroutines, branches, calls, "for" loops, and conditional processing.

{-- *comment*} puts a comment into a macro. This macro keyword is two hyphens (--) with no spaces between them.

{BRANCH *location*} transfers macro control from the current macro instruction to *location* and does not return to the calling macro.

{DEFINE *location1,location2,...,location n*} specifies where to store arguments passed to a subroutine in a {*subroutine*} command. You must include a {DEFINE} command in any subroutine to which you pass arguments, and the {DEFINE} command must come before the point in the subroutine where the arguments are used.

{DISPATCH *location*} performs an indirect branch by transferring macro control to the cell whose name or address is entered in *location*.

{FOR *counter,start,loop,step,subroutine*} creates a For loop that repeatedly performs a subroutine call to *subroutine*.

{FORBREAK} cancels a For loop created by a {FOR} command.

{IF *condition*} evaluates *condition* as true or false. If *condition* is true, 1-2-3 continues with the next instruction immediately following the {IF} command in the same cell. If *condition* is false, 1-2-3 goes immediately to the next cell in the column, skipping any further instructions in the same cell as the {IF} command.

{LAUNCH *"command",[window]*} starts a Windows application using the *command* string, usually with a directory path. The *window* argument is an optional argument that controls the initial state of the application.

{LOTUS-LAUNCH *command,[window],[switch-to]*} starts and optionally switches to a Windows application.

{ONERROR *branch-location,[message-location]*} traps and handles errors that occur while a macro is running.

{QUIT} ends a macro, returning control to the user.

{RESTART} clears the subroutine stack, ending the macro when the current subroutine ends.

{SYSTEM *command*} temporarily suspends the 1-2-3 session, switches to the operating system (DOS), and executes the specified operating system command.

Data Manipulation Commands

The Data Manipulation commands are designed to enter, edit, erase, and recalculate data, typically (but not exclusively) involving a database.

{APPENDBELOW *target location,source location*} is used with the {FORM} command to transfer records from an entry form to a database table by copying the contents in the *source location* to the rows immediately below the *target location*.

{APPENDRIGHT} is used with the {FORM} command to transfer records from an entry form to a database table by copying the contents in the *source location* to the rows immediately to the right of the *target location*.

{BLANK *location*} erases the contents of *location*. {BLANK} does not change the formatting of the cells in *location* and does not force recalculation.

{CONTENTS *target-location,source-location,[width],[format]*} copies the contents of *source-location* to *target-location* as a label.

{LET *location,entry*} enters a number or left-aligned label in *location*.

{PUT *location,column-offset,row-offset,entry*} enters a number or left-aligned label in a cell within *location*.

{RECALC *location,[condition],[iterations]*} recalculates the values in *location*, proceeding row by row.

{RECALCCOL *location,[condition],[iterations]*} recalculates the values in *location*, proceeding column by column.

{FORM *input range,[call table],[include range],[exclude range]*} temporarily suspends macro execution so you can enter and edit data in the unprotected cells in the unprotected *input range*. The optional *call table* range lists acceptable user keystrokes in one column and corresponding macro commands in the next column. The optional *include range* lists acceptable keystrokes, and the *exclude range* lists keystrokes to be ignored (use one or the other, not both).

{FORMBREAK} is used within a call-table subroutine to end a {FORM} command so 1-2-3 can continue macro execution at the instruction immediately following the {FORM} command.

Database Commands

The database commands are designed to control how 1-2-3 for Windows handles databases.

{COMMIT *["driver",database]*} finalizes (commits) all pending external database transactions if no optional arguments are included, or finalizes specific transactions pending for the SQL server *driver* and external *database* you designate.

{CROSSTAB *db-table,rowheadings,col-headings,summary-field,summary-method*} Creates a cross-tabulation table.

{DATABASE-APPEND *source-range,database-table*} adds new records to database-table.

{DATABASE-CONNECT *driver-name*, [*driver-user-id*], [*driver-password*], [*connection-string*], *db-name*, [*db-user-id*], [*db-password*], [*owner-name*], *table-name*, [*range-name*]} establishes a connection to an external database table so you can use the table with other 1-2-3 commands.

{DATABASE-CREATE-TABLE *driver-name*, [*driver-user-id*], [*driver-password*], *db-name*, [*db-user-id*], [*db-password*], [*owner-name*], *table-name*, [*range-name*], [*creation-string*]*model-table*} sets up the structure for and connects to a new table in an external database.

{DATABASE-DELETE *database-table,criteria*} deletes the records from *database-table* that meet criteria.

{DATABASE-DISCONNECT *range-name*} disconnects an external table, ending all data exchange between 1-2-3 and the external table.

{DATABASE-FIND *database-table,criteria*} locates and selects records in *database-table* that meet *criteria*.

{DATABASE-SEND-COMMAND *driver-name*, [*driver-user-id*], [*driver-password*], [*connection-string*], *db-name*,[*db-user-id*], [*db-password*], *command*} sends a command to an external database.

{QUERY-ADD-FIELD *field*} adds a field to the currently selected query table. The field is displayed as the last field in the query table.

{QUERY-AGGREGATE *function,field-name*} performs calculations on groups of data from a query table. For example, you can calculate sales by salesperson, by month of sale, or by account.

{QUERY-CHOOSE-FIELDS [*field1*], [*field2*],..., [*field15*]} specifies the fields that you want to appear in the currently selected query table.

{QUERY-COPY-SQL} copies to the Clipboard the SQL command equivalent to the current query.

{QUERY-CRITERIAL [*criteria*]} specifies criteria to determine which records appear in a new or currently selected query table.

{QUERY-DATABASE-TABLE *database-table*} specifies a database table or changes the database table for the currently selected query table without changing the criteria, sort settings, aggregate, or the location of the query table if the new database table contains all the fields in the current table.

{QUERY-JOIN [*join-criteria*]} allows you to query multiple database tables that contain a common field.

{QUERY-NAME *new-name*} assigns a new name to the currently selected *query table*.

{QUERY-NEW *database-table,output-range*, [*criteria*], [*query-name*], [*record-limit*], [*field1*], [*field2*],...,[*field10*]} creates a query table that contains the records you extract from a database table.

{QUERY-OPTIONS *option,on-off*,[*record-limit*]} specifies options for manipulating data in the currently selected query table.

{QUERY-REFRESH} updates records in the currently selected query table to reflect changes made to the database table, query options, criteria, or aggregate.

{QUERY-REMOVE-FIELD *field*} removes a field from the currently selected query table.

{QUERY-SHOW-FIELD *field,field-alias*} specifies an alias field name for *field* to display in the currently selected query table. Doing so does not change the field name in the database table, but only changes the field name in the query table.

{QUERY-SORT} [*key1*],[*order1*],[*key2*],[*order2*],[*key3*],[*order3*]} arranges data in the currently selected query table in the order you specify.

{QUERY-SORT-KEY-DEFINE *key-num,key-field,key-order*} defines a sort key to be used by a subsequent {QUERY-SORT} command.

{QUERY-SORT-RESET} clears all sort keys for the currently selected query table.

{QUERY-UPGRADE *input-range,output-range,criteria-range*, [*query-name*]} upgrades a query from a previous version of 1-2-3 so that it works with the Query commands in 1-2-3 Release 4.1.

{QUERY-UPDATE} applies any changes you make to records in the currently selected query table to the corresponding database table.

{ROLLBACK [*driver-name*],[*database*]} cancels pending external database transactions.

{SEND-SQL *range,command*,[*output-range*],[*error-code-location*]} sends an SQL syntax command string to an external database driver.

Dynamic Data Exchange (DDE) Commands

The Dynamic Data Exchange (DDE) commands are designed to manipulate conversation level (low-level) links between 1-2-3 for Windows and other Windows applications.

{INSERT-OBJECT} embeds a new OLE (Object Linking and Embedding) object in 1-2-3 for Windows.

{UPDATE-OBJECT} updates a 1-2-3 object embedded in another application file.

{EDIT-OBJECT} executes either the PRIMARY or SECONDARY verb for the currently selected OLE object.

{DDE-ADVISE [*branch-location*], item-name, [*format*], [*destination*], [*acknowledge*]} specifies the macro routine to branch to when data in the *topic item* of an external server application's file changes.

{DDE-CLOSE [*conversion-number*]} ends the current conversation with a Windows application last initiated by the {DDE-OPEN} command or made current by the {DDE-USE}. If no conversation is open, or if multiple conversations are open but none is current, this command has no effect.

{DDE-EXECUTE *execute-string*} sends a command to the external server application that can be interpreted by the application as a macro or one of its own commands.

{DDE-OPEN *application,topic-name,[location]*} starts a conversation with a Windows application, linking to a specific *file* of an *application* (and optionally, a specific cell or range address location), making that the current conversation.

{DDE-POKE *range, item-name,[format]*} sends a *range* of data to a server application during the current conversation where *item-name* is the name of the topic item you want to link and send data to.

{DDE-REQUEST *range, item-name,[format]*} transfers data from a Windows application to a specific *range* in 1-2-3.

{DDE-TABLE *location,[type]*} creates a table of conversations associated with all active files that were created with {DDE} commands.

{DDE-ADVISE [*branch-location*],item-name,[format],[destination], [*acknowledge*]} specifies the macro that is executed when data changes in the server application.

{DDE-UNADVISE *item-name,[format]*} ends a {DDE-ADVISE} command.

{DDE-USE *conversation-number*} establishes the current conversation based on the designated *conversation number* from all conversation numbers assigned by Windows.

Object Linking and Embedding (OLE) Commands

The Linking commands are designed to manipulate link level (low-level) links between 1-2-3 for Windows and other Windows applications.

{LINK-ASSIGN *link name,range[clear-styles]*} uses the *link name* to refer to an existing link, specifies a *range* to link to, clearing all properties in the range or (optionally) clearing styles.

{LINK-CREATE *link name,app,topic,item*, [*format*], [*mode*], [*branch-location*]} uses the *link name* to create a link without using the

Clipboard between the current worksheet file and another Windows *app* (application) that supports DDE as a server. The *topic* is the name of the application worksheet or file to link to, and the *item* is the name of the topic item to link to.

{LINK-DEACTIVATE [*link-name*]} deactivates the link specified by the *link-name* in the current worksheet, but leaves it intact. When a link is inactive, 1-2-3 does not update values in the destination range.

{LINK-DELETE *link-name*} erases the link specified by the *link-name* in the current worksheet, but leaves the values obtained through the link in the worksheet.

{LINK-REMOVE *link name*} removes the currently used destination range for the DDE link specified by the *link name* in the current worksheet, but does not delete the data in the range.

{LINK-TABLE *location*} creates a table at the *location* address showing all DDE links associated with the current file.

{LINK-UPDATE [*link name*]} updates the active DDE and OLE links specified by the *link-name* in the current worksheet, or activates and updates links deactivated with the {LINK-DEACTIVATE} command.

Printing Commands

{SET "Printer-Setup-Name"} selects the printer to use.
{SET "Printer-Setup-Papersize"} selects the paper size for the printer.
{SET "Printer-Setup-Bins"} selects the printer bin.

Mapping Commands

{MAP-NEW *destrange[,mapname]*} creates a new map.
{MAP-REDRAW} updates the maps in the spreadsheet.

User Interface Commands

{MENU-CREATE} replaces the current 1-2-3 menu bar with a customized menu bar.
{MENU-COMMAND-ADD} adds a menu command to a custom menu.

Interactive Commands

{CHOOSE-ONE} displays a dialog box and waits for the user to select an option and then choose OK or Cancel. It then runs the macro associated with the option chosen.

{CHOOSE-MANY} displays a dialog box and waits for the user to select one or more check boxes and then choose OK or Cancel.

{DIALOG} displays a custom dialog box.

{MODELESS-DISPLAY} displays a modeless message box that stays active on the screen while a macro is running. One application is for displaying status information from a 1-2-3 macro while using another application.

Screen Control Commands

{SET "SMARTICONS",OFF} sets SmartIcons palette off.

{SET "STATUSBAR",ON} sets Statusbar on.

Navigation Commands

{CELL-ENTER *data,[target-location]*} enters *data* in *target-location*.

{EDIT-GOTO *name,[part],[type]*} selects all or part of a range, query table, chart, or other drawn object, and then scrolls to it. Any items in the same file that were previously selected become unselected.

{SCROLL-COLUMNS *[amount]*} scrolls horizontally by column in the current worksheet.

{SCROLL-ROWS *[amount]*} scrolls vertically by row in the current worksheet.

{SCROLL-TO-CELL *location*} scrolls in the current worksheet so that the first cell of *location* is in the top left corner of the worksheet window.

{SCROLL-TO-COLUMN *location*} scrolls left or right in the current worksheet so that the leftmost column of *location* is the leftmost column of the worksheet window.

{SCROLL-TO-OBJECT *name,[type]*} scrolls to but does not select a range, query table, chart or other drawn object in the current worksheet.

{SCROLL-TO-ROW *location*} scrolls up or down in the current worksheet so that the top row of *location* is the top row in the worksheet window.

{SELECT *name,[part],[type]*} selects all or part of a range, chart, query table, or other drawn object, without scrolling to it. Any items in the same file that were previously selected become unselected.

{SELECT-ALL *[type]*} selects the active area of the current worksheet, or all charts or drawn objects in the current worksheet, or all worksheets in the current file.

{SELECT-APPEND *name,part*} selects all or part of a range, chart, or other drawn object without deselecting those currently selected.

{SELECT-RANGE-RELATIVE *[col],[row],[wksht],[cp-col-off],[cp-row-off],[cp-sheet-off]*} moves the cell pointer and then selects a range whose address is represented by offsets of the current cell (the current cell is 0). Any items in the same file that were previously selected become unselected.

{SELECT-REMOVE *name*} removes a range, chart, or other drawn object from the currently selected collection.

{SELECT-REPLACE *old-range,new-range*} replaces *old-range* with *new-range* in a collection.

Charting Commands

{CHART-ASSIGN-RANGE *range,method*} assigns the data ranges in a chart.

{CHART-AXIS-INTERVALS *axis,[major],[minor],[major-interval],[minor-interval]*} changes the intervals between X-axis, Y-axis, or 2nd Y-axis tick marks in the current chart.

{CHART-AXIS-LIMITS *axis,[upper],[lower],[upper-limit],[lower-limit]*} creates, for the current chart, a scale for the X-axis, Y-axis, or 2nd Y-axis that displays only the data that falls between (and includes) *upper-limit* and *lower-limit*.

{CHART-AXIS-SCALE-TYPE *axis,type*} specifies the type of scale to use for an axis in the current chart.

{CHART-AXIS-TICKS *axis,[major],[minor],[space]*} used to specify major and minor tick marks for an axis in the specified chart.

{CHART-AXIS-TITLE *axis,[title],[title-cell]*} changes an axis title in the current chart.

{CHART-AXIS-UNITS *axis,[manual-calc],[manual-title],[exponent],[title], [title-cell]*} changes the magnitude of the axis units and the axis-unit titles for the current chart.

{CHART-COLOR-RANGE *series,[color-range]*} sets the color for each value in a data series in the current chart, using values in *color-range*.

{CHART-DATA-LABELS *series,[label-range],[position]*} creates labels for data points or bars in the current chart, using data in *label-range* as the labels.

{CHART-FOOTNOTE [*line1*],[*line2*],[*position*],[*cell1*],[*cell2*]} adds chart footnotes to the current chart.

{CHART-GRID *axis*,[*major*],[*minor*]} displays or hides grid lines for an axis in the current chart.

{CHART-LEGEND *series*,[*legend*],[*position*],[*legend-range*]} creates legend labels that identify the colors, symbols, or patterns or the current chart's data series.

{CHART-NEW *location* [*type*],[*style*],[*name*]} draws a chart at *location*, using data from the currently selected range.

{CHART-PATTERN-RANGE *series*,[*pattern-range*]} sets the pattern for each value in a data series in the current chart.

{CHART-PIE-LABELS [*values*],[*percentage*],[*x-range*],[*c-range*]} creates labels for the current pie chart.

{CHART-PIE-SLICE-EXPLOSION *explosion-type*,[*all-by-%*]} explodes slices in the current pie chart.

{CHART-RANGE *series*,[*series-range*],[*series-type*],[*2y-axis*]} sets the data range, series type, and 2nd Y axis flag for a data series in the current chart.

{CHART-RANGE-DELETE *series*} deletes the *series* from the current chart.

{CHART-RENAME *old-name*,*new-name*} renames a chart.

{CHART-SET-PREFERRED} saves the settings of the currently selected chart as the "preferred" chart type.

{CHART-TITLE [*line1*],[*line2*],[*position*],[*cell1*],[*cell2*]} adds chart titles to the current chart.

{CHART-USE-PREFERRED} defines current chart's type as the default chart type and defines the selected chart's grid settings as the default grid settings.

Range Commands

Range macro commands correspond to the Range menubar commands.

{DATA-TABLE-1 [*output-range*],[*input-cell-1*]} substitutes values for one variable in one or more formulas and enters the results in *output-range*.

{DATA-TABLE-2 [*output-range*],[*input-cell-1*],[*input-cell-2*]} substitutes values for two variables in one formula and enters the results in *output-range*.

{DATA-TABLE-3 [*output-range*],[*input-cell-1*],[*input-cell-2*],[*input-cell-3*], [*formula*]} substitutes values for three variables in one formula and enters the results in *output-range*.

{DATA-TABLE-RESET} clears the ranges and input-cell settings for all what-if-tables in the current file.

{DISTRIBUTION [*values-range*],[*bin-range*]} creates a frequency distribution that counts how many values in *values-range* fall within each numeric interval specified by *bin-range*.

{FILL [*range*],[*start*],[*step*],[*stop*],[*units*]} enters a sequence of values in a specified range.

{FILL-BY-EXAMPLE [*range*]} fills *range* with a sequence of data. 1-2-3 creates a pattern for the sequence, based on data you include in the *range*.

{MATRIX-INVERT [*matrix-to-invert*],[*output-range*]} inverts a square matrix.

{MATRIX-MULTIPLY [*matrix1*],[*matrix2*],[*output-range*]} multiplies the matrix in *matrix1* by the matrix in *matrix2* to create a matrix in *output-range* that contains the results.

{PARSE [*parse-range*],[*output-range*],[*format-line*]} converts long labels from an imported text file into separate columns of data of one or more types (values, dates, times, and labels).

{RANGE-NAME-CREATE *range-name*,[*range-location*]} assigns a name to a range address.

{RANGE-NAME-DELETE *range-name*} deletes a range name in the current file.

{RANGE-NAME-DELETE-ALL} deletes all range names in the current file.

{RANGE-NAME-LABEL-CREATE [*direction*],[*label-range*]} assigns an existing label as the range name for a single cell immediately above, below, to the right of, or to the left of the label.

{RANGE-NAME-TABLE [*table-location*]} creates a two-column table with the names of all defined ranges in the current file listed alphabetically in the left column, and the corresponding range addresses listed in the right column.

{RANGE-TRANSPOSE *destination*,[*transpose*],[*origin*]} copies data from *origin* to *destination*, transposing the copied data and replacing any copied formulas with their current values.

{RANGE-VALUE *destination*,[*origin*]} copies the contents and styles from *origin* to *destination*, and replaces all copied formulas with their current values.

{REGRESSION [*X-range*],[*Y-range*],[*output-range*],[*intercept*]} performs multiple linear regression analysis and also calculates the slope of the line that best illustrates the data.

{SHEET-NAME *new-name*,[*old-name*]} names a 1-2-3 worksheet in the current file.

{SHEET-NAME-DELETE [*worksheet-name*]} deletes the name of a 1-2-3 worksheet in the current file.

{SORT [*range*],[*key1*],[*order1*],[*key2*],[*order2*],[*key3*],[*order3*]} arranges data in *range* in the order you specify.

{SORT-KEY-DEFINE *key-number,key-range,key-order*} defines a sort
key to be used by a subsequent {SORT} command.
{SORT-RESET} clears all sort keys for sorting range data.

SmartIcon commands

The SmartIcon commands correspond to several frequently-used
SmartIcons.

{SMARTSUM} sums values in the selected or adjacent range, if you
include empty cells below or to the right of the range.
{SORT-ASCENDING} sorts a range or database table in ascending
order (A-Z and smallest to largest values), using the selected column as the key.
{SORT-DESCENDING} sorts a range or database table in descending
order (Z-A and largest to smallest values), using the selected column as the key.
{TOGGLE-OUTLINE} adds or removes a border.
{TOGGLE-SHADOW} draws or removes an outline around a cell or
range and adds or removes a drop shadow.

Solver Commands

Solver commands correspond to the Range Analyze Backsolver and Solver
menu commands.

{BACKSOLVE *formula-cell,target-value,adjustable-range*} finds values
for one or more cells that make the result of a formula equal to a
value you specify.
{SOLVER-ANSWER *answer*} displays in the worksheet the answers or
attempts 1-2-3 finds.
{SOLVER-ANSWER-SAVE *scenario,[comment]*} saves the current
answer or attempt as a scenario.
{SOLVER-DEFINE *[adj-cells],[constraint-cells],[optimize],[opt-cell], [opt-
type],[answers]*} analyzes data in a worksheet and returns a number of possible answers to a problem you define.
{SOLVER-DEFINE? *[adj-cells],[constraint-cells],[optimize],[opt-cell], [opt-
type],[answers]*} displays the Solver Definition dialog box, optionally displaying defaults you specify.
{SOLVER-REPORT *type,[comp1],[comp2],[diff-value]*} creates a new
.WK4 file that contains a report based on the current answer.

User Environment

{ALERT *message,[buttons],[icon-type],[results-range],[x],[y]*} displays a message box and waits for the user to choose OK or Cancel.

{CHOOSE-FILE *file-type,results-range,title,[x],[y]*} displays a Windows common dialog box that contains a list of files and waits for the user to select one.

{CHOOSE-ITEM *list-range,results-range,prompt,title,[x],[y]*} displays a dialog box that contains a list of data items, waits for the user to select one and then choose OK or Cancel; and enters the index number of the user's choice in the worksheet.

{CHOOSE-MANY *choices-range,results-range,prompt,title,[x],[y]*} displays a dialog box with data items and waits for the user to select one or more and then choose OK or Cancel.

{CHOOSE-ONE *choices-range,results-range,prompt,title,[x],[y]*} displays a dialog box with data items and waits for the user to select one and then choose OK or Cancel; then runs the macro associated with the option.

{DIALOG *range*} displays a custom dialog box created with the Lotus Dialog Editor.

{DIALOG? *name*} displays a 1-2-3 dialog box, and waits for the user to choose OK or press Enter.

{GET-FORMULA [*prompt*]} displays a dialog box and waits for the user to enter a formula; then enters the formula in a cell.

{GET-LABEL [*prompt*]} displays a dialog box and waits for the user to enter a label; then enters the label in a cell.

{GET-NUMBER [*prompt*]} displays a dialog box and waits for the user to enter a number; then enters the number in a cell.

{GET-RANGE [*prompt*]} displays a dialog box and waits for the user to enter a range or address; then enters the name or address in a cell as a number.

{LOOK *location*} checks the typeahead buffer for keystrokes and records the first keystroke (if any) as a left-aligned label in *location*.

{MENU-COMMAND-ADD *menu-description-range,menu-index,command-index*} adds a command to a custom pull-down menu.

{MENU-COMMAND-REMOVE *menu-description-range,menu-index, command-index*} removes a command from a custom pull-down menu.

{MENU-COMMAND-ENABLE *menu-index,command-index*} enables a command enabled with {MENU-COMMAND-DISABLE}.

{MENU-COMMAND-DISABLE *menu-index,command-index*} disables a command in a custom menu. Disabled commands appear dimmed.

Other Commands

{AUDIT} audits a 1-2-3 worksheet file or files.

{SEND-MAIL} sends an electronic mail message from within a 1-2-3 session.

{SPELLCHECK} launches a 1-2-3 spell checker.

{SCENARIO-CREATE} creates a new, named scenario.

{VERSION-CREATE} creates a new version.

{REGISTER} makes a function in a Dynamic Link Library (DLL) available as an @function.

{DEL} deletes a single character in the Input Line or deletes the cell contents, format, style, and graph at the cell pointer location or contained in a highlighted range.

B

Translating 1-2-3 Macros to Excel

Translating a 1-2-3 macro to Microsoft Excel can be a difficult and frustrating task due to the completely different macro languages the two spreadsheet programs use. As you've seen, it's fairly easy to write a straight keystroke macro in 1-2-3 with little more than a knowledge of the letters you would type to accomplish the task manually. For example, to write a macro to sum a column of numbers, you only need to type

```
@sum({u}.{end}{u})~
```

and give the macro a name like \A. In Excel, on the other hand, you would need to go to a separate macro sheet (where macros for the current sheet must reside), and type nine lines of code like:

=REFTEXT(ACTIVE.CELL())	(Entered in cell A2)
=SELECT("R[-1]C")	(Entered in cell A3)
=SELECT.END(3)	(Entered in cell A4)
=ROW(ACTIVE.CELL())	(Entered in cell A5)
=SELECT(TEXTREF(A2))	(Entered in cell A6)
=ROW(ACTIVE.CELL())	(Entered in cell A7)
=DEFINE.NAME("up1","=R[-1]C")	(Entered in cell A8)
=FORMULA("=SUM(R["&A5-A7&"]C:up1)")	(Entered in cell A9)
=RETURN()	(Entered in cell A10)

This code starts by storing the address for the current cell pointer position, moves the cell pointer up one cell, moves to the top of the column of numbers to be summed, stores the row number of that top cell, returns to the original cell, captures its row number, creates the range name "up1" at the cell above, uses the information stored by the code in lines A5 and A7 to create the summing formula, and quits.

This is just one example of the added complexity you'll encounter in Excel macros, and it's fairly typical.

Fortunately, Microsoft has added one feature to make the task of converting 1-2-3 macros to Excel a little easier. If you click on the control panel in the upper left corner of the Excel Window (just to the left of Excel's application titlebar) you can gain access to the Macro Translation Assistant (otherwise known as MTA). Using this mini-application, you can get a worst-case translation of your 1-2-3 macros to use as a starting point for doing your macro conversions.

Be aware, however, that the MTA generally has problems converting 1-2-3 macros of even the slightest complexity or sophistication. In those cases, plan on spending considerable time doing a line-by-line audit of the code this program generates. And in some cases, the MTA simply cannot make a direct translation for you. For example, it has no way at all of translating the one-line summing macro above.

However, on the positive side, the MTA does provide a good starting point for most macro conversions. By seeing how the MTA tries to translate macro code, you can get a good idea of ways to approach the translation, and over time you'll learn the Excel method of macro writing.

To help you with your 1-2-3 macro conversions to Excel, Table A2.1 below lists the macro equivalents for Excel menu commands, and Table A2.2 lists and describes Excel macro commands by category:

Table A2.1 Excel Macro Functions by Category

Chart Menu Commands	*Macro Commands*
Add Arrow	ADD.ARROW
Add Legend	LEGEND
Add Overlay	ADD.OVERLAY
Attach Text	ATTACH.TEXT
Axes	AXES
Calculate Now	CALCULATE.NOW
Delete Arrow	DELETE.ARROW
Delete Overlay	DELETE.OVERLAY
Edit Series	EDIT.SERIES
Gridlines	GRIDLINES
Select Chart	SELECT.CHART
Select Plot Area	SELECT.PLOT.AREA

Table A2.1 (*Continued*)

Control Menu Commands	Macro Commands
Close	CLOSE
Maximize (application)	APP.MAXIMIZE
Maximize (window)	WINDOW.MAXIMIZE
Minimize (application)	APP.MINIMIZE
Minimize (window)	WINDOW.MINIMIZE
Move (application)	APP.MOVE
Move (document)	MOVE
Move (window)	WINDOW.MOVE
Restore (application)	APP.RESTORE
Restore (window)	WINDOW.RESTORE
Size (application)	APP.SIZE
Size (window)	WINDOW.SIZE

Data Menu Commands	Macro Commands
Consolidate	CONSOLIDATE
Delete	DATA.DELETE
Extract	EXTRACT
Find	DATA.FIND
Form	DATA.FORM
Parse	PARSE
Series	DATA.SERIES
Set Criteria	SET.CRITERIA
Set Database	SET.DATABASE
Set Extract	SET.EXTRACT
Sort	SORT
Table	TABLE

Edit Menu Commands	Macro Commands
Clear	CLEAR
Copy	COPY
Copy Chart	COPY.CHART
Copy Picture	COPY.PICTURE
Copy Tool Face	COPY.TOOL
Create Publisher	CREATE.PUBLISHER
Cut	CUT
Delete	EDIT.DELETE
Fill Down	FILL.DOWN
Fill Group	FILL.GROUP
Fill Left	FILL.LEFT
Fill Right	FILL.RIGHT
Fill Up	FILL.UP
Insert	INSERT
Insert Object	INSERT.OBJECT

Table A2.1 (*Continued*)

Edit Menu Commands	Macro Commands
Paste	PASTE
Paste Link	PASTE.LINK
Paste Picture	PASTE.PICTURE
Paste Picture Link	PASTE.PICTURE.LINK
Paste Special	PASTE.SPECIAL
Repeat	EDIT.REPEAT
Share	SHARE
Share	SHARE.NAME
Undo	UNDO

File Menu Commands	Macro Commands
Close	FILE.CLOSE
Close All	CLOSE.ALL
Delete	FILE.DELETE
Exit	QUIT
Links	CHANGE.LINK
Links	LINKS
Links	OPEN.LINKS
Links	UPDATE.LINK
New	NEW
Open	OPEN
Open Mail	OPEN.MAIL
Page Setup	PAGE.SETUP
Print	PRINT
Print Preview	PRINT.PREVIEW
Quit	QUIT
Save	SAVE
Save As	SAVE.AS
Save Workbook	SAVE.WORKBOOK
Send Mail	SEND.MAIL

Format Menu	Macro Commands
3-D View	VIEW.3D
Alignment	ALIGNMENT
AutoFormat	FORMAT.AUTO
Border	BORDER
Bring to Front	BRING.TO.FRONT
Cell Protection	CELL.PROTECTION
Column Width	COLUMN.WIDTH
Font	FORMAT.FONT
Group	GROUP
Legend	FORMAT.LEGEND
Main Chart	FORMAT.MAIN

Table A2.1 *(Continued)*

Format Menu	*Macro Commands*
Number	DELETE.FORMAT
Number	FORMAT.NUMBER
Object Placement	PLACEMENT
Object Properties	OBJECT.PROPERTIES
Object Protection	OBJECT.PROTECTION
Overlay	FORMAT.OVERLAY
Patterns	PATTERNS
Row Height	ROW.HEIGHT
Scale	SCALE
Send to Back	SEND.TO.BACK
Style	APPLY.STYLE
Text	FORMAT.TEXT
Ungroup	UNGROUP

Formula Menu Commands	*Macro Commands*
Apply Names	APPLY.NAMES
Create Names	CREATE.NAMES
Define Name	DEFINE.NAME
Find	FORMULA.FIND
Goal Seek	GOAL.SEEK
Goto	FORMULA.GOTO
Note	NOTE
Outline	OUTLINE
Paste Function	FORMULA
Paste Names	LIST.NAMES
Replace	FORMULA.REPLACE
Scenario Manager	SCENARIO.ADD
Select Special	SELECT.LAST.CELL
Select Special	SELECT.SPECIAL
Show Active Cell	SHOW.ACTIVE.CELL

Gallery Menu Commands	*Macro Commands*
3-D Area	GALLERY.3D.AREA
3-D Bar	GALLERY.3D.BAR
3-D Column	GALLERY.3D.COLUMN
3-D Line	GALLERY.3D.LINE
3-D Pie	GALLERY.3D.PIE
3-D Surface	GALLERY.3D.SURFACE
Area	GALLERY.AREA
Bar	GALLERY.BAR
Column	GALLERY.COLUMN
Combination	COMBINATION

Table A2.1 *(Continued)*

Gallery Menu Commands	*Macro Commands*
Line	GALLERY.LINE
Pie	GALLERY.PIE
Preferred	PREFERRED
Radar	GALLERY.RADAR
Set Preferred	SET.PREFERRED
XY (Scatter)	GALLERY.SCATTER
Assign to Object	ASSIGN.TO.OBJECT
Assign to Tool	ASSIGN.TO.TOOL
Resume	RESUME
Run	RUN

Options Menu Commands	*Macro Commands*
Calculate Document	CALCULATE.DOCUMENT
Calculate Now	CALCULATE.NOW
Calculation	CALCULATION
Calculation	PRECISION
Color Palette	COLOR.PALETTE
Color Palette	EDIT.COLOR
Display	DISPLAY
Group Edit	WORKGROUP
Protect Document	PROTECT.DOCUMENT
Remove Page Break	REMOVE.PAGE.BREAK
Set Page Break	SET.PAGE.BREAK
Set Print Area	SET.PRINT.AREA
Set Print Titles	SET.PRINT.TITLES
Spelling	SPELLING
Toolbars	SHOW.TOOLBAR
Workspace	SHOW.INFO
Workspace	WORKSPACE

Window Menu Commands	*Macro Commands*
Arrange	ARRANGE.ALL
Hide	HIDE
Freeze Panes	FREEZE.PANES
New Window	NEW.WINDOW
Show Clipboard	SHOW.CLIPBOARD
Show Info	SHOW.INFO
Split	SPLIT
Unhide	UNHIDE
View	VIEW.SHOW
Zoom	ZOOM

Table A2.2 Macro Commands by Category

Note: In the following table, required arguments are in bold italics, while optional arguments are in italics only.

Information Macro Commands

ACTIVE.CELL()
    Returns the active cell reference

CALLER()
    Returns the calling function reference

DIRECTORIES(***path_text***)
    Returns an array of specified path's subdirectories

DIRECTORY(*path_text*)
    Sets current drive and directory to a specified path

DOCUMENTS(*type_num,match_text*)
    Returns names of the specified open documents

FILE.EXISTS(***path_text***)
    Tests for the existence of a file or directory

FILES(*directory_text*)
    Returns the filenames in a specified directory

GET.BAR(***bar_num,menu,command***)
    Identifies menu bars, menus, and commands

GET.CELL(***type_num,****reference*)
    Returns information about the specified cell

GET.CHART.ITEM(***x_y-index,****point_index,item index*)
    Returns information about a chart item

GET.DEF(***def_text,****document_text,type_num*)
    Returns a name matching a definition

GET.DOCUMENT(***type_num,****name_text*)
    Returns information about a document

GET.FORMULA(***reference***)
    Returns the contents of a cell

GET.LINK.INFO(***link_text,type_num,****type_of_link,reference*)
    Returns information about a link

GET.NAME(***name_text***)
    Returns the definition of a name

GET.NOTE(*cell_ref,start_char,num_chars*)
    Returns characters from a note

GET.OBJECT(***type_num,****object_id_text,start_num*)
    Returns information about an object

GET.TOOL(***type_num,bar_id,position***)
    Returns information about a tool or tools on a toolbar

GET.TOOLBAR(***type_num,***bar_id)
    Retrieves information about a toolbar

GET.WINDOW(***type_num,****window_text*)
    Returns information about a window

Table A2.2 *(Continued)*

Information Macro Commands

GET.WORKBOOK(***type_num**,name_text*)
   Returns information about a workbook document

GET.WORKSPACE(***type_num***)
   Returns information about the workspace

LAST.ERROR()
   Returns the reference of the cell where the last error occurred

LINKS(*document_text,type_num*)
   Returns the name of all linked documents

NAMES(*document_text,type_num,match_text*)
   Returns the names defined in a document

REPORT.GET(***type_num**,report_name*)
   Returns information about reports defined for the active document

SCENARIO.GET(*type_num*)
   Returns the specified information about the scenarios defined on your worksheet

SELECTION()
   Returns the reference of the selection

SLIDE.GET(***type_num**,name_text,slide_num*)
   Returns information about a slide or slide show

SOLVER.GET(***type_num,sheet_name***)
   Returns information about the current settings for Solver

VIEW.GET(***type_num**,view_name*)
   Returns an array of all the views in the active document

WINDOWS(*type_num,match_text*)
   Returns the names of all open windows

Lookup and Reference Commands

ABSREF(***ref_text,reference***)
   Returns the absolute reference of a range of cells to another range

DEREF(***reference***)
   Returns the value of the cells in the reference

EVALUATE(***formula_text***)
   Evaluates a formula or expression that is in the form of text and returns the result

FORMULA.CONVERT(***formula_text,from_a1***,to_a1,to_ref_type,rel_to_ref)
   Changes the reference style and type

REFTEXT(***reference**,a1*)
   Converts a reference to text

RELREF(***reference,rel_to_ref***)
   Returns a relative reference

TEXTREF(***text**,a1*)
   Converts text to a reference

Table A2.2 *(Continued)*

Database Commands

CROSSTAB.CREATE(*rows_array,cols_array,values_array,create_outline,*
    create_names,multiple_values,auto_drilldown,new_sheet)
    Creates a cross-tabulation table

CROSSTABL.DRILLDOWN()
    Returns the records in the active result table in a cross-tabulation table

CROSSTAB.RECALC(*rebuild*)
    Recalculates an existing cross-tabulation table

DATA.DELETE()
    Deletes data that match the current criteria

DATA.FIND(*logical*)
    Finds records in a database

DATA.FINDNEXT()
    Finds next matching record in a database

DATA.FIND.PREV()
    Finds previous matching record in a database

DATA.FORM()
    Displays the data form

EXTRACT()
    Copies database records that match the criteria into a separate extract range

SET.CRITERIA()
    Defines the name Criteria for the selected range on the active sheet

SET.DATABASE()
    Defines the name Database for the selected range on the active sheet

SET.EXTRACT()
    Defines the name Extract for the selected range on the active sheet

Scenario Commands

SCENARIO.ADD(*scen_name,value_array*)
    Defines the specified values as a scenario

SCENARIO.CELLS(*changing_ref*)
    Defines the changing cells for a model on your worksheet

SCENARIO.DELETE(*scen_name*)
    Deletes the specified scenario

SCENARIO.SHOW(*scen_name*)
    Recalculates a model using the specified scenario and displays the result

SCENARIO.SHOW.NEXT()
    Recalculates a model using the next scenario and displays the result

SCENARIO.SUMMARY(*result_ref*)
    Generates a table summarizing the results of all the scenarios for the model
    on your worksheet

Table A2.2 (*Continued*)

Slide Show Commands

SLIDE.COPY.ROW()
> Copies the selected slides, each of which is defined on a single row, onto the Clipboard

SLIDE.CUT.ROW()
> Cuts the selected slides and pastes them onto the Clipboard

SLIDE.DEFAULTS(*effect_num,speed_num,advance_rate_num,soundfile_text*)
> Specifies the default values for the active slide show document

SLIDE.DELETE.ROW()
> Deletes the selected slides

SLIDE.EDIT(*effect_num,speed_num,advance_rate_num,soundfile_text*)
> Changes the attributes of the selected table

SLIDE.PASTE(*effect_num,speed_num,advance_rate_num,soundfile_text*)
> Pastes the contents of the Clipboard onto a slide

SLIDE.PASTE.ROW()
> Pastes previously cut or copied slides onto the current selection

SLIDE.SHOW(*initialslide_num,repeat logical,dialogtitle_text,allownav_logical, allowcontrol_logical*)
> Starts the slide show in the active document

Solver Commands

SOLVER.ADD(***cellref,relation,****formula*)
> Adds a constraint to the current problem

SOLVER.CHANGE(***cellref,relation,****formula*)
> Changes the right side of an existing constraint

SOLVER.DELETE(***cellref,relation,****formula*)
> Deletes an existing constraint

SOLVER.FINISH(*keepfinal,reportarray*)
> Allows you to specify whether and where to keep the Solver results

SOLVER.LOAD(***load_area***)
> Allows you to load a model

SOLVER.OK(*setcell,max_min_val,value_of,****by_changing***)
> Specifies options in the Solver dialog box

SOLVER.OPTIONS(*max_time,iterations,precision,assume_linear,step_thru, estimates,derivatives,search,int_tolerance,scaling*)
> Specifies available options in the Solver dialog box

SOLVER.RESET()
> Erases all cell selections and restraints from the Solver dialog box

SOLVER.SAVE(***save_area***)
> Specifies a cell range in which to save the current problem specification

Window and Workbook Commands

WINDOW.MAXIMIZE(*window_text*)
> Maximizes a window

Table A2.2 (*Continued*)

Window and Workbook Commands

WINDOW.MINIMIZE(*window_text*)
>   Minimizes a window

WINDOW.MOVE(*x_pos,y_pos,window_text*)
>   Moves a window

WINDOW.RESTORE(*window_text*)
>   Restores a window to its previous size

WORKBOOK.ACTIVATE(*sheet_name,new_window_logical*)
>   Activates the specified workbook document

WORKBOOK.ADD(***name_array****,dest_book,position_num*)
>   Adds the specified document to the specified workbook

WORKBOOK.COPY(***name_array****,dest_book,position_num*)
>   Copies one or more documents from the current workbook into another
>   workbook

WORKBOOK.MOVE(***name_array****,dest_book,position_num*)
>   Moves documents from one workbook to another or to another position in
>   the same workbook

WORKBOOK.OPTIONS(***sheet_name****,workbook_name,bound_logical*)
>   Changes the settings of a workbook document

WORKBOOK.SELECT(*name_array,active_name*)
>   Selects the specified documents in a workbook

ZOOM(*magnification*)
>   Enlarges or reduces a document in the active
>   window

Other Macro Commands

A1.R1C1(***logical***)
>   Displays A1 or R1C1 location references

ACTIVATE(*window_text,pane_num*)
>   Switches to a window

ACTIVATE.NEXT(*workbook_text*)
>   Switches to the next window or document in a workbook

ACTIVATE.PREV(*workbook_text*)
>   Switches to the previous window or document in a workbook)

CANCEL.COPY(*render_logical*)
>   Cancels the copy marquee

CHART.WIZARD(*long,**ref**,gallery_num,type_num,plot_by,categories,ser_titles,
legend,title,x_title,y,z*)
>   Creates and formats a chart

CONSTRAIN.NUMERIC(*numeric_only*)
>   Constrains handwriting recognition to numbers and punctuation only

CREATE.DIRECTORY(***path_text***)
>   Creates a directory or folder

Table A2.2 *(Continued)*

Other Macro Commands

CREATE.OBJECT(***object_type,ref_1,x***_offset1,y_offset1,***ref_2,x***_offset2,y_offset2,text, *fill*)
  Creates an object

CREATE.OBJECT(***object_type,ref_1,x***_offset1,y_offset1,***ref_2,x***_offset2,y_offset2,***array,****fill*)
  Creates an object

CREATE.OBJECT(***object_type,ref_1,x***_offset1,y_offset1,***ref_2,x***_offset2,y_offset2,xyseries,fill, gallery_num,type_num)
  Creates an object

CUSTOMIZE.TOOLBAR?(*category*)
  Displays the Customize Toolbar dialog box

DELETE.DIRECTORY(***path_text***)
  Deletes an empty directory

DELETE.FORMAT(***format_text***)
  Deletes a number format

DEMOTE(***row_col***)
  Demotes the selection in an outline

DUPLICATE()
  Makes a copy of an object

EXTEND.POLYGON(***array***)
  Adds vertices to a polygon

FILL.AUTO(*destination_ref,copy_only*)
  Copies cells or automatically fills a selection

FORMAT.AUTO(*format_num,number,font,alignment,border,pattern,width*)
  Formats the selected range of cells from a built-in gallery of formats

FORMAT.MOVE(***x_offset,y_offset,****reference*)
  Moves the selected object

FORMAT.SHAPE(***vertex_num,insert,****reference,x_offset,y_offset*)
  Inserts, moves, or deletes vertices of the selected polygon

FORMAT.SIZE(*x_off,y_off,***reference***)
  Sizes an object

FORMAT.SIZE(*width,height*)
  Sizes an object

FORMULA(***formula_text,****reference*)
  Enters values into a cell or range or onto a chart

FORMULA.ARRAY(***formula_text,****reference*)
  Enters an array

FORMULA.FILL(***formula_text,****reference*)
  Enters a formula in the specified range

FULL(*logical*)
  Changes the size of the active window

Table A2.2 *(Continued)*

Other Macro Commands

HIDE.OBJECT(*object_id_text,hide*)
>   Hides objects

HLINE(***num_columns***)
>   Horizontally scrolls through the active window by columns

HPAGE(***num_windows***)
>   Horizontally scrolls through the active window one window at a time

HSCROLL(***position,***col_logical*)
>   Horizontally scrolls through a document by percentage or by column number

LINE.PRINT(***command,***file,append*)
>   Prints the active document using 1-2-3 compatible methods

LINE.PRINT(***command,***setup_text,leftmarg,rightmarg,topmarg,botmarg,*
>   *pglen,formatted*)
>   Prints the active document using 1-2-3 compatible methods

LINE.PRINT(***command,***setup_text,leftmarg,rightmarg,topmarg,botmarg,*
>   *pglen,wait,autolf,port,update*)
>   Prints the active document using 1-2-3 compatible methods

OBJECT.PROPERTIES(*placement_type,print_object*)
>   Determines an object's relationship to underlying cells

PROMOTE(*rowcol*)
>   Promotes the selection in an outline

REPORT.DEFINE(***report_name,views_scenarios_array,***pages_logical*)
>   Creates or replaces a report definition

REPORT.DELETE(***report_name***)
>   Removes a report definition from the active document

REPORT.PRINT(***report_name,***copies_num,show_print_dlg_logical*)
>   Prints a report

RESUME(*type_num*)
>   Resumes a paused macro

SAVE.WORKBOOK(*doc_text,type_num,prot_pwd,backup,write_res_pwd,*
>   *read_only_rec*)
>   Saves the workbook to which the active document belongs

SELECT(*selection,active_cell*)
>   Selects a cell

SELECT(***object_id_text,***replace*)
>   Selects a worksheet object

SELECT(***item_text,***single_point*)
>   Selects a chart item

SELECT.END(***direction_num***)
>   Selects the last cell in a range

SHOW.CLIPBOARD()
>   Displays the contents of the Clipbaord in a new window

Table A2.2 *(Continued)*

Other Macro Commands

SHOW.DETAIL(***rowcol,rowcol_num,****expand*)
> Expands or collapses a portion of an outline

SHOW.LEVELS(*row_level,col_level*)
> Displays a specific number of levels of an outline

SOUND.NOTE(*cell_ref,file_text,resource*)
> Imports sound from another file

SOUND.NOTE(*cell_ref,erase_snd*)
> Recrods or erases sound from cell notes

SOUND.PLAY(*cell_ref,file_text,resource*)
> Plays the sound from a cell note or a file

SPELLING.CHECK(***word_text,****custom_dic,ignore_uppercase*)
> Checks the spelling of a word.

SPLIT(*col_split,row_split*)
> Splits a window

TEXT.BOX(***add_text,object_id_text,****start_num,num_chars*)
> Replaces text in a text box

UNLOCKED.NEXT()
> Goes to the next unlocked cell

UNLOCKED.PREV()
> Goes to the previous unlocked cell

VIEW.DEFINE(***view_name,****print_settings_log,row_col_log*)
> Creates or replaces a view

VIEW.DELETE(***view_name***)
> Removes a view from the active document

VIEW.SHOW(***view_name***)
> Shows a view

VLINE(***num_rows***)
> Vertically scrolls through the active window by rows

VPAGE(***num_windows***)
> Vertically scrolls through the active window one window at a time

VSCROLL(***position,****row_logical*)
> Vertically scrolls through a document by percentage or by column number

Macro Control Commands

ARGUMENT(***name_text,****data_type_num*)
> Passes an argument to a macro

ARGUMENT(*name_text,data_type_num,****reference***)
> Passes an argument to a macro

BREAK()
> Interrupts a FOR-NEXT, FOR, CELL-NEXT, or WHILE-NEXT loop

ELSE()
> Specifies an action to take if an IF function returns FALSE

Table A2.2 *(Continued)*

Macro Control Commands

ELSE.IF(*logical_test*)
> Specifies an action to take if an IF or another ELSE.IF function returns FALSE

END.IF()
> Ends a group of macro functions started with an IF statement

FOR(*counter_text,start_num,end_num,step_num*)
> Starts a FOR-NEXT loop

FOR.CELL(*ref_name,area_ref,skip_blanks*)
> Starts a FOR.CELL-NEXT loop

GOTO(*reference*)
> Directs macro execution to another cell

HALT(*cancel_close*)
> Stops all macros from running

IF(*logical_test*)
> Specifies an action to take if a logical test is TRUE

NEXT()
> Ends a FOR-NEXT, FOR, CELL-NEXT, or WHILE-NEXT loop

PAUSE(*no_tool*)
> Pauses a macro

RESTART(*level_num*)
> Removes return addresses from the stack

RESULT(*type_num*)
> Specifies the data type a custom function returns

RETURN(*value*)
> Ends the currently running macro

SET.NAME(*name_text,value*)
> Defines a name as a value

SET.VALUE(*reference,values*)
> Sets the value of a cell on a macro sheet

STEP()
> Turns on macro single-stepping

VOLATILE(*logical*)
> Makes custom functions recalculate automatically

WAIT(*serial_number*)
> Pauses a macro

WHILE(*logical_test*)
> Starts a WHILE-NEXT loop

Customizing Commands

ADD.BAR(*bar_num*)
> Adds a menu bar

ADD.COMMAND(*bar_num,menu,command_ref,position*)
> Adds a command to a menu

Table A2.2 (*Continued*)

Customizing Commands

ADD.MENU(***bar_num,menu_ref***,*position*)
Adds a menu to a menu bar

ADD.TOOL(***bar_id,position,tool_ref***)
Adds one or more tools to a toolbar

ADD.TOOLBAR(***bar_name***,*tool_ref*)
Creates a new toolbar with the specified tools

ALERT(*message_text,type_num,help_ref*)
Displays a dialog box and a message

APP.TITLE(*text*)
Changes the title of the application workspace

ASSIGN.TO.TOOL(***bar_id,position***,*macro_ref*)
Assigns a macro to a tool

BEEP(*tone_num*)
Sounds a tone

CANCEL.KEY(***enable***,*macro_ref*)
Disables macro interruption

CHECK.COMMAND(***bar_num,menu,command,check***)
Adds or deletes a check mark to or from a command

COPY.TOOL(***bar_id,position***)
Copies a tool face to the Clipboard

CUSTOM.REPEAT(*macro_text,repeat_text,record_text*)
Specifies a macro to run when the Repeat command is chosen from the Edit menu

CUSTOM.UNDO(***macro_text***,*undo_text*)
Specifies a macro to run to undo a custom command

DELETE.BAR(***bar_num***)
Deletes a menu bar

DELETE.COMMAND(***bar_num,menu,command***)
Deletes a command from a menu

DELETE.MENU(***bar_num,menu***)
Deletes a menu

DELETE.TOOL(***bar_id,position***)
Deletes a tool from a toolbar

DELETE.TOOLBAR(***bar_name***)
Deletes custom toolbars

DIALOG.BOX(***dialog_ref***)
Displays a custom dialog box

DISABLE.INPUT(***logical***)
Blocks all input to Microsoft Excel

ECHO(*logical*)
Controls screen updating

ENABLE.COMMAND(***bar_num,menu,command,enable***)
Enables or disables a menu or custom command

Table A2.2 (*Continued*)

Customizing Commands

ENABLE.TOOL(*bar_id,position,enable*)
　　Enables or disables a tool on a toolbar

ENTER.DATA(*logical*)
　　Turns Data Entry mode on and off

ERROR(*enable_logical,macro_ref*)
　　Specifies what action to take if an error is encountered while a macro is running

HELP(*help_ref*)
　　Displays a custom Help topic

INPUT(*message_text,type_num,title_text,default,x_pos,y_pos,help_ref*)
　　Displays a dialog box for user input

MESSAGE(*logical,text*)
　　Displays a message in the status bar

MOVE.TOOL(*from_bar_id,from_bar_position,to_bar_id,to_bar_position,*
　　copy,width)
　　Moves or copies a tool from one toolbar to another

ON.DATA(*document_text,macro_text*)
　　Runs a macro when data is sent to Microsoft Excel by another application

ON.DOUBLECLICK(*sheet_text,macro_text*)
　　Runs a macro when you double-click any cell or object on the specified document or chart

ON.ENTRY(*sheet_text,macro_text*)
　　Runs a macro when data is entered

ON.KEY(*key_text,macro_text*)
　　Runs a macro when a specified key is pressed

ON.RECALC(*sheet_text,macro_text*)
　　Runs a macro when a document is recalculated

ON.TIME(*time,macro_text,tolerance,insert_logical*)
　　Runs a macro at a specified time

ON.WINDOW(*window_text,macro_text*)
　　Runs a macro when you switch to a window

PASTE.TOOL(*bar_id,position*)
　　Pastes a tool face from the Clipboard to a specified position on the toolbar

PRESS.TOOL(*bar_id,position,down*)
　　Formats a tool so it appears either normal or depressed into the screen

RENAME.COMMAND(*bar_num,menu,command,name_text*)
　　Changes the name of a command or menu

RESET.TOOL(*bar_id,position*)
　　Resets a tool to its original tool face

RESET.TOOLBAR(*bar_id*)
　　Resets a built-in toolbar to its initial default setting

SAVE.TOOLBAR(*bar_id,filename*)
　　Saves one or more toolbar definitions to a specified file

Table A2.2 *(Continued)*

Customizing Commands

SHOW.BAR(*bar_num*)
    Displays a menu bar

SHOW.TOOLBAR(**bar_id,visible,dock,x_pos,y_pos,***width*)
    Hides or displays a toolbar

WINDOW.TITLE(*text*)
    Changes the title of the active window

DDE/External Functions

APP.ACTIVATE(*title_text,wait_logical*)
    Switches to another application

EDIT.OBJECT(*verb_num*)
    Starts the selected object's application for editing or other actions

EDITION.OPTIONS(**edition_type,***edition_name,ref,option,appearance,size, formats*)
    Sets publisher and subscriber options

EMBED(**object_type,***item*)
    Displayed in the formula bar when an embedded object is selected

EXEC(**program_text,***window_num*)
    Starts another application

EXEC(**program_text,***background,preferred_size_only*)
    Starts another application

EXECUTE(**channel_num,execute_text**)
    Carries out a command in another application

FCLOSE(**file_num**)
    Closes a text file

FOPEN(**file_text,***access_num*)
    Opens a file with the type of permission specified

FPOS(**file_num,***position_num*)
    Sets the position in a text file

FREAD(**file_num,num_chars**)
    Reads characters from a text file

FREADLN(**file_num**)
    Reads a line from a text file

FSIZE(**file_num**)
    Returns the size of a text file

FWRITE(**file_num,text**)
    Writes a line to a text file

FWRITELN(**file_num,text**)
    Writes a line to a text file

INITIATE(**app_text,topic_text**)
    Opens a channel to another application

INSERT.OBJECT(**object_class**)
    Creates an embedded object whose source data is supplied by another application

Table A2.2 *(Continued)*

DDE/External Functions

POKE(***channel_num,item_text,data_ref***)
  Sends data to another application

REGISTER(***module_text,****procedure,type_text,function_text,arg_text,macro_type,category,shortcut_text*)
  Registers a code resource

REGISTER(***file_text,****resource,type_text,function_text,arg_text,macro_type, category,shortcut_text*)
  Registers a code resource

REGISTER.ID(***module_text,procedure,****type_text*)
  Returns the register ID of the resource

REGISTER.ID(***file_text,procedure,****type_text*)
  Returns the register ID of the resource

REQUEST(***channel_num,item_text***)
  Returns data from another application

SEND.KEYS(***key_text,****wait_logical*)
  Sends a key sequence to an application

SET.UPDATE.STATUS(***link_text,status,****type_of_link*)
  Controls the update status of a link

SUBSCRIBE.TO(***file_text,format_num***)
  Inserts contents of an edition into the active document

TERMINATE(***channel_num***)
  Closes a channel to another application

UNREGISTER(***register_id***)
  Removes a registered code resource from memory

UNREGISTER(***module_text***)
  Removes a registered code resource from memory

UNREGISTER(***file_text***)
  Removes a registered code resource from memory

INDEX

425

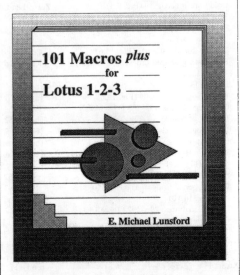